McDonaldization
The Reader

McDonaldization
The Reader

SECOND EDITION

GEORGE RITZER
University of Maryland

PINE FORGE PRESS
An Imprint of Sage Publications, Inc.
Thousand Oaks • London • New Delhi

For information:

Pine Forge Press
A Sage Publications Company
2455 Teller Road
Thousand Oaks, California 91320
E-mail: order@sagepub.com

Sage Publications Ltd.
1 Oliver's Yard
55 City Road
London EC1Y 1SP
United Kingdom

Sage Publications India Pvt. Ltd.
B-42, Panchsheel Enclave
Post Box 4109
New Delhi 110 017 India

Printed in the United States of America

Library of Congress Cataloging-in-Publication Data

Mcdonaldization: The reader / George Ritzer, editor.– 2nd ed.
    p. cm.
Includes index.
ISBN 1-4129-2600-9 (pbk.: alk. paper)
    1. Civilization, Modern—1950- 2. Standardization—Social aspects—United States. 3. United States—Social conditions—1980- I. Ritzer, George.
HN59.2.M423 2006
306′0973—dc22   2005027635

This book is printed on acid-free paper.

06   07   08   09   10   9   8   7   6   5   4   3   2   1

Acquisitions Editor:	Ben Penner
Editorial Assistant:	Annie Louden
Production Editor:	Denise Santoyo
Typesetter:	C&M Digitals (P) Ltd.
Indexer:	Kathy Paparchontis
Cover Designer:	Ravi Balasuriya

Contents

Preface to the
Second Edition

E ven though the first edition of this book was quite successful, I have substantially revised it for this new edition. The following are the major changes:

Part IV, "The Debate Over the Relationship Between McDonaldization and Globalization" is entirely new, although two of the chapters (Chapter 31 by Waters and Chapter 32 by Watson) were in the first edition under a different heading. The addition of this part, of course, reflects the increasing importance of globalization and the need to relate McDonaldization (which, in part, but *only* in part, involves globalization) to it. It also deals with some of the criticisms of the McDonaldization thesis from the point of view of globalization (in addition to Waters and Watson, a critical orientation is clear in Turner and Caldwell, Chapters 33 and 34, respectively). Although all of the critics have reasonable points to make, I particularly like the positions taken by Bryman in Chapter 35 and Ram in Chapter 36. They understand that McDonaldization is not only, or even mainly, about food (and adaptations of McDonald's menus to local realities), but about its principles, structures, and systems and their globalization. Chapter 37 in Part IV is an excerpt from the 2004 edition of *The McDonaldization of Society* (which, in turn, is derived from *The Globalization of Nothing* [also 2004]) in which I relate the broader thesis of *The Globalization of Nothing* to McDonaldization. Both theses are then critiqued by Veseth in Chapter 38.

Three new and original essays, written especially for this edition, are included here. They are all in Part II, "The McDonaldization of Social Structures and Institutions": Sara Raley on the McDonaldization of the Family (Chapter 13), Suzanne Hudd on the McDonaldization of character education and the creation of McMorals (Chapter 15), and Andrew Knight on supersizing farms and the creation and expansion of McAgriculture (Chapter 19). In addition, Mathew Robinson has revised and updated his essay on criminal justice written especially for the first edition of this book (Chapter 11).

A number of other entries are new to this edition, although they have been published previously in a variety of other venues. In Part I, "McDonaldization: Basics, Studies, Applications, and Extensions," these include my essays on Weber and precursors to McDonaldization (Chapter 2) and the social geography of McDonaldization (Chapter 3, "Islands of the Living Dead"), Bryman on McDonald's as, in his terms, a Disneyized institution (Chapter 6); and conversations with the author of *Fast Food Nation*, Eric Schlosser (Chapter 8), and the director of the movie documentary *Super Size Me*, Morgan Spurlock (Chapter 9). Part I closes with a discussion by Bryan Turner of the major general criticisms of the McDonaldization thesis.

Part II includes an excerpt from a piece by Kemmesies on the McDonaldization of the care of drug addicts in Germany (Chapter 14) and an adaptation by John Drane of his essay on the McDonaldization of the church (Chapter 20).

Part III, "Cross-Cultural Analysis, Social Movements, and Social Change" remains much as it was, although two of the essays from the original edition, now Chapters 31 and 32, have been moved to Part IV.

The opening chapter in the book, in effect an introduction to McDonaldization, is drawn from the first chapter of the 2004 edition of *The McDonaldization of Society* and thus constitutes an updating of the parallel entry from the first edition of this anthology, which was taken from the first chapter of the 2000 edition of that book.

Overall, this new edition is chock full of new material. It devotes a great deal of attention to globalization, it includes much more critical analysis of the McDonaldization thesis, and it includes much else that is new or updated. There are approximately 10 more readings in this edition than the last. In order to keep the size (and price) of the book manageable, I have chosen to edit heavily and cut many of the entries rather than drop any. This editing has also made the book crisper and more to the point; many tangents have been ruthlessly deleted. Other changes include the addition of broad pedagogical questions at the end of each Part of the book, more focused critical thinking questions at the end of each chapter, and each reading is now prefaced by a brief introduction by the editor.

I believe that this edition is a great improvement over the first (already strong and popular) edition. It is much more ambitious, it includes a more balanced appraisal of the McDonaldization thesis, and several of the essays point to new directions in work on the topic.

A word on citations . . . or rather the lack, in most cases, of them. In order to make this book attractive and accessible to students, I have systematically deleted citations and references where they existed in the original texts and urged authors of essays written especially for this volume not to use them, to delete them, or to put them at the end of their entries. For those readers who are interested, the necessary citations can be found in various places, usually in the original publications or from the authors of essays found only in this book.

Great thanks in this edition go to my new editor at Pine Forge Press, Ben Penner, as well as his predecessor (and now boss), Jerry Westby (just realized that they are Ben & Jerry!). They, as well as the Pine Forge/Sage people in general, are great to work with. We all work hard but have great fun as well. I'd like to share some of those laughs with all of you, including those at a memorable quail dinner in San Francisco, but a discussion of them would never survive the copyeditor's red pen. Finally, much gratitude to Zeynep Atalay, my very able assistant on this project and the author of the pedagogical questions at the end of each part.

EXCERPTS FROM THE PREFACE TO THE FIRST EDITION

Students will, I think, not only like this book but also learn a great deal from it. As with many of my other works, this volume deals with a broad area—the McDonaldization of society—with which students are intimately familiar. Furthermore, it looks at this process within an array of settings—for example, fast-food restaurants, the family, the university, the Internet—that they are quite knowledgeable about (or, in the case of another—the sex industry—might like to be) and that are at the heart of their daily lives. While they are quite knowledgeable about such areas, they have almost certainly never looked at any one of them, let alone such a wide diversity of settings, through the lens of McDonaldization. This book will allow students to look at such settings, as well as their daily lives, in a whole new way.

A second attraction to students is the discussion of another set of areas that they may not have thought much about, and certainly not from the perspective of McDonaldization. For example, analyses of Disney World, mountain climbing, the church, and politics from this perspective should prove quite eye-opening and provocative to students. Who would have ever thought that the church, to take one example, could have been thought of as McDonaldized?

A third issue that should prove very interesting to students is the worldwide existence and implications of McDonaldization. They will see that this is not only an American phenomenon (although most of its roots are there) but that it has also penetrated deeply into much of the rest of the world. Furthermore, it has helped lead to movements, sometimes quite violent, against this process. Given the events of September 11, 2001, and their relationship to the concerns in this book (e.g., Jihad as an alternative to McDonaldization or "McWorld"), this discussion could not be more timely. Furthermore, with McDonaldization continuing to expand and proliferate, especially in domains of greatest interest and concern to students, this book should be highly relevant to them and their lives.

More generally, this book stems from the strong and continuing interest in the "McDonaldization thesis." One aspect of that interest is a growing body of literature on McDonaldization. As the wide array of books and articles on the topic came to my attention over the last decade, I came to realize that there is a need for an anthology that offers a sampling of this burgeoning body of work. In preparing this volume, I reviewed well over a hundred works on McDonaldization and its relationship to various aspects of the social world. Of course, I could only use a small percentage of those works in this volume, and that required some difficult decisions. To keep the size of this book manageable, I have had to leave out a number of important and interesting works. However, the final product is, I think, a tight and manageable survey of work on the McDonaldization of society.

I envision a variety of different uses for this book. First, it is a significant extension of ideas developed in *The McDonaldization of Society* and can be used in various courses in sociology, and many other disciplines, as a supplement to that book. Second, it is a self-contained volume and therefore could be used instead of *The McDonaldization of Society*, especially by instructors who have used that book through several years (and editions) and are looking for something different. Third, it could be used in a wide variety of courses—theory, social problems, social organizations, and especially introductory sociology—as one of several texts or as a supplement to a basic textbook. Most of the major topics in introductory sociology are covered in this book, pretty much in the order they are dealt with in such courses. Although this anthology does not include the breadth of offerings that one finds in the typical reader for introductory sociology, it has the advantage of covering all the basic topics from a single, coherent perspective. As students make their way through the book, they will quickly become quite expert on the topic and increasingly better able to understand and critically analyze the material presented. When they complete the book, I believe that students in introductory courses (and others) will know not only a lot more about sociology and McDonaldization but also how to critically analyze the social world and the sociological study of it.

Beyond its pedagogical utility in various courses, this book, like *The McDonaldization of Society*, should also be useful to those sociologists interested in extending the McDonaldization thesis empirically and theoretically. The basics are provided for those who want to extend our knowledge of the McDonaldization of specific social structures and institutions, apply the fundamental ideas to various settings, develop alternative ideas (e.g., "Disneyization"), and think about issues related to globalization and global responses to McDonaldization. In addition, this survey also reveals areas and topics that have not yet been studied or theorized from this perspective.

PART I

McDonaldization

Basics, Studies, Applications, and Extensions

Part I opens with the Introduction from the "New Century" (fourth) edition of The McDonaldization of Society *(2004), in which the term "McDonaldization" is defined, and some of the indicators of the success of the model of this process, the McDonald's chain, are outlined. The effect of this process on many other businesses in the United States is discussed, as is the extension of this model to other businesses in many other parts of the world. In fact, the model has been adopted so widely elsewhere that McDonaldized firms overseas are exporting back to the United States, heightening the level of McDonaldization in the nation that lies at its source.*

Although much of the United States has experienced a high degree of McDonaldization and other parts of the world have been McDonaldized to some degree, it remains the case that many other sectors in the United States (see the discussion of rib joints below), and many more throughout the world, have experienced little or no McDonaldization. That being said, such sectors are likely to experience increasing McDonaldization in the coming years.

1

An Introduction to McDonaldization

George Ritzer

◆◆◆ ───

Ray Kroc (1902–1984), the genius behind the franchising of McDonald's restaurants, was a man with big ideas and grand ambitions. But even Kroc could not have anticipated the astounding impact of his creation. McDonald's is the basis of one of the most influential developments in contemporary society. Its reverberations extend far beyond its point of origin in the United States and in the fast-food business. It has influenced a wide range of undertakings, indeed the way of life, of a significant portion of the world. And in spite of McDonald's recent and well-publicized economic difficulties, that impact is likely to expand at an accelerating rate.

However, this is *not* a book about McDonald's, or even about the fast-food business, although both will be discussed frequently throughout these pages. I devote all this attention to McDonald's (as well as the industry of which it is part and that it played such a key role in spawning) because it serves here as the major example of, and the paradigm for, a wide-ranging process I call *McDonaldization*—that is,

Editor's Note: From Ritzer, G. (2004). An Introduction to McDonaldization. *The McDonaldization of Society, Revised New Century Edition* (pp. 1–23). Thousand Oaks, CA: Sage.

the process by which the principles of the fast-food restaurant are coming to dominate more and more sectors of American society as well as of the rest of the world.

As you will see, McDonaldization affects not only the restaurant business but also education, work, the criminal justice system, health care, travel, leisure, dieting, politics, the family, religion, and virtually every other aspect of society. McDonaldization has shown every sign of being an inexorable process, sweeping through seemingly impervious institutions and regions of the world.

The success of McDonald's (in spite of recent troubles; see the closing section of this chapter) itself is apparent: In 2002, its total sales was over $41 billion, with operating income of $2.1 billion. McDonald's, which first began operations in 1955, had 31,172 restaurants throughout the world as of early 2003. Martin Plimmer, a British commentator, archly notes: "There are McDonald's everywhere. There's one near you, and there's one being built right now even nearer to you. Soon, if McDonald's goes on expanding at its present rate, there might even be one in your house. You could find Ronald McDonald's boots under your bed. And maybe his red wig, too."

McDonald's and McDonaldization have had their most obvious influence on the restaurant industry and, more generally, on franchises of all types:

1. According to the International Franchise Association, there were 320,000 small franchised businesses in the United States in 2000 and they did about $1 trillion in annual sales. Although accounting for less than 10% of retail businesses, over 40% of all retail sales come from franchises and they employ more than 8 million people. Franchises are growing rapidly with a new one opening every 8 minutes in the United States. Over 57% of McDonald's restaurants are franchises.

2. In the restaurant industry, the McDonald's model has been adopted not only by other budget-minded hamburger franchises, such as Burger King and Wendy's, but also by a wide array of other low-priced fast-food businesses. Yum! Brands, Inc. operates nearly 33,000 restaurants in 100 countries under the Pizza Hut, Kentucky Fried Chicken, Taco Bell, A&W Root Beer, and Long John Silver's franchises and has more outlets than McDonald's, although its total sales ($24 billion in 2002) are not nearly as high. Subway (with almost 19,000 outlets in 72 countries) is one of the fastest-growing fast-food businesses and claims to be—and may actually be—the largest restaurant chain in the United States.

3. Starbucks, a relative newcomer to the fast-food industry, has achieved dramatic success of its own. A local Seattle business as late as 1987,

Starbucks had over 6,000 company-owned shops (there are no franchises) by 2003, more than ten times the number of shops in 1994. Starbucks has been growing rapidly internationally and is now a presence in Latin America, Europe (it is particularly omnipresent in London), the Middle East, and the Pacific Rim.

4. Perhaps we should not be surprised that the McDonald's model has been extended to casual dining—that is, more upscale, higher-priced restaurants with fuller menus (for example, Outback Steakhouse, Chili's, Olive Garden, and Red Lobster). Morton's is an even more upscale, high-priced chain of steakhouses that has overtly modeled itself after McDonald's: "Despite the fawning service and the huge wine list, a meal at Morton's conforms to the same dictates of uniformity, cost control and portion regulation that have enabled American fast-food chains to rule the world." In fact, the chief executive of Morton's was an owner of a number of Wendy's outlets and admits: "My experience with Wendy's has helped in Morton's venues." To achieve uniformity, employees go "by the book"; "an ingredient-by-ingredient illustrated binder describing the exact specifications of 500 Morton's kitchen items, sauces, and garnishes. A row of color pictures in every Morton's kitchen displays the presentation for each dish."

5. Other types of business are increasingly adapting the principles of the fast-food industry to their needs. Said the vice chairman of Toys 'R Us, "We want to be thought of as a sort of McDonald's of toys." The founder of Kidsports Fun and Fitness Club echoed this desire: "I want to be the McDonald's of the kids' fun and fitness business." Other chains with similar ambitions include Gap, Jiffy Lube, AAMCO Transmissions, Midas Muffler & Brake Shops, Great Clips, H&R Block, Pearle Vision, Bally's, Kampgrounds of America (KOA), KinderCare (dubbed "Kentucky Fried Children"), Jenny Craig, Home Depot, Barnes & Noble, PETsMART.

6. McDonald's has been a resounding success in the international arena. Over half of McDonald's restaurants are outside the United States (in the mid-1980s, only 25% of McDonald's were outside the United States). The majority (982) of the 1,366 new restaurants opened in 2002 were overseas (in the United States, the number of restaurants increased by less than four hundred). Well over half of McDonald's revenue comes from its overseas operations. McDonald's restaurants are now found in 118 nations around the world, serving 46 million customers a day. The leader, by far, is Japan with almost 4,000 restaurants, followed by Canada with over 1,300, and Germany with over 1,200. As of 2002, there were 95 McDonald's in Russia, and the company plans to open many more restaurants in the former Soviet Union and in the vast new territory in Eastern Europe that has been

laid bare to the invasion of fast-food restaurants. Great Britain has become the "fast-food capital of Europe," and Israel is described as "McDonaldized," with its shopping malls populated by "Ace Hardware, Toys 'R Us, Office Depot, and TCBY."

7. Many highly McDonaldized firms outside of the fast-food industry have also had success globally. Although most of Blockbuster's 8,500 sites are in the United States, more than 2,000 of them are to be found in twenty-eight other countries. Wal-Mart is the world's largest retailer with 1.3 million employees and $218 billion in sales. Over three thousand of its stores are in the United States (as of 2002). It opened its first international store (in Mexico) in 1991, but it now has more than one thousand units in Mexico, Puerto Rico, Canada, Argentina, Brazil, China, Korea, Germany, and the United Kingdom. In any week, more than 100 million customers visit Wal-Mart stores worldwide.

8. Other nations have developed their own variants of this American institution. Canada has a chain of coffee shops, Tim Hortons (merged with Wendy's not long ago), with 2,200 outlets (160 in the United States). Paris, a city whose love for fine cuisine might lead you to think it would prove immune to fast food, has a large number of fast-food croissanteries; the revered French bread has also been McDonaldized. India has a chain of fast-food restaurants, Nirula's, that sells mutton burgers (about 80% of Indians are Hindus, who eat no beef) as well as local Indian cuisine. Mos Burger is a Japanese chain with over fifteen hundred restaurants that, in addition to the usual fare, sells Teriyaki chicken burgers, rice burgers, and "Oshiruko with brown rice cake." Perhaps the most unlikely spot for an indigenous fast-food restaurant, war-ravaged Beirut of 1984, witnessed the opening of Juicy Burger, with a rainbow instead of golden arches and J. B. the Clown standing in for Ronald McDonald. Its owners hoped that it would become the "McDonald's of the Arab world." Most recently, in the immediate wake of the 2003 war with Iraq, clones of McDonald's (sporting names like "MaDonal" and "Matbax") opened in that country complete with hamburgers, french fries, and even golden arches.

9. And now McDonaldization is coming full circle. Other countries with their own McDonaldized institutions have begun to export them to the United States. The Body Shop, an ecologically sensitive British cosmetics chain had, as of early 2003, over nineteen hundred shops in fifty nations, of which three hundred were in the United States. Furthermore, American firms are now opening copies of this British chain, such as Bath & Body Works. Pret A Manger, a chain of sandwich shops that also originated in Great Britain (interestingly, McDonald's purchased a 33% minority share of the company in 2001), has over 130 company-owned and -run restaurants, mostly in the United Kingdom but now also in New York, Hong Kong, and Tokyo.

10. Ikea, a Swedish-based (but Dutch-owned) home furnishings company, did about 12 billion euros in business in 2002 derived from the over 286 million people (equal to about the entire population of the United States) visiting their 150-plus stores in 29 countries. Purchases were also made from the 118 million copies of their catalog printed in over 45 languages. In fact, that catalog is reputed to be the second largest publication in the world, just after the Bible. An international chain to watch in the coming years is H&M clothing, founded in 1947 and now operating over 900 stores in 17 countries with plans to open another 110 stores by the end of 2003. It currently employs over 39,000 people and sells more than 500 million items a year.

McDONALD'S AS A GLOBAL ICON

McDonald's has come to occupy a central place in American popular culture, not just the business world. A new McDonald's opening in a small town can be an important social event. Said one Maryland high school student at such an opening, "Nothing this exciting ever happens in Dale City." Even big-city newspapers avidly cover developments in the fast-food business.

Fast-food restaurants also play symbolic roles on television programs and in the movies. A skit on the legendary television show *Saturday Night Live* satirized specialty chains by detailing the hardships of a franchise that sells nothing but Scotch tape. In the movie *Coming to America* (1988), Eddie Murphy plays an African prince whose introduction to America includes a job at "McDowell's," a thinly disguised McDonald's. In *Falling Down* (1993), Michael Douglas vents his rage against the modern world in a fast-food restaurant dominated by mindless rules designed to frustrate customers. *Moscow on the Hudson* (1984) has Robin Williams, newly arrived from Russia, obtain a job at McDonald's. H. G. Wells, a central character in the movie *Time After Time* (1979), finds himself transported to the modern world of a McDonald's, where he tries to order the tea he was accustomed to drinking in Victorian England. In *Sleeper* (1973), Woody Allen awakens in the future only to encounter a McDonald's. *Tin Men* (1987) ends with the early 1960s heroes driving off into a future represented by a huge golden arch looming in the distance. *Scotland, PA* (2001) brings *Macbeth* to the Pennsylvania of the 1970s. The famous murder scene from the Shakespeare play involves, in this case, plunging a doughnut king's head into the boiling oil of a deep fat fryer. The McBeths then use their ill-gotten gains to transform the king's greasy spoon café into a fast-food restaurant featuring McBeth burgers.

Further proof that McDonald's has become a symbol of American culture is to be found in what happened when plans were made to raze Ray

Kroc's first McDonald's restaurant. Hundreds of letters poured into McDonald's headquarters, including the following:

> Please don't tear it down!. . .Your company's name is a household word, not only in the United States of America, but all over the world. To destroy this major artifact of contemporary culture would, indeed, destroy part of the faith the people of the world have in your company.

In the end, the restaurant was rebuilt according to the original blueprints and turned into a museum. A McDonald's executive explained the move: "McDonald's. . . is really a part of Americana."

Americans aren't the only ones who feel this way. At the opening of the McDonald's in Moscow, one journalist described the franchise as the "ultimate icon of Americana." When Pizza Hut opened in Moscow in 1990, a Russian student said, "It's a piece of America." Reflecting on the growth of fast-food restaurants in Brazil, an executive associated with Pizza Hut of Brazil said that his nation "is experiencing a passion for things American." On the popularity of Kentucky Fried Chicken in Malaysia, the local owner said, "Anything Western, especially American, people here love. . . . They want to be associated with America."

One could go further and argue that in at least some ways McDonald's has become *more important* than the United States itself. Take the following story about a former U.S. ambassador to Israel officiating at the opening of the first McDonald's in Jerusalem wearing a baseball hat with the McDonald's golden arches logo:

> An Israeli teen-ager walked up to him, carrying his own McDonald's hat, which he handed to Ambassador Indyk with a pen and asked: "Are you the Ambassador? Can I have your autograph?" Somewhat sheepishly, Ambassador Indyk replied: "Sure, I've never been asked for my autograph before."
>
> As the Ambassador prepared to sign his name, the Israeli teen-ager said to him, "Wow, what's it like to be the ambassador from McDonald's, going around the world opening McDonald's restaurants everywhere?" Ambassador Indyk looked at the Israeli youth and said, "No, no. I'm the American ambassador—not the ambassador from McDonald's!"
>
> Ambassador Indyk described what happened next: "I said to him, 'Does this mean you don't want my autograph?' And the kid said, 'No, I don't want your autograph,' and he took his hat back and walked away."

Two other indices of the significance of McDonald's (and, implicitly, McDonaldization) are worth mentioning. The first is the annual "Big Mac Index" (part of "burgernomics") published by a prestigious magazine, *The*

Economist. It indicates the purchasing power of various currencies around the world based on the local price (in dollars) of the Big Mac. The Big Mac is used because it is a uniform commodity sold in many different nations. In the 2003 survey, a Big Mac in the United States cost an average of $2.71; in China it was $1.20; in Switzerland it cost $4.52. This measure indicates, at least roughly, where the cost of living is high or low, as well as which currencies are undervalued (China) and which are overvalued (Switzerland). Although *The Economist* is calculating the Big Mac Index tongue-in-cheek, at least in part, the index represents the ubiquity and importance of McDonald's around the world.

The second indicator of McDonald's global significance is the idea developed by Thomas Friedman that "no two countries that both have a McDonald's have ever fought a war since they each got McDonald's." Friedman calls this the "Golden Arches Theory of Conflict Prevention." Another half-serious idea, it implies that the path to world peace lies through the continued international expansion of McDonald's. Unfortunately, it was proved wrong by the NATO bombing of Yugoslavia in 1999, which had sixteen McDonald's as of 2002.

To many people throughout the world, McDonald's has become a sacred institution. At that opening of the McDonald's in Moscow, a worker spoke of it "as if it were the Cathedral in Chartres . . . a place to experience 'celestial joy.'" Kowinski argues that indoor shopping malls, which almost always encompass fast-food restaurants, are the modern "cathedrals of consumption" to which people go to practice their "consumer religion." Similarly, a visit to another central element of McDonaldized society, Walt Disney World, has been described as "the middle-class hajj, the compulsory visit to the sunbaked holy city."

McDonald's has achieved its exalted position because virtually all Americans, and many others, have passed through its golden arches on innumerable occasions. Furthermore, most of us have been bombarded by commercials extolling McDonald's virtues, commercials tailored to a variety of audiences and that change as the chain introduces new foods, new contests, and new product tie-ins. These ever-present commercials, combined with the fact that people cannot drive very far without having a McDonald's pop into view, have embedded McDonald's deeply in popular consciousness. A poll of school-age children showed that 96% of them could identify Ronald McDonald, second only to Santa Claus in name recognition.

Over the years, McDonald's has appealed to people in many ways. The restaurants themselves are depicted as spick-and-span, the food is said to be fresh and nutritious, the employees are shown to be young and eager, the managers appear gentle and caring, and the dining experience itself seems fun-filled. People are even led to believe that they contribute through their purchases, at least indirectly, to charities such as the Ronald McDonald Houses for sick children.

THE LONG-ARM OF McDONALDIZATION

McDonald's strives to continually extend its reach within American society and beyond. As the company's chairman said, "Our goal: to totally dominate the quick service restaurant industry worldwide. . . . I want McDonald's to be more than a leader. I want McDonald's to dominate."

McDonald's began as a phenomenon of suburbs and medium-sized towns, but in more recent years, it has moved into smaller towns that supposedly could not support such a restaurant and into many big cities that are supposedly too sophisticated. You can now find fast-food outlets in New York's Times Square as well as on the Champs-Elysées in Paris. Soon after it opened in 1992, the McDonald's in Moscow sold almost thirty thousand hamburgers a day and employed a staff of twelve hundred young people working two to a cash register. (Today McDonald's controls an astounding 83% of the fast-food market in Russia.) In early 1992, Beijing witnessed the opening of the world's largest McDonald's, with seven hundred seats, twenty-nine cash registers, and nearly one thousand employees. On its first day of business, it set a new one-day record for McDonald's by serving about forty thousand customers.

Small satellite, express, or remote outlets, opened in areas that cannot support full-scale fast-food restaurants, are also expanding rapidly. They are found in small storefronts in large cities and in nontraditional settings such as department stores, service stations, and even schools. These satellites typically offer only limited menus and may rely on larger outlets for food storage and preparation. McDonald's is considering opening express outlets in museums, office buildings, and corporate cafeterias. A flap occurred not long ago over the placement of a McDonald's in the new federal courthouse in Boston. Among the more striking sites for a McDonald's restaurant are the Grand Canyon, the world's tallest building (Petronas Towers in Malaysia), a ski-through on a slope in Sweden, and in a structure in Shrewsbury, England, that dates back to the 13th century.

No longer content to dominate the strips that surround many college campuses, fast-food restaurants have moved onto many of those campuses. The first campus fast-food restaurant opened at the University of Cincinnati in 1973. Today, college cafeterias often look like shopping-mall food courts (and it's no wonder, given that campus food service is a $9.5 billion-a-year business). In conjunction with a variety of "branded partners" (for example, Pizza Hut and Subway), Marriott now supplies food to many colleges and universities. The apparent approval of college administrations puts fast-food restaurants in a position to further influence the younger generation.

We no longer need to leave many highways to obtain fast food quickly and easily. Fast food is now available at many, and in some cases all, convenient rest stops along the road. After "refueling," we can proceed with our trip, which is likely to end in another community that has about the same density and mix of fast-food restaurants as the locale we left behind. Fast food is also increasingly available in hotels, railway stations, and airports.

In other sectors of society, the influence of fast-food restaurants has been subtler but no less profound. Food produced by McDonald's and other fast-food restaurants has begun to appear in high schools and trade schools; over 20% of school cafeterias offer popular brand-name fast foods such as Pizza Hut or Taco Bell at least once a week. Said the director of nutrition for the American School Food Service Association, "Kids today live in a world where fast food has become a way of life. For us to get kids to eat, period, we have to provide some familiar items." Few lower-grade schools as yet have in-house fast-food restaurants. However, many have had to alter school cafeteria menus and procedures to make fast food readily available. Apples, yogurt, and milk may go straight into the trash can, but hamburgers, fries, and shakes are devoured. The attempt to hook school-age children on fast food reached something of a peak in Illinois, where McDonald's operated a program called, "A for Cheeseburger." Students who received As on their report cards received a free cheeseburger, thereby linking success in school with rewards from McDonald's.

The military has also been pressed to offer fast food on both bases and ships. Despite the criticisms by physicians and nutritionists, fast-food outlets increasingly turn up inside hospitals. Although no homes yet have a McDonald's of their own, meals at home often resemble those available in fast-food restaurants. Frozen, microwavable, and prepared foods, which bear a striking resemblance to meals available at fast-food restaurants, often find their way to the dinner table. There are even cookbooks—for example, *Secret Fast Food Recipes: The Fast Food Cookbook*—that allow one to prepare "genuine" fast food at home. Then there is also home delivery of fast foods, especially pizza, as revolutionized by Domino's.

Another type of expansion involves what could be termed "vertical McDonaldization." That is, the demands of the fast-food industry, as is well documented in Eric Schlosser's *Fast Food Nation,* have forced industries that service it to McDonaldize in order to satisfy its insatiable demands. Thus, potato growing and processing, cattle ranching, chicken raising, and meat slaughtering and processing have all had to McDonaldize their operations, and this has led to dramatic increases in production. However, that growth has not come without costs. Meat and poultry are more likely to be disease-ridden, small (often non-McDonaldized) producers and ranchers have been driven out of business, and millions of people have been forced to work in low-paying, demeaning, demanding, and sometimes outright dangerous jobs. For example, in the meatpacking industry, relatively safe, unionized, secure, manageable, and relatively high-paying jobs in firms with once-household names like Swift and Armour have been replaced by unsafe, nonunionized, insecure, unmanageable, and relatively low-paying positions with largely anonymous corporations. While some (largely owners, managers, and stockholders) have profited enormously from vertical McDonaldization, far more have been forced into a marginal economic existence.

McDonald's is such a powerful model that many businesses have acquired nicknames beginning with Mc. Examples include "McDentists" and "McDoctors," meaning drive-in clinics designed to deal quickly and efficiently with minor dental and medical problems; "McChild" care centers, meaning child care centers such as KinderCare; "McStables," designating the nationwide racehorse-training operation of Wayne Lucas; and "McPaper," describing the newspaper *USA TODAY*.

McDonald's is not always enamored of this proliferation. Take the case of We Be Sushi, a San Francisco chain with a half dozen outlets. A note appears on the back of the menu explaining why the chain was not named "McSushi":

> The original name was *McSushi*. Our sign was up and we were ready to go. But before we could open our doors we received a very formal letter from the lawyers of, you guessed it, McDonald's. It seems that McDonald's has cornered the market on every McFood name possible from McBagle [sic] to McTaco. They explained that the use of the name McSushi would dilute the image of McDonald's.

So powerful is McDonaldization that the derivatives of McDonald's in turn exert their own influence. For example, the success of *USA TODAY* has led many newspapers across the nation to adopt, for example, shorter stories and colorful weather maps. As one *USA TODAY* editor said, "The same newspaper editors who call us McPaper have been stealing our McNuggets." Even serious journalistic enterprises such as the *New York Times* and *Washington Post* have undergone changes (for example, the use of color) as a result of the success of *USA TODAY*. The influence of *USA TODAY* is blatantly manifested in *The Boca Raton News,* which has been described as "a sort of smorgasbord of snippets, a newspaper that slices and dices the news into even smaller portions than does *USA TODAY,* spicing it with color graphics and fun facts and cute features like 'Today's Hero' and

'Critter Watch.'" As in *USA TODAY*, stories in *The Boca Raton News* usually start and finish on the same page. Many important details, much of a story's context, and much of what the principals have to say is cut back severely or omitted entirely. With its emphasis on light news and color graphics, the main function of the newspaper seems to be entertainment.

Like virtually every other sector of society, sex has undergone McDonaldization. In the movie *Sleeper,* Woody Allen not only created a futuristic world in which McDonald's was an important and highly visible element, but he also envisioned a society in which people could enter a machine called an "orgasmatron," to experience an orgasm without going through the muss and fuss of sexual intercourse.

Similarly, real-life "dial-a-porn" allows people to have intimate, sexually explicit, even obscene conversations with people they have never met and probably never will meet. There is great specialization here: Dialing numbers such as 555-FOXX will lead to a very different phone message than dialing 555-SEXY. Those who answer the phones mindlessly and repetitively follow "scripts" that have them say such things as, "Sorry, tiger, but your Dream Girl has to go. . . . Call right back and ask for me." Less scripted are phone sex systems (or Internet chat rooms) that permit erotic conversations between total strangers. The advent of the webcam now permits people even to see (though still not touch) the person with whom they are having virtual sex. As Woody Allen anticipated with his orgasmatron, "Participants can experience an orgasm without ever meeting or touching one another." "In a world where convenience is king, disembodied sex has its allure. You don't have to stir from your comfortable home. You pick up the phone, or log onto the computer and, if you're plugged in, a world of unheard of sexual splendor rolls out before your eyes." In New York City, an official called a three-story pornographic center "the McDonald's of sex" because of its "cookie-cutter cleanliness and compliance with the law." These examples suggest that no aspect of people's lives is immune to McDonaldization.

THE DIMENSIONS OF McDONALDIZATION

Why has the McDonald's model proven so irresistible? Eating fast food at McDonald's has certainly become a "sign" that, among other things, one is in tune with the contemporary lifestyle. There is also a kind of magic or enchantment associated with such food and its settings. However, the focus here is the four alluring dimensions that lie at the heart of the success of this model and, more generally, of McDonaldization. In short, McDonald's has succeeded because it offers consumers, workers, and managers efficiency, calculability, predictability, and control.

Efficiency

One important element of McDonald's success is *efficiency,* or the optimum method for getting from one point to another. For consumers, McDonald's offers the best available way to get from being hungry to being full. In a society where both parents are likely to work or where a single parent is struggling to keep up, efficiently satisfying hunger is very attractive. In a society where people rush from one spot to another, usually by car, the efficiency of a fast-food meal, perhaps even a drive-through meal, often proves impossible to resist.

The fast-food model offers, or at least appears to offer, an efficient method for satisfying many other needs, as well. Woody Allen's orgasma-tron offered an efficient method for getting people from quiescence to sexual gratification. Other institutions fashioned on the McDonald's model offer similar efficiency in losing weight, lubricating cars, getting new glasses or contacts, or completing income tax forms.

Like their customers, workers in McDonaldized systems function efficiently following the steps in a predesigned process. They are trained to work this way by managers who watch over them closely to make sure that they do. Organizational rules and regulations also help ensure highly efficient work.

Calculability

Calculability is an emphasis on the quantitative aspects of products sold (portion size, cost) and services offered (the time it takes to get the product). In McDonaldized systems, quantity has become equivalent to quality; a lot of something, or the quick delivery of it, means it must be good. As two observers of contemporary American culture put it, "As a culture, we tend to believe deeply that in general 'bigger is better.'" Thus, people order the Quarter Pounder, the Big Mac, the large fries. More recent lures are the "double" this (for instance, Burger King's "Double Whopper with Cheese") and the "super-size" that. People can quantify these things and feel that they are getting a lot of food for what appears to be a nominal sum of money (best exemplified by McDonald's current "dollar menu"). This calculation does not take into account an important point, however: The high profit margin of fast-food chains indicates that the owners, not the consumers, get the best deal.

People also tend to calculate how much time it will take to drive to McDonald's, be served the food, eat it, and return home; then, they compare that interval to the time required to prepare food at home. They often conclude, rightly or wrongly, that a trip to the fast-food restaurant will take less time than eating at home. This sort of calculation particularly supports home delivery franchises such as Domino's, as well as other chains that emphasize time saving. A notable example of time saving in another sort of chain is LensCrafters, which promises people, "Glasses fast, glasses in one hour."

Some McDonaldized institutions combine the emphases on time and money. Domino's promises pizza delivery in half an hour, or the pizza is free. Pizza Hut will serve a personal pan pizza in five minutes, or it, too, will be free.

Workers in McDonaldized systems also tend to emphasize the quantitative rather than the qualitative aspects of their work. Since the quality of the work is allowed to vary little, workers focus on things such as how quickly tasks can be accomplished. In a situation analogous to that of the customer, workers are expected to do a lot of work, very quickly, for low pay.

Predictability

McDonald's also offers *predictability*, the assurance that products and services will be the same over time and in all locales. The Egg McMuffin in New York will be, for all intents and purposes, identical to those in Chicago and Los Angeles. Also, those eaten next week or next year will be identical to those eaten today. Customers take great comfort in knowing that McDonald's offers no surprises. People know that the next Egg McMuffin they eat will not be awful, although it will not be exceptionally delicious, either. The success of the McDonald's model suggests that many people have come to prefer a world in which there are few surprises. "This is strange," notes a British observer, "considering [McDonald's is] the product of a culture which honours individualism above all."

The workers in McDonaldized systems also behave in predictable ways. They follow corporate rules as well as the dictates of third managers. In many cases, what they do, and even what they say, is highly predictable. McDonaldized organizations often have scripts (perhaps the best-known is McDonald's, "Do you want fries with that?") that employees are supposed to memorize and follow whenever the occasion arises. This scripted behavior helps create highly predictable interactions between workers and customers. While customers do not follow scripts, they tend to develop simple recipes for dealing with the employees of McDonaldized systems. As Robin Leidner argues,

> McDonald's pioneered the reutilization of interactive service work and remains an exemplar of extreme standardization. Innovation is not discouraged . . . at least among managers and franchisees. Ironically, though, "the object is to look for new, innovative ways to create an experience that is exactly the same no matter what McDonald's you walk into, no matter where it is in the world."

Control Through Nonhuman Technology

The fourth element in McDonald's success, *control, is* exerted over the people who enter the world of McDonald's. Lines, limited menus, few options, and uncomfortable seats all lead diners to do what management wishes them to do—eat quickly and leave. Furthermore, the drive-through (in some cases, walk-through) window leads diners to leave before they eat. In the Domino's model, customers never enter in the first place.

The people who work in McDonaldized organizations are also controlled to a high degree, usually more blatantly and directly than customers. They are trained to do a limited number of things in precisely the way they are told to do them. The technologies used and the way the organization is set up reinforce this control. Managers and inspectors make sure that workers toe the line.

McDonald's also controls employees by threatening to use, and ultimately using, technology to replace human workers. No matter how well they are programmed and controlled, workers can foul up the system's operation. A slow worker can make the preparation and delivery of a Big Mac inefficient. A worker who refuses to follow the rules might leave the pickles or special sauce off a hamburger, thereby making for unpredictability. And a distracted worker can put too few fries in the box, making an order of large fries seem skimpy. For these and other reasons, McDonald's and other fast-food restaurants have felt compelled to steadily replace human beings with machines. Technology that increases control over workers helps McDonaldized systems assure customers that their products and service will be consistent.

THE ADVANTAGES OF McDONALDIZATION

This discussion of four fundamental characteristics of McDonaldization makes it clear that McDonald's has succeeded so phenomenally for good, solid reasons. Many knowledgeable people such as the economic columnist, Robert Samuelson, strongly support McDonald's business model. Samuelson confesses to "openly worship[ing] McDonald's," and he thinks of it as "the greatest restaurant chain in history." In addition, McDonald's offers many praiseworthy programs that benefit society, such as its Ronald McDonald Houses, which permit parents to stay with children undergoing treatment for serious medical problems; job-training programs for teenagers; programs to help keep its employees in school; efforts to hire and train the handicapped; the McMasters program, aimed at hiring senior citizens; an enviable record of hiring and promoting minorities; and a social responsibility program with social goals improving the environment and animal welfare.

The process of McDonaldization also moved ahead dramatically undoubtedly because it has led to positive changes. Here are a few specific examples:

♦ A wider range of goods and services is available to a much larger portion of the population than ever before.

♦ Availability of goods and services depends far less than before on time or geographic location; people can do things, such as obtain money at the grocery store or a bank balance in the middle of the night, that were impossible before.

♦ People are able to get what they want or need almost instantaneously and get it far more conveniently.

♦ Goods and services are of a far more uniform quality; at least some people even get better quality goods and services than before McDonaldization.

♦ Far more economical alternatives to high-priced, customized goods and services are widely available; therefore, people can afford things they could not previously afford.

♦ Fast, efficient goods and services are available to a population that is working longer hours and has fewer hours to spare.

♦ In a rapidly changing, unfamiliar, and seemingly hostile world, the comparatively stable, familiar, and safe environment of a McDonaldized system offers comfort.

♦ Because of quantification, consumers can more easily compare competing products.

♦ Certain products (for example, diet programs) are safer in a carefully regulated and controlled system.

♦ People are more likely to be treated similarly, no matter what their race, gender, or social class.

♦ Organizational and technological innovations are more quickly and easily diffused through networks of identical operators.

♦ The most popular products of one culture are more easily diffused to others.

A CRITIQUE OF McDONALDIZATION: THE IRRATIONALITY OF RATIONALITY

Although McDonaldization offers powerful advantages, it has a downside. Efficiency, predictability, calculability, and control through nonhuman technology can be thought of as the basic components of a rational system. However, rational systems inevitably spawn irrationalities. Another way of saying this is that rational systems serve to deny human reason; rational systems are often unreasonable. The downside of McDonaldization will be dealt with most systematically under the heading of the irrationality of rationality; in fact, paradoxically, the irrationality of rationality can be thought of as the fifth dimension of McDonaldization.

For example, McDonaldization has produced a wide array of adverse effects on the environment. One is a side effect of the need to grow uniform potatoes from which to create predictable french fries. The huge farms of the Pacific Northwest that now produce such potatoes rely on the extensive use of chemicals. In addition, the need to produce a perfect fry means that much of the potato is wasted, with the remnants either fed to cattle or used for fertilizer. The underground water supply in the area is now showing high levels of nitrates, which may be traceable to the fertilizer and animal wastes. Many other ecological problems are associated with the McDonaldization of the fast-food industry: the forests felled to produce paper wrappings, the damage caused by packaging materials, the enormous amount of food needed to produce feed cattle, and so on.

Another unreasonable effect is that fast-food restaurants are often dehumanizing settings in which to eat or work. Customers lining up for a burger or waiting in the drive-through line and workers preparing the food often feel as though they are part of an assembly line. Hardly amenable to eating, assembly lines have been shown to be inhuman settings in which to work.

Such criticisms can be extended to all facets of the McDonaldizing world. For example, at the opening of Euro Disney, a French politician said that it will "bombard France with uprooted creations that are to culture what fast food is to gastronomy.

As you have seen, McDonaldization offers many advantages. However, this book will focus on the great costs, and enormous risks of McDonaldization. McDonald's and other purveyors of the fast-food model spend billions of dollars each year outlining the benefits of their system. However, critics of the system have few outlets for their ideas. For example, no one is offering commercials between Saturday-morning cartoons warning children of the dangers associated with fast-food restaurants.

Nonetheless, a legitimate question may be raised about this critique of McDonaldization: Is it animated by a romanticization of the past and an impossible desire to return to a world that no longer exists? Some critics do base their critiques on nostalgia for a time when life was slower and offered more surprises, when people were freer, and when one was more likely to deal with a human being than a robot or a computer. Although they have a point, these critics have undoubtedly exaggerated the positive aspects of a world without McDonald's, and they have certainly tended to forget the liabilities associated with earlier eras. As an example of the latter, take the following anecdote about a visit to a pizzeria in Havana, Cuba, which in many respects is decades behind the United States:

The pizza's not much to rave about—they scrimp on tomato sauce, and the dough is mushy.

It was about 7:30 P.M., and as usual the place was standing-roam-only, with people two deep jostling for a stool to come open and a waiting line spilling out onto the sidewalk.

The menu is similarly Spartan. . . . To drink, there is tap water. That's it— no toppings, no soda, no beer, no coffee, no salt, no pepper. And no special orders.

A very few people are eating. Most are waiting. . . . Fingers are drumming, flies are buzzing, the clock is ticking. The waiter wears a watch around his belt loop, but he hardly needs it; time is evidently not his chief concern. After a while, tempers begin to fray.

But right now, it's 8:45 P.M. at the pizzeria, I've been waiting an hour and a quarter for two small pies.

Few would prefer such a restaurant to the fast, friendly, diverse offerings of, say, Pizza Hut. More important, however, critics who revere the past do not seem to realize that we are not returning to such a world. In fact, fast-food restaurants have begun to appear even in Havana. The increase in the number of people crowding the planet, the acceleration of technological change, the increasing pace of life—all this and more make it impossible to go back to the world, if it ever existed, of home-cooked meals, traditional restaurant dinners, high-quality foods, meals loaded with surprises, and restaurants run by chefs free to express their creativity.

It is more valid to critique McDonaldization from the perspective of the future. Unfettered by the constraints of McDonaldized systems, but using the technological advances made possible by them, people would have the potential to be far more thoughtful, skillful, creative, and well-rounded than they are now. In short, if the world were less McDonaldized, people would be better able to live up to their human potential.

We must look at McDonaldization as both "enabling" and "constraining." McDonaldized systems enable us to do many things that we were not able to do in the past. However, these systems also keep us from doing things we otherwise would not do. McDonaldization is a "double-edged" phenomenon. We must not lose sight of that fact, even though this book will focus on the constraints associated with McDonaldization—its "dark side."

WHAT ISN'T McDONALDIZED?

This chapter should give you a sense not only of the advantages and disadvantages of McDonaldization but also of the range of phenomena discussed throughout this book. In fact, such a wide range of phenomena can be linked to McDonaldization that you may be led to wonder what isn't McDonaldized. Is McDonaldization the equivalent of modernity? Is everything contemporary McDonaldized?

Although much of the world has been McDonaldized, at least three aspects of contemporary society have largely escaped the process:

- ♦ Those aspects traceable to an earlier, "premodern" age. A good example is the mom-and-pop grocery store.
- ♦ New businesses that have sprung up or expanded, at least in part, as a reaction against McDonaldization. For instance, people fed up with McDonaldized motel rooms in Holiday Inns or Motel 6s can instead stay in a bed-and-breakfast, which offers a room in a private home with personalized attention and a homemade breakfast from the proprietor.
- ♦ Those aspects suggesting a move toward a new, "postmodern" age. For example, in a postmodern society, "modern" high-rise housing projects would make way for smaller, more livable communities.

Thus, although McDonaldization is ubiquitous, there is more to the contemporary world than McDonaldization. It is a very important social process, but it is far from the only process transforming contemporary society.

Furthermore, McDonaldization is not an all-or-nothing process. There are degrees of McDonaldization. Fast-food restaurants, for example, have been heavily McDonaldized, universities moderately McDonaldized, and mom-and-pop groceries only slightly McDonaldized. It is difficult to think of social phenomena that have escaped McDonaldization totally, but some local enterprise in Fiji may yet be untouched by this process.

McDONALD'S TROUBLES: IMPLICATIONS FOR McDONALDIZATION

McDonald's has been much in the news in the early 21st century, and most of the time, the news has been bad (at least for McDonald's)—bombings (some involving fatalities) and protests at restaurants overseas, lawsuits claiming that its food made people obese and that it mislabeled some food as vegetarian, declining stock prices, and its first-ever quarterly loss. McDonald's has responded by withdrawing from several nations, settling lawsuits, closing restaurants, reducing staff, cutting planned expansions, replacing top officials, and remodeling restaurants.

It is hard to predict whether the current situation is merely a short-term downturn to be followed by renewed expansion or the beginning of the end of McDonald's (after all, even the Roman Empire, to say nothing of A&P and Woolworth's, among many others, eventually declined and disappeared).

For the sake of discussion, let's take the worst-case scenario—McDonald's imminently turning off the griddles in the last of its restaurants.

This would clearly be a disastrous event as far as stockholders, franchisees, employees, and devotees of Big Macs and Chicken McNuggets are concerned, but what of its broader implications for the McDonaldization of society? The hypothetical demise of McDonald's would spell the end of the model for this process, but it would be of *no consequence* to the process itself. We might need to find a new model and label—"Starbuckization" suggests itself at the moment because of Starbucks' great current success and its dramatic expansion around the globe—but whatever we call it, the process itself will not only continue but grow more powerful. Can we really envision an alternative future of increasing inefficiency, unpredictability, incalculability, and *less* reliance on new technology?

In the restaurant industry, the decline and eventual disappearance of McDonald's would simply mean greater possibilities for its competitors (Subway, Wendy's) and open the way for more innovative chains (In-N-Out Burger). However, which fast-food chains dominate would be of little consequence to the process of McDonaldization since *all of them* are highly McDonaldized and all are based on the model pioneered by McDonald's. What would be of consequence would be a major revival of old-fashioned, non-McDonaldized alternatives like cafes, "greasy spoons," diners, cafeterias, and the like. However, these are not likely to undergo significant expansion unless some organization finds a way to successfully McDonaldize them. And if they do, it would simply be the McDonaldization of yet another domain.

What is certainly *not* going to happen is a return to the pre-McDonald's era dominated by the kinds of alternatives mentioned above. Can we really envision the approximately 13,000 sites currently occupied by McDonald's restaurants in the United States being filled by a like number of independently owned and operated cafes and diners? The problem of finding skilled short-order cooks to staff them pales in comparison to the difficulty in finding people who will frequent them. It's been nearly fifty years since the franchise revolutionized the fast-food industry with the opening of the first of the McDonald's chain. The vast majority of Americans have known little other than the McDonaldized world of fast food, and for those born before 1955, the alternatives are increasingly dim memories. Thus, McDonaldized systems for the delivery of fast food (e.g., drive-through lanes, home-delivered pizzas), and the McDonaldized food itself (Whoppers, Taco Bell's watered-down version of the taco), have become the standards for many people. A hamburger made on the grill at a diner or a taco from an authentic taco stand are likely to be judged inferior to the more McDonaldized versions. Furthermore, those who are accustomed to the enormous efficiency of the fast-food restaurant are unlikely to put up with the relative inefficiencies of diners or taco stands. Those who have grown used to great predictability are not likely to be comfortable with food served in wildly different quantities and shapes. The greater human involvement in preparing and serving food in non-McDonaldized alternatives is likely to be off-putting to most consumers who have grown acclimated to the dehumanization associated with the nonhuman technologies and scripted counter people found throughout today's fast-food industry. The key point is that McDonald's current difficulties do not auger a return to earlier non-McDonaldized alternatives or even to the widespread creation (if one could even envision such a thing) of some new non-McDonaldized form.

McDonald's is doing better outside the United States, and it is there that we are likely to see a continued expansion of it, and other American fast-food chains, for the foreseeable future (by all accounts, the American market for fast-food restaurants is saturated, and this is a big source of McDonald's problems). More important, as pointed out earlier, many other nations have witnessed the emergence of their own fast-food chains modeled, naturally, after McDonald's. Not only are they expanding within their own borders, but they are also increasingly interested in global expansion (Britain's Pizza Express is expanding into Eastern European countries as San Marzano restaurants), even into the American market. Interesting recent examples include the opening in Manhattan of a number of Pret A Manger (the British chain that, as we have seen, is partly owned by McDonald's) shops offering higher-quality, prewrapped sandwiches, and Polio Capero (from Guatemala) fried-chicken restaurants in Los Angeles and Houston (with plans for big expansion in the United States). In fact, the center of McDonaldization, as was previously the case with many forms of factory production, is increasingly shifting outside the United States. Whether it occurs under the name of Mos Burger (Japan) or Nirula's (India), it is still McDonaldization.

If the principles have proven successful and have proliferated so widely, why is McDonald's in trouble? There are obviously a number of reasons, including many bungled opportunities and initiatives such as efforts to be more attractive to adults, to create new menu items, and to restructure restaurants as well as the chain as a whole. While McDonald's could have done better, the fact is that in the end it has been undercut by its own success. Many competitors have adopted its principles and entered the niche created by McDonald's for fast food. Like many other innovators, McDonald's now finds itself with many rivals who learned not only from McDonald's successes but also from its failures. (One could say that these competitors are "eating McDonald's lunch.") McDonald's, too, may now be better able to overcome its problems and learn from the hot new companies in the fast-food industry. However, whether or not it does, fast-food restaurants and, more generally, the process of McDonaldization are with us for the foreseeable future.

Thinking Critically

◆◆◆

1. Is there really any such thing as McDonaldization?

2. Is McDonald's the best example of McDonaldization? In light of its problems, and the rise of Starbucks, would the latter now be a better example? Should we relabel the process "Starbuckization"?

3. Is the fast food-restaurant really as important as is suggested here?

4. Can you think of any other dimensions of McDonaldization?

5. Can rationality ever really be irrational?

This chapter, from The McDonaldization of Society, *deals with the precursors to the fast-food restaurant and the concept of McDonaldization. The key figure in this history is the German social theorist Max Weber (1864–1920), who pioneered the contemporary sociological conception of the bureaucracy and created the best-known theory of rationalization. The bureaucracy was the paradigm for the rationalization process in Weber's day. That process is described here using the same dimensions as were used in Chapter 1 to define the essence of McDonaldization. This should not be surprising because my theory of McDonaldization is based on, and closely related to, Weber's theory of rationalization. One key difference, however, is that whereas Weber focused largely on production, the focus of McDonaldization is consumption, which has come to rival, even exceed, the importance of production, especially in highly developed nations like the United States. It is this that leads to the conclusion that the fast-food restaurant, whose home is obviously in the realm of consumption, is a better paradigm today for the rationalization or McDonaldization of society than the bureaucracy.*

I also explore Weber's famous idea that rationalization (now McDonaldization) creates an "iron cage" from which it is increasingly difficult for us to escape. Although this continues to be a useful image, I reexamine it in Chapter 3, which offers another way of thinking about the structure of McDonaldization.

2

Precursors

Bureaucracy and Max Weber's Theory of Rationality, Irrationality, and the Iron Cage

George Ritzer

M cDonaldization did not emerge in a vacuum; it was preceded by a series of social and economic developments that not only anticipated it but also gave it many of the basic characteristics touched on in Chapter 1. In this chapter, I will look briefly at the notion of bureaucracy and Max Weber's theories about it and the larger process of rationalization.

BUREAUCRATIZATION: MAKING LIFE MORE RATIONAL

A *bureaucracy* is a large-scale organization composed of a hierarchy of offices. In these offices, people have certain responsibilities and must act in

Editor's Note: From Ritzer, G. (2004). McDonaldization and Its Precursors: From the Iron Cage to the Fast-Food Factory. *The McDonaldization of Society, Revised New Century Edition* (pp. 24–24). Thousand Oaks, CA: Sage.

accord with rules, written regulations, and means of compulsion exercised by those who occupy higher-level positions.

The bureaucracy is largely a creation of the modern Western world. Although earlier societies had organizational structures, they were not nearly as effective as the bureaucracy. For example, in traditional societies, officials performed their tasks because of a personal loyalty to their leader. These officials were subject to personal whim rather than impersonal rules. Their officers lacked clearly defined spheres of competence, there was no clear hierarchy of positions, and officials did not have to obtain technical training to gain a position.

Ultimately, the bureaucracy differs from earlier methods of organizing work because of its formal structure, which, among other things, allows for greater efficiency. Institutionalized rules and regulations lead, even force, those employed in the bureaucracy to choose the best means to arrive at their ends. A given task is broken down into components, with each office responsible for a distinct portion of the larger task. Incumbents of each office handle their part of the task, usually following preset rules and regulations, and often in a predetermined sequence. When each of the incumbents has, in order, handled the required part, the task is completed. In handling the task in this way, the bureaucracy has used what its past history has shown to be the optimum means to the desired end.

Weber's Theory of Rationality

The roots of modern thinking on bureaucracy lie in the work of the turn-of-the-century German sociologist Max Weber. His ideas on bureaucracy are embedded in his broader theory of the *rationalization* process. In the latter, Weber described how the modern Western world managed to become increasingly rational—that is, dominated by efficiency, predictability, calculability, and nonhuman technologies that control people. He also examined why the rest of the world largely failed to rationalize.

As you can see, McDonaldization is an amplification and extension of Weber's theory of rationalization. For Weber, the model of rationalization was the bureaucracy; for me, the fast-food restaurant is the paradigm of McDonaldization.

Weber demonstrated in his research that the modern Western world had produced a distinctive kind of rationality. Various types of rationality had existed in all societies at one time or another, but none had produced the type that Weber called *formal rationality*. This is the sort of rationality I refer to when I discuss McDonaldization or the rationalization process in general.

What is formal rationality? According to Weber, *formal rationality* means that the search by people for the optimum means to a given end is shaped by rules, regulations, and larger social structures. Individuals are not left to their own devices in searching for the best means of attaining a given objective. Weber identified this type of rationality as a major development in the history of the world: Previously, people had been left to discover such mechanisms on their own or with vague and general guidance from larger value systems (religion, for example). After the development of formal rationality, they could use institutionalized rules that help them decide—or even dictate to them—what to do. An important aspect of formal rationality, then, is that it allows individuals little choice of means to ends. In a formally rational system, virtually everyone can (or must) make the same, optimal choice.

Weber praised the bureaucracy, his paradigm of formal rationality, for its many advantages over other mechanisms that help people discover and implement optimum means to ends. The most important advantages are the four basic dimensions of rationalization (and of McDonaldization).

First, Weber viewed the bureaucracy as the most efficient structure for handling large numbers of tasks requiring a great deal of paperwork. As an example, Weber might have used the Internal Revenue Service, for no other structure could handle millions of tax returns so well.

Second, bureaucracies emphasize the quantification of as many things as possible. Reducing performance to a series of quantifiable tasks helps people gauge success. For example, an IRS agent is expected to process a certain number of tax returns each day. Handling less than the required number of cases is unsatisfactory performance; handling more is excellence.

The quantitative approach presents a problem, however, little or no concern for the actual quality of work. Employees are expected to finish a task with little attention paid to how well it is handled. For instance, IRS agents who receive positive evaluations from their superiors for managing large numbers of cases may actually handle the cases poorly, costing the government thousands or even millions of dollars in uncollected revenue. Or the agents may handle cases so aggressively that taxpayers become angered.

Third, because of their well-entrenched rules and regulations, bureaucracies also operate in a highly predictable manner. Incumbents of a given office know with great assurance how the incumbents of other offices will behave. They know what they will be provided with and when they will receive it. Outsiders who receive the services that bureaucracies dispense know with a high degree of confidence what they will receive and when they will receive it. Again, to use an example Weber might have used, the millions of recipients of checks from the Social Security Administration know precisely when they will receive their checks and exactly how much money they will receive.

Finally, bureaucracies emphasize control over people through the replacement of human judgment with the dictates of rules, regulations, and structures. Employees are controlled by the division of labor, which allocates to each office a limited number of well-defined tasks. Incumbents must do those tasks, and no others, in the manner prescribed by the organization. They may not, in most cases, devise idiosyncratic ways of doing those tasks. Furthermore, by making few, if any, judgments, people begin to resemble human robots or computers. Having reduced people to this status, leaders of bureaucracies can think about actually replacing human beings with machines. This replacement has already occurred to some extent: In many settings, computers have taken over bureaucratic tasks once performed by humans. Similarly, the bureaucracy's clients are also controlled. They may receive only certain services and not others from the organization. For example, the Internal Revenue Service can offer people advice on their tax returns but not on their marriages. People may also receive appropriate services in certain ways and not others. For example, people can receive welfare payments by check, not in cash.

Irrationality and the "Iron Cage"

Despite the advantages it offers, bureaucracy suffers from the *irrationality of rationality*. Like a fast-food restaurant, a bureaucracy can be a dehumanizing place in which to work and by which to be serviced. Ronald Takaki characterizes rationalized settings as places in which the "self was placed in confinement, its emotions controlled, and its spirit subdued." In other words, they are settings in which people cannot always behave as human beings—where people are dehumanized.

In addition to dehumanization, bureaucracies have other irrationalities. Instead of remaining efficient, bureaucracies can become increasingly inefficient because of tangles of red tape and other pathologies. The emphasis on quantification often leads to large amounts of poor-quality work. Bureaucracies often become unpredictable as employees grow unclear about what they are supposed to do and clients do not get the services they expect. Because of these and other inadequacies, bureaucracies begin to lose control over those who work within and are served by them. Anger at the nonhuman technologies that replace them often leads employees to undercut or sabotage the operation of these technologies. All in all, what were designed as highly rational operations often end up quite irrational.

Although Weber was concerned about the irrationalities of formally rationalized systems, he was even more animated by what he called the "iron cage" of rationality. In Weber's view, bureaucracies are cages in the sense that people are trapped in them, their basic humanity denied. Weber feared most that bureaucracies would grow more and more rational and that rational principles would come to dominate an accelerating number of sectors of society. He anticipated a society of people locked into a series of rational structures, who could move only from one rational system to another—from rationalized educational institutions to rationalized workplaces, from rationalized recreational settings to rationalized homes. Society would eventually become nothing more than a seamless web of rationalized structures; there would be no escape.

A good example of what Weber feared is found in the contemporary rationalization of recreational activities. Recreation can be thought of as a way to escape the rationalization of daily routines. However, over the years, these escape routes have themselves become rationalized, embodying the same principles as bureaucracies and fast-food restaurants. Among the many examples of the rationalization of recreation are Club Med, chains of campgrounds, and package tours. Take, for example, a thirty-day tour of Europe. Buses hurtle through only the major cities in Europe, allowing tourists to glimpse the maximum number of sites in the time allowed. At particularly interesting or important sights, the bus may slow down or even stop to permit some picture taking. At the most important locales, a brief stopover is planned so visitors can hurry through the site, take a few pictures, buy a souvenir, then hop back on the bus to head to the next attraction. With the rationalization of even their recreational activities, people do live to a large extent in the iron cage of rationality.

Thinking Critically

1. Is the bureaucracy as important today as it was in Weber's day (circa 1900)?

2. Was the bureaucracy in Weber's day a good example of what he called rationalization?

3. In what ways is today's bureaucracy different from what it was when Weber wrote?

4. Is today's bureaucracy a good example of rationalization?

5. Can a bureaucracy ever truly be an iron cage?

One way to think about the "iron cage" is that it represents a vision of the social geography of McDonaldization. That is, our social landscape is so dominated by McDonaldized settings of all types that we are imprisoned in them; there is no escape from them. However, when one thinks about this geographically (and in many other ways), it is clear that as ubiquitous as these settings are, there is certainly ample room for escape. Thus, this chapter posits an image of contemporary society as being characterized by "islands" of McDonaldization in a "sea" (the rest of society) that is either less or non-McDonaldized. This image seems to fit today's reality better than the iron cage because we are able to move easily from McDonaldized islands (e.g., a fast-food restaurant) to the less- or non-McDonaldized settings that surround them (e.g., the family, although it, too, is becoming McDonaldized; see Chapter 13) and are still predominant (although perhaps not for much longer).

These islands are described, following the film maker George Romero and his cult classic, Dawn of the Dead, *as housing the "dead." That is, people may be viewed as being dead in these settings in various senses, especially because they are expected to conform to what is expected of them and not to act creatively. Although this is certainly true, it is also the case that much life is found in these McDonaldized settings (think of Disneyland, or better yet, Las Vegas). Combining the ideas of death and life with islands, the image of the social geography of McDonaldization that is communicated here is "islands of the living dead." To some degree how alive or dead these islands are, and even how dominant they become, is up to us as consumers, workers, managers, owners, and so on. After all, we can either accept the death they offer us, or we can choose to enliven them. Of course, we can also reject them completely leading to a less-, or even a non-, McDonaldized society.*

3

Islands of the Living Dead

The Social Geography of McDonaldization

George Ritzer

◆◆◆ ————————————————————————————————

I focus in . . . this article on the social geography . . . of the McDonaldization of society. This, of course, is based on Max Weber's famous work on rationalization and his vision of the social world as being increasingly encased in an "iron cage" of rationalization. This metaphor can be interpreted in various ways, but one that has not been explored systematically is from the perspective of social geography.

On the surface, when examined from this geographic point of view, the image of an iron cage seems to convey the sense of an entire society, or even world, enclosed by an overarching system of rationalization. Although this is one geographic image, the fact is that Weber famously lacked a sense of society (let alone the world) as a whole but instead focused on specific structures, institutions, and domains. Thus, it could be argued that it would be more accurate to say that Weber envisioned a series of iron cages rather than a single, overarching cage. He did see such cages growing more numerous

Editor's Note: From Ritzer, G. (2003, Oct). Islands of the Living Dead: The Social Geography of McDonaldization." *American Behavioral Scientist, 42*(2). Reprinted with permission from Sage Publications, Inc.

with more and more sectors of society coming to be rationalized. In addition, he believed that the bars on these cages were growing stronger, thicker, and harder. However, this does not yield a view of a society as a whole (or the world) growing increasingly rationalized . . .

Whatever the real possibilities of . . . a seamless system of McDonaldized sites arising in the future, the fact remains that today it is more accurate to think of those sites as islands of McDonaldization.

In fact, Weber's actual image of the social geography of rationalization comes closer to another social geography—Foucault's sense of a "carceral archipelago"—to which it is often contrasted. On the surface, the image of an iron cage communicates a totally enclosed system, whereas that of a "carceral archipelago" conveys a sense of relatively individual, even isolated, rationalized systems with great gaps—the relatively free and open "seas"— between them. However, as we have already seen, Weber, like Foucault, envisions just such a series of "islands" of rationalization and the iron cage imagery is clearly in line, at least on each of the islands, with Foucault's carceral vision of what those islands are like. For his part, Foucault, especially in his thoughts on "discipline," has a rationalized view of the world— or at least of the islands in the archipelago—not unlike that of Weber.

However, when we turn to the contemporary rationalized world—one that I have described in terms of McDonaldization—the issue arises as to whether either of these images—iron cage (at least in the totalistic sense in which it is usually interpreted) or carceral archipelago—is an adequate description of it. In fact, it is clear almost immediately that both are inadequate. In no way can we think of society as a whole as an iron cage of rationality. Although we can certainly think in terms of islands of McDonaldization, those islands lack bars; they are not carceral in any sense of the term; people are *not* locked into these islands. Thus, I would like to use this article as an occasion to develop a vision of the social geography of McDonaldization that, although it is related to Weber's "iron cage" and Foucault's "carceral archipelago," differs from both in significant ways . . . .

The appropriate phantasmagoric social geographic image, with a bow to Hollywood and its "B" movies, is islands of the living dead. Notable sources for this view are George Romero's movies *The Night of the Living Dead* (1968) and especially its sequel *Dawn of the Dead* (1979). The latter, in fact, takes place in . . . one of the most important of these islands: a shopping mall.

ISLANDS

Foucault's vision of an archipelago is far closer to the metaphor being developed here than the image conveyed by those who interpret Weber as offering a sense of an overarching iron cage. It is clear that there is no way that we can think of society today in terms of an iron cage and, furthermore, it is almost impossible to envision a scenario—especially one involving the increasing prevalence and preeminence of consumption settings—in which the result is such an all-embracing phenomenon in the future. The abysmal failure of the Soviet Union to create such a system would seem to make it clear that its successful development and implementation is, to put it mildly, unlikely. Developments in capitalist societies indicate that McDonaldized systems are likely to grow more numerous, and the "bars" that surround them are likely to grow thicker and stronger, but they are likely to remain enclaves of rationalization in a larger society that is less—or even not—rationalized.

It is far more accurate to think in terms of islands of rationalization or McDonaldization:

- ♦ Factories are increasingly rare in the United States and those comparatively few that continue to exist are likely to be surrounded by decaying and destroyed remnants of the far greater number of factories that used to dot the American landscape;
- ♦ in the city, any given block might have a fast-food restaurant or a Gap store, but in between we are still likely to find traditional, individually owned and operated, small shops and businesses and even abandoned shops or empty lots;
- ♦ the suburbs are likely to be dotted with highly rationalized shopping malls composed almost exclusively of McDonaldized shops and businesses;
- ♦ small towns are likely to see their downtown business areas decimated by fast-food restaurants and a Wal-Mart, all built on the road out of town or on its periphery;
- ♦ every 20 miles or so on the main highway from Washington, D.C., to New York City (and many other highways) one finds rest stops now exclusively offering food from one of the many fast-food franchise systems that are so increasingly prevalent;
- ♦ even on the Las Vegas Strip with its famous, and highly McDonaldized, casino-hotels, there are numerous non-McDonaldized small businesses remaining in the spaces between them;
- ♦ on a cruise ship, the tourist may be trapped on a McDonaldized "island," and may visit the areas of "real" islands along the way that are almost as McDonaldized, but just beyond the ship's railing, as well as the borders of the island enclaves that are visited, are far less rationalized, even non- or irrational, worlds; and
- ♦ Disney World is clearly a McDonaldized island and innumerable other such islands have grown up around it in Orlando, Florida (as well as around the other Disney theme parks in California, Japan, and France [and now Hong Kong]), but there remain areas in the environs that have not yet been McDonaldized.

One could extend such examples but it is obvious that in none of these locales do we find an iron cage of McDonaldization but rather many islands defined by their high degree of rationalization. Although it is true that there are an increasing number of such islands, and that number is likely to increase even further in the future, this allows us to see that there remain non-McDonaldized areas, often quite vast in scope, in the interstices that exist between the islands. These interstices can be undeveloped land; non-McDonaldized settings; non-rational or irrational domains; areas that once were, but are no longer, McDonaldized; as well as areas that have not-yet-been, but likely soon-will-be, McDonaldized. Thus, it is not only possible but remains quite easy, at least from a social geographic point of view, for those who so wish to avoid the McDonaldized islands and seek out and find non-McDonaldized alternatives.

Of course, that leads, almost immediately, to the issue of why so many people are increasingly drawn to the McDonaldized islands and, conversely, are so unwilling to venture off into the non-McDonaldized spaces that offer alternatives to them. There is clearly a kind of magnetism associated with McDonaldized settings and consumers are increasingly drawn to them. That magnetism comes, of course, from the clever, attractive, and aggressive marketing and advertising campaigns undertaken by the firms that own McDonaldized settings. Thus, the magnetism is not intrinsic to the systems but manufactured by them, especially their public relations, marketing, and advertising arms or firms hired by them. The non-McDonaldized alternativeses—for example, independently owned businesses—lack the resources to make themselves similarly magnetic. Thus, although the "sea" of settings continues to be overwhelmingly populated by non-McDonaldized systems, many consumers are drawn to the islands of rationalization and routinely bypass the numerous nonrationalized or less-rationalized alternatives along the way. Why people do this is also linked to the next section of this analysis: the "living" that takes place on these islands.

LIVING

There is a great deal of living taking place on the McDonaldized islands being analyzed here; there is much that is lively, full of life, associated with them. This is often lost sight of in the focus on the critiques of rationalization and McDonaldization, especially the irrationalities of rationality intimately associated with them. We must attend to the fact that large numbers of people are drawn to these islands and seem to derive a great deal of pleasure from their visits. For example, people seem to enjoy the food at fast-food chains such as McDonald's, Burger King, Taco Bell, Pizza Hut, and Starbucks. Egg McMuffins, burgers, tacos, pizzas, and double espressos are downed with great gusto and in huge quantities. Furthermore, in many senses, it is more the fun associated with fast-food restaurants than the food consumed in them that attracts consumers. This is most obvious in the case of children drawn by the toy and movie promotions and the carnival-like atmosphere of at least some fast-food restaurants. Adults seem to enjoy watching their children having fun and, in addition, derive their own gratifications from visiting fast-food restaurants. Similarly, the shoppers at the Gap, Old Navy, and Banana Republic arrive in droves and joyously grab clothing from the racks, try on various garments, and bring them home in great numbers. Whatever scholars may say of a critical character about such settings—how they manipulate customers, the mediocre quality of what they have to offer—we cannot ignore the fact that so many people seem to be having such a terrific time in them and in consuming what they have to offer.

This is even more true of the large and famous islands in the archipelago of McDonaldized consumption. The Mall of America, Disney World, the Las Vegas Strip, and the Destiny cruise ship are among the most desired destinations for not only American consumers, travelers, and tourists but those from much of the rest of the world as well. Disney World's self-designation as "the happiest place on earth" also could be employed by these other settings, and the behavior of visitors to these settings does little to belie such claims. At the Mall of America, people seem to be having a great time shopping and shuttling between the mall and the amusement park found under the same roof. For children, and their parents, a visit to Disney World seems like the culmination of a lifelong ambition. Joyous faces abound on the rides, in the attractions, and in the various hotels, shops, and restaurants. Gamblers in Las Vegas are in the world mecca of gambling, and they act like it (at least until they have to tote up the inevitable losses), and the transformation of the town into more of a family tourist attraction makes even the nongamblers happy as they can visit indoor malls attached to casino-hotels, see circus acts at Circus Circus, watch a sea battle at Treasure Island, view the water show at Bellagio, and take a gondola ride at the Venetian.

Thus, a great deal of living takes place on these McDonaldized islands; there is a lot of life to them. The critical orientation to be discussed in the following section should not cause us to lose sight of this fact. There is certainly a paradox here; a paradoxical relationship between the life of these islands and the "death" we are about to discuss, a paradox we will deal with in the conclusion to this article.

DEATH

In what senses can we think of McDonaldized islands as "dead," as being associated with "death"? Of interest, Jean Baudrillard focuses on the cemetery, which in terms of this article can be considered a means of consuming death and the dead. Indeed, at least some cemeteries (the famous Forest Lawn Cemetery in Los Angeles) have, similar to other cathedrals of consumption, sought to become spectacular to attract a larger "clientele." However, the key point is that modern cemeteries represent the separation of death from life, whereas in earlier societies the two were intimately related. Cemeteries were (and are) "ghettos" for the dead and, in a sense, the McDonaldized islands being discussed here are similar ghettos separated from life. According to Baudrillard, death is controlled "in anticipation of the future confinement of life in its entirety." We can think of McDonaldized islands as settings in which large portions of life have come to be confined—in which some of life has clearly come to be separated from the rest of life. Furthermore, Baudrillard is making it clear here (as we have above) that the confinement of life in its entirety—Weber's iron cage—is not yet a reality. Baudrillard seems to believe unequivocally that such a fully carceral system is an inevitability, but at this point, such a reality only looms in the distance. Regardless of whether Baudrillard is right about the future, his vision of the present is consistent with the island metaphor being employed here.

People are, as we have seen, living on these islands, but it is a life that, by definition, is clearly separated from the rest of existence (the "sea" surrounding the islands). Separation implies alienation, and it could be argued that life in those settings is alienated from the rest of life. Instead of life flowing naturally into and out of these islands, the living that takes place on them tends rather to take place in largely autonomous settings; it is a relatively segregated form of living that takes place in these settings. Furthermore, the life on one island is different and separated from the living that is to be found on other islands. Thus, one is virtually forced to leave one's everyday life to participate in the living found on the Vegas Strip, Disney World, or Mall of America. This is even true of more local and everyday islands such as the nearby mall, superstore, or even franchise restaurant. Furthermore, one must leave the life experienced in one setting to experience the form of living to be found on another island. All of this is certainly living, but it is a ghettoized form of living taking place in a similarly ghettoized context. It is living, but a form of living separated from the rest of life.

Although there is life on McDonaldized islands, it is arguably at least a different form of life, if not less of a form of life, than that found in at least some of the non-McDonaldized interstices between the islands. One way of looking at what is different about life on McDonaldized islands is Weber's conception of life in the rationalized world and its cold skeletal hands. Clearly, Weber associates death with rationalization in general and, more specifically, with the death of the life-affirming character of sex. However, we need not go back to Weber for a theoretical resource on this—Baudrillard offers a similar view in his discussion of the segregated world of death and cemeteries as "a meticulously regulated universe." Thus, McDonaldized islands fit Baudrillard's view that life "is no longer anything but a doleful, defensive bookkeeping, locking every risk into its sarcophagus." Thus, in contrast to Ulrich Beck's view that we live in a risk society and the fact that risk undoubtedly remains a reality in the interstices between the islands, life on McDonaldized islands is virtually risk free. Although in some senses this is highly desirable, in many other senses it is undesirable, especially in leading to a dull, boring, routine form of existence. This is at least one of the senses in which we can say that those who "live" on these islands are "dead." This is clearly the case for the workers who do nothing but dull, boring, and routine work. Furthermore, the workers spend a considerable part of their day on the islands. However, it is also true for customers, although they spend far less time there. For example, the food that they eat, and what they are required to do to get the food, are well described as being dull, boring, and routine.

Following Baudrillard, death characterizes life on these islands in another way. McDonaldized settings seek to optimize rationalization; according to Baudrillard, they seek "perfection." That is, they seek to be all positivity, to eliminate all negativity. However, such an approach renders a world in which everything resembles "the smile of a corpse in a funeral home." A more lively setting would permit positivity and negativity to coexist. To put it in other Baudrillardian terms, McDonaldized systems are dead because they lack "evil" (as well as "seduction" and "symbolic exchange"). Therefore, what they need is an injection of such evil. That is, they need more of the things associated with life—instability, seduction, ambivalence, "the natural disorder of the world."

McDonaldized systems are also, again in Baudrillard's terms, "ecstatic" systems. That is, they are hypertelic, expanding in a seemingly limitless manner (see Stephenson's association of franchises with viruses). Expansion seems out of control with the result that the system as a whole "shines forth in its pure and empty form." One of Baudrillard's major examples of ecstasy is cancer, and thus, the association of McDonaldization with this process clearly also links it to death. The ecstatic expansion of the growth of McDonaldization not only means more islands of McDonaldization but also more empty, dead, or dying settings.

Furthermore, in Baudrillard's view, the dead are transformed into a "stuffed simulacrum of life." One is tempted to describe the diners who have finished their massive "value meals" in fast-food restaurants in similar terms, but the idea of simulacra has broader applicability to the islands of McDonaldization. That is, these islands are characterized, even dominated, by simulations. Examples are legion, including the various casino-hotels in Las Vegas (Paris, Mandalay Bay), all of the "worlds" in Disneyland, "eatertainment" sites such as Rainforest Cafe, and so on. Is real life going on there, or is the living that we find there merely a faint copy of what life should be all about? If we answer yes to the second question then this is a second sense in which we can associate what transpires on the islands as being associated with death. That is, it is nothing more than a simulation of life, not life itself. Furthermore, living, at least for a time, in these simulated worlds, can people do anything but live a life dominated by simulation?

The most direct association between the geographic settings of concern here and death is Kowinski's work on the shopping mall and what he calls the "Zombie Effect." That is, the structure of malls induces consumers to wander about them for hours in a near-endless pursuit of goods and services. Of course, the idea of zombies brings us back to the living dead, specifically the movies of George Romero. In *Dawn of the Dead* (1979), Romero's zombie-consumers are set loose in a Cleveland shopping mall. This image can be extended to all consumers in all McDonaldized settings who are simultaneously alive and dead: the living dead—zombies.

CONCLUSION

This article has made the case not only for a social geography of the McDonaldized world but a specific social geographic image—"islands of the living dead." This is seen as a more accurate image, at least for the time being, of the state of McDonaldization in society. It may be that at some point in the future, Foucault's vision of a "carceral" archipelago or even the view . . . associated with Weber of an all-encompassing "iron cage" might be more accurate, but that remains to be seen. The strength of the image presented here is that it accurately conveys a sense of still-isolated "islands" of McDonaldization; it makes it clear that there is much that is positive about these islands (the "living" that takes place on them); and it offers a critical orientation toward them, their "dead" structures, and their tendency to deaden the life that transpires within their confines.

Thinking Critically

◆◆◆

1. Do you feel like you live in a carceral archipelago?

2. Do you feel like you live in an iron cage?

3. Do you feel like your life is spent moving from one island of the living dead to the next?

4. In what ways are you alive on these islands?

5. In what ways are you dead on these islands?

Chapter 4 reports on an empirical study to determine whether the entire restaurant business in the United States has been McDonaldized, specifically whether it has come to be dominated by chains. The author distinguishes between fast-food and full-service restaurants and finds that while, as expected, fast-food restaurants are dominated by chains, the latter have made only minimal inroads into the full-service sector. The implication is that full-service restaurants have not been highly McDonaldized. Of course, being part of a chain is related to, but far from a perfect indicator of, a high degree of McDonaldization. That is, it is possible that full-service restaurants have grown increasingly McDonaldized even though they are not part of chains.

4

On Mass Distribution

A Case Study of Chain Stores in the Restaurant Industry

Joel I. Nelson

◆◆◆──

M y argument in this chapter is straightforward: The presence of chains or systems of mass distribution is neither total nor fully explained. Considerable literature argues that mass production is not a monolithic development, and I argue the same case with respect to retail trade. I focus on one segment of the retail industry—restaurants. Restaurants have been singled out as the quintessential instance of chain store organization (Ritzer), and eating outside the home represents a burgeoning segment of consumer expenditures. If mass distribution follows mass consumption, then chains ought to develop throughout the industry. Using the idea that innovations occur oppositionally in proximate or adjacent fields, I suggest that there is good reason to believe that substantial segments of the industry are composed of single, independent establishments, and this in spite of the growing and substantial size of the market. My research draws on the distinction between full-service and fast-food restaurants and shows that mass distribution

Editor's Note: Excerpts from "On Mass Distribution: A Case Study of Chain Stores in the Restaurant Industry" by Joel I. Nelson, 2001, *Journal of Consumer Culture* 1: 141–160. Used with permission.

develops in a bipolar fashion—in a manner at odds with the popular conception of a world of restaurants awash in chain store development. . . .

CHAINS IN FAST-FOOD AND FULL-SERVICE RESTAURANTS

Industry Background

Figure 4.1 provides the historical backdrop for examining the distribution of chains in the restaurant industry. The figure graphically juxtaposes two indicators across the 30-year period covered by this research: the comparative distribution of fast-food and full-service restaurants and changing expenditures for eating out. As to the first of these issues, the bar columns indicate the distribution of restaurant types; the respective number in each type are shown along the axis on the left. The figure indicates the dramatic rise of fast-food restaurants over this nearly 30-year time period . . . [but] there is no indication that full-service restaurants are increasingly peripheral. While full-service restaurants do not grow at the same rate as fast-food restaurants, their numbers over the 30-year period have hardly diminished and in fact have increased by about 9%.

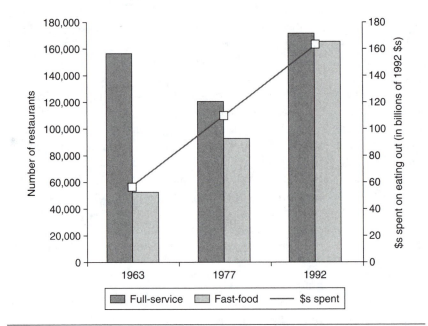

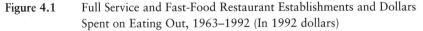

Figure 4.1   Full Service and Fast-Food Restaurant Establishments and Dollars Spent on Eating Out, 1963–1992 (In 1992 dollars)

. . . Growth in all of these restaurants reflects (and indeed may partially have caused) rising consumer expenditures in eating outside of the home. Changes in expenditures are displayed by the trendline and the axis on the right-hand side of the figure indicating the actual dollars spent on eating out.

The juxtaposition of the trendline for expenditures and the changing proportions of restaurants suggest that the full-service sector remains a forceful competitor for consumer spending. While full-service restaurants increasingly garner smaller proportions of the market than in the past, the dollar sums involved are substantial and rose over the three time periods—$47 billion in 1963, $64 billion in 1977, and $85 billion in 1992 (all in 1992 dollars). If chains as mass distribution systems are a function of mass consumer markets, then chains ought to proliferate across various types of restaurants. But my data indicate that they do not. . . .

CONCLUSIONS AND DISCUSSION

In the context of the widespread growth of chains throughout the fast-food sector, it is somewhat surprising that chains in a related industry would be as minimal as they are, particularly in light of the substantial size of the market. To explain this apparent paradox, I suggested that proximate markets grow oppositionally and further that the full-service sector—with extensive menus, service, and on-site preparation—has provided few opportunities for the high-profit margins of interest to large-scale capital development. Data . . . documented that growth in chains in the full-service sector was indeed minimal and additionally outlined the possible ways full-service chains might cope with restraints on profits by generating high-volume sales. In this review, restaurants overall are not as commonly chained as Ritzer, for example, suggested.

Equally important are the findings suggesting that restaurants are not marginalized by the growth of fast-food chains. The data in Figure 4.1 indicate continual erosion of the proportions of the market controlled by the full-service sector, but not at a level reflective of increasing marginality. Furthermore, this pattern persists into 1997 as well. . . .

The conclusions here are straightforward: Different profit environments generate different market structures and different strategies for survival.

Thinking Critically

♦♦♦

1. Are full-service restaurants themselves becoming increasingly McDonaldized?

2. What do you think of McDonaldized, full-service chains of restaurants like Olive Garden, Red Lobster, and Outback?

3. What is the future of the gourmet restaurant?

4. What is the relationship of social class and economic standing to the growth of both full-service and fast-food restaurants?

5. Given the range of options, where would you rather eat most of the time? Why? Given the spread of McDonaldization, will you still have much of a choice in the future?

Chapter 5 on "rib joints" describes another aspect of the restaurant business that has not been McDonaldized to any great degree. As the authors put it, "There is no fast food in a rib joint. The food arrives as dictated by the desire of the proprietor or by the dictates of cooking the ribs, which 'takes as long as it takes.'" The authors see the rib joint as a kind of deviant setting in which behavior that rebels against modern society in general, and McDonaldized society in particular, is encouraged. Similarly, the shady characters who run rib joints are very unlike the straight businesspeople who operate McDonald's franchises.

My distinction among three types of people—those who see McDonaldization as creating a "velvet," an "iron," or a "rubber" cage—is used to distinguish among rib joint patrons. Those who see McDonaldization as a velvet cage love such enterprises and are unlikely to ever make their way into a rib joint. Those who view it as rubber cage will venture out of their McDonaldized world on occasion for a change of pace but quickly return to it. Those who view the McDonaldized world as an iron cage are the real hope for non-McDonaldized settings such as rib joints because they are likely to become loyal patrons of such settings. That is, if they see themselves in an iron cage, and such a position offends them, they are likely to try to escape to places such as rib joints.

While the rib joint can be seen as an alternative to McDonaldization, such joints could come to be McDonaldized, but that would mean their demise as a genuine alternative to the increasingly ubiquitous McDonaldized meal.

5

A Sociology of Rib Joints

P. D. Holley and D. E. Wright, Jr.

◆◆◆ ───

O nly barbeque restaurants that feature ribs may be classified as "rib
joints." . . . This ideal type includes the following deviant aspects.

1. A location that is usually difficult to find. . . . This joint seldom
advertises; patrons learn about it by "word of mouth" and by the occasional
"lifestyles" section of some metropolitan newspaper or magazine written by
a reporter looking for an "offbeat" story, or by an annual exercise of rating
local restaurants. The best rib joints must be searched out . . . utilizing refer-
rals from locals, such as service station attendants.

2. The location may seem "shady," "suspicious," or "questionable,"
even to a typical patron. The normal reaction to such locations would be
uncertainty, if not fear, as to whether one should be in this part of town or
in this neck of the woods. . . .

───────────

Editor's Note: Excerpts from "A Sociology of Rib Joints" by P. D. Holley and
D. E. Wright, Jr., pp. 73–74, 75–82 in *McDonaldization Revisited: Critical Essays
on Consumer Culture,* edited by Mark Alfino et al. Copyright © 1998, Praeger
Publishing Company, Westport, CT. Used with permission.

3. A building or facility itself may be of dubious nature, with a run-down exterior, messy woodpile, smokers, and parts scattered around. The interior should represent a mixture of plain and gaudy . . . This is to be opposed to the brightly lit, spic-and-span atmosphere of the mainstream eatery. The restroom may only minimally meet health department standards and may even have a Portapotty out back. . . . The furnishings are "odd," perhaps reminiscent of the 1950s era. Soot from the smoker may be visible on the ceiling, fan blades, and other places routinely inaccessible to cleaning. Thus, patrons are left to wonder about health department regulations.

4. The staff of a rib joint, and especially the proprietor, may seem of a dubious, shady, deviant nature. Such staff may treat patrons, especially first-time patrons, with what appears as indifference.

5. "Regulars" of the rib joint are disdainful of newcomers, especially if these newcomers seem ill at ease or if the novices are "dressed up."

THE RIB JOINT EXPERIENCE

Eating ribs is a greasy and messy enterprise. . . .

The attraction of barbeque . . . may well incorporate a unique style of preparation, dependent on the experience, ability, and passion of the pit-boss. Even with a desire for consistency in outcome, unpredictability from one time to the next may reign supreme. Further, there are elements of mystery in that ingredients of the sauces are matters of extreme secrecy. The recipes for everyday eating fail the patron of a rib joint, especially the novice . . . who must abandon the old recipes for eating out and create or learn a new one. In this, one can expect the novice to be uncomfortable and probably not to enjoy the first experience in a rib joint—there is often no menu to be leisurely examined and reviewed. The sometimes impatient server recites a jargon-filled menu that must typically be explained and repeated so that one simply can be sure of what one is hearing. The novice either blindly selects something or is assured by a regular ribber or server to "trust me" on a particular order. In other joints, the menu is posted on the wall, with little in the way of item description or explanation.

Absent are menu items for children; unless they eat ribs, they are out of place. The ideal rib joint is not prepared to serve children and serves them regular meals, allows children to eat off their parents' plates, or improvises on the spot. Rib eating is for "adults."

There is no fast food in a rib joint. The food arrives as dictated by the desire of the proprietor or by the dictates of cooking the ribs, which "takes as long as it takes." Furthermore, when the ribs run out, nothing else can substitute, since there are no other entrée items on the menu.

Dining with others is a social occasion . . . in which to create and demonstrate invidious comparisons among people in terms of respectability. . . . Alternatively, especially in fast-food eateries, dining becomes a safe and routinized activity with no special meaning beyond merely providing sustenance.

None of this is true in ribbing. First, the basics of fire-cooked meat brings to mind something of a dangerous experience. . . . Second, a rib meal is anything but routinized and fast. . . . Further, in its very essence, a rib meal is antisnob, antiyuppie, antihierarchical. Traditionally, a meal wholly or primarily of meat is a sign of egalitarianism among the select few who together partake of the meal. Such a meal meant a time of celebration, a special occasion. The rib meal, consisting of the basics of fire-cooked meat, is interpreted by many ribbers as a return to "primal," basically a return to times before status hierarchies became institutionalized and the practice of eating became cluttered with "manners" and a seemingly endless variety of equipment.

Ribbing is an "earthy" experience. It is difficult if not impossible to pretend to be better than others with food in one's hand, with grease and sauce on one's mouth and hands, and wearing a bib and/or a napkin stuck in the neck of one's shirt.

The rib joint's fare itself is messy. And, even with the improvements in pork quality, it is in opposition to the current "health food" craze which emphasizes small and infrequent helpings of low-fat, well-cooked meat.

It is difficult to have what most etiquette books would consider to be "bad table manners" in a rib joint. One is expected to have a "dirty-fingers, greasy mouth, crunchy-bone experience." In a rib joint, one eats with one's hands; puts one's elbows on the table; wears a bib or even places a napkin in one's shirt or uses many paper towels as napkins (from a paper towel roll prominently displayed on the table); gets one's face smeared; passes food from one person to another and/or from one plate to another; smacks one's lips; exclaims loudly about how good the food is; licks one's fingers and lips so as not to miss a drop of meat, juice, and sauce; and freely and openly uses toothpicks. As one eats, one begins to stack the gnawed-bare bones in a pile on the table, clearly as a trophy of one's accomplishments. In short, one must unlearn "good table manners." Neither Julia Child nor Emily Post— both of whom would heartily disdain rib table manners—is likely to show up for a meal at a rib joint. . . .

Part of the meaning of ribbing is counter to modern society; it is a rebellious act. Further, it is an act imbued with a "we against the world" attitude, or at least a "we against the 'straights,'" that is to say against those who do not "do ribs." In doing ribs, one is, among other things, thumbing one's nose at mainstream society. Ribbers see themselves as independent from mainstream customs, free from the need to be well thought of. Last, there develops among ribbers an ethnocentrism, an aloofness toward the outside world, toward those who put on airs, and toward those who eschew ribs. Ribbers are smug in their knowledge that they understand what truly fine food and good eating are. Simultaneously, ribbers pity and ridicule those not initiated to ribs.

THE RIB JOINT PROPRIETOR

There are few true "individualists" any longer, but the rib joint proprietor may qualify. Typically, the proprietor is male and something of a reprobate, someone who has chosen to avoid or leave the mainstream of typical employment and working for someone else, having chosen to enter one of the most failure prone of businesses, the food-services business. Further, the proprietor is in a business little known and little appreciated by the society at large, as evidenced by the small number of rib joints in the United States. . . . To open a rib joint would seem like "risky business" indeed. However, success in the common sense seems not to be the major motivating force. While not opposed to financial success, most rib joint proprietors appear to be motivated more by a desire to get out of the mainstream and by the desire to provide a good meal for their patrons. . . . Many . . . refuse to do what would be necessary for fame and fortune, choosing instead to serve friends and to enjoy themselves. In this, most rib joint proprietors have a demeanor that seems to say "take me as I am—I am not changing; if I cannot make it as I am, I will do something else.". . .

At best a marginal person, the proprietor has the ability to interact with and serve those of varying socioeconomic and ethnic backgrounds, and to make the dining experience an enjoyable one, to which many return. Usually serving as owner, manager, cashier, server, and cook (or pit-boss), the proprietor presents himself to the customer in active, multiple, and unique ways. . . .

One rule intimately known by ribbers is "call first." Rib joints are notorious for opening and closing at odd hours. In many joints, the proprietor prepares a certain number of slabs of ribs per day—when those are sold, the doors are closed. Often, the owner will close the joint for a month or so while on vacation, fully expecting the clientele to return when he is ready to get back to work.

The rib joint proprietor possesses a passion, a vision, a method, and a secret. The passion is for ribs—real barbeque. His vision is to serve up the best ribs there are, and on a regular basis. The method he has perfected over time, combining particular woods, a certain type of smoker, the application of a marinade, a rub and/or sauce, particular cuts of meat, involves slow cooking with periods of doing nothing interspersed with the attention and care of a perfectionist. Sauces, sometimes invented by the pit-boss, and at other times inherited from family members or friends, represent a crowning achievement. Unique sauces . . . have certain ingredients as carefully guarded secrets. Unique dry rubs . . . maintain ingredients as mysterious.

When the rib joint proprietor dies (or for some reason closes the operation), the continuation of the joint is not at all certain. Sauce secrets may be taken to the grave. Children or other employees may have neither the skill, experience, or passion possessed by the proprietor. Food quality may not be consistent with that of the founder. Or, there may be conflict among spouses, children, other relatives, and others over ownership, control, and management of the joint, as in the case of the Wild Horse Bar-B-Que. These factors seem to explain the tenuous life of the rib joint.

RIB JOINT PATRONS

Ritzer delineates three types of people based on their attitudes and behavior toward "McDonaldization." The first type refers to those who view the consequences of rationalization as constituting a "velvet cage" connoting that these patrons like McDonald's and welcome it. The second view the consequences as a "rubber cage" with both advantages and disadvantages from which they occasionally and temporarily seek escape. The third group shares with Weber the belief that the disadvantages are more numerous and are similar to an ever-expanding "iron cage" from which ultimately there may be no escape. The velvet cagers always eat at the McDonald's of the modern world, the rubber cagers eat there during the work week and when pressed for time, and the iron cagers never eat there and are fearful that McDonald's will soon be the only type of eatery available.

The velvet cagers would of their volition never select a rib joint. Such persons, when found in rib joints, arrive reluctantly, in the company of others who persuaded them against their "better judgment," and are unlikely to return again. These people are not likely to order ribs, unless there is nothing else on the menu; if they have ribs, they may attempt to cut the meat from the bone and consume the meat with a fork. These patrons are noticeably uncomfortable and consider rib joints as barbaric and archaic. They are people who do not want eating and dining to be an adventure.

Patrons who are in the rubber cage category are like "weekend warriors" who are looking for an alternative to the ho-hum routine of the week and not content with certain features of the fast-food eateries. They are willing to risk some uncertainty in finding alternatives—on occasion. While frequenting "barbeque restaurants," these patrons may also wander into a rib joint by accident but are adventurous enough to brave the deviant (or is it, in their eyes, "cute"?) aspects of the joint to stay and try the main dish. Such patrons will even follow the local custom of throwing good table manners to the winds and dine in appropriate rib fashion; in short, they enjoy themselves. Such rubber cagers may return on more than one occasion and bring others with them. However, these people view ribbing as a sometime thing to do when one has time and as only one of numerous alternatives to fast-food eateries. Last, rib joint patrons of this second type do not qualify as the ideal type patron in that they remain attached to the highly rationalized fast-food eateries and do not internalize an image of themselves as being first and foremost rib connoisseurs.

It should be noted that the rubber cagers are both boon and bane to the rib joint proprietor. On the one hand, they constitute a healthy portion of the joint's clientele, help to popularize particular joints, and introduce first-timers who may eventually become aficionados. On the other hand, these patrons tend truly not to understand the culture and significance of rib joints and from time to time contaminate the joint with culture from the outside world; examples would be for these patrons, who have dined in the joint on occasion, to believe that the proprietor is indebted to them, to expect that they can make special requests, or to be in a hurry. Further, by popularizing the joint, the rubber cagers may serve, unintentionally, to destroy the joint by making it too successful.

The third type of patron is those who view the McDonald's of the world as anathema—pure disaster. As patrons of rib joints, these people do so by choice—indeed, the rib joint is the first thought when eating out occurs. These regulars view themselves as "ribbers" or "rib addicts" and thoroughly delight in the ambiance, decor, food, and manners (or lack thereof) of the joint. These people also differ from the previous type in that for the true rib joint patron, eating here is not a sometime affair to be done when one happens to think about it or when one has enough time. The true patron *always* thinks first of ribs and makes time for them. These patrons are like "sojourners" who "pine for the old days" and view themselves as out of touch with the modern, as alienated from modern food culture. They do not necessarily romanticize the past, but they prefer it when it comes to dining. Further, these patrons view the velvet cagers with disdain and the rubber cagers with wariness. True patrons may even attempt to discourage the first-timers or velvet cagers from staying or returning. The wariness toward the rubber cagers is because of the possibility that they may over-popularize the joint, or make it so successful that the joint and proprietor become upscale.

THE FUTURE OF THE RIB JOINT

In sum, the rib joint and a rib meal are anachronisms. The very nature of the rib joint makes it unlikely that ribbing will catch on as has Mexican and Italian dining. Franchises, drive-up windows, faster service, and so on may all find their way into fringes of the rib culture. Barbeque establishments may be located in malls. However, the uniqueness of the food, the proprietor, and the patrons guarantees restricted popularity and limited expansion. . . .

The steady pace of modernization with its emphasis on speed, efficiency, impersonalization, and processing is another source of concern for the rib joint subculture. The very success of some rib joints has caused some proprietors and some businesspeople (ever attentive to making a buck) from outside the subculture to attempt "rationalizing" the rib meal and to make of it the next "McDonald's." Were the rib joint given too much attention, were it to be mass marketed and mainstreamed, the rib joint as described here would die. . . .

But, it is our prediction that the rib joint will persist. We further predict that the rib joint will remain outside the mainstream food culture. . . .

A major factor in the perpetuation of the rib joint is the modernization process and its tendency to "McDonaldize" everything it touches. Rib joints are out-of-step anachronisms, throwbacks to other times, like the "mom and pop" corner stores with their more personalized and less mechanized, less standardized services. To the extent there is a backlash to the modern, whether this backlash is for only the weekend experiment or as a way of life, rib joints will find a niche in the effort to correct for the alienating effects of modernity. To the extent that poor, yet entrepreneurial men and women are produced in this culture, the rib joint will persist . . .

Long live the rib joint!

Thinking Critically

◆◆◆

1. What is the future of the "rib joint" in the age of McDonaldization?

2. What is it about rib joints that might lead people to eat in them?

3. What is it about rib joints that might lead people to pass them up and eat in fast-food restaurants?

4. In what ways is the rib joint an anachronism?

5. In what ways is the critique of McDonaldization animated by a romanticization of places like rib joints?

In this chapter, Bryman applies his four elements of Disneyization to McDonald's and finds that the latter is, to a large degree, Disneyized. (In other words, he has shown how Disney is McDonaldized in various ways.) The following are the basic dimensions of Disneyization that characterize McDonald's.

Theming. *This is the "story," really "stories," that McDonald's tells about itself and communicates aggressively to everyone it comes into contact with— suppliers, workers, and especially consumers. There actually are many different stories (for children, parents, teenagers, grandparents, etc.), but one overall theme is that this is a "happy" place for all. This happiness is found in the smile of counter people and of Ronald McDonald, as well as in the "Happy Meal."*

Merchandising. *McDonald's sells all sorts of stuff beyond the food on offer at the restaurants. Most notable are various toy promotions as well as the merchandise for sale on its Web site.*

Dedifferentiation of Consumption. *This involves the interpenetration of various forms of consumption, for example, when McDonald's promotes Disney movies and McDonald's restaurants are found in Disney theme parks. Another is the existence of McDonald's restaurants in shopping malls where many other things are for sale.*

Emotional Labor. *McDonald's employees are expected not only to smile, but to be friendly and happy.*

6

McDonald's as a Disneyized Institution

Alan Bryman

◆◆◆ ───

M cDonaldization is a trend that George Ritzer has argued is enveloping more and more spheres of contemporary society, but it is by no means the only way of conceptualizing change. Ritzer himself remarks at one point that for him it "is simply one important trend, one important way of thinking about contemporary developments." This comment provides an admission ticket for a number of different narratives of change. Such further ways of conceptualizing change should not be seen as contestants in a struggle for our attention but as additional ways of getting to grips with what is happening around us. They are not alternatives: They provide leverage on those areas that notions such as McDonaldization do not fully allow us to encapsulate.

One such additional way of thinking about change that I have suggested in earlier work is the idea of Disneyization. This notion was deliberately set up as a parallel set of changes to those associated with McDonaldization. Ritzer argued that McDonald's provided a paradigm whose underlying

Editor's Note: From Bryman, A. (2002, Oct.). McDonald's as a Disneyized Institution. *American Behavioral Scientist, 47*(2). Reprinted with permission of Sage Publications, Inc.

principles were spreading their tentacles around more and more sectors of society, even though the principles themselves preexisted the first McDonald's restaurant. In a similar vein, I developed the idea of Disneyization as "the process by which *the principles* of the Disney theme parks are coming to dominate more and more sectors of American society as well as the rest of the world." In other words, I substituted the phrase "Disney theme parks" for "the fast-food restaurant" in Ritzer's definition of McDonaldization in coming up with a definition of Disneyization.

An interesting twist on this issue is provided by several suggestions in Ritzer's work that theme parks, and the Disney ones in particular, exemplify McDonaldization. Although I have expressed some doubts about whether the Disney theme parks fit the McDonaldization picture in terms of calculability, in other words, whether the parks emphasize quantity at the expense of quality, it fits well in terms of the other three dimensions. The Disney theme parks and all theme parks modeled on them provide predictable tourist entertainment, exert considerable control over their guests (including control through the use of nonhuman technologies), and are highly efficient in their processing of guests.

However, as with other spheres in which McDonaldization has wrought its impact, to describe the Disney theme parks as McDonaldized does not capture entirely their significance or impact. And, indeed, the quotation from Ritzer's work cited above leads us to think that he is unlikely to subscribe to such a view either. The notion of Disneyization was born out of this kind of reflection: What do the Disney theme parks express that is significant and that is having a growing impact on modern society? In formulating Disneyization, I came up with four dimensions or aspects:

1. *Theming*: the use of a narrative that is consciously imposed on a particular sphere and which envelops consumers,

2. *Dedifferentiation of consumption*: denotes simply the general trend whereby the forms of consumption associated with different institutional spheres become interlocked with each other and increasingly difficult to distinguish,

3. *Merchandising*: a term I use simply to refer to the promotion of goods in the form of, or bearing, copyright images and logos, including such products made under license, and

4. *Emotional labor*: entails control over the employee so that socially desired emotions are exhibited during service transactions.

Walt Disney and the Disney company did not invent any of these principles any more than the McDonald brothers and Ray Kroc invented the principles of

McDonaldization. Instead, the Disney theme parks exemplify these principles. The high-profile nature and huge success of the Disney theme parks may have played an important role in promoting the spread of the principles but the parks should not be seen as their wellspring.

It was previously noted that Ritzer depicted the Disney theme parks as McDonaldized. But could we turn the picture around and ask whether McDonald's is a Disneyized institution? The fit may not be a perfect one but the four principles that underpin Disneyization have come to the fore in more recent times than those associated with McDonaldization. The latter can be traced back, as Ritzer frequently observes, to F. W. Taylor and Henry Ford, but the principles of Disneyization are much more closely connected with the rise of consumerism. If we take the view that, if nothing else, consumerism refers to people's purchase of goods and services they do not need and the sustained efforts of a host of organizations to supply consumers with these unnecessary goods and services, this is a collection of features that has become especially prominent in more recent times.

Can a case be made, then, that McDonald's is a Disneyized organizational form? We should not be overly surprised if this were the case because there are numerous ways in which the two are connected. They were both built up by visionary entrepreneurs, they both have strong corporate cultures, they both have universities, they both emphasize the advantages of automation, they both emphasize the family, and so on. It is even the case that when Ray Kroc joined the Red Cross at the end of World War I, he says in his biography that there was another young man who had lied about his age to get in. Kroc writes, "He was regarded as a strange duck, because whenever we had time off and went out on the town to catch girls, he stayed in camp drawing pictures." So, by a strange quirk of fate, the two men who nurtured two of the most prominent brands and companies of the last 100 years spent time together in a Red Cross company.

McDONALD'S AS A DISNEYIZED INSTITUTION

I will turn now to the question of how far McDonald's corresponds to the four dimensions of Disneyization that have been outlined.

Theming

McDonald's can be viewed as themed in different ways and at different levels. As Gottdiener has observed, franchised chains of restaurants such as McDonald's essentially provide a theme that is themselves. This theme is expressed in the corporate decoration, modes of service delivery, staff clothing, and various architectural cues that are pervasive features of these establishments. Beardsworth and Bryman have referred to such theming as *reflexive theming,* whereby the theme, the brand, and its expression become coterminous. With reflexive theming, the organization does not draw on external devices for its narratives; instead, the thematic elements are internally generated and then continuously reproduced. "Each themed setting refers reflexively to itself and to the population of clones which reflect it and are reflected by it."

Such theming, then, is essentially self-referential and refers to those relatively rare instances in which a brand provides its own organizational narrative, a feature that also can be seen in the Disney theme parks and other realms of the Disney empire. McDonald's as a company is acutely aware of its self-referential theming. It portrays its eating environments as experiences. Benjamin Barber quotes Jim Cantalupo, then president of international operations, who explains how McDonald's "is more than just price. It's the whole experience which our customers have come to expect from McDonald's. It's the drive-thrus . . . it's the Playlands . . . it's the smile at the front counter . . . it's all those things . . . the experience." When Ray Kroc once observed, "when you are in this business you are in show business," he was drawing attention to the way in which the development of a brand has to do with turning the perception of it into an experience by which it becomes instantly recognizable. Certainly, both Shelton and Manning and Callum-Swan have drawn attention to the way in which there are theatrical or dramatic connotations to a McDonald's visit. Thus, when it is suggested by the latter writers that "McDonald's is a brilliantly conceived dramatic production," it is the brand as a unique eating experience that is crucial. Similarly, in an interview for *Foreign Policy* in 2001, chief executive officer Jack Greenberg was quoted as saying, "When you enter the restaurant, you enter the brand. And so the challenge for all of our local franchisees and local management around the world is to ensure a minimum level of consistency." The opening in 2001 of the Golden Arch hotel in Zurich, where the headboards on the beds are in the shape of a golden arch, is an interesting illustration of the use of a brand as mechanism for theming. Such extensions of the McDonald's theme reflect the faith in brands such as McDonald's that have come to connote consistency of quality. As Twitchell has observed, with branding, "what is being bought is place, prestige, comfort, security, confidence, purpose, meaning." Thus, McDonald's as a company is acutely aware of the significance of its brand as a provider of meaning and organizer of experiences.

But theming in McDonald's does not rest solely at the level of reflexive theming. There are other ways in which theming reveals itself. One is that there is a constant overlay of a narrative of family in the advertising and images associated with the company. It is routinely depicted (or perhaps it would be more accurate to say that it routinely depicts itself) as a clean, safe haven for families to refuel at relatively low cost. As Law points out, this appeal to families is emphasized through a tendency to personalize its advertising and through the suggestion that in this fun place the family will be reinforced. Kincheloe observes that family values are frequently deployed in McDonald's advertising as part of a nostalgic reference to an idealized past.

This familial discourse is a powerful one in that the company is well aware of its appeal to children and indeed engages in many tactics to enhance that appeal. The image of the family at McDonald's renders parents more amenable to children's pester power and the association with low-risk eating in a safe environment provides a reassuring setting for families. Watson also has noted the intensive use of family imagery in McDonald's advertising in East Asia.

However, there is also evidence of McDonald's becoming increasingly attracted to the use of external narratives in its restaurants. Chicago's own rock 'n' roll McDonald's serves as an illustration of the use of this kind of development. In 2001, an article in the *New York Times* announced that a huge McDonald's was planned for Times Square that would have the ambience of a Broadway theatre. Schlosser wrote that when he visited the McDonald's near Dachau concentration camp, it had a Wild West theme. Yan describes a themed McDonald's in Beijing in which the restaurant was decorated like a ship and crew members wore sailor uniforms rather than conventional McDonald's garb. The narrative was one of Uncle McDonald's Adventure, which is meant to entail a round-the-world trip with Uncle McDonald. Also, the company has announced that it is going to refurbish some of its outlets as traditional diners, thereby drawing on a motif that is an extremely popular thematic focus for American restaurant chains. Bone reported in the *Times* that not only was Denny's remodeling some of its restaurants "to give the nostalgic feel of traditional diners" but McDonald's was doing the same and had just opened its "first diner-style outlet in Kokomo, Indiana, and customers are lining up to eat such old-fashioned American fare as turkey steak and mashed potato." A second has since opened in another town in Indiana. It remains to be seen whether these McDonald's diners will be rolled out more widely but the fact that they are experimenting with such theming is very telling about the directions that the company is considering.

A further sign of theming is the use of ethnic theming. In the United Kingdom, for example, the company often features lines that are themed in terms of Indian or Italian cooking (both of which are very popular among the British). Gordon and Meunier report that in spring 2000, McDonald's launched a raft of locally themed meals. In one month, the enthusiast could buy a burger with a different French cheese on each day of the week. The following month, "gourmet" meals were available in the south of France.

Gourmet was signified by being able to eat burgers topped with ratatouille or by ice cream with a black currant sauce topping.

Therefore, in several ways, McDonald's restaurants can be viewed as themed. The growing use of theming that goes beyond reflexive theming and theming in terms of family may be due to a belief that although the company does provide a certain kind of experience, as Cantalupo suggests, it increasingly needs to do more in this regard. Pine and Gilmore have suggested that with regard to what they call the *experience economy,* companies increasingly need to raise consumers' experiences to new levels that will be highly memorable. Although it is unlikely that McDonald's would want to turn itself into a chain of themed restaurants that become destinations in their own right, especially in view of the financial difficulties experienced by such chains in the past few years, the slow move in some of its outlets to a more distinctive kind of theming may prove an interesting long-term development in terms of Disneyization.

Merchandising

There is evidence of merchandising in McDonald's as well as theming. It can be seen in the availability of a wide range of merchandise bearing its logos or characters. The McDonald's Web site has a very large amount of merchandise for sale at a variety of prices. These include clothing items such as baseball caps and t-shirts to nostalgia items such as cookie jars. The McDonald's in the Disney Marketplace in Orlando had a particularly wide range of merchandise when I visited the area in 2000. Merchandising has to a certain extent been extended by the McKids range of children's clothing. Referring to this range in his *Foreign Policy* interview, Greenberg said, "It happens to be licensed to Wal-Mart, but it's our brand and we get a royalty for it." Although merchandising in McDonald's is by no means as extensive as in Disney theme parks, there is evidence that the restaurant chain has incorporated this element of Disneyization.

Dedifferentiation of Consumption

There are two main ways in which dedifferentiation of consumption can be seen in relation to McDonald's. One is through the way its tie-ins with companies such as Disney become the context for the distribution of toys or when it latches onto new toy crazes such as the Beanie Babies. These toys have attracted enthusiasts who collect them; there is a Web site for sharing of information about them and an annual convention for collectors. Most new Disney films are involved in cross-promotional tie-ins with McDonald's so that as Pecora and Meehan report in the context of their U.S.

component of the Global Disney Audiences Project, "Given Disney's promotional agreement with McDonald's, the McDonald's in the mall had been decorated with *Hunchback* streamers and promotional displays. It offered special *Hunchback* meals with *Hunchback* place mats, napkins, paper cups, etc." But it is the distribution of free toys that is the key feature for us in terms of dedifferentiation of consumption. Wolf points out that the exclusive McDonald's/Disney alliance produced a 23% increase in Happy Meals in the United States. In 1997, this made for a 7% increase in sales. In the process, McDonald's became the largest distributor of toys in the world. It is not surprising, therefore, that the participant researchers in the Global Disney Audiences Project noted that their interviewees in several countries frequently noted the prominence of tie-ins with Disney films. However, it is not just Disney films that are tied in to McDonald's—films such as *Space Jam* also have been involved in this way. Although writers, for example, Wolf, claim that such tie-ins can result in very significant improvements in food sales for McDonald's, the movie tie-in with food is by no means a recipe for success, as Taco Bell found with its cross-promotion with *Godzilla*. The significance of such tie-ins for the present discussion is simply that the distribution of free toys as a lure for children can be viewed as evidence of the dedifferentiation of consumption because it involves elements of the sale of both food and toys. It also should be noted that this form of the dedifferentiation of consumption is often a focus for criticism because it is seen as evidence of the manipulation of consumers and of children in particular. The Archbishop of Canterbury has criticized such tie-ins and singled out Disney for particular disapproval, saying, "The Disney empire has developed this to an unprecedented pitch of professionalism."

The second main way in which we find dedifferentiation of consumption in relation to McDonald's is the way in which it is frequently implicated in settings that bring together a variety of forms of consumption. Examples are the obvious ones, such as the presence of McDonald's in malls, but there are others too, such as its location in theme parks. Ritzer has observed that McDonald's is often found in the modern ballpark. He and Stillman depict the growth of food courts featuring McDonald's and other chains as one of the ways in which the modern ballpark seeks to make the overall experience of spectatorship "more spectacular and enchanted." Certainly, the company's plans in terms of this feature of Disneyization are ambitious. In the Afterword to Kroc's autobiography, Kroc's coauthor Robert Anderson mentions the appearance of McDonald's in a hospital, tollway services plazas, military bases, shopping malls, and amusement parks. He quoted from the 1985 annual report, "Maybe—someday—McDonald's will be found on aircraft carriers and commercial airliners. In sports stadiums and fine department stores." As a strategy, this is not always successful, as the company found when it was forced because of poor levels of patronage to close many of its outlets that were located in Wal-Mart stores.

Emotional Labor

Emotional labor is a key feature of McDonald's restaurants. It is a component of the Quality Service and Value ethos from Ray Kroc's days that remains a central tenet of the faith. Its importance is drilled into franchisees and managers at the Hamburger Universities. Crew members at the customer interface are widely expected to engage with diners in a friendly way to enhance the pleasurable nature of the dining experience and to increase the likelihood of more items being purchased. Royle, for example, on the basis of his European research on McDonald's, has written that the company's employees "are expected to control themselves *internally* by being pleasant, cheerful, smiling and courteous to customers, even when customers are rude and offensive." It is very much part of the show business atmosphere that Kroc felt was such an important component of the success of the restaurants. It can be seen in the previously quoted remark by Jim Cantalupo, then president of international operations, when he refers to the significance of "the smile at the front counter." As Fantasia points out in connection with the reception of McDonald's in France, the American ambience is a very important aspect of its success there among youth, and it is the deployment of emotional labor that plays an important role in creating that ambience. It is striking that when Kincheloe interviewed a woman originally from Hong Kong, she explained how as a girl her enthusiasm for McDonald's was such that she used to play role-playing games in which she would "churn up a big smile, and say, 'How can I help you today? May I please have your order?'"

Emotional labor is not without its problems for crew members. As Leidner has shown, the scripted nature of interactions with clients and the need to act in a way that can be inconsistent with how one actually feels—especially in the face of difficult customers—can be a deeply alienating experience. However, the main point in relation to the current discussion is that McDonald's exhibits this dimension of Disneyization.

However, there is a further dimension to emotional labor at McDonald's, and it is one that was neglected in the original exposition of Disneyization. It is not just crew workers who are involved in exhibiting emotional labor; managers are also involved in a form of emotional labor in that they are trained and encouraged to become subservient to the McDonald's corporate ethos and culture. Leidner writes that the company seeks to produce managers with "ketchup in their veins." The Hamburger University plays a significant role in inculcating this corporate spirit. In part, the training is conducted to instruct managers in the correct operational procedures to maximize the kind of uniformity of process and product for which the company is famous. But also, as Leidner observes, managers' zeal is worked on to ensure they understand as fully as possible the reasons for adherence to protocol so that they are more likely to ensure that there is no transgression. The training is concerned, therefore, with "building commitment and motivation" as much as instruction in McDonald's ways of doing things. The kind of company loyalty that is required and engendered is a form of emotional labor on the part of those who are required to exhibit it. Much like Disney's University, the managers also are introduced to the company's history and to the words of its founder to enhance the emotional appeal of the corporate culture.

Reflection

There does, then, seem to be evidence to support my contention that McDonald's is a Disneyized institution. Once again, I am not suggesting that McDonald's has copied the Disney theme parks, although that may sometimes have occurred. In particular, it may be worth drawing a distinction between *structural* and *transferred* Disneyization. The former "reflects a complex of underlying changes of which the Disney theme parks are exemplars." Transferred Disneyization is where the principles of the Disney theme parks are transferred into another sphere. A similar kind of distinction also could be made in relation to McDonaldization, although in practice it is difficult to distinguish between concrete cases of Disneyization or McDonaldization in terms of which process has taken place. However, the point is that McDonald's exhibits tendencies that are *exemplified* by the Disney theme parks. There may be an element of imitation in many cases (as with transferred Disneyization), but this is by no means necessarily the case.

Thinking Critically

◆◆◆

1. Is the world growing more Disneyized than McDonaldized?

2. What are the similarities/differences between Disneyization and McDonaldization?

3. Does the theory of Disneyization accord too much importance to an amusement park? to Disney?

4. In what ways does the string of Disney Worlds around the world form an iron cage? A carceral archipelago? Islands of the living dead?

5. In what ways are both Disneyization and McDonaldization expressions of American culture?

As we have already seen, and will see to an increasing degree as this book proceeds, McDonaldization has spread far beyond the fast-food industry. Among the many things that would seem to be impervious to McDonaldization are daredevil acts such as mountain climbing. Yet as Ian Heywood shows in Chapter 7 even mountain climbing has been McDonaldized to some degree. He sees climbing as a "recreational escape attempt," and clearly one of the things that people attracted to such an activity are escaping is the McDonaldization of society. Yet because it attracts a number of people, climbing comes under pressure to rationalize from social, political, and especially commercial sources.

Heywood focuses on adventure climbing, a distinctive British tradition that is perceived as something close to pure sport. It involves things such as physical skill, technical ability, moral qualities, and character. There is a great deal of unpredictability and risk associated with it. The joy comes from the climbing itself and not necessarily the end of reaching the top. Adventure climbing represents genuine escape to those who practice it. However, Heywood identifies three things that make this form of climbing less adventurous and more rationalized. First, there are now guidebooks that greatly reduce the predictability of climbing. Second, there now exists an enormous amount of scientifically tested and technologically sophisticated equipment created by commercial interests to generate profits. All of this equipment makes previously difficult routes easier and safer. Third, training for mountain climbing has also been McDonaldized so that climbers have greater control over potential risks. As a result of all this, adventure climbing has become "more predictable and controllable." Those who want risky and unpredictable climbs can still find them, but the majority, especially those who are new to the sport and have been raised in the McDonaldized society, will gravitate toward more McDonaldized ways of climbing mountains.

7

Urgent Dreams

Climbing, Rationalization, and Ambivalence

Ian Heywood

◆◆◆————————————————————————————————

CLIMBING AS ESCAPE?

The efforts of a sport like climbing to evade societal rationalization invariably become deeply paradoxical under contemporary conditions. Climbing, like other escape attempts, shows every indication of coming under rationalization pressure. There are "external" pressures, deriving from commercial sources (markets, competition, etc.) but also from social or political circumstance—for example, the need . . . for climbing to present itself to the rest of society, or at least to the media, as a legitimate recreation or sport able to make reasonable claims, sometimes against the arguments of competing groups, for access to increasingly scarce natural resources.

There are also less obvious but in some ways more interesting internal pressures, which I will outline by discussing the contrast, much debated

———————————

Editor's Note: Excerpts from "Urgent Dreams: Climbing, Rationalization, and Ambivalence" by Ian Heywood, 1994, *Leisure Studies*, 13, 179–194. Used with permission.

recently within the climbing world, between "sport climbing" and "adventure climbing."

The term "adventure climbing" is an attempt to describe a distinctive British climbing tradition and to contrast this tradition with a new approach, initially developed in Europe: "sport climbing." In adventure climbing, the climbing team (usually of two or three) starts from the ground, without much in the way of preliminary inspection, and ascends to the top relying on a brief guidebook description, direct observation and experience, and protecting themselves with ropes and leader-placed, removable devices which do not damage the rock surface. In high standard sport climbing, generally short (one pitch) routes are "worked," perhaps over days or weeks, with the climber repeatedly resting or falling onto the frequent bolts or pitons which provide security; in most sport climbs, the climber is very unlikely to suffer serious injury however many times he or she falls, jumps, or rests on the protection. The same could not be said for many adventure climbs.

Adventure climbing, its adherents argue, is inherently and uniquely challenging and satisfying, it is a pure or authentic form of the sport. For many, it . . . stands out against the rationalizing tide engulfing so many other areas of social life. For its critics, sport climbing reduces a complex activity involving the whole person to technique and strength, to what is determined by genetic inheritance or acquired by intensive training. "Real" climbing is seen to demand, from time to time, not just physical performance, not just *technical* qualities, but *moral* qualities and qualities of *character* as well.

Treated as a cultural phenomenon, adventure climbing represents for many participants a genuine escape attempt, a small but important challenge to the encroachments of rationalization. This is not of course to say that the practice of adventure climbing is routinely disorganized, impulsive, conducted in a kind of romantic stupor; on the contrary, it demands an approach which is ordered, deliberate, clear-headed, and circumspect.

This said, there is about the notion of adventure climbing something fundamentally at odds with the outlook and values belonging to the process of rationalization as it has been understood and described by writers from Weber onward. Rationalization demands the objectification of the phenomena it confronts; it must make them into its "materials," more or less discrete entities related to one another in relatively simple, potentially intelligible and manipulable ways. It is interested in predictability, simplicity, and effective control. The powerful rhetoric associated with rationalization restricts self-reflection to operational considerations. It is typically thought of as value-neutral, focused on devising and implementing effective means, so that the primary satisfactions available to rationalizers derive from the results of the process, not the process itself.

Adventure climbing, on the other hand, does not treat rock as a material to be subjugated and mastered technically. The rock surface is not to be modified to provide better holds or protection; it must be encountered as it is, "phenomenologically," in all its rich complexity of texture, form, and angle. The climber does not really know from one moment to another whether the next move will be possible or not, the process is unpredictable and the outcome uncertain. The satisfactions of climbing are intrinsic rather than extrinsic; neither "getting to the top" nor even "surviving" is really intelligible as a satisfactory end unless it is thought of as part of the process of climbing itself. Finally, authentic climbing is always accompanied by risk, the possibility of injury or even death. This is profoundly alien to rationalization, in which risk is to be minimized and death constitutes a limit condition; it must be avoided for as long as possible.

Yet might we not want to question just how "adventurous" a lot of adventure climbing is? I shall consider three ways in which it is perhaps a bit less "raw," a little more "processed," than its protagonists might like to admit. First, for most climbers a current guidebook is almost as important as a rope. Guidebooks are an invaluable source of information not just about where the route goes but about its grade of difficulty, its degree of danger, its atmosphere, the amount of "exposure" (big drops which are difficult to ignore), whether it is likely to be enjoyable in the wet, whether an escape onto an easier route nearby can be engineered if things get unpleasant, and so on. For middle grade and harder routes, a modern guidebook will provide an overall grade for the climb, which incorporates a view of technical difficulty, whether or not the difficulties are sustained, and how "serious" (difficult to protect, dangerous) the climb is. Individual pitches are given the technical grade of the hardest move; this is meant to indicate the objective physical difficulty of a move irrespective of its dangers or situation. Experienced climbers can often read between the lines of a route description to extract additional information in the form of inferences, significant omissions, the first ascent date, and so forth. Thus guidebooks contain enormous amounts of information, much of it in a codified, convention-governed form; with these descriptions the competent interpreter approaches the climb with a considerable amount of reliable, intersubjectively verified knowledge. Unpredictability is significantly reduced, while the climber's ability to objectify and control the climbing environment increases. Objectification, predictability, and control are, of course, hallmarks of rationalization.

Second, I want to consider climbing gear: footwear, clothes, protection devices. A vast amount could be written on this topic. Briefly however, each of these categories of equipment has been, and continues to be, the subject of scientific and technological research. Rock climbing footwear has improved steadily over the postwar period; light boots or slippers now fit closely, enable the climber to feel the texture and shape of the rock, and are shod with high-friction "sticky" rubber originally developed for aircraft tires. Rock climbers, and more particularly mountaineers, can now buy (if they can afford them!) well-designed garments which are, to some extent, water-resistant, breathable, and windproof. Protection equipment, including ropes, harnesses, belay plates, wire alloy "nuts," and advanced camming devices have all improved the safety of the climber beyond anything that those of us who stared climbing in the 1960s could have imagined possible. Literally thousands of high-quality routes, for years considered too dangerous for all but an elite of "hardmen," can now be enjoyed by a much wider constituency of ordinary mortals. For the experienced climber placing protection devices properly and using knowledge of the route derived from the guidebook, the activity is usually, under controlled circumstances, controlled, predictable, and relatively safe. Or perhaps it would be more accurate to say that uncertainty and danger can be, if the climber so chooses, controlled.

Third, I turn to the importance of training. Prior to the 1970s, few climbers trained seriously. Some had strenuous manual jobs, which helped with strength and stamina, but usually people got "climbing fit" by climbing. During the 1970s, elite climbers began to realize the advantages of specialized, systematic work with weights on climbing walls and boulders. Dieting, flexibility exercises, and even mental training to produce a relaxed but focused attitude all became commonplace. These ideas have spread in recent years so that now most climbers who consider themselves at all serious about their sport train: running, watching their diets, using weights and walls, stretching, and so on. Many develop rigorous "scientific" or systematic routines based on up-to-date sport research and training practice. All this can give the climber more control, it can render the activity more predictable, it can make it less likely that, at a given grade, the climber will be confronted by physical or even mental demands that exceed available resources.

To summarize, I have argued that recent developments in so-called adventure climbing, in particular the information quality of contemporary guidebooks, the effectiveness of new equipment, and the evolution of training methods, have progressively rendered the activity more predictable and controllable. Now the danger, the unpredictability, the risk, the irrationality of climbing are substantially matters of *choice*; climbers can have their activity raw, medium, or well-done according to how they feel or what they want from the sport. . . . Adventure climbing has itself already gone a considerable way toward its rational transformation.

Thinking Critically

◆◆◆

1. Can mountain climbing, especially of something like Mt. Everest, ever be McDonaldized to a high degree?

2. Would you want to climb mountains in a non-McDonaldized way?

3. Would you want to climb mountains in a McDonaldized way?

4. Would McDonaldized mountain climbing still represent an escape?

5. Aren't the gains in safety from McDonaldizing mountain climbing worth the disadvantages associated with it?

Eric Schlosser is the author of the international bestseller, Fast Food Nation. *In the following interview, Schlosser discusses, and expresses surprise over, the wide-reaching influence of the fast-food industry. Although he sees positive effects, Schlosser focuses on the costs associated with this industry such as increasing uniformity and conformity, the obesity epidemic, deskilled labor, and the horrendous working conditions in the slaughterhouses that supply the fast-food industry with its meat products. Schlosser goes beyond describing these problems to suggest reforms such as a prohibition on advertising unhealthy food to children, better pay and working conditions, and a stronger federal food safety program. Concerned about these and other problems, Schlosser has sworn off fast food, at least until the industry mends its ways and seeks to deal with its worst abuses.*

8

A Conversation With Eric Schlosser, Author of *Fast Food Nation*

◆◆◆ ————————————————————————

Q: Whether the product is furniture, books, clothes, or food, chains are taking over independent businesses across the country and the world. What prompted you to focus on fast food?

A: The fast-food industry is enormous—and enormously influential. The fast-food chains demonstrated that you could create identical retail environments and sell the same products at thousands of different locations. The huge success of McDonald's spawned countless imitators. The founders of the Gap later said they'd been inspired by McDonald's and Kentucky Fried Chicken. The key to all these businesses is uniformity and conformity. So by looking at fast food I'm trying to explain how communities throughout the United States have lost a lot of their individuality over the past 20 years and have started to look exactly the same.

Q: Fast Food Nation begins with a look at Cheyenne Mountain and the Colorado Springs area. Why did you focus on this part of the country?

Editor's Note: From "A Conversation with Eric Schlosser, author of *Fast Food Nation,* published by Houghton Mifflin."

Http://www.houghtonmifflinbooks.com/booksellers/press_release/schlosser/. Reprinted with permission of The Houghton Mifflin Company.

A: Well, I could have chosen just about any suburban community and told much the same story. But Colorado Springs appealed to me because its growth has neatly paralleled the growth of the fast-food industry. The city feels like a place on the cutting edge—like Los Angeles in the 1950s—a glimpse, maybe, of America's future. The high-tech economy there, and the kind of thinking that goes with it, seems linked to the fast-food industry's worship of new gadgets and technology. And I wanted to set the book somewhere in the American West, the part of the country that embodies our whole spirit of freedom and independence and self-reliance. Those are the very qualities that the fast-food industry is now helping to eliminate.

Q: Why has the fast-food industry grown so quickly around the world?

A: Here in the States, I think, fast food is popular because it's convenient, it's cheap, and it tastes good. But the real cost of eating fast food never appears on the menu. By that I mean the cost of the obesity epidemic fast food has helped to unleash, the social costs of having such a low-wage workforce, and the health costs of the new industrialized agriculture that supplies the big restaurant chains.

Overseas, much of fast food's appeal stems from its Americanness. Like Hollywood movies, MTV, and blue jeans, fast food has become one of our major cultural exports.

Q: How do fast-food restaurants benefit from "de-skilled" jobs and from high turnover among their employees?

A: A reliance on cheap labor has been crucial to the fast-food industry's success. It's no accident that the industry's highest rate of growth occurred during a period when the real value of the U.S. minimum wage declined by about 40 percent. The chains have worked hard to "de-skill" the jobs in their kitchens by imposing strict rules on how everything must be done, selling highly processed food that enters the restaurant already frozen or freeze-dried and easy to reheat, and relying on complex kitchen machinery to do as much of the work as possible. Instead of employing skilled short-order cooks, the chains try to employ unskilled workers who will do exactly as they're told. The chains are willing to put up with turnover rates of 300 to 400 percent in order to keep their labor costs low. It doesn't really matter to them who comes or goes, since this system treats all workers as though they're interchangeable.

Q: When you were doing your research for the book, what surprised you the most?

A: I guess it was the far-reaching influence of this food that surprised me most. Because it's something you never really think about. Fast food is everywhere, it seems so mundane, taken for granted. But it has changed what we eat, how we work, what our towns look like, and what we look like in the mirror. I also was amazed to learn that much of fast-food's taste is manufactured at a series of chemical plants off the New Jersey Turnpike.

Q: *Do you feel that the fast-food industry has made any positive impressions on our culture?*

A: In the early days, I think the industry embodied some of the best things about this country. It was started by high school drop-outs who had little training, by entrepreneurs who made it big by working hard. Guys like the McDonald brothers didn't rely on focus groups, marketing surveys, or management consultants with MBAs. They just set up their grills and started cooking. It's ironic that what they created turned into such a symbol of faceless, ruthless corporate power. It's a very American story, both good and bad. . . .

Q: *One of the book's most arresting passages describes your visit to a slaughterhouse in which the working conditions are atrocious. How have slaughterhouses gotten away with such poor management and treatment of employees for so long? Do you foresee any changes in this industry in the near future?*

A: The meatpacking industry now employs some of the poorest, most vulnerable workers in the United States. Most are recent immigrants. Many of them are illiterate and don't speak English. Many are illegals. A generation ago, meatpacking workers belonged to strong unions that could fight for better pay and working conditions. But today's workers often feel that they can't speak out, rightly afraid they will be fired or deported. It's amazing to me how well hidden these abuses remain. I think the media's lack of interest in the plight of meatpacking workers has to do with their skin color. If blond-haired, blue-eyed workers were being mistreated this way, there'd be a huge uproar.

I think the working conditions in the nation's meatpacking plants could improve very quickly—almost overnight. The fast-food chains have the power to say to their suppliers: treat your workers better or we won't buy meat from you anymore. McDonald's is the world's largest purchaser of beef. It recently issued strict guidelines to its suppliers on the humane treatment and slaughter of animals. I think McDonald's should now show the same kind of compassion for human beings.

Q: *What changes would you like to see instituted within the fast-food industry and the government agencies regulating it?*

A: I'd like the fast food industry to start assuming some of the real costs it now imposes on the rest of society. And I don't think the chains are going to pay those costs willingly. The right legislation will have to do the job. I'd like to see a total ban on the advertising of unhealthy food to children. If a grown man or woman wants to buy a bacon-double-cheeseburger with large fries, well, great, it's a free country. But the fast-food chains should not be allowed to spend millions advertising fatty, unsafe food for children. Obesity is now the second leading cause of death in the United States, after smoking. In the interest of public health, we've banned cigarette ads directed at adults. We should do at least as much to protect children. Such a ban, among other things, would encourage McDonald's to sell Happy Meals that aren't so laden with fat.

I'd like to see a rise in the minimum wage, tougher enforcement of overtime laws, and new OSHA regulations designed to protect employees who work at restaurants late at night. All of these things will help improve the lives of fast food workers-the biggest group of minimum wage earners in the United States.

And I'd like to see a complete overhaul of the federal food safety system, which at the moment is spread across a dozen separate agencies. We should have a single food safety agency, completely separate from the Department of Agriculture, that has power over the fast food industry and its suppliers. We should be able to demand recalls of tainted food, and we should be able to impose fines on companies that deliberately sell bad meat. Right now millions of Americans are needlessly being sickened by what they eat.

Q: *Are you a vegetarian? Do you eat fast food?*

A: I have a lot of respect for people who are vegetarian for religious or ethical reasons. Despite all my research, however, I'm still a carnivore. My favorite meal, by far, is a cheeseburger with fries. But I don't eat ground beef anymore. I've seen firsthand what goes into it, and I'm angry about the careless greed of the meatpacking industry. I still eat beef, though I always try to buy meat that's been produced by ranchers who care about their animals and the land. And no, I won't eat fast food anymore. Not until the industry changes its ways.

Thinking Critically

1. Have communities lost their individuality because of the spread of the fast-food restaurant and McDonaldization?

2. How would you feel about working in a de-skilled job?

3. Is the fast-food industry "a symbol of faceless, ruthless corporate power"?

4. Do you think the federal government should get involved in legislating the fast-food industry so that, for example, it is prevented from advertising unhealthy food to children?

5. Could vegetarianism be McDonaldized?

Morgan Spurlock achieved fame in 2004 with the release of his acclaimed, Academy Award–nominated documentary, Super Size Me. *As is well known, he spent a month eating nothing but McDonald's food, accepting supersized portions whenever they were offered to him. He gained 25 pounds, and his health deteriorated in a variety of ways. Indeed, his health grew much worse than the doctors had predicted when he began. Although the documentary is quite focused, Spurlock recognizes that he is really addressing a larger cultural problem, one that is called here "McDonaldization."*

9

The Real Price of a Big Mac

Filmmaker Morgan Spurlock Discusses Life as a Human Guinea Pig

Brian Braiker

Sometimes inspiration strikes in the unlikeliest places. After gorging himself on Thanksgiving dinner in 2002, Morgan Spurlock was watching TV with his belt unbuckled and his pants unzipped. On the news was a report about two girls in New York who were suing McDonald's because, they claimed, the food made them overweight and sick. At one point in the report, recalls Spurlock, a representative for the fast-food chain claimed its food was, in fact, nutritious. It was at that precise moment that Spurlock, who runs his own production company, says "the bells went off." He decided to make a documentary—his first feature-length film—in which he would, in an attempt to explore why Americans are so fat, eat at McDonald's three times a day for 30 solid days.

. . .

[T]he viewer gets a front-row seat as the formerly fit filmmaker eats everything on the menu, packing on the pounds, and looking—and feeling—worse in each successive frame. McDonald's' response? The home of the Happy Meal declined to comment in the film but has released statements saying that its menu offers an array of choices, some healthier than others. . . .

Q: You ate three meals a day at McDonald's for 30 days for this film. What happened to your body over the course of that month?

A: My body just basically falls apart over the course of this diet. I start to get tired; I start to get headaches; my liver basically starts to fill up with fat because there's so much fat and sugar in this food. My blood sugar skyrockets, my cholesterol goes up off the charts, my blood pressure becomes completely unmanageable. The doctors were like "You have to stop."

Q: You saw more than one doctor?

A: I was seeing three different doctors over the course of this, just so I would really have a fair balance between all the people so nobody could say "oh, it was doctor bias; it was physician bias." Each of these doctors was doing their own blood tests and each of the blood tests were going to three different labs so there was no way lab error could be an issue. Everything that happens to my body over the course of the film was caused by this diet. And everything that happened to my body was caused by this food that I got at this restaurant. I didn't eat anything—no gum, no candy, not even a Tic Tac—everything that I put in my mouth came from over the counter at McDonald's. Even the water. I wouldn't even drink water from outside, that way there would never be a question that "oh there was probably something in the water somewhere else when he was traveling around." I only drank bottled water from McDonald's.

Q: How much weight did you put on?

A: I put on about 25 pounds in a month.

Q; How did you feel at the end of the month?

A: [*Laughs*] I felt terrible! I felt so bad because I put on this weight so quickly my knees hurt. I was so depressed. I would eat, and I would feel so good because I would get all that sugar and caffeine and fat and I would feel great. And an hour later I would just crash—I would hit the wall and be angry and depressed and upset. I was a disaster to live with. My girlfriend by the end was like "You have to stop because I've had it." It really affects you in so many ways that I think a lot of people don't realize, very subtle little things. Over the course of the film you see my transformation, and it's not pleasant.

Q: Why McDonald's specifically? Why not Burger King; why not Subway?

A: McDonald's is an icon, a cultural icon, a cultural phenomenon and nothing represents America and the American fast-food way of life more than McDonald's. The chain has 30,000 restaurants in more than 100 countries on six continents around the world. It has truly influenced how we eat, how food is made and how, really, other cultures are starting to eat. All these other food companies have started to follow suit, from franchising and how they manufacture and distribute their food, McDonald's is a trendsetter. So for me, the idea of picking McDonald's was, one, to pick it as the icon for what it represents. It represents every food, in my opinion; it represents every company. Also in my opinion it represents the one company that more than anybody else could really make a difference. McDonald's could institute change that everyone else would also follow. It could do away with super-size portions and everyone else would say, "Wow, you know what? We don't need to do this anymore either. We need to make a difference." If they would truly champion a change for healthier menu option—it would happen across the board.

Q: But doesn't it boil down to individual choice?

A: I think there is a level of personal choice. In the film it's not like I'm saying fast food is the sole problem. In the film we examine a multitude of issues that cause the obesity epidemic, personal choice being one of them. McDonald's every day feeds 46 million people worldwide—that's more than the entire population of Spain. You're talking about one company that has a huge impact. I think that sure you can argue personal choice, but on the same point, if there aren't healthy menu options available, and there isn't nutrition information available to people who come there to make a choice about what they're going to eat, you're really limiting your argument on some levels. Their marketing and advertising from the very beginning really targets kids. Children from such an early age are just so washed over with the idea of the happy clown and the Happy Meals and, oh, look, there's a playground, let's go there for fun. I know kids whose parents have never taken them to McDonald's, but if you ask them what their favorite restaurant is and they'll say McDonald's—and they've never even been in one! That's pretty scary.

Q: This sounds a lot like Eric Schlosser's book Fast Food Nation. *Did you read that?*

A: *Fast Food Nation* is a tremendous book and was definitely something that we referenced while we were making the film. Eric Schlosser and I were e-mailing one another back and forth but never really connected, and that was not really an influence on my doing the film. I read *Fast Food Nation* when it first came out two years ago, and it's a great book.

. . .

Q: McDonald's has argued that the premise of your film is unfair, that its stores offer a wide array of food.

A: It's a very extreme route I took. That's the other argument that's made: nobody's supposed to eat this food that often, no wonder all these bad things happen. But the thing is, there are people who go to these restaurants and do eat very heavy fat-laden foods and sugar-laden foods every day. Maybe not every day but six days a week or five days a week. And while they may not get the dramatic impacts that I had—things may not happen at such an exaggerated rate—these things will happen over the long run if they don't exercise, if they're not taking care of themselves. You have to exercise a lot to run off a super-sized Big Mac meal. You're talking about 1,500 calories. You eat 1,500 calories, you have to run for three or four miles, for 45 minutes to an hour.

. . .

Thinking Critically

---◆◆◆

1. Was Morgan Spurlock fair to McDonald's?

2. Could you eat any single kind of food for a month without experiencing physical and health problems?

3. Why do Americans have such a love affair with large sizes in their fast food (and elsewhere)?

4. Was *Super Size Me* a wake-up call for Americans? Is there any evidence that Americans are eating less fast food because of it?

5. What would constitute a wake-up call for Americans? For you?

The McDonaldization thesis is not without its critics. In this chapter, one of today's leading social thinkers outlines some of the major criticisms. The first is that in looking at McDonald's around the globe, it is clear that it adapts to, and is modified by, local cultures. Thus, McDonald's is not nearly as uniform as suggested by the McDonaldization thesis (this issue will be addressed in much more detail in Part IV of this volume). Second, the perspective is accused of giving insufficient attention to the opposition to it (some of this is dealt with in Part III). Finally, there is the issue of whether McDonaldization adds anything new to earlier theories, especially Weber's theory of rationalization. Overall, Turner concludes that none of these, or other, criticisms constitute a fundamental challenge to the validity and utility of the McDonaldization thesis.

10

McDonaldization

The Major Criticisms

Bryan S. Turner

◆◆◆ ─────────────────────────────────────

The McDonaldization thesis has been an important and influential debate in contemporary sociology because it illustrates an issue that has been central to the sociological account of modernity. *The McDonaldization of Society* was explicitly a study in Weberian sociology insofar as it described the rationalization of contemporary society. It also can be seen correctly as a contribution to the study of global consumption. The book was revised partly in response to critics and has produced a variety of valuable research projects in modern sociology. . .

───────────

Author's Note: For advice and information on McDonald's in developing this analysis, I would like to thank the following people: Ayca Alemdaroglu (University of Cambridge), Mona Abaza (American University of Cairo), Greg Burton and Sue Kenny (Deakin University, Australia), and Bill Thornton (National Cheng University, Taiwan).

Editor's Note: From Turner, B. (2003, Oct.). McDonaldization: The Major Criticisms. *American Behavioral Scientist, 47*(2). Reprinted with permission of Sage Publications, Inc.

The major lines of criticism and comment on the McDonaldization thesis have been fairly well developed. First, there has been an issue about the extent and uniformity of McDonald's as an illustration of cultural standardization where critics have argued that around the world, McDonald's products and packaging are adjusted to and modified by local cultures. In Asia, ethnographic studies, for example, in James Watson's *Golden Arches East*, have demonstrated that McDonaldization is not a uniform process. . . . Second, in the original study, Ritzer failed to provide an account of how McDonaldization as an iron cage could be resisted. In his subsequent work and in the debate, the avenues of resistance have been given considerable attention. The rise of the antiglobalization movement has been a vivid, and occasionally violent, testimony to global political responses to McDonald's as a symbol of Americanization. The negative social, health, and economic consequences of McDonald's have been fully explored in both serious political economy and popular critique, for example, in Eric Schlosser's *Fast Food Nation* or John Vidal's *McLibel*. Finally, there are various contributions to sociological theory that broadly address the question as to whether the debate has contributed anything new to the rationalization thesis that we have inherited from Weber and critical theory. Perhaps the best answer to that criticism comes from Barry Smart, who has observed that the real value of Ritzer's study has been to force us to attempt a general sociological understanding of the central feature of modern society, thereby "provoking a theoretical and practical debate concerning key novel and defining features of our contemporary world and forcing us to define our response to crucial aspects of our everyday world." We can take this statement as a broad translation of Weber's injunction that our duty as sociologists is to understand the characteristic uniqueness of the times in which we live.

Much of the critical debate with Ritzer's analysis is not, however, a fundamental challenge to his account of McDonald's because the criticisms often amount merely to extensions, corrections, or additions to the thesis. For example, the ethnographic illustrations about localization or glocalization have primarily brought an empirical richness to the abstract theorization of rationalized production and consumption. We need to develop these ethnographic observations to another level as a genuine theoretical step beyond the Weberian model of rationalism. To engage in a debate over McDonaldization, we need to see the McDonald's case study as a contribution to Weberian economic sociology in the sense that Ritzer has shown us how the rationalization of distribution and popular consumption is a historical elaboration of Weber's analysis of the rationalization of production. To address Ritzer's thesis more directly, we might ask what social or economic transformations of the McDonaldization process would result in the falsification of the rationalization theory?

Thinking Critically

1. Does the fact that McDonald's adapts to local cultures around the world undermine the McDonaldization thesis?

2. In what ways have you resisted McDonaldization?

3. In what ways have others resisted McDonaldization?

4. Should McDonaldization be resisted?

5. In what ways could we falsify the McDonaldization thesis; that is, find data that questions, if not undermines, it?

Part I

1. Define the "McDonaldization of society." What are the four dimensions of McDonaldization?

2. What are the structural and administrative transformations that industries go through as they McDonaldize? Discuss the effects of McDonaldization on the national and global labor force.

3. What does "irrationality of rationality" mean? Cite examples of it beyond those discussed in this part of the book.

4. What key characteristics distinguish the bureaucratic system from the prebureaucratic system? Compare these two systems in terms of efficiency, calculability, predictability, and control through nonhuman technology.

5. How does Weber define formal rationality? Why does formal rationality limit substantive rationality?

6. Bureaucratic organization expands in modern societies to perform many complex tasks efficiently. However, it also generates dysfunctions that lead to alienation and inefficiency. Identify some of the rationalities and the irrationalities of bureaucracy in the daily rounds of life.

7. What is Disneyization? What are the common characteristics of Disneyization and McDonaldization? How does Disneyization operate in McDonaldized spaces?

8. How does the college education system adapt to McDonaldization? Are the offered classes and their requirements McDonaldized?

9. How does McDonaldization transform personal space and the presentation of the self? Does it leave room for individuality?

10. How have cultural standardization and the trend toward globalization affected you, your family, and your community? List both the pros and the cons. Have the benefits outweighed the drawbacks?

11. Spend a few hours walking or driving around your local community. Do the types of chain stores differ according to the residential patterns? Does each neighborhood have the same stores? Are there economic, social, and ethnic patterns in the neighborhoods that have the same types of chain stores?

12. Could the organic food movement be a challenge to the intensity of McDonaldization in agriculture and food industry? Is the spread of organic food chains a demonstration of McDonaldization?

13. McDonaldization theory suggests that the organizational principles that underlie McDonald's are increasingly dominating the entire society. If you have computer access, visit the Web site of your college and look at the application procedures. How is academic success measured? Examine the importance of nationally standardized tests as indicators of a student's qualifications.

14. Find a copy of the book *1984*, George Orwell's satire of a totalitarian bureaucracy. How do the rationally enacted rules and regulations operate in the depicted monumental state bureaucracy? How does bureaucracy invade privacy in the book? Draw parallels to our contemporary society. How do data mining, electronic records of credit card purchases, surveillance cameras, and new information technologies threaten privacy?

PART II

The McDonaldization of Social
Structures and Institutions

Part II begins with Chapter 11, which offers an overview of the McDonaldization of America's police, courts, and corrections. Matthew Robinson describes how the four dimensions of McDonaldization fit all these elements of the legal system. Efficiency is manifest in the police force in the shift from two- to one-person patrol cars, in the courts with the increasing frequency of plea bargaining, and in corrections with the current efforts to expedite executions. In terms of calculability, there is within the police an emphasis on available funds and number of officers on the street; in the courts we find longer sentences and offenders serving a larger proportion of their sentences; and in prisons there is a focus on more prisons, more prisoners, and more executions. Greater predictability is exemplified by police profiling, "going rates," and "three strikes and you're out" in the courtroom, as well as risk classification in the prisons. Finally, increasing control is best exemplified by the new "supermax" prisons. Most distinctive about this essay is its discussion of the irrationality of this seemingly rational process—especially that, in spite of, or perhaps because of, McDonaldization, Americans are less sure of receiving justice from the justice system than they have been in the past.

11

McDonaldization of America's Police, Courts, and Corrections

Matthew B. Robinson

◆◆◆———————————————————————————————————

There is no aspect of people's lives that is immune to McDonaldization. This includes crime and criminal justice. To date, there is only one published examination of how crime and criminal justice are McDonaldized.

David Shichor's article, "Three Strikes as a Public Policy: The Convergence of the New Penology and the McDonaldization of Punishment" (1997), demonstrates how the metaphors of getting "tough on crime" and fighting a "war on drugs" have led to penal policies based exclusively on deterrence and incapacitation. These policies have resulted in longer prison sentences, a rapid growth in prison populations, and prison overcrowding. Three-strikes state laws, now in place in more than half of the United States, were meant to increase the *efficiency* of the criminal justice process, were to be based on scientific *prediction* of dangerousness, and were to protect citizens in a *cost-efficient* manner. In fact, the opposite of what was expected has occurred, at least in the state of California, where its three-strikes law is

---

Editor's Note: This chapter was revised for this volume from the first edition of *McDonaldization: The Reader* (2002).

the most widely used among all the states. Billions of dollars have been spent in the application of the state's three-strikes law on relatively minor offenders, courts are backlogged with additional trials, and correctional facilities are overpopulated. Although crime fell, it fell everywhere across the country, in states with three-strikes laws and without. California counties that used the laws more had smaller declines in crime than those counties that used the laws less. Similar to the fast-food industry, "rationalized" methods of delivering products have produced irrational results. California citizens are getting the opposite of what they were promised.

This chapter builds on Shichor's preliminary analysis by linking the trend of McDonaldization to increasingly efficient, scientific, costly, and control-oriented systems of police, courts, and corrections in the United States. Using its basic elements, I illustrate how the McDonaldization of U.S. criminal justice has resulted in irrational criminal justice policy.

CRIMINAL JUSTICE IN THE UNITED STATES

The "criminal justice system" is a term that represents the three interdependent components of police, courts, and corrections. There are actually 51 criminal justice systems in the United States, one for each state and one for the federal government. Police agencies are responsible for investigating alleged criminal offenses, apprehending suspected criminal offenders, assisting the prosecution with obtaining criminal convictions at trial, keeping the peace in the community, preventing crime, providing social services, and upholding Constitutional protections. Courts are responsible for determining guilt or innocence of suspected offenders at trial (adjudication), sentencing the legally guilty to some form(s) of punishment, interpreting laws made by legislative bodies, setting legal precedents, and upholding Constitutional protections. Finally, corrections agencies are responsible for carrying out the sentences of the courts by administering punishment and providing care and custody for accused and convicted criminals in line with Constitutional protections.

Although each of these agencies of criminal justice has its own goals, they also share the goals of the larger criminal justice system, which include reducing crime and doing justice. The meaning of reducing crime is clear; doing justice implies both catching, convicting, and punishing criminals *and* assuring that innocent people do not fall victim to wrongful punishment by assuring that individual Constitutional rights are protected.

Our nation's justice systems face a continual balancing act attempting to achieve both forms of justice. The pendulum shifts back and forth between an emphasis on catching, convicting, and punishing criminals and an emphasis on assuring that Constitutional rights of suspected offenders are protected.

This chapter demonstrates that the U.S. criminal justice system has become McDonaldized; the result is that U.S. police, courts, and corrections favor the former conception of justice (crime control) at the expense of the latter (due process).

EFFICIENCY AND CRIMINAL JUSTICE

The importance of efficiency in America's criminal justice system has always been stressed, but perhaps never in our nation's history as in the past three decades. When systems of criminal justice are more focused on catching, convicting, and punishing criminals than assuring fairness and impartiality, efficiency of the systems becomes the most important value; informal processes are used in place of formal processes to expedite criminal justice operations and to hold a larger proportion of criminals accountable for their criminal acts.

To the degree that cases move through the criminal justice system like an "assembly line," criminal justice practice is much like a fast-food production line. Modern criminal justice practice aims to be efficient, even at the cost of due process rights of defendants. Adherence to efficiency can be seen within each of the components of the justice system, including police, courts, and corrections.

Policing

The increased use of directed and aggressive patrol techniques (aimed at high crime areas), as part of a problem-oriented policing strategy, provides evidence for the emphasis on efficiency in policing. Police occupy certain areas of the city more than others to most efficiently use their resources. The zero-tolerance policing in our nation's largest cities, aimed at eliminating social and physical incivilities (untended people and places), is further evidence of an allegiance to efficiency. These efforts are aimed at doing away with signs of disorder before they become major crimes. The fact that directed and aggressive patrol is disproportionately used against the nation's poor and that zero-tolerance policing produces unnecessary use of police force and hostility between inner-city residents and police seems to be irrelevant to most police agencies because the goal of efficient crime control takes precedence.

The shift from two- to one-officer police cars, based on the realization that one-officer cars are just as effective as those occupied by two officers, provides further evidence for the importance of efficiency in policing. Then, there is the growth of technology in policing, from crime analysis and crime mapping, to fingerprinting and computers in squad cars, suggesting that policing is much more focused on proactive strategies than it has been historically. Changes such as these to police practice in the United States are aimed at making policing more efficient at detecting crime. For sure, police are discovering more crime, and the use of additional evidence makes it easier to convict alleged criminals. The effect on the other conception of justice, however, is rarely considered by police.

Courts

The popularity of plea bargaining provides strong evidence for the significance of efficiency in U.S. courts. The ideal of U.S. justice is an "adversarial" process, whereby prosecutors and defense attorneys fight for the truth and justice in a contest at trial. Yet, an administrative system is in effect, as evidenced by the substantial use of plea bargaining in courts; these cases are handled informally in hallways and offices rather than in courtrooms. Instead of criminal trials where prosecutors and defense attorneys clash in an effort to determine the truth and do justice for all concerned parties, prosecutors, defense attorneys, and sometimes judges "shop" for "supermarket" justice through plea bargaining.

Criminal trials are now the exception to the rule of plea bargaining. Plea bargaining is an informal process whereby defendants plead guilty to lesser charges in exchange for not taking up the court's valuable time and spending the state's money on trials. In this process, individuals give up their Constitutional rights to cross-examine witnesses, to present a defense, to not incriminate themselves, to testify on their own behalf, and to appeal their convictions, all in exchange for a dismissal or reduction in charges, and/or a lesser sentence. This is an irrational process driven by efficiency as a value, especially given the evidence that some innocent people plead guilty to crimes they did not commit in the face of overwhelming coercion to plead guilty.

The original approval of plea bargaining by the Supreme Court in 1971 was based more on the pragmatic concern that the criminal justice system could not assure every accused criminal his or her Constitutional rights rather than a concern for justice. In other words, plea bargaining achieves only one thing—a more efficient court. Most criminologists and criminal justice scholars view plea bargaining as an unjust process driven by large numbers of caseloads, understaffed courts, and the renewed emphasis on using law enforcement to solve drug use and public order offenses.

Corrections

A renewed emphasis on efficiency can be found in the increased use of incarceration to achieve incapacitation and deterrence of large numbers of inmates. The United States has shifted its focus away from the treatment of individuals to the handling of aggregates, creating the illusion of a more efficient system of justice. The net of criminal justice is now cast much wider than in previous decades. Increased use of imprisonment is discussed in the following section on calculability. Here, it simply should be noted that a greater use of imprisonment implies to consumers that the criminal justice system will be more efficient in preventing crime because it will prevent criminality by those currently locked up (hence serving the function of incapacitation) and instill fear in those considering committing crimes (hence serving the function of deterrence). In fact, prisons offer little protection from crime, especially in the long run; approximately 90% of inmates will be released. Criminals typically enter prisons uneducated, unskilled, and unemployable. They typically exit the same way, but also angry, bigger physically, stigmatized, and to a large degree, dependent on the government.

Other evidence of increased efficiency in corrections includes legislative efforts to expedite executions by limiting appeals and the elimination of gain time and parole by states and the federal government. In terms of the former issue, speeding up the application of the death penalty is an effort to increase the deterrent effect of the punishment. Convicted murderers on death row will now spend an average of more than 10 years on death row. This has led states to push for expediting the process. Federal law now allows death row inmates only one federal appeal unless new evidence proves clearly and convincingly that the person is innocent. The elimination of gain time and parole (early release from prison) is a major factor contributing to prison overcrowding, which is another irrational result of the supposedly rational criminal justice system. More than a dozen times, federal courts have ordered state correctional facilities to reduce overcrowding or face major fines and withdrawal of federal funding.

CALCULABILITY AND CRIMINAL JUSTICE

A greater emphasis has been placed on calculability in criminal justice during the past three decades—policymakers seem much more satisfied with *more* criminal justice (quantity) than with *better* criminal justice (quality). Victimless crimes have at virtually all times in our nation's history been criminalized, and we have fought numerous wars on drugs; yet, the most recent such war under Presidents Ronald Reagan, George H. Bush, Bill Clinton, and George W. Bush has stressed much more criminal justice intervention than at any time in our nation's history. As a nation, we have spent hundreds of billions on the war on drugs since 1980; the cost of the drug war increased from more than $1 billion in 1981 to more than $20 billion in 2004. The largest portion of drug war funding is intended for domestic law enforcement (policing in the U.S.) as opposed to treatment and prevention; domestic social programs (such as welfare) have also been cut dramatically to pay for the war on drugs. The largest spending increases between the end of the Clinton presidency and the latest year of the George W. Bush presidency (1996 and 2004) were for international spending and interdiction, whereas prevention and treatment increased less. Research shows that the most effective means of curbing drug abuse is through prevention and treatment; yet, the justice system operates on the dubious premise that if we just do more of what has already proven ineffective, eventually it will work.

Policing

Politicians in the 1990s promised to place "100,000 *more* cops on the street." In September 1994, President Clinton signed the Violent Crime Control and Law Enforcement Act; the stated purpose of which was "to prevent crime, punish criminals, and restore a sense of safety and security to the American people." This law allowed for the hiring of 100,000 new police, the construction of thousands of new prison cells, and the expansion of the death penalty to dozens of additional types of murders. Assuming that we ever achieve the goal of 100,000 more police, there will never actually be anything close to 100,000 more police on the streets *at one time*. It takes at least five additional officers to provide one additional officer on the street around the clock because of varied shifts, vacations, illnesses, and so forth. An additional 100,000 new police officers would only account for 20,000 additional officers around the clock. An additional 100,000 police on the street would increase the ratio of police officers to citizens from 2.7 per 1,000 citizens to 3.1 per 1,000 citizens. This largely symbolic promise was aimed at little more than appealing to Americans' allegiance to calculability, a value promoted by the fast-food industry. In other words, citizens will not actually be safer, even though they may intuitively be satisfied with the government for trying.

We also see calculability in asset forfeitures in the nation's drug war. The reward for police is being allowed to confiscate and keep some drug-related assets. To some degree, law enforcement officials have come to rely on drug assets to purchase equipment and conduct training so that police can exterminate drug use. The majority of law enforcement agencies in the United States have asset forfeiture programs in place. Federal agencies seize hundreds of millions in cash and property annually. The irony of police using drug assets to fight drug use is lost on taxpayers, who are the primary criminal justice consumers.

Courts

Longer sentences have been put in place for virtually all crimes, which is indicative of calculability because citizens have been sold on the idea that more punishment is better. It is also evident in laws that require offenders to serve greater portions of their sentences—the so-called "truth in sentencing" laws. A truth in sentencing law was first enacted in 1984, the same year that parole eligibility and good-time credits were restricted or eliminated. At the dawn of the 21st century, approximately 30 states and the District of Columbia met the Federal Truth-in-Sentencing Incentive Grants program eligibility criteria. Eleven states adopted truth in sentencing laws in 1995, one year after funding was established by Congress. Incentive grants were awarded by the federal government to 27 states and the District of Columbia, and another 13 states adopted a truth in sentencing law requiring some offenders (usually violent offenders) to serve a specific percentage of their sentence.

Corrections

Calculability means building *more* prisons, sending *more* people to prison, and sending *more* people to their deaths through capital punishment. The imprisonment rate in the United States has historically been relatively constant. It has fluctuated over the years, but never until the 1970s did it consistently and dramatically increase. In fact, scholars had written about the "stability of punishment" because there was so little fluctuation in the nation's incarceration rate for so long. Beginning in 1973, the United States began an "imprisonment orgy." Since the early 1970s, there has been approximately a 6.5% increase each year in imprisonment, although this slowed in the 21st century. Approximately half of the increases have occurred because of violent criminal incarceration, and much of the remainder is because of drug incarcerations; from 1980 to 1993, the percentage of prisoners in state prisons serving sentences for drug offenses more than tripled and in federal prisons more than doubled. The United States now has more than twice the rate of prisoners per 100,000 citizens as any other democracy, and more than 5 times the rate of democracies such as Canada, England, Germany, and France.

The ironic fact remains, however, that drug use trends have largely been unaffected since 1988, and drug abuse levels have actually increased. An increased commitment to calculability—more criminal justice—has not resulted in substantial reductions in crime rates or drug use and abuse.

PREDICTABILITY AND CRIMINAL JUSTICE

If one were to assess fairly the performance of our nation's criminal justice system in terms of crime control over the past century, one could conclude that there is little likelihood of being subjected to it; that is, the most predictable thing about it has been its futility. Even today, the chance of being apprehended, convicted, and sentenced to imprisonment is highly unlikely for all crimes other than murder.

The criminal justice system operates on the assumption that catching, convicting, and punishing criminals serves as a deterrent to crime (it causes fear in people, and thus they do not commit crimes). The most important factor in the effectiveness of deterrence is the certainty of punishment, that is, the likelihood of being punished. Research on deterrence has consistently found that the severity of a sentence has less of a deterrent effect than sentence certainty. United States criminal justice performs poorly in providing certain, swift punishments that outweigh the potential benefits of committing crimes. For every 100 serious street crimes (as measured in the National Crime Victimization Survey), about 40%, or 40, are known to the police (as measured in the Uniform Crime Reports). Of these 40, only one-fourth (approximately 10) will lead to an arrest. Of these 10, some will not be prosecuted, and others will not be convicted. Only about 3% of the original 100 serious street crimes will lead to an incarceration.

Putting more cops on the street and increasing the use of prison sentences are efforts to make criminal justice outcomes more predictable. Yet, these efforts do not result in crime prevention. The criminal justice system will never know about most crime unless we put a police officer on every street corner in the United States and give police greater freedom to investigate alleged crimes. As long as Americans desire freedom from an overzealous government and value their Constitutional protections, the criminal justice system will largely be a failure.

Policing

Police officers now attempt to apprehend suspects by using offender profiling methods, which allow them to develop a picture of the offender based on elements of his or her crime. The scientific method has always been a part of modem policing, at least since the 1830s under Sir Robert Peel in England. Only in the past two decades, however, has offender profiling been used by police. The aims of this are to increase the accuracy of predictions about who committed crimes based on the characteristics of the crime scenes left behind by offenders.

Police also try to accurately predict who is likely to get into trouble with the law before they commit criminal acts. They focus on particular types of people because of their own personal experience or that of their institution and profession, which suggests that certain people are more likely to violate the law. This practice, known as "police profiling," results in startling disparities in police behavior based on class and race. Police use "extralegal" factors such as race, ethnicity, gender, and so forth, as a proxy for risk. This is supported by courts as legitimate when extralegal factors are used in conjunction with some legal factor. For example, courts have stated that as long as the totality of the circumstances warrants the conclusion of the officer that the subject was acting suspiciously, race can be part of the circumstances considered by the officer. So, an African American male driving the speed limit on a major highway would be suspicious, not just because of the man's skin color, but because no one drives the speed limit on a major highway. In this scenario, police officers may suspect the man of transporting drugs. These elements of predictability in policing lead to difficulties in police–minority interactions, disproportionate use of force against people of color, and disrespect for the law generally.

Courts

Courts in the United States are highly predictable in much of what they do. The main actors in this process within the criminal courts—the prosecutor, the defense attorney, and the judge—enter the courtroom daily knowing essentially what will happen each day. The courtroom workgroup is made up of this collective of individuals who interact, share goals, follow court norms, and develop interpersonal relationships. This concept is important because it helps us understand why their overriding concern is speeding up the process and finishing cases as efficiently as possible, often to the detriment of doing justice. It also helps us understand how legal issues can be predictably resolved. Ideally, members of the courtroom workgroup play their own roles and have their own goals; in reality, each member's main job is not to rock the boat in the daily operations of U.S. courts.

Because of the strong interpersonal relationships among workgroup members, *going rates* are established in bail and sentencing. The process of plea bargaining, discussed earlier, serves as an excellent example. In studies of plea bargaining, cases are disposed of with great regularity and predictability meaning that the resulting sentence is reliably predicted based on the nature of the charges and the defendant's prior record. A going rate is established for particular types of crimes committed by particular types of people, one which becomes established over time and which is learned by each member of the courtroom workgroup. Plea bargains typically closely parallel this going rate, and defendants charged with particular crimes can easily learn what sentence they are likely to face if they plead guilty.

At the sentencing phase in the courts, criminal penalties are highly predictable. Generally, the most important factors include the seriousness of the offense and the offender's prior record, so that the more serious the offense and the longer the prior record, the more severe the sentence will be.

Mandatory sentences now establish a minimum sanction that must be served on a conviction for a criminal offense. Thus, everyone who is convicted for a crime that calls for a mandatory sentence will serve that amount of time. Indeterminate sentences that allowed parole and determinate prison sentences that could be reduced by good-time or earned-time credits have been replaced by mandatory sentences across the country. Furthermore, sentencing guidelines have been established to make sentences more predictable and scientifically based on a set of criteria including prior record, offense seriousness, and previous interactions with the justice system. Sentencing grids reduce the discretion of judges and thus shift power to government prosecutors. The guidelines at the federal level have been successfully challenged all the way up to the Supreme Court level by inmates who had been sentenced to very long prison terms for relatively minor crimes.

The best example of mandatory sentences are the three-strikes laws, discussed earlier, which are in effect in more than half of our states. The logic of three-strikes laws is to increase penalties of second offenses and to require life imprisonment without possibility of parole for third offenses. These laws usually do not allow sentencing courts to consider particular circumstances of a crime, the duration of time that has elapsed between crimes, and mitigating factors in the background of offenders. The offender's potential for rehabilitation, ties to community, employment status, and obligations to children are also not taken into account. In other words, sentencing laws aimed at increasing predictability end up also producing illogical sentencing practices. A large share of people sentenced under three-strikes laws are actually very minor offenders who have created little harm to society; yet, each will be incarcerated in a prison at a cost of approximately $30,000 per inmate per year.

Corrections

Risk classification in corrections entails a great degree of prediction, as well. Individuals convicted of crimes can be put on probation, incarcerated in jail or prison, or subjected to some intermediate sanction; one's punishment is determined largely by offense seriousness, prior record, and behavior during previous criminal justice interventions. Each form of punishment entails more or less supervision, fewer or greater rules to follow (e.g., probation versus intensive supervision probation), and/or greater restrictions on movement and activities (e.g., minimum versus maximum security). The most violent and/or unmanageable inmates are now placed in isolation or incarcerated for 23 hours of the day in super-maximum security (supermax) prisons. These issues are discussed in the section on control that follows.

CONTROL AND CRIMINAL JUSTICE

In the past three decades, the United States has witnessed a rapid expansion of criminal justice, an expansion that is driven not by facts about crime or increasing crime rates but instead by politics, fear, and an increasingly punitive attitude about crime and toward criminals. This expansion is literally unparalleled in history; yet corresponding decreases in crime have not been achieved. Indeed, street crime decreased throughout the 1990s, but only a moderate portion of this decrease is attributable to imprisonment.

Policing

Under the guise of the war on crime and the war on drugs (and now the war on terrorism), U.S. police have been freed to gather and use much more evidence against suspects to obtain criminal convictions in court. For example, police are empowered to stop, detain, and question people who fit the "profile" of drug couriers in airports, even without probable cause. They are permitted to use dogs to search travelers' luggage without probable cause. Police are entitled to stop motorists without probable cause and to conduct searches of automobiles without a warrant. They are permitted to obtain warrants based on informants' tips. Police enjoy the "good-faith exception" that allows courts to use evidence obtained in error by the police as long as police erred in good faith. Police also can claim exigent circumstances to justify gathering and using unlawful evidence, including evidence that was in their plain view or within reach.

Also, police can seize a person's property through asset forfeiture programs based on suspicion of drug activity. The burden of proof falls on the accused to prove that he or she is not involved in the drug trade; even when this is accomplished, the government can keep up to 30% of the property for administrative purposes. All of this is inconsistent with the presumption of innocence and due process, as well as at least one conception of justice defined earlier. More importantly, these changes in the law enlarge the net of control cast on citizens of the United States.

Courts

As noted earlier, these changes in policing abilities are largely because of court decisions. The federal judiciary and the Supreme Court in particular have become more firmly entrenched in crime control values rather than due process values. That is, judges nominated by conservative presidents and appointed by conservative senators have, during the past three decades, eroded many of the gains for U.S. civil liberties won during the Warren

Supreme Court of the 1960s. They have done so, at least in theory, to make it easier for the criminal justice system to exert control over criminals.

The Rehnquist Court was the least likely Court in the past four decades to decide cases in favor of individual defendants and most likely to decide cases in favor of state governments, respectively. The Rehnquist Court was associated, at least in part, with the strongly conservative nature of the Chief Justice himself. For example, Rehnquist's successful efforts to limit federal habeas corpus appeals stemmed from his disgust over what he saw as abuses of such appeals by criminal defendants during his career as a lawyer and judge.

Since the 1980s and especially in the 1990s, the federal government has exerted more and more influence over state and local governments when it comes to crime control efforts. As a result, federal courts are empowered to restrict the rights of criminal defendants and to broaden the power of crime control agencies, thereby increasing the power of the government and the amount of control it has over the lives of citizens.

Corrections

In the 1970s and 1980s, state spending for correctional budgets dramatically increased but fell for non-Medicare welfare, highways, and higher education. These figures are evidence of increased control efforts by the criminal justice system. They are also criticized for being a disinvestment in the nation's future.

The clearest control issue in criminal justice revolves around corrections. Correctional facilities are now state of the art in terms of their use of technology to manage inmates. Increased use of other technologies include electronic monitoring of offenders under house arrest.

The so-called supermax prisons are the epitome of control. Offenders in supermax prisons have restricted contact with other inmates and with correctional personnel. Many inmates are locked in their cells for most of the day. The stark cells have white walls and bright lights on at all hours of the day and night. Front doors are completely closed, and there are no windows. Examples of supermax facilities include Marion (Illinois) and Pelican Bay (California). In such prisons, prisoners are confined to their cells for 23 hours per day and can only take showers 2 to 3 times per week. When inmates are transferred, they are shackled in hand cuffs and sometimes leg irons. Temperatures inside these facilities consistently register in the 80s and 90s.

The supermax facility gives us another interesting parallel between criminal justice and the fast-food industry. Technically, nothing can be *more* maximum than "maximum" custody, yet now we have supermax custody. In fast food, french fries used to come in small, medium, and large. Now they come in medium, large, and extra large: The extra-large sizes are "supersized," "biggie sized," and even "super supersized" and "great biggie sized." French fries provide the fast-food industry top profit margins. The McDonaldized fast-food industry tricks consumers into paying very high prices for a very small portion of potato using deceptive terms such as those just mentioned to convince consumers they are getting a good deal; the McDonaldized criminal justice system creates the illusion through the term "supermax custody" that these institutions keep Americans safe. In fact, most supermax inmates will one day be released into society, having to read-just to living with other people. And the costs to taxpayers just to build such facilities can be more than $130,000 per inmate.

Despite a rallying cry against big government, the nation's federal gov-ernment controls states by mandating certain criminal justice activities for funding. It assures control over state efforts to reduce crime by promising billions of dollars to states that follow its lead. Two examples include allo-cating prison funds to states that require offenders to serve at least 85% of their sentences and encouraging states to try juveniles as adults. States agree to engage in such criminal justice practices so that they will not lose resources from the federal government. Hence, criminal justice policy at the state level flows less from its potential efficacy than from the state's finan-cial concerns. The politicization of crime at the national level has created this paradox, another irrationality of U.S. criminal justice.

Control in criminal justice affects not only those subjected to policing and criminal penalties, but also has great effects on those who work within the nation's criminal justice system, including police, members of the court-room workgroup, probation and parole officers, and personnel inside our nation's correctional facilities. Much like workers in the fast-food industry, workers in criminal justice agencies are trained *not* to think and question but to simply operate in a preordained way. Police officers act in ways consistent with the values of their subculture, members of the courtroom workgroup act in ways consistent with the norms of the court, and courtroom personnel, correctional officers, and parole and probation officers are constrained by large numbers of caseloads. This is McDonaldization at its finest. In the fast-food industry, workers have been de-skilled to the point of absurdity in an effort to produce a consistent, predictable product and to minimize the like-lihood of employee error. Many of the jobs in criminal justice are also requiring fewer and fewer critical-thinking skills.

CONCLUSION

This chapter specified some of the relationships between McDonaldization and the U.S. systems of police, courts, and corrections. From the analysis presented, it is clear that our criminal justice system has fallen victim to McDonaldization and its basic dimensions. Given the frequency of exposure to our nation's fast-food establishments, Americans have probably come to expect these qualities from many institutions and services other than fast-food restaurants. Americans now expect easy solutions to complex problems such as crime. This makes it easier for politicians to tout and sell fast and easy solutions to the nation's crime problem.

Unfortunately, as U.S. police, courts, and corrections have become McDonaldized, irrational policies have resulted. That is the major point of this chapter: The criminal justice system, much like the fast-food industry, has rationalized, but in the process has delivered something entirely different; because of its increased devotion to the values of McDonaldization—efficiency, calculability, predictability, and control—irrational policies have developed out of a rationalized system of criminal justice. Americans are now less sure of receiving justice from their justice systems. This is true even though we have created *more* criminal justice today, even though we have made criminal justice practice *more* predictable, and even though Americans may now believe they are safer because of *more* control over criminals exerted by the government.

Thinking Critically

♦♦♦

1. What are the advantages of McDonaldizing the police, courts, and corrections?

2. What are the disadvantages of McDonaldizing the police, courts, and corrections?

3. If you could choose one of these to McDonaldize, which one would it be? Why?

4. If you could choose one of these that it would be a bad idea to McDonaldize, which one would it be? Why?

5. Is U.S. criminal justice better or worse off because of McDonaldization?

The reading (Chapter 12) "McDonaldization of the Sex Industries?" by Kathryn Hausbeck and Barbara Brents does an excellent job of taking all the dimensions of McDonaldization and applying them in a very systematic manner to the sex industry. One of the distinctive characteristics of this essay is the discussion of resistance to each of these dimensions by sex workers, customers, owners, and the sex industry itself. However, there is far greater acquiescence than resistance in this realm and most other areas of the social world.

Like many other commodities, sex has been McDonaldized. There is something unique and particularly disturbing, however, about the infiltration of this process into this area of our lives. While the McDonaldization of public aspects of our lives is disturbing enough, when it affects this most private, mysterious, and intimate of realms, it seems particularly troubling. Nevertheless, we have witnessed the rationalization and bureaucratization of sex even though it seems particularly intrusive and injects sterility into something that is supposed to be anything but sterile. The authors close this essay by relating their argument to that of Weber: "It also threatens to entrap us in Weber's fearsome iron cage: coldly colonizing our imaginations and brushing up against our skins." This image of McDonaldized systems touching us physically, and even entering and controlling our consciousness, brings concerns over McDonaldization to a whole new level.

12

McDonaldization of the Sex Industries?

The Business of Sex

Kathryn Hausbeck and Barbara G. Brents

◆◆◆ ────────────────────────────────────

Taken together the topless or nude dance clubs, live Internet stripping, cyber-sex services, sex toy stores, adult bookstores, pornographic magazines, adult comics, erotic trading cards, adult CD-ROMs, adult pay per view TV, sadomasochistic stores, services and dungeons, adult videos, TV and films, phone sex services, escort services, street prostitution, and legalized brothel prostitution constitute a huge and burgeoning sex industry in the United States. . . .

Does this expansion of the sex industry reflect the same pattern of rationalization and McDonaldization that characterizes other rapidly growing segments of the service economy?

───────────────

Editor's Note: Excerpts from "McDonaldization of the Sex Industries? The Business of Sex" by Kathryn Hausbeck and Barbara G. Brents, McGraw-Hill Primis [n.d., n.p.]

DIMENSIONS OF McDONALDIZATION: PUTTING THE SEX INDUSTRY TO THE TEST

We will explain each of the four dimensions of McDonaldization, consider the ways in which various parts of the sex industry are acquiescing to rationalization; discuss how this process affects owners, workers, and customers; and then examine the ways in which other parts of the adult industry continue to resist these trends.

Efficiency: Rule #1 for Fast-Food Sex

. . . In the sex industry, consumer desire for easy access and fast choices requires the compartmentalization of sexual relations into efficient units of consumption. This way of being sexual results in commodified and often superficial interactions. Further, where sex is defined as simply experiencing an orgasm, it is reduced to a mechanistic act in which the most efficient means to achieve the desired goal of climax is the most rational. This is the Taylorization of sex. Sexual efficiency becomes commercially defined human sexuality, disconnected from human spirituality or long-term emotional connection between participants. It is this version of sexuality that is marketed and sold in McDonaldized aspects of the adult industry.

Acquiescence: Owners

The legal brothels in Nevada are organized so that, for men, obtaining sex is much more efficient than typical ways of meeting and negotiating sex with potential female partners. A customer entering the brothel will generally ring a buzzer at the entrance gate, and by the time the customer gets inside and is greeted by the house matron, bartender, or manager, the working women are lined up and waiting for the customer to choose among them. This "line-up" demands that women stand in a prescribed manner (no special posing, no gestures, no sales pitches allowed!) while each makes a brief introduction. In the larger brothels, the manager usually encourages the customer to make a choice quickly, so as not to waste anyone's time. Most brothels and/or working women have hand-designed or printed menus (designed to look like restaurant menus) listing available services, though the customer will have to go to the prostitute's room to actually negotiate prices and services. Typically, a deal is struck between "working girl" and client that specifies the acts, the amount of time allocated for completion, and the cost of the transaction. The customer pays prior to service, the money is removed from the room for the safety of the worker, and a timer is set by management to keep track of the length of the exchange. When the time that was paid for is up, a manager will knock on the prostitute's door and advise her to end the transaction immediately, or "renegotiate" with the "john" for more money and more time. Efficiency dominates in this world of timed intimacy; both owner and prostitute benefit from this rationalized model of sexual exchange.

Acquiescence: Workers

For the workers, on the one hand, efficiency can mean streamlining interactions with clients while maximizing earnings and tips. On the other hand, efficiency can result in de-skilling and rationalizing workers in a manner that alienates them from their own labors.

A good example of the former trend has emerged in the exotic dance business. Many gentlemen's clubs are trying to make the purchase of private dances from strippers and drinks from cocktail waitresses more efficient by using "club money." These are vouchers that may be purchased from a waitress or at the door so that a client can use a credit card (without the name of the club on the charge to protect the purchaser from any disapproving spouse, parent, or boss who may see the bill) to tip or buy private dances. This is an efficient way for customers to turn a single credit card charge into a cash-like form which allows them to buy dances from multiple dancers and tip easily. It is also efficient for cocktail waitresses and dancers to receive "club money" instead of having to go through all the steps to run a credit card charge for each purchase. Clearly, though, the owner benefits most in this arrangement as "club money" is an extremely easy, efficient, and tempting way to separate a customer from his or her money. It is not possible to redeem the "club money" for cash, so it is either spent entirely or wasted.

On the other hand, workplaces that are organized around efficiency can de-skill workers and result in alienation. A good example is the phone sex industry. Here, many companies have "scripts" or guides that direct the phone sex worker to say certain things in particular ways in order to generate the highest fees from the customer. While this is an efficient business move, it curtails the creativity of employees and reduces the interaction between phone sex workers and clients to formulaic and scripted encounters.

Acquiescence: Customers

The sex industry has grown the most where it breaks sexual pleasures down to their most basic, easily packaged, mass-produced components, allowing maximum profitability while offering the customer easy access to goods and services, quick and convenient choices, and hassle-free exit from the encounter. This trend is seen regardless of whether we are talking about a client in a brothel, a customer in a strip club, or a shopper in an adult store.

Technology has been absolutely critical in the growth of the sex industry. The implications of technology can be seen in all four areas of McDonaldization. Technology has developed in ways that has met consumers' demands for efficiency at the same time as owner demands for profits. Consumers' calls to escort services are routed from a centralized telephone operator to workers via cell phones and beepers. This allows the escort or dancer to get to the customer as quickly as possible. This also allows owners to advertise speedy delivery of the dancer, sometimes claiming that she will be at your door in less than 30 minutes—quicker than take-out Thai food! The advent of home video technology in the 1980s produced porn "to go." For consumers, public adult movie theaters of the 1970s have been replaced by the easy and cheap availability of a wide variety of pornographic videos to be viewed in the privacy and convenience of their own homes.

Perhaps the most efficiently organized arena of the sex industry is in the growth of Internet sex. It is efficient for the consumers because not only can they meet, screen, date, and have virtual sex with individuals in online chat rooms without leaving their home, but customers can have real-time individual dancers appear on their computer screen and respond immediately to their sexual requests for money. It is efficient for the owners of the business since they only need a designated computer line, video equipment, a room, and a willing worker. This is considerably cheaper and more efficient than setting up an elaborate "gentlemen's club." This is why efficiency is the dominant operating principle in much of the sex industry: It creates a market of consumers for the products and offers services for sale that are quick, safe, and convenient, while at the same time increasing profitability for owners.

Resistance

The sex industry is a service industry that involves, even more than other aspects of the service industry, emotional labor. Emotional labor has an interesting and contradictory relation to McDonaldization. At the same time as the industry moves to rationalize, package, make efficient, quantify, and control the emotions surrounding sex and sexuality, the very nature of emotions breeds a resistance to McDonaldization that is important to examine. Efficiency, especially, is one of those contradictory areas. Both customers and service providers have resisted the reduction of sexual pleasure to a Taylorized assembly line. They avoid sexual fantasy and desire that is so efficient that it becomes sterile, unexciting, and cold (especially in what are called "gentlemen's clubs," strip clubs oriented to conventioneers and businessmen). A German visitor to Atlanta's gentlemen's clubs commented, "For Europeans . . . it has the sex appeal of a dishwasher." Similarly, many

American consumers want more from their sex industry purchase than simply a quick and convenient exchange. It is common for sex workers to report that customers want at least the appearance of intimacy, or the simulation of closeness during the exchange. Customers, on the one hand, seek ease in attaining this intimacy. But customers also value listening, flirting, complimenting, and feigning pleasure as important parts of the fantasy world of the sex industry. While these affective and emotive interactions are commodified for sale, they simultaneously resist easy reduction to purely efficient profit-driven exchange.

To make the sex industry fully efficient means dissolving the veil of fantasy that is a critical component of the adult industry. For example, it would be much cheaper for porn magazines to do what the advertising industry is increasingly doing and replace expensive models with flawless computer-generated men and women. However, this would obliterate the fantasy of seeing a real person with a "real" story to tell, thus making the possibility for "really" having sex with her or him impossible. This would not sell subscriptions.

It is the legal business of selling intercourse itself that has most strongly resisted the trend toward efficiency. In Nevada's legal brothels, too much formalized interaction (i.e., being assigned a number and a prostitute, having predesignated packages of services with fixed prices that set strict limits on the physical contact and interaction, etc.) and the resulting efficiency is unlikely to either generate new customers or encourage repeat business. While a "line-up" allows for fast and efficient choice of sexual partners, most brothels will allow men to bypass the line-up and have a drink at the bar, if the brothel has one. Some customers make a choice from there. But a person can also simply have a drink and leave. In addition, prices and services are still individually negotiated between customer and prostitute. None of these options is very efficient from the perspective of owners. Probably the most significant resistance to efficiency in the brothel is the fact that there are no standardized ways of performing sexual acts. While some women claim to know efficient ways to bring a man to climax in a set period of time, these procedures have not been standardized or systematized. As yet, there is still no assembly-line approach to the provision of sex; all the "tricks of the trade" that prostitutes report using to encourage an efficient sexual encounter with a client still require customization to the part'   ᵊᵉds, desires, and physiological capacities of each "john."

Resistance to efficiency also comes in the organization of try. The fastest growth within the sex industry is coming fro of the larger, more rationally organized, corporate busines we see the best examples of McDonaldization. The exotic (probably the best example of this trend. Chain-like busine' visible in gentlemen's strip clubs. But the industry still remains very fragmented. . . . The largest number of strip clubs, as is the case in other segments of the sex industry, are small, independently owned, and run as they have always been run by entrepreneurs who dared to oppose society's sexual norms. As a result, these businesses are not highly rationalized; there are no standard wages, skills, training, or workplace rules. Only the largest adult businesses have developed enough staff, capital investment, legal security, or customers to maximize efficiency through a fully rationalized organization. So, while the fastest growing sectors of the adult industry may appear to be acquiescing to efficiency—customers getting more convenient ways to purchase sexual products and services, and workers experiencing more standardization—the bulk of the industry resists the trend toward corporate efficiency.

Ironically, too much efficiency threatens to become inefficient in the adult industry: For customers, efficiency emphasizes outcomes over process, which can be alienating; for workers, efficiency can limit employee autonomy and alienate employees from their own embodied labors; and for owners, too much efficiency either in the rationalization of workers or in the rationalization of services to clients can easily result in the destruction of the very desires that sustain their profitability. There is a fine line between too little and too much efficiency when it comes to rationalizing sexual exchanges.

Predictability: Standardizing Sexuality and Desiring the Familiar

. . . The complexities of sexual desire are reduced to marketable commodities in the commercial arena of public life. There is an implied predictability inasmuch as only sexual desires that are recognizable and able to be reproduced are available for mass production. For business owners, mass production makes replication possible, desirable, and profitable. For consumers, there is safety and comfort in knowing what to expect around every corner: each burger tasting like the last, each hotel room looking like the last, each experience feeling like the last.

Acquiescence: Owners

Owners of adult businesses benefit from predictability in their industry in two ways. First, cultivating a desire for predictable interactions in their clientele allows owners to mass-produce sexual goods and services using a formulaic approach to commercializing sexuality, significantly increasing profits. Diversity, unpredictability, unique sexual products and services are more expensive, resource-intensive, and difficult to generate and sell.
's is why in much of the industry the sexuality that is for sale is

heterosexual sexuality dominated by traditional gender roles and hegemonic notions of beauty. Second, to the extent that predictability requires conformity and standardization, owners may use formal models for the production of their services by routinizing their employees, their business practices, and, to the extent the market will allow, their interactions with clients. As we have shown, owners have difficulty reducing all interactions to assembly-line efficiency, but many at times do conform to a predictable set of repertoires. This reinforces corporate efficiency and streamlines business through its simplified predictability.

Owners can capitalize on this predictability as well in the organization of business. While not a trend that has hit all parts of the sex industry, the more chain-like gentlemen's clubs have begun to share some management functions, manager training, and legal advice. The advantage is in making some of the unpredictabilities of the market disappear.

Acquiescence: Workers

The requirement of predictability offers guidelines for the behavior and appearance of sex workers, which can be liberating to the extent that formalized scripts require less personal innovation and investment; but it also can stifle creativity, individual choice, and style among laborers in the adult industry. For example, in pornographic videos, there is a language of pleasure and desire scripted into the plot line (however simplistic it may be), encoded in the camera angles, and reinforced by the soundtracks. Certain facial expressions, close-up shots, and noises are blended to give the viewing audience a sense of the intensity of the sexual encounter, as well as a sense of what is "really" desirable, exciting, and clear evidence of pleasure. While this formula may reveal itself to savvy viewers as simplistic, even a caricature, the repetitious nature of American pornography attests to the application of a tested and marketable model of sexual intimacy that is produced with only slight variations for consumption by the mass viewing public.

So, too, with strip clubs: While the decor, the clientele, the bodies and attire of the dancers, and the norms of the establishment may differ, the basic formula for the interaction between dancer and client is predictable. Sexuality in strip clubs is constructed through a subtle but repetitive series of moves, gestures, interactions, and props. Sexy clothing that is removed to the rhythm of loud music, gyrating hips, seductive flirtations with customers which reveal enough flesh to entice, but not enough to satisfy without the client offering more money, are all part of the commercial construction and sale of sexual fantasy in dimly lit strip clubs throughout the sex industry.

The more we, as a society, become accustomed to affordable, mass-produced products, the more consumers desire the predictable. As pornographic magazines, videos, and the Internet mass-produce images, a model's physical appearance becomes predictable. Women and men working as dancers, models, or actors must conform to cultural norms of stereotypical beauty. They must be of a particular size, within a range of predictable hair colors, makeup, and body dimensions. Plastic surgery increases the uniformity and predictability of body types, and what the actual body may lack in uniformity, computer enhancement can add.

Acquiescence: Customers

The sex industry has grown where it has provided consumers the comfort of predictability in an industry that is often associated with the exotic and unexpected: "Adult superstars" mimic the predictable look of a Blockbuster Video or Kmart; upscale gentlemen's clubs—dark, smoky rooms with neon or strobe lights, loud throbbing music, small tables, and couches with bars around the perimeter—also design their spaces to be predictable. The chain-like gentlemen's clubs are opening with uniform slogans, similar or at least recognizable names, the result being that a customer can go to a Deja Vu strip club in Atlanta and trust it will be as familiar as the one in Nashville or Las Vegas. The comfort of a friendly woman taking money at the door and large male bouncers roaming the crowd exudes an aura of predictable safety from any uncontrollable libidinal urges or jealous tempers.

The brothel industry, while in many ways resisting total predictability, has grown to the extent that it can provide consumers with legal sexual services in a manner that is basically the same from house to house and relatively unchanging over time. Women working in brothels are required by Nevada state law to be totally disease-free before beginning a shift at the brothel. They are checked for gonorrhea and chlamydia once a week and for HIV and syphilis once a month. Condoms are always required. The "guarantee" that a brothel will provide clean, disease-free women has been important in the continued existence of the legal brothel industry in Nevada. The resulting predictability has opened the brothel industry to a wide range of customers who might otherwise be frightened away from purchasing sex because of the potential for contracting sexually transmitted diseases.

Resistance

Again, the majority of adult businesses are small independent businesses, and they resist predictability just as much as they resist efficiency. Even in upscale gentlemen's strip clubs there are no uniforms, no scripts for dancers, and the rules of the house vary greatly. Regulations and zoning ordinances that have a huge impact on the development of the sex industries vary from one locale to the other, so it is difficult to ensure predictability of location or legal parameters governing adult industry interactions between geographic regions. And again, because both customers and services resist rationalizing all aspects of human interaction, there is wide variability in what dancers, prostitutes, and performers will do to fulfill sexual fantasies. There is a market value for at least the illusion of unpredictable and "special" sexual encounters.

The bottom line is that a certain amount of predictability in the presentation and purchase of sexual goods and services seems to be necessary to increase consumer comfort and participation in the adult industry, at the same time too much predictability diminishes the unique and private expression of sexuality. Moreover, perfect predictability seems to take away the very things that customers crave so much—personal attention, some element of surprise, exotic settings, and personally erotic situations.

Control: Robotic Sexuality?

Acquiescence: Owners

As we described above, little has done more to facilitate the growth of the sex industry than technology. Technology has been developed not only to increase efficiency for consumers but also to increase owners' control over the work environment in a way that increases profits. Technology has been harnessed to help frame, monitor, and limit both the work environment and the provision of sexual services. Automatic screens in peep shows strictly control how much a customer gets to see. Security systems watch and record everything in gentlemen's clubs. Even the simplest technology of a kitchen timer regulates the customer's time with prostitutes in brothels, ensuring both safety and profitability.

Reliance on technology allows business owners to control the sexual exchange in ways that are increasingly reducing the need for physical human interaction. From phone sex businesses, to virtual sex in chat rooms, to live Internet stripping, owners can provide a wide range of sexual services to customers without their ever leaving their homes or touching another human body. Computer technology means owners can record and replay workers, thus reducing the need for actual live temperamental bodies or workers. Internet pornography means more exchanges can be sold using less labor. Surveillance equipment allows owners to monitor workers more closely, thus ensuring their compliance with work rules as well as adherence to legal regulations. Violation of local regulations can be very dangerous and expensive for owners who legally have to defend themselves to protect their business interests.

Acquiescence: Workers

Medical technology, especially plastic surgery, has allowed workers to extend control over the body itself. Diversity in women's bodies can be reigned in—fat cut off here, implants added there, scars removed, makeup permanently added. Women's performing bodies literally become cyborg-like machines, carefully crafted for a particular look, with interchangeable parts. Success for dancers in the gentlemen's clubs, on the Internet, or in pornographic videos demands rigid control over the appearance of bodies, as well as over workers' labors.

Technological control in the sex industry reaches beyond the cyborgian reconstruction of bodies to simulate mass-produced images of beauty into the control of workers' time, movements, and interactions. Strip club dancers are surveilled by remote camera as they interact with clients. They are surveilled as they interact with one another in dressing rooms. They are required to take a Breathalyzer test at the end of their shift. Brothel prostitutes are timed as they are providing services to their "johns." Phone sex workers' conversations are taped and timed. Sex workers experience technological control both as a means to offer a safer workplace and as a means to regulate and control all of their movements, labors, and dealings with customers. While this control primarily means more profits for owners, it also means more safety for workers. Control over interactions means control over potentially unruly customers. A prostitute who is with a client after the kitchen timer sounds is usually immediately checked both to help her negotiate for more money and to make sure she is safe. Surveillance protects against customers who demand too much.

Acquiescence: Customers

For customers in the sex industry, technological control is often an insignificant part of McDonaldization. That is, consumers are so accustomed to being surveilled, timed, and rationally structured in their commercial dealings that this experience is not significantly different in the adult industry.

Resistance

However, here, too, there is resistance. In some ways the industry is less restrictive of workers than in the past. For example, the development of satellite systems in the phone industry has transformed the way in which labor is organized in the phone sex industry. The business of phone sex has in some cases evolved from being provided from a central location where women sit in large rooms with headsets and can be easily monitored by supervisors to being provided by women who work out of their homes. The pressures to provide the cheapest labor possible combined with changes in technology allow a business to seek out women wherever they are cheapest and least regulated by governments. Increasingly, a customer may be speaking to a phone sex worker anywhere in the world without even knowing it. This brings a whole new level of simulation to the fantasy of the girl next door!

As we have indicated, much of what is produced and sold in the sex industry involves emotional labor and at least feigned intimate interactions. Just as customers and workers resist efficiency and predictability, so too they resist complete control. Phone sex workers do have scripts, but workers report that it is their ability to act, impersonate, and respond to particular desires and needs that brings customers back. There is little use of computerized recordings. Although simulated dancers are well within the Internet's technological capability, customers still prefer live dancers who can interact, via computer, in real time. In sum, technology has been the handmaiden to the emergence of, and explosive growth within, the sex industry, and yet technology has not yet been fully deployed in the control of workers or in the Taylorization of sex.

Calculability: Bigger, More, Faster, Cheaper, Better

Acquiescence: Owners

In rationalized systems, quantification and calculability supersede quality in rank importance. "Good, better, best" corresponds to "big, bigger, biggest"; "Large fries only $.99" or "Now, 50% more . . . FREE!" are examples of calculability at work. Calculability ensures the greatest and most efficient profit possible for business owners, and it allows consumers to know what to expect of their transactions.

Acquiescence: Workers

Quantification is not just apparent in the time it rakes to purchase particular interactions, it also becomes a part of the measure of quality of service provided by workers. The "quality" of the goods—usually bodies—is measured in inches. For most body measurements, "more" is typically equated with "better." Many pornographic magazines advertise "more" of whatever is being sold. It is common in ads to boast more pictures, more sex acts, bigger penises, larger breasts, better bodies. The slogan of one gentlemen's club chain is "1000s of beautiful girls and three ugly ones." In a society where the breast has become fetishized, the bigger is praised as better. *Exotic Dancer* magazine contains stories of dancers whose income increased dramatically as they were surgically transformed from a 38D to a 42EEE bra size.

Acquiescence: Customers

As we discussed above, the process of McDonaldization in the sex industry has broken sexual interactions into component parts and sold them back to us. Moreover, these parts have been quantified in ways that can be easily measured. As we have shown, in brothels, phone sex, and live and Internet exotic dancing, interactions are typically negotiated and sold by the minute. Pleasure becomes measured in minutes; the purchase of sex is based on an agreed-upon act (or set of acts) in a fixed amount of time, for an agreed-upon price. Phone sex is measured and paid for by the minute, gentlemen's club dances are measured and paid for in the time it takes for a song, Internet dancing is measured and paid for by the minute. Basically, in a McDonaldized sex industry, the standard unit of sexual pleasure is the minute.

Resistance

The most resistance to McDonaldization comes in the small and fragmented businesses, where calculability and economies of scale are not common routes to economic success. At a businesswide level, most sex industries are strictly regulated and regulations vary from locale to locale. This means that it becomes difficult, if not impossible, for most businesses to rationalize costs in a predictable way. While the few chain-like gentlemen's clubs are centralizing tasks like management training and legal advice, their licensing fees, taxes, legal costs, and so on still vary greatly from location to location. The small businesses, because of a variety of legal and liability issues, hire dancers, escort workers, and prostitutes as independent contractors, and most of the pay for support staff comes from tips by the dancers. It becomes difficult to quantify and predict their input and output in calculating costs of business. Owners of brothels, for example, still do not calculate in any precise way their customer demographics. Financial figures are nearly impossible to locate, as large sections of the industry are still cash-based, which makes it even more difficult to tally, count, and keep track of profits.

And finally, the reliance on emotional labor means that it is hard to quantify and calculate all services provided. Desires and fantasies of customers are widely variable, difficult to measure or quantify, and hard to sell with a slogan like "Large fries, $.99." Calculability is difficult when an important part of the product or service being sold is amorphous: attitude, emotions, intimacy.

Acquiescence or Resistance?

In sum, McDonaldization is based upon efficiency, predictability, control, and calculability. In the sex industry, there is a complex pattern of both acquiescence and resistance to these trends. A good example comes from a recent article about the Nevada brothels in a local tourist magazine. Advertising the Chicken Ranch, the author boasts, ". . .[T]he cat-house has been the greatest Western institution. Today, it is bigger, better, glossier than ever and it is operated more efficiently than ever. . . . [T]he girls often display a genuine concern for the male patrons beyond 'satisfying their needs, and often their dreams.'" However, given that efficiency, predictability, control, and calculability are, perhaps, the most common and sought-after conditions of consumer life as we move into the 21st century, and continued McDonaldization is a likely path in the ongoing expansion and normalization of the adult industry in the United States.

McDONALDIZING SEX? FAST FOOD VS. FLESH AND FANTASY

Why focus on the McDonaldization of sex? In doing so, are we asserting that there is something about sex that is different from fast food, that is special, even sacred? After all, in many ways the business of selling sex/sexuality is just like commodifying other products and selling them for profit. In modern, capitalist society most of us take for granted that almost anything can be packaged, marketed, and sold. Regardless of whether or not we are critical of this process of commodification—and as sociologists, a healthy skepticism of this trend is well warranted—the empirical reality is that shopping and nearly constant consumption have become hallmarks of our American lifestyle at the end of the 20th century. The use of sex to sell other nonsexual products and the sale of sexuality itself are part of the trend toward a service-industry-based consumer society. To sell sex, in any one of its many forms, is to sell a product within a licensed, regulated, business environment for the purpose of generating profit. Structurally, then, this is no different than commercialization of other social interactions or services in order to sell products and generate profit.

On one hand, if this is convincing, then a paper investigating trends toward the McDonaldization of the sex industry would be somewhat passé; after all, Ritzer explains the general historical, sociocultural, and economic trend toward McDonaldization quite well. On the other hand, there *is* something different when the commodity being sold is sex. The question is *why*, sociologically, does it seem that the commercialization of sexuality warrants special consideration?

Even when the context of the exchange of sexual products or services occurs in an efficient, rational, calculable environment that feels comfortable, clean, and safe, this McDonaldization of sex is still distinctive compared to the McDonaldization of other aspects of our lives. Perhaps this should not be surprising, given that sex is typically seen as most appropriately located deep within the private sphere, and human sexuality is often thought of as a highly individual alchemy of desire. This is the crux of the question of how rationalized sex in a McDonaldized adult industry differs from other rationalized, McDonaldized business endeavors. First, sex is typically associated with the private realm of everyday life where the imperatives of the government, the marketplace, and public life do not tread; to sell sex as a commercial venture is to intrude on the sanctity of private life. Second, sexuality is not simply private, it is an expression of our innermost desires. Most of us rarely discuss the intimacies and precise details of our sex lives with others. Third, there is often an aura of uncertainty and mystery that shrouds the reality of desiring bodies, the physicality of sexual contact, the specific enactments of intimacy that characterize our sex lives. Taken together, sex(uality), being located in the private sphere and being thought of as uniquely personal and shrouded in mystery, distinguishes its rationalization from the rationalization of other commercial services. When sex is sold, there is often a fascination with its introduction into public life; uncloseting certain variations of sexual desires by codifying them in commercial enterprises makes visible that which is typically unseen and offers a public glimpse at the ways in which "others" experience parts of their sexuality.

The McDonaldization of sex is a pragmatic business endeavor in the context of an increasingly rationalized public sphere, where standardization allows the service industry to commodify social exchanges for profit. At the same time, however, the McDonaldization of sex marks the encroachment of the iron cage into the depths of the private sphere, into one of the most personal and apparently uniquely individual areas of human interaction: sexuality. Its commodification intrigues us by suggesting that desires and sexual interactions might be patterned, knowable recipes that lend themselves easily to packaging and standardization. For example, where a person may not feel fully secure with the secrets of great sex or the intricate intimacies of what others experience as "normal" sexuality or desires, it is fascinating—sometimes positive and interesting and sometimes alienating or worse—to see how corporate enterprises have apparently identified these secrets and developed formulaic sexual exchanges that are marketable and enticing to a large consuming public while remaining intimate enough to be fulfilling. This is the enigmatic nature of the rationalization of sex; it is a microcosm of the contradictory nature of American discourses and attitudes toward sex and sexuality in general.

Our society celebrates Viagra and restricts access to birth control. We fuel a rapidly growing adult industry, even as most American children do not receive any substantive, formal sex education. We collectively fixate on descriptions of [former] President Clinton's sex life, even as we alternately condemn him and dismiss it all as unimportant nonsense. Given this, it is not surprising that rationalized commercial sex is apparently a trend that many Americans crave (evidenced by growth of the sex industry in its McDonaldized forms), even as so many of us decry the commodification and McDonaldization of our bodies, our desires, and our private, intimate lives.

THE BOTTOM LINE: EROTIC BUREAUCRACY AND SEX IN A McDONALDIZED WORLD

. . . McDonaldization *is* "bureaucratic seduction." At first glance, this might seem to be a contradictory term. After all, where is the sensuality in red tape? Where is the mystery and eroticized anticipation in scripted, staged, and hurried commercial interactions? Upon further examination, however, it is clear that McDonaldized industries offer a plethora of products, full of consumer choices that are safe, colorful, relatively inexpensive, apparently convenient, reliable, and familiar; this is potentially very profitable for workers and owners. In short, then, McDonaldization *is* seductive; at the same time, however, the bureaucratic regimentation of rationalized economies of desire and standardized commercial sex are a sterile intrusion of the public sphere into the private, of the social into the personal, which makes any uncritical endorsement of McDonaldization seductively and deceptively simple. Beneath the aura of ease, opportunity, and freedom in a rationalized adult industry is a cold, alienating bureaucratic formation that employs bodies and desires in the profit-making enterprise of global capitalism.

This, then, is the sublime irony of McDonaldized sex. It is the bureaucratically ordered structure that makes certain kinds of consumer pleasures possible and that creates a larger range of consumers for the growing adult industry, even as this process leads to greater dehumanization, less diversity of desires, and more stratification. A McDonaldized sex industry is convenient for some consumers, safer and more lucrative for some workers, and profitable for owners, but it also threatens to entrap us in Weber's fearsome iron cage: coldly colonizing our imaginations and brushing up against our skin.

Thinking Critically

◆◆◆

1. In what ways is sex impervious to McDonaldization?

2. What aspects of sex would be benefited by McDonaldization? How?

3. What aspects of sex would be adversely affected by McDonaldization? How?

4. In what ways is your own sex life McDonaldized?

5. In what ways do we (you) resist the McDonaldization of sex?

Sara Raley examines contradictory developments and changes in the family from the perspective of McDonaldization. On the one hand, the structure of the family seems to be de-McDonaldizing. That is, the once highly predictable nuclear family (mom, dad, and 2.2 children) is in decline, and a whole range of different and highly unpredictable family forms are on the rise (never-married single parents; unmarried cohabiting heterosexual couples who may never marry; gay and lesbian couples who, with few exceptions, cannot marry; blended families with children from various marriages; married couples that are childless by design; grandparents tending to grandchildren; and so on). This change from a highly McDonaldized form to one far less McDonaldized is traceable to many factors including the fact that although the early form was efficient (as well as having many of the other characteristics of McDonaldization), many found it (like the fast-food restaurant) unsatisfying, even oppressive, perhaps even an "iron cage." The emphasis now is more on the quality of the relationship (e.g., romance, a good marriage) and on the lives of the children that result rather than such quantitative factors as number of years in a perhaps unfulfilling marriage or the number of children reared.

On the other hand, when one looks at everyday family life one finds a considerable trend in the direction of McDonaldization. This is seen, for example, in the impatience of married (or cohabiting) partners to move into a relationship and to see quick results, their reliance on the quick fixes offered by popular books and TV shows, their dependence on a variety of nonhuman technologies, their utilization of a wide range of McDonaldized settings for family activities, and so on. In spite of these and other changes, Raley hypothesizes that the family may be uniquely suited to retard the spread of McDonaldization.

13

McDonaldization and the Family

Sara Raley

◆◆◆ ──────────────────────────────────────

Any discussion about "the family" invariably must begin with a description of what is meant by the term "family." At midcentury, the conceptualization of what constituted a family was narrow. The ideal typical family (and also the most prevalent) was white, middle class, and nuclear with a husband sole-earner, a stay-at-home wife, and children. However, this conceptualization as the ideal has come under fire during the past few decades, as the "cookie cutter" nuclear family has been replaced by a widely diverse set of family types, including the never-married single parent, unmarried cohabiting heterosexual couples who eschew marriage, same sex unions who cannot marry even if they desire it, blended families made up of couples with children from their previous marriages, married couples who choose to remain child free, and grandparents residing with their grandchildren. The trend toward greater family diversity (and greater recognition of diversity that existed even at midcentury) reflects a process of de-McDonaldization as families place more emphasis on the quality of bonds between family members than the predictability offered by the heterosexist, gender-specialized arrangement of the 1950s.

─────────────

Editor's Note: This chapter was written for this volume.

In stark contrast to what is happening with the shifts in family structure, however, are the day-to-day realities of family life. The daily activities of families seem to have undergone a process of McDonaldization as people look for instant gratification in their relationships, and family time is governed more and more by technology such as television, cell phones, video game systems, and computers. Thus, shifting family structures pose a challenge to the process of McDonaldization, and aspects of the McDonaldized world continue to seep into family life.

THE DE-McDONALDIZATION OF THE FAMILY STRUCTURE

Perhaps the most obvious indication that family structure has undergone a process of de-McDonaldization is the wide variety of paths to forming a family. In the 1950s, this was fairly straightforward and easily predicted: A man meets a woman, they marry, and if all goes well with his job, he becomes the breadwinner, and she stays at home to raise children. Although this did not characterize all families at midcentury, it fit the majority (even among racial minority and low-income families). Today, however, even the expectation that a man will partner up with a woman is uncertain. Gay and lesbian couples are a small, but increasingly visible type of family that calls the notion that a family begins with the union of a man and woman into question.

Although marriage is not as inevitable as it once was, it is still very common. Most people who can legally marry, do. But just as the pathway to marriage has shifted, so too has the structure of marriage itself. The slow erosion of rigid gender roles in addition to declines in male wages and expanded opportunities for women in the workplace have made dual-earning the modal arrangement among married couples, including those with children. In most dual-earning couples, the male is still the primary earner, but a growing number of couples include cobreadwinners and wives who outearn their husbands. Families with stay-at-home fathers are still a very small group, but even employed married fathers have stepped up their participation in child-rearing and pick up more of the housework slack. Therefore, families are exercising a wider range of earning and care-taking arrangements that do not always fall along the predictable gender-specialized lines.

Not only are breadwinning and caregiving arrangements more fluid in contemporary marriages, but it is also no longer a given that the marriage will be a lifetime partnership. The slow rise in divorce rates over time and high rates of remarriage imply that marriage is not a once-in-a-lifetime experience; it may happen two, three, or even four times (especially if you are a celebrity). This makes familial relationships incredibly complex and highly unpredictable. For example, a woman may experience several immediate family relationships over the course of her life: her parents (who may or may not be married, may or may not be living together, and may or may not be heterosexual), siblings, step-siblings, half-siblings, a first husband, a same-sex cohabitating partner, step-children, half-children, and nonresident biological children.

In addition to marriage, most people have children at some point in their lives. Yet, even this dimension of family life has become less certain over time. A small but growing minority of couples, not limited by infertility, is opting for a childfree lifestyle. Rather than seeking fulfillment through having children, these couples take pleasure in fulfilling careers and maybe a pet or two. For those who do become parents, it is no longer a social prerequisite that mothers and fathers be married, or even that there *is* a mother and father. It is more common now than in previous decades for childbearing to take place outside of marriage, particularly among low-income men and women.

These trends raise the question: why did family structure shift? Particularly given how stable the conventional nuclear family was, and that U.S. society has placed a higher value on efficiency, rationality, and predictability as time goes on, it seems odd that so many Americans would choose to reject this model. This rejection seems to come at the hands of many who found the arrangement oppressive. Despite all of the McDonaldized advantages it had to offer, it did not offer fulfillment to people who did not wish to have children, to women who found housework depressing, to men who found breadwinning to be stressful, to homosexuals who did not wish to partner up with someone of the opposite sex, or to couples who were trapped in unsatisfying marriages. So underlying the changes in family structure was a movement toward building rewarding relationships and having satisfying family relationships (e.g., remaining married out of want rather than out of obligation or having children because you want them, not because you are "supposed" to have them).

Today, there is an intense focus on the quality of family life, particularly on raising high-quality children and forming high-quality marital relationships. Demographers argue that families have transitioned from wanting a high "quantity" of children to desiring high "quality" children. This emphasis on "quality" children is evidenced by the cultural shift toward "intensive mothering" and "involved fathering," two terms that have received a great deal of popular press in the past decade.

Among middle- and upper-class parents, these parental investments in children start as early as the pregnancy. Expectant parents (both women *and* men) immerse themselves in books about pregnancy and parenting, enroll in Lamaze and prebirthing classes, put earphones of classical music against their pregnant bellies, settle on names long before the fetus reaches full term, and carry around sonogram pictures as if the child were already born. Once babies are born, the nurturing continues and accelerates. Children are enrolled in preschool classes to enhance their cognitive development, even in families with nonemployed mothers. The very best preschools can have waiting lists several years long, so that children need to be put on the list before they are even born. Then parents race to sign their children up for various extracurricular activities such as art classes, sports teams, and music lessons. Although poor parents do not necessarily have the means or desire to enroll their children in countless activities to enhance their development, this group of parents often has some of the highest educational and occupational aspirations for their children. Parental involvement in poor families is more likely to be characterized by protecting children's physical safety in urban areas and providing their children's material needs (perhaps by forgoing some of their own material needs).

The trend toward high parental investment might seem counterintuitive given that as time goes on, children are less economically useful to their parents. Children no longer offer the benefit of unpaid labor on the farm, neither do they offer much help in the form of paid labor given child labor laws in the United States. Further, the establishment of the federal Social Security system and Medicare as well as the availability of nursing centers, means children are not as essential for parents' old age security (although the Social Security system is facing a bit of a crisis in recent years, it was growing strong at the time of declining fertility).

Not only do children not offer much economic utility, they are expensive. For many middle- and upper-class families, it is even normative for children to expect their parents will pay for their college tuition, and sometimes their postgraduate educations. Indeed, young adults are attending college at record rates, many on their parents' dime. Children also reside in their parents' homes longer, often through young adulthood (and often rent-free). This has many parenting experts wondering why Americans have any children at all, particularly low-income men and women, who have less disposable income to devote to childrearing. Children now cost much more money than they give in return, and yet parents seem to be investing in their children more than ever.

Obviously, children offer something other than economic value to their parents, and this is probably why people have them. Today, emotional bonds more aptly characterize the parent-child relationship than economic ones. Parents get joy from their children's accomplishments rather than their financial return. This is not to say that parents did not get joy or have love for their children in years past, only that there was an economic component of the relationship that does not seem to be as strong today.

In addition to high-quality children, people also aspire to enter high-quality romantic partnerships. The importance of romantic love in contemporary relationships is a relatively recent phenomenon, given that historically marriage has been conceptualized as a committed economic partnership.

In the past, economic gains to marriage were clearer: Men gained unpaid labor and women gained economic security. Now that gendered roles are changing (albeit slowly), and marital stability has decreased, the gains to marriage are ambiguous and less tangible. Women can earn a living outside the home, and so they do not necessarily need men for economic security (although gender discrimination and the gendered wage gap persist, so women are still disadvantaged in the labor market). Women may also be less willing to do the unpaid labor in the home. Hence, when men and women do cohabitate or marry, their marriages may be of higher quality because there may be a greater focus on companionship and romantic love than on economic exchange. Women have expanded opportunities to work outside the home if they so desire, may be more empowered to voice their opinions pertaining to family matters, and enjoy greater agency to leave unfulfilling marriages. Men may have lost a bit of power inside the home, but they might feel less pressure to be the sole breadwinner (a job loss might not be as devastating to the family) and find relationships with their children more rewarding.

Expectations about what partners should get from relationships, and marriages in particular, still have some economic basis, but added to it is the expectation that a partner should also be a lover and a friend. This is evidenced by the fact that a woman's standard of living generally declines after a divorce, and yet women remain much more likely to initiate a divorce than men. Therefore, women are obviously seeking more than just economic support when they marry.

Among some groups, the aspirations for a good marriage are so high that people will delay marriage until midlife or indefinitely. For example, some scholars argue that low-income men and women have disproportionately lower marriage rates than middle- and high-income couples because they do not feel they have achieved the necessary prerequisites for a good marriage, such as economic stability and a long-standing romance. For many men and women, being "happily married" seems more important than just being married.

In sum, shifts in family structure offer some of the more striking examples of trends toward de-McDonaldization. Families, or perhaps more appropriately, individuals within families, have successfully challenged the dominant arrangement of the white, middle-class, nuclear family with the breadwinner father and stay-at-home mother. This arrangement, which seemed to offer the most predictability for organizing family life, has been replaced by a wide variety of family structures. These additional arrangements may not offer as much stability as the 1950s ideal, but they may create satisfying (i.e., better quality) relationships for people. Although there are movements to reinstate the traditional nuclear family of yesteryear as the ideal, the increasing tolerance for family structures that deviate from this family type gives people more choices to construct relationships in unique ways that fit their wants and needs.

McDONALDIZATION OF EVERYDAY FAMILY LIFE

Although it might seem that people are more interested in forming emotion-ally fulfilling partnerships than those in previous generations, it also seems as if many people are falling short of this goal. It is difficult to ignore the rise in marital instability as well as the high level of volatility of cohabitating rela-tionships—many cohabitating relationships dissolve because they turn into marriages, but not all. Part of this may have to do with expanded life spans—as people live longer, they have to live together longer, and the prospect of spending the next 60 to 70 years together may seem more daunting than just spending the next 30 or 40. At the same time, it seems as if some degree of calculation might be going on in marital relationships. Just as people expect instantaneous results when they dine in fast-food restaurants, people may expect instant gratification from their romantic partnerships. The impatience to "see results" may be part of the reason a high percentage of marriages that end in divorce do so within a few years and why so many cohabitating rela-tionships are short-lived. When couples run into obstacles or disagreement, they may be more likely to exit the relationship than stay the course. The extreme examples of this are the widely publicized celebrity marriages, such as that of Britney Spears, which last only hours or a few days.

When spouses do not get the immediate results they expect from the rela-tionship, they might turn to prepackaged advice in the form of self-help books rather than seeking in-depth, personalized marriage counseling. These self-help books are written by people who may or may not be professionals and who are completely removed from the unique circumstances of any individual marriage. Although these books might offer some small insights to a couple, they are unlikely to single-handedly save a relationship. Yet, the appeal of quick and easy fixes to conflict is reflected in the near universal familiarity with John Gray's, *Men Are From Mars, Women Are From Venus*, which argues men and women must learn to accept the "natural" differences between the sexes to establish healthy communication and develop deep connections. Essentially, the book offers advice for couples who accept and follow gendered stereotypes.

The popularity of quick fixes to family issues is further evidenced by one of the most popular daytime television talk shows, *Dr. Phil*. Dr. Phil, a tele-vision personality, offers succinct solutions to a variety of complex family issues in less than an hour. His straight talk one-liners make navigating family relationships sound easy. In fact, Dr. Phil's advice is so revered that he even wrote a best-selling dieting book despite being a bit overweight himself. (It is also worth noting that the "relationship expert" Dr. John Gray lost little credibility after divorcing his first wife.)

One caveat to these relationship books is that they still underscore the trend toward high-quality relationships. This is because the interest alone in these types of self-help books and television shows indicates that people are looking for more out of their relationships than just financial gain. There may not have been a market for these kinds of books or shows in previous decades, because the concerns over having a happy marriage and/or maximizing a child's cognitive development were not nearly as intense as they are today. The idea of seeking marriage counseling or needing to read to their child every night would have seemed foreign to a young couple in the 1950s. Yet today, some couples seek counseling, or listen to John Gray's *Men Are From Mars, Women Are From Venus* book on tape, before they are even married.

In addition to the impatience to make a marriage work, there may be impatience to see the marital relationship come to fruition. This may seem like an odd perspective given that young people are more likely to delay marriage than in the past. How could people be impatient to marry or partner up if they are increasingly putting off this decision? First, it does not seem as if marriage is delayed because people are spending more time hunting around for Mr. or Ms. Right. A more common, and probable, explanation of delayed marriage is that people are investing more time in educational and leisure pursuits. Their sole focus as young adults is not on finding a good mate, but rather finding a good job. It was often joked that when women went to college in the 1970s, they were seeking their "Mrs." degree, whereas now that argument does not seem to carry much weight for recent cohorts of women who are actually graduating from college at higher rates than their male counterparts. In fact, *because* young people are focusing so intensely on their studies or burgeoning careers, they may arrive at their late 20s in a state of panic, realizing they have not yet connected with a mate.

Popular reality television shows such as *The Bachelor* and *Who Wants to Marry My Dad?* are prime examples of the impatience with which some segments of the American population are approaching marriage. Even though these programs are made for television, they are reflective of what is going on in some segments of the viewing public. For example, "speed dating" has become quite popular in major cities. Potential dating partners gather together in a group, have a one-on-one conversation with each individual in the group for a few minutes, and then make a list of the people they find worthy of further dates. Internet matchmaking, another example of this, has virtually exploded over the past decade. People select dating partners by scanning online McDonaldized profiles, which include short snippets of a person's occupation, interests, and hobbies that generally offer no credible insight into a person's depth or originality. People may still form high-quality relationships as a result (or perhaps in spite of) this process, but the process itself is certainly McDonaldized.

Perhaps the most striking evidence of how the family has McDonaldized is the extent to which families have embraced nonhuman technology. Families are allowing the technology to seep into their homes and pervade their most intimate relationships. In fact new technologies are increasingly targeted toward families, particularly parents and children. Verizon's "Family Share Plan" for cellular phones is a prime example, where cell phone communication between family members is "free" (after you pay for phones for each family member, activation fees, and the flat monthly fee). This encourages families to hook up all of their members to cell phones, controlling the means of their communication. Cell phones in hand, families no longer have to be together to stay in touch. Although this may mean that families are more closely connected than ever before, it can also mean spotty cell phone calls ("Can you hear me now?") replace quality face-to-face dinner conversations. The implications of this technology for family life are unclear.

What is clearer is that family time may increasingly involve convening around the television rather than the dinner table given that families (1) spend large amounts of time watching television and (2) are less likely to have one member of the family devoting time solely to household work such as preparing home-cooked dinners. Ready-made dinners might be picked up from grocery stores or take-out restaurants on the way home, or perhaps frozen dinners are zapped in the microwave. Parents may contend with "vanishing children" who come home from school and immerse themselves in technology—heading straight to the television to watch their favorite programs or to the computer to play video games, surf the Internet, download music, or "instant message" their friends. Although not all families can afford to own a computer or to be hooked up to the Internet, families are more likely than other types of households to both own a computer and have the Internet streaming into their households. Hence, the technology is increasingly affecting how families spend their time.

Family time is also increasingly structured and scripted. Families may even incorporate time management strategies they learn at the workplace into their family life so that they "make the most" of family time. Examples include creating a family calendar where family dinners or talks and spousal "date nights" are squeezed between sports practices, music lessons, birthday parties, sleepovers, and parental work schedules. When families want to get away together, they travel to McDonaldized amusement parks such as Six Flags or every child's media-generated fantasy, Disneyland. Almost every experience is preplanned in these parks, so parents do not have to come up with creative ways to entertain and interact with their children—Disney has done all the work. Families only need to decide which ride to go on first and what time to stop and eat at the McDonaldized restaurants to refuel. In addition to amusement parks, shopping malls are another hot spot for families to spend time together. Malls are popular because there is something for everyone: toy stores for young children, music and apparel stores for teenagers, and electronic, home, and department stores for parents. Eating is simplified by the food court where everyone can select their favorite fast food and dine together in the centralized seating area.

Finally, family celebrations such as birthdays, anniversaries, and graduations may also be homogenized, taking place at the nearest chain restaurant, complete with singing waiters and a brownie sundae for dessert. In sum, virtually every aspect of the day-to-day lives of families has been McDonaldized in one way or another.

THE FAMILY AS AN INSTITUTION: CAN IT RETARD THE McDONALDIZATION OF U.S. SOCIETY?

Although family life has been highly influenced by the process of McDonaldization, it is also an institution uniquely suited to hinder and challenge the principles of McDonaldization governing U.S. society. Perhaps the most distinctive characteristic of contemporary U.S. families is that they are (presumably) made up of people who care for each other and perhaps even have love or altruistic feelings toward one another. Unlike other social institutions, such as corporations or governments, families are not motivated strictly by profit. At least for the parent-child relationship, an emotional connection is a major, if not the primary, dimension of the bond. Although financial gain or efficiency may be a component of the familial relationship, families seem to be less focused on economic gain than in years past.

Within families, people have the freedom to construct their own family norms and create unique traditions together (or at least the adults in the family can). As employees and consumers, however, people are subject to the McDonaldized norms and stipulations dictated by corporations and the government. In fact as the workplace and the consumption landscape become increasingly rationalized, homogenized and impersonal, people can, and probably do, seek refuge in their family life. The "nothingness" of the outside world may be part of the reason why families are investing so heavily in their children and raising the standards for their marital relationships.

Although not wholly free of restraint, family life may be a space where they can choose to value authenticity and creativity. It may also be one of the few areas people can get a reprieve from the focus on efficiency, calculability, predictability, and control that they experience at work and in consuming.

Additionally, families have the power to hijack elements of the McDonaldized world, such as the nonhuman technologies that control people's lives, and use them to humanize relationships and create authenticity. This is in direct conflict with the way such technology has traditionally created distance between people and depersonalized nonfamily interactions. Rather than allowing the technology to govern their lives, which is all but inescapable in corporate America, families have the opportunity to use technology to bring family members closer. Returning to the cell phone example used earlier, such technology can actually be used to strengthen family bonds. Verizon's mission is not to bring families closer, but to maximize its profits by hooking as many people as possible up to its cell phones. It wants everyone to be talking on cell phones as often as possible, racking up those minutes. Families, however, can subvert these goals by making careful decisions about how they use the technology in their family life. So, rather than allowing cell phone conversations to replace face-to-face interactions or keeping people connected to bosses when they are supposed to be spending time together as a family, the technology could be used by employees on business trips as a means to have more contact with their family members. Further, extended family bonds, which may grow distant over time as people move and are geographically separated, may be rekindled with the magic of cell phone technology. Adult siblings and parents with adult children living on separate coasts who may not otherwise be able to afford the costly plane travel or high landline telephone bills, may remain in close contact via low-cost cell phone programs and free e-mail, which they may access at work or the public library if they do not have a home computer.

CONCLUSION

Even though the process of McDonaldization continues, structural changes in the family pose a threat to the trend. People seem to want deep, authentic connections in their family relationships, and they seem willing to sacrifice some level of predictability to achieve these goals (hence the movement away from the white, middle-class nuclear ideal). However, what the McDonaldized world has to offer them in the way of "enchanting" technologies such as television shows, cell phones, and Web surfing may be difficult for families to reject, even when such technologies are likely to control and erode quality family time. Families have the power to use these technologies for their own non-McDonaldized purposes (using e-mail to keep in close and meaningful contact with distant relatives rather than sending meaningless forwards to acquaintances), but only if they make conscious efforts to do so.

Thinking Critically

1. Is the de-McDonaldization of the family structure more of a good or a bad thing? Why?

2. Is the McDonaldization of everyday family life more of a good or a bad thing? Why?

3. Think about the relationship between the McDonaldization of family structure and everyday family life.

4. Would you rather raise your family in a McDonaldized or a de-McDonaldized fashion? Explain your choice.

5. Would you expect the greatest resistance to McDonaldization to come from within the family?

In the following cross-cultural and cross-institutional analysis, drug abuse treatment is analyzed from the point of view of the four basic dimensions of McDonaldization. The author of this chapter finds it a near prototype of that process in that drug abuse treatment in Germany was thought of in singular linear terms with drug abuse seen as a steady irreversible progression. Treatment, as a result, involved preventing initial use, stopping use as quickly as possible after initial use, and urging abstinence on long-term users. This led to a McDonaldized system that, among other things, sought to maximize efficiency by, for example, focusing on the limited goal of abstinence and giving those being treated no options in terms of their treatment. Stages were clearly defined en route to the objective of drug abstinence.

However, as with at least some other efforts to extend the idea, the McDonaldized approach to drug treatment was not highly successful. Recent thinking has led to the view, for example, that there is not one linear pattern to drug abuse, but a multitude of paths, some of which do not culminate in drug addiction. As a result, a variety of approaches to treating drug abuse have emerged in recent years, many of them less or even de-McDonaldized (e.g., highly individualized treatment plans).

14

What Do Hamburgers and Drug Care Have in Common?

Some Unorthodox Remarks on the McDonaldization and Rationality of Drug Care

Uwe E. Kemmesies

PROLOGUE

While a hamburger and its raw materials are well-known, tangible entities, drug policy and approaches to drug treatment seem to be largely amorphous, much less objective concepts. The conceptual basis for drug policy and treatment is determined by countless established institutions, associations, departments within particular ministries, and the like that cope with its different facets. Proponents of current drug prohibitionist policy envision a world completely free of individuals who consume mind altering substances. . . .

Editor's Note: From Kemmesies, U. E. (2002). Hamburgers and Drug Care. *Journal of Drug Issues*, pp. 691–695. Reprinted with permission of Florida State University.

If we leave aside qualitative differences, a hamburger will keep its phenotypic manifestation; if that is lost, it ceases to be a hamburger or would not be identified as one. On the other hand, the drug care system changes its appearance every time its intentions and objectives change, as was the case in the mid 1980s when AIDS first became an issue. Since then the shift from abstinence to harm reduction has led to a dramatic change in and diversification of drug treatment approaches (syringe exchange, injection rooms, methadone substitution, etc.).

INTRODUCTION

The (stylized) hamburger appears as the outstanding (pop-art) icon of a rapidly spreading fast-food culture. This culture can be seen as a symbol of a completely rationalized society, one that is strictly oriented toward calculability and the rapid pace of life; this societal structure now appears to be spreading as part of a global process. One of, if not the most, prominent representative of this development is the fast-food chain McDonald's. This company, representing modern fast-food culture, has been featured in a thesis developed by the astute American sociologist, George Ritzer, which he has subsequently elaborated on in many publications. Ritzer's thesis is aptly titled the "McDonaldization" of society (Ritzer, 2000). . . .

This paper asks the reader to think about how far the drug care system has already progressed in terms of Ritzer's McDonaldization process.

THE McDONALDIZATION OF DRUG POLICY AND TREATMENT

. . . Until the late 1980s, drug treatment discourse in Germany was dominated by a 'linear' image/idea of addiction. In other words, addiction was conceptualized as a career model, a steadily progressing condition that over time leads to increasing involvement in a drug related lifestyle. Furthermore, addiction was held to be irreversible, as reflected in the colloquial adage "once addicted, always addicted." Based on this concept of drug use, treatment was aimed at preventing initial use (primary prevention), aborting the addiction process as early as possible once it has begun (secondary prevention), or facilitating abstinence status among long-term users (tertiary prevention). This linear concept of addiction and drug treatment was formulated early on and became the classic approach to the problem. It was focused on abstinence and designed to remove drug users from the diverse career stages of their addiction (disease), in order to abort the process.

Ultimately drug treatment was based on an action model that has been discussed by experts as the "abstinence paradigm."

The classic drug treatment system satisfies the four core dimensions of McDonaldization. Drug treatment facilities have been strictly oriented towards the addiction-model and the abstinence-paradigm, and these were—as regards both content and conception—closely linked in order to foster optimal efficiency. Seen from this perspective, the calculability of the treatment processes and especially the predictability of therapeutic interventions should have been improved. This was relatively easy because the system limited its goals to drug abstinence (though this was seldom achieved). The ideal-typical model of drug care was visualized as an interlocking system or therapy chain based on a division of labor (counseling centers, therapy facilities, and aftercare facilities). It was thought that this could ensure the efficient achievement of abstinence. Drug treatment providers thought of this system as a paragon of efficiency because the people it was designed to treat did not have any choices to make. The long-term objective and the stages involved in getting there were clearly defined and institutionalized. In a general sense, this classic interlocking system of drug treatment appears to be a prototype of the McDonaldization thesis.

In practice, however, research and experience revealed that drug use does not follow such a logical sequence. This system failed to produce an acceptable level of success, despite its efficiency and predictability. From about the mid 1980s on, partially driven by the rapidly emerging challenges posed by HIV, it became possible to discuss the system "outside the box," that is outside the framework of these earlier dogmatic ideas of addiction and drug consumption. Several drug researchers helped to bring about this change of thinking regarding the earlier uni-directional development of drug use. Recent research findings—especially those concerned with the controlled use of psychoactive substance and self-recovery—make clear that drug addiction, seen as a phase of compulsive use, represents only one *possible* stage in a longer lasting, and also reversible development. Moreover, addiction is not a kind of final, inevitable stage in a drug career. There are other "career patterns" that never lead to any kind of compulsive, addictive drug use. Progressive groups in the drug treatment debate notwithstanding, the following facts were discovered in the 1980s: drug use patterns develop heterogeneously, drug use does not inevitably lead to addiction, and use does not necessarily have to be stopped entirely in therapy. These theoretical shifts led to an increase in the diversity of drug treatment options that have been made available since the mid 1980s. These changes would not have occurred without the enormous socio-medical challenges posed by HIV/ AIDS. For example, since that time it has become acceptable to consider methadone substitution as a legitimate treatment form in Germany. In fact, this form of treatment has now become well established—methadone is an accepted form of maintenance substitution, and the medical prescription of heroin has even been given serious consideration. Furthermore, the older counseling centers, whose primary aim was to motivate drug consumers to participate in a therapeutic recovery process have been supplemented by numerous and diverse low-threshold facilities. The latter facilities, often termed "contact cafés," offer a variety of supports for everyday life in order to prevent a progressive impoverishment of the marginalized drug consumer who is, in most cases, experiencing serious health problems. These centers offer sleeping facilities, medical care, and food, and they also include needle-exchange programs (the first of these were established during the early 1990s) and the recently emerging safe-injection rooms (the first of these opened in 1994 in Frankfurt am Main). The latter two programs are now legally protected, so long as they do not violate the German drug law, the BtMG (Betaeubungsmittelgesetz). The diverse programs that have endured during the last decade need to be interpreted as examples of de-McDonaldization. That is, there are now more rather than fewer facilities and there are more individualized treatment options rather than less—the opposite of what one would expect in a McDonaldized system. However, we should not attach too much significance to this because the symptoms of McDonaldization are still dominant.

Thinking Critically

♦♦♦

1. Are you surprised that there was an effort to McDonaldize drug treatment? Why, or why not?

2. Are you surprised that in more recent years there has been movement in the direction of de-McDonaldizing drug care? Why, or why not?

3. Do you foresee problems in a society that is increasingly McDonaldized, but drug treatment is growing more de-McDonaldized? If so, what kind?

4. Are there signs that drug-taking is growing more (or less) McDonaldized?

5. What would happen to the rate of drug use if it was McDonaldized to a high degree?

Education is one of the areas that has been most addressed from the perspective of McDonaldization. Although the public schools have undoubtedly been McDonaldized to a very high degree, it is the universities that have been most often examined from this perspective. In the following chapter written especially for this volume, Suzanne Hudd examines the public schools, but rather than focusing on any number of rather obvious topics, she looks at one—character education—that would, on the surface, seem less likely to be McDonaldized. After all, such a moral issue would appear to be less amenable to McDonaldization than, say, curriculum or lesson plans. Yet, Hudd details a significant level of McDonaldization in character education, much of it traceable to federal involvement as a result of the 2001 No Child Left Behind Act. Hudd discusses the paradox that McDonaldizing character education in the schools may actually lower the ability of students to make moral decisions once they are outside the school setting, or cause them to leave such moral training behind in later life. In addition to analyzing character education from the point of view of McDonaldization, Hudd also usefully employs the ideas of disenchantment (Chapter 22) and McDonaldized "islands of the living dead" (Chapter 3) to cast additional insight into character education.

15

McMorals Revisited

Creating Irrational Characters?

Suzanne S. Hudd

◆◆◆ ───

> *We must take care lest we impoverish morality in the process of rationalizing it; and we must anticipate the complications that it entails and prepare for them.*
>
> Emile Durkheim, *Moral Education*, 1961

C haracter education has made a comeback in our schools. As a group of students at an elementary school assembly I recently attended described it, "citizenship is hip." Formal instruction in character has long been an important part of the U.S. education system. In its current form, character education emphasizes understanding, caring, and acting on core values such as respect, honesty, and responsibility. Ideally, it is infused throughout the curriculum and the school.[1]

The resurgence of interest in character education has occurred with much support from educators, parents, and policymakers. In a 1994 Gallup

─────────────

Editor's Note: This chapter was written for this volume.

poll, 57% of parents expressed support for the inclusion of character education in school curricula. The support for teaching specific virtues such as caring, honesty, and moral courage was nearly unanimous.[2] Teachers affirm the need for character education with this same enthusiasm: They see character education as an important component in the school curriculum, and they feel generally confident in their ability to serve as role models and teach character.[3] Policymakers have also encouraged the development of character education curricula. The vast majority of states have adopted legislation pertaining to character education and the No Child Left Behind Act of 2001 authorized nearly $25 million of funding to support school-based character instruction.[4]

It has been argued that character education seems to have replaced "apple pie and motherhood"[5] as an essential element in our culture. We do not object because the hidden curriculum is an inherent part of school-based instruction: Character education simply shifts it to a more central and visible place. Statistics that suggest character is on the wane also make character education compelling. A 1998 study of 3,123 students listed in "Who's Who Among High School Students" raises concerns about morality among our youth; 80% of those surveyed admit to having cheated, and more than half perceive that cheating is not a serious violation.[6]

This chapter will not dwell on the purported moral decline within our culture, however. Nor is it my intention to debate whether character education is a panacea for our social ills. Instead, here I will focus on *how* we have chosen to administer character education programs in our schools nationwide as well as some of the possible consequences of school-based character instruction. I will argue that many of the contemporary processes of character instruction, which we are in the midst of adopting are, to a certain extent, being driven by our cultural impetus to "McDonaldize" virtually every aspect of our lives. Although we may lament the evolution of McDonaldized systems for shopping or theme parks, the McDonaldization of character represents perhaps the ultimate example of how deeply embedded our drive for efficient and predictable outcomes has become.

Ironically, rational, school-based systems offering character education may sometimes limit opportunities for thoughtful reasoning to achieve their ultimate goal of creating reasonable adults. Why is this so? How does rationalized character education work? Are there irrational results? My aim in this chapter is not to criticize character educators, whose goals are well-intentioned, and who frequently speak to the complexity inherent in their discipline.[7] Rather, my core concern is that our social compulsion to develop efficient and rational solutions for even our most complex problems will affect the development of character education curricula in our schools. The creation of formal, rational systems for character education, may bring us to

an era of McMorals; character education that encompasses the core principles of efficiency, calculability, predictability, and control.[8] In this chapter,
I will consider the extent to which character development that occurs within
a McDonaldized system is likely to produce irrational results: a disenchantment, homogenization, and dehumanization that will come to characterize
our moral culture and daily aspects of our moral lives.

MORALS ARE THE PROBLEM, CHARACTER IS THE SOLUTION

A variety of behavioral trends are cited as evidence of a growing moral crisis in our country, among them: rising youth violence, increasing dishonesty, growing disrespect for authority, increasing peer cruelty, the
deterioration of language, a rise in hate crime, cheating at school, stealing,
and sexual precocity and abuse.[9] The list of problems seems virtually endless, and it incorporates behaviors that occur both in and out of school. The
sources of this purported moral decline are complex, and in many cases
they lie beyond school walls: the erosion of institutional values, the decline
of family time because of divorce and the rise in dual-income households,
growing economic disparity, and the increasing acceptability of violence in
the media.[10] It has been argued that the decline of "functional communities
with intergenerational closure"[11] has changed the role of the school. Put
more simply: Today's parents lack access to informal social networks that
can provide them with both information on their children's behavior as well
as surrogate discipline when they cannot be present. To a certain extent,
character education, in its many forms, has arisen to fill this social void.

Educators use various strategies to instill character. The term character
education encompasses a wide range of learning and reasoning techniques
intended to encourage personal and moral development. The ultimate objective of many character education programs is to develop a consistency of
"moral knowing, feeling, and action"[12] in students that is reinforced in their
daily activities. In its ideal form, character education is infused throughout
the curriculum, and it becomes a routine aspect of school life. Effective character education is incorporated throughout school activities, both inside and
outside the culture, and it seeks to engage actors beyond school walls,
namely parents and community leaders. When it is implemented holistically,
character education can become a vehicle for school reform and a driving
force for altering the prevailing school culture.[13]

There are two primary categories into which the vast majority of
character education efforts can be grouped: direct and indirect.[14] Direct
character education methods involve role modeling, rules, and discipline.
According to this approach, students attain 'moral literacy' through the

use of classic stories and works of literature that exemplify proper moral attitudes. Direct character instruction also encourages students to participate in classroom discussion related to a specific set of values with the goal of enhancing their understanding of these attributes and thereby increasing the frequency of moral action. Indirect methods of character education (e.g., values clarification and discussion of moral dilemmas) do not espouse a limited set of virtues, but rather, they employ methods that enable students to identify and understand their own and others' moral values with the goal of stimulating moral growth and development.

Irrespective of the method through which it is provided, there is an explicit set of principles that character educators accept. A successful character education program typically

- ♦ Emphasizes a set of core ethical principles
- ♦ Includes thinking, feeling, and behaving
- ♦ Promotes core values throughout the school
- ♦ Encourages the development of a caring school community
- ♦ Provides students with occasion for moral action
- ♦ Is reflected in the academic curriculum
- ♦ Is oriented toward intrinsic motivation
- ♦ Involves the entire school staff, not just the faculty
- ♦ Encourages moral leadership from staff and students
- ♦ Involves members of the community and parents as partners
- ♦ Assesses its effects[15]

Thus, in its ideal form, character education is comprehensive, and when it is implemented appropriately, it should affect broadly both students and the school culture.

Effective character education is not simple because the process of character development itself is complex. High-quality character education must create an emotional attachment between student and school and involve parents and offer opportunities for reflection on social and moral issues:[16] a tall order. Schools seeking to alleviate behavioral problems they associate with our moral crisis, however, may be tempted to implement character education programs with more immediate goals in mind. Some character education scholars have expressed concern that character education programs do not become oriented to increasing student compliance and encouraging good manners.[17] Others have been harsher in their criticism, describing contemporary character programs as a "fix the kids" approach rooted in a pessimistic view of human nature and the innate behavioral tendencies of children.[18] Given the acknowledged complexity of character and the vast array of factors that foster its development, why are we inclined to consider simple, standardized methods of moral instruction? Our systems for character instruction mimic the cultural conditions from which they emanate.[19] Thus, we can only expect that character education based in a culture that espouses efficient, predictable, calculable, and controllable processes will come to reflect these tendencies in its methodology, and potentially in its outcomes.

THE RISE OF McMORALS?

In many school-based programs, character seems to have become a commodity, a by-product of our educational process that we seek to instill and measure to document our success. Although many scholars in the field of character education do their best to remind schools of the complexity of effective character development, I fear their warnings may be overridden by our cultural impetus to create systems characterized by a McDonaldization mode. Formal, standardized systems for character education are imbued with the risk of creating McMorals, character development that is guided by the principles of efficiency, predictability, calculability, and control.

The creation of *efficient* character education programs has, in part, been fostered by the increased demand for character education created by state and federal legislation that funds, and in some cases, mandates it.[20] A visit to the World Wide Web offers a plethora of options for school curricula to foster character, many of which can be accompanied by posters, handouts, and school supplies embossed with character principles. A pencil labeled with the word "integrity" may make a student think twice about cheating on a standardized test. Although these materials offer a quick and easy solution for instilling character, such "prepackaged" character education curricula[21] may remove depth of thought on the teachers' part. It is the difference between deciding "what's for dinner," and visiting the drive-up window at McDonald's where the choices are constrained. Although standardized curricula may be efficient because they ensure that certain topics are being covered in a certain order, they may de-skill and disempower teachers. Criticisms of customized textbooks apply here; prepackaged character education may create a "factorylike" atmosphere where students and faculty are made to feel like automatons.[22] Although these conditions may serve to socialize students for their experiences in the McDonaldized work world on graduation, it is unclear whether they will foster long-term moral development.

An important element in efficient McDonaldized systems is streamlining the process. Character educators sometimes employ an approach that is similar to those used by fitness instructors: Practice makes perfect.[23] Such repetition ignores the importance of information construction, as opposed to information transmission. Efficient models of character education may sometimes simply be used to convey values and norms rather than providing students with essential opportunities to make sense and construct personal images of what they have learned and how they might apply it.[24] In situations requiring character, there sometimes is no one, right answer. Because the process is stream-lined in a McDonaldized approach, however, the opportunity to acknowledge and work with differential understandings may be missed.

The movement to increase the *calculability* of character education outcomes represents probably the most important trend within the field at the present time. No Child Left Behind (NCLB) stipulates that funding will only be made available to programs that are founded on scientific research. Programs must also undertake rigorous evaluation efforts that employ empirical methods involving multiple measurements and experimental and quasi-experimental designs.[25] Leaders in the field tout the importance of evaluation as an essential component of an effective character education pro-gram.[26] The Character Counts! Web site now proudly displays the slogan, "Meets NCLB requirements."[27]

Our understanding of effective practices in character education is only nascent, however. Although they aspire to quantifiable results, proponents of character education admit that assessment data are limited in relation to the number of programs that are operating.[28] The drive to calculate charac-ter is perhaps best evidenced in the emphasis on quantitative findings in research designed to assess the effectiveness of character education initia-tives. We know much less about the qualitative effects of character educa-tion.[29] Does it affect moral conversations among students? Between students and teachers? Does it change the tone of conversations in the home? If so, how? Given the contemporary movement to provide character education through a McDonaldized system with quantifiable outcomes, such questions are not likely to be addressed any time soon.

To many critics, *predictability* of student behavior seems to be the underlying goal of character educators. Likewise, to a certain extent, stan-dardized curricula in character education may yield predictable teaching methods. "Scripted interactions with customers"[30] are a key feature of McDonaldized systems that can serve to increase their predictability. The quote library on the Character Counts! Web site offers a daily reading that either a teacher or principal can share with the students. The library enables quotes and conversations to be scripted by topic: Caring and wisdom are among the choices. Because research suggests that teachers are sometimes reluctant to discuss moral issues for fear of controversy or lawsuits,[31] scripted programs may be especially attractive because they reduce the liability teach-ers associate with providing character instruction.

To achieve predictable results, character educators may first need to consider narrowing the scope of behaviors they seek to affect. Congressional testimony in support of character education outlines its wide-ranging goals that suggest character education might be used to reduce unwanted pregnancy and limit alcohol use, while at the same time, teaching honesty and respect. Congressional leaders also identify school shootings and low voter turnout as additional reasons to support funding for school-based character education.[32] The Character Education Partnership,[33] a national advocacy organization for the character education movement, maintains a Web site that includes a variety of assessment tools that can be used to evaluate the effectiveness of character education programs. These evaluation instruments are organized under various headings, and they encompass everything from academic attitudes to at-risk behaviors and the assessment of individual traits such as empathy and honesty. Of course, by defining their goals so broadly, educators potentially enhance the probability that they will be effective in some way.

Critics of school-based character education have argued that it can appear as indoctrination.[34] Even advocates have expressed fear that when it is delivered inappropriately, character education will not foster the development of strong, independent character.[35] Thus, there is a risk that character education, if not implemented well may simply serve as a vehicle for *control*. Certainly, instruction within a prescribed set of virtues and a reward system designed to reinforce desired behavior patterns is an effective way to constrain behavioral options within the school setting. It has been argued that offering rewards to students who exemplify good behaviors is a surefire way to reduce the likelihood that the behavior will be repeated over time.[36] Thus, if long-term character development is the goal, the methods some educators have chosen may be questionable.

The fact that much of the evidence that supports the effectiveness of character education typically covers a short time frame (i.e., two to three years),[37] suggests that fundamental, long-term changes in character may be a less important goal than behavioral control, at least for some educators. A Character Counts! program in one state was deemed effective because "students reported improvement in every category of misdeed assessed" and "teachers reported better student behavior towards others and authority." The success of this program was also based on the observation that "the more exposures per month students had to Character Counts! the better they behaved."[38] In such cases, it seems that educators are equating situational compliance with programmatic success.

RATIONAL CHARACTER EDUCATION: CREATING "IRRATIONAL CHARACTERS"?

At face value, the movement to implement school-based character education is rational: Moral instruction is inherently part of the curriculum, therefore why not be methodical in how we do it? This same preference for rationality has served as a source of motivation to adopt McDonaldized systems in various aspects of our culture. Sociologists have long understood, however, that humans are only "intendedly rational"[39] and that many of our seemingly well-reasoned decisions produce irrational outcomes.

The goals of school-based character education programs, although they are laudable, are not likely to be adequate to eliminate our perceived moral crisis. School busing did not alleviate racist attitudes or segregation.[40] Likewise, the implementation of school-based character training, in and of itself, is not likely to create character in the world at large or to alter our prevailing social norms in any dramatic way.[41] If character education fails, it will *not* be because of the scope of our "moral crisis" or because character educators' efforts were misguided. Instead, it may fail because character education implemented through a McDonaldized model is not appropriate to the complexity of the outcome we are seeking to achieve. A McDonaldized system for character education may produce any number of irrational results, most important among them, a disenchantment, homogenization, and dehumanization of our moral culture.

Disenchantment

The system can become disenchanted when logic overrides a process in such a way that the unknowns are removed. Rational systems emphasize quantity over quality and reduce the opportunity for enchantment to occur because enchantment often emerges from less tangible processes. In McDonaldized systems, the "magic" is gone.[42] Character education formalized in school curricula exemplifies this trend. The shift of character from the hidden curriculum to a more formal, standardized form of instruction has created the potential for assessing character as a measurable organizational output. The school becomes a processing plant, and outcomes with quantifiable character evolve as an organizational goal.[43]

Organizations tend to become detached from individual concerns. Rather, they seek to redefine personal needs in ways that are organizationally convenient and easy to control.[44] So, as we have increasingly embedded character education in formalized school curricula, we have also tended to emphasize simple and rational indicators to quantify its effects. Outcomes such as reductions in theft, alcohol and drug consumption, vandalism, and teasing are all presented as evidence that character education works.[45] Although these statistics demonstrate that behaviors at school have been improved— an organizationally desirable goal—they are not necessarily indicative of fundamental changes in attitudes, character, or moral thinking. In the worst case, these results may only indicate that students are better at hiding or postponing their misdeeds where they are less likely to be sanctioned.

In rationalizing character instruction, we risk removing many of its enchanted features. The "magic" of character is sustained in the hidden curriculum, in the daily, unpredictable, but often positive interactions between teachers and students. The magic of character also exists in the unknown: There is often more than one good way to resolve a moral dilemma, and it is interesting to observe the unsolicited creativity and compassion of students. Essentially, the "magic" of character is inherent in the surprises and unique opportunities it offers us. Formalized character education can lead to disenchantment because it creates a single lens through which teachers and students may come to interpret their character experiences.

Rationalized systems often call for the re-creation of enchantment to attract customers.[46] Thus, in the case of the new unhidden form of character education, posters exemplifying character traits and ceremonies honoring students who exhibit character are made very public with the goal of drawing in teachers and students. Are these efforts directed at re-enchantment necessary? Because the failure to comply with character education can often result in sanctions against students, there is really no need to excite them as customers. Perhaps, then, the re-enchantment of character education is designed to sustain the engagement of teachers? Although teachers recognize character instruction as an inherent part of the curriculum, at least one qualitative study suggests that they may at times resist becoming engaged with formalized curricular efforts to instill character.[47] Worse than noncompliance, however, is the potential for teachers to behave in ways that contradict the goals of character curricula. The pressure placed on teachers to improve scores on standardized academic tests has produced one unintended outcome, albeit in a small number of documented cases: teacher cheating.[48] It would be quite unfortunate if our efforts to rationalize character instruction and quantify its effects should yield a similar result.

Homogenization

Homogenization, or the tendency for the same products to be offered in the same way,[49] is also on the rise in character education. A leading provider of character education curricula, Character Counts! has contracted with more than 500 member organizations. Members who employ the Character Counts! curriculum include national organizations such as the Boys and Girls Clubs of America, communities, schools, service organizations, and businesses.[50] These organizations have the option to purchase supplemental instructional materials such as posters, banners, and school planners emblazoned with the "six pillars" of character: trustworthiness, respect, responsibility, fairness, caring, and citizenship. Although it is recommended that the Character Counts! program be tailored to meet individual school goals, there is enough standardization in the materials that a child could conceivably move across the country and enroll in a school that at least superficially appears to convey an identical approach to instilling character: the same posters and lessons. In a homogenized curriculum, the complexity of character may be lost as discussion is contained around a limited set of attributes.

There has been an increasing tendency to homogenize efforts to assess the effectiveness of character education programs as well. The phrase "scientifically based research" occurs more than 100 times in the No Child Left Behind legislation.[51] Although researchers have acknowledged that it is not appropriate to assess character through standardized tests,[52] the allure of federal funding tagged to scientific models of program implementation may override this prevailing logic. The concern is whether legislators who fund character education will be willing to wait for long-term results and to wade through detailed, qualitative descriptions of program effects. We may never know whether formalized character education influences how students actually practice or think about character in their daily lives because in a McDonaldized system, we will not likely prioritize the collection of data to document these results.

Because character is a multifaceted concept, the creation of homogenized character curricula is essentially character boiled down to a few of its core components. Much as McDonald's offers three flavors of milk shakes—vanilla, chocolate, and strawberry—many character education programs espouse a limited set of principles to create a predetermined set of outcomes. By offering instruction centered on a homogenized, limited list of character attributes, we disregard the fact that in the world outside of school, what is "appropriate" character in a given setting is not always universally agreed upon. Because our children are increasingly exposed to homogenized character programs, they may be ill-equipped to handle the diversity of character experiences they will ultimately encounter in their everyday lives.

Dehumanization

In McDonaldized systems, dehumanization occurs when "prefabricated interaction takes the place of authentic interaction." These dehumanized processes of communication lead to subtle forms of rejection and alienation on the part of workers.[53] Dehumanized character education offers potentially grave consequences because it seems unlikely character will be sustained unless there are opportunities for individualized response. Students, teachers, families, and moreover society at large, all stand to be affected detrimentally if we continue to constrain the definition of character in such a way that it thwarts individual expression.

It is ironic that character education may dehumanize the very individuals it seeks to energize, the customers themselves, students. At McDonald's, the meal is efficient and quick. The inclusion of character in the formal curriculum has the potential to be counterproductive in that it may create the perception that character is no longer an essential aspect of everyday life, but rather, a subject to be taught.[54] In addition, when students are rewarded with a ticket for each good deed they perform, the intrinsic, personal experience of demonstrating character may begin to erode.[55] Much like performing for a standardized test, students may simply be regurgitating what they have learned as exemplary behavior rather than reacting from the mind and heart.

Teachers have expressed diverse views about character education. Research tells us that among a number of barriers to widespread implementation of character education, the varied perspectives of teachers on the issue are a key constraint. Educators disagree on what character is, what constitutes character education, and whether it is appropriate.[56] Standardized character education curricula do little to understand or incorporate these differences. As such, they dehumanize the experience of teaching character. As the curriculum takes precedence, educators may feel compelled to downplay personal orientations in order to administer it effectively.

Formalized character education also has the potential to dehumanize moral conversations in the family. As McDonaldization is in part responsible for the demise of the family meal,[57] it has also likely altered the location of moral conversations: Discussions of character have been shifted from the dinner table to the back seat of the car. Perhaps dad can talk with Jane about what she should have done when Ellen asked for her homework while they wait at the drive-up window for their supersized meal. Lost in this interaction is facial contact and lengthy, open-ended discussion. Often, only one parent is present. As the trip ends, the conversation may be disrupted: Dad stops to collect the discarded wrappers from the car floor, and Jane enters the house to do her homework. As the evening evolves, the conversation may never be continued. While the school is not responsible here, it is important to recognize that McDonaldization in other aspects of life may serve to exacerbate the effects of formalized character education in unforeseen ways.

Although the changing locations of moral conversations may serve to affect negatively interactions about character, the content of the discussion represents another potential source of dehumanization. When students receive instruction in character curricula, which they then bring home to their parents, the dynamic between parent and child is changed. Parents may struggle to fulfill their role in moral conversations guided by school curricula and terminology that they only vaguely understand or might not otherwise use. As such, they may begin to shut down, feeling that their role as moral educator is being supplanted by the school. For their part, character educators seek to engage parents, stressing that parental involvement is integral to the success of school-based programs.[58] While we know that when parents are disengaged, the results are less than optimal, we do not fully understand the long-term consequences when parental behavior contradicts what students learn about character at school. This is perhaps an even greater risk in our society where declining morality is evident as often in the behavior of adults, as it is in children.

CONCLUSION: LAND OF THE MORALLY DEAD?

We can not blame teachers or character educators for the threat of McMorals. Rather, we can only blame ourselves. It is our unceasing desire for efficient, calculable, predictable, and controlled lives that has created the drive to rationalize character. Contemporary approaches to character education that emphasize a specific list of virtues or values are rooted in our cultural emphasis on simple, efficient systems. We long to take what is complex and break it down. This is true even when simplification destroys the integrity of the concept. So it is with character.

The world in which our children must act—the world beyond school walls—is characterized by moral ambiguity.[59] Character education delivered through a McDonaldized model may not provide our children with skills in moral reflection and reasoning that will be necessary in the real world with all of its diverse values. By their nature, McDonaldized systems minimize choice. Rather than striving to be responsive, they seek to control: to suppress diversity and independent thought. We have come to tolerate these constraints in the fast-food setting. Rather than stepping out of line to wait for my burger without ketchup, I go with the flow because it is quicker; it simply requires too much energy to assert my preference. The development of character through McDonaldized systems holds potentially grave consequences for our children. Will they be adequately prepared for a situation that will require them to defy organizational prerequisites for action to demonstrate morality? At best, the answer is unclear.

It has been argued that a morality that is not connected to the larger culture is doomed to fail.[60] Although we have linked the *process* through which we are delivering school-based character education to our cultural values for efficiency, calculability, predictability, and control, we cannot link these values to the *product*. Character, with all of its depth and complexity will never be well served or well developed by a model in which it must be overly simplified to be taught. In addition, we are currently experiencing a disconnection, perhaps even opposition between our prevailing cultural values and the values we strive to impart in character education curricula. Social norms of individualism and achievement sit in direct contrast to school lessons that encourage community and sharing.[61] How will our children respond to the mixed messages that we are giving them? How will they rectify these discrepancies?

One possible answer to these questions is that our children will shut down. Their moral lives will become deadened because we do not provide them with ample opportunities to exercise complex moral thought, i.e., to explore and make sense of these contradictions. Ritzer describes the social geography of McDonaldized systems as "islands of the living dead,"[62] places where the human experience is isolated from the rest of life. On these islands, both workers and customers exist as if they are dead. Natural behaviors are constrained by risk-free structures that are characteristic of McDonaldized institutions seeking to facilitate only perfection and positivity. This speaks to my primary concern for contemporary character education in that school may become one of these islands where moral life is segregated and experienced in a simulated fashion, away from the moral complexity students face when they leave school grounds. The end result of our emphasis on McMorals may be large numbers of morally dead adults who once spent time on an island (i.e., school) where character seemed possible, but who have no sense of how to evoke it in their daily lives. Instead, they will have been trained to respond to the prevailing social climate within the institutions in which they find themselves.

Trends describing the integrity of today's college students suggest we are moving in this direction. Statistics related to the values of college-aged students reveal that there has been a dramatic increase in the number of students who cheat. Surveys of college students reveal that they learn in an environment where cheating is rampant, faculty members do not take the time to notice, and when students are sanctioned for their dishonesty, they face only trivial penalties.[63] This research suggests that students cheat for a variety of reasons, but primary among them are parental pressure and the fact that "everyone is doing it." Thus, the lives of college students exemplify an important dualism we sustain in our society: practice integrity, but above all else, achieve. Will we perpetuate and perhaps worsen this problem for the next generation, our school-aged children, with formalized character education curricula that will be difficult to sustain in the face of a cultural ethos emphasizing personal success?

Among a list of several important questions that scholars of character education are, as yet, unable to answer is the following: What are the long-term effects of character education?[64] One possible outcome is that moral character developed in school-based programs will wither and die when confronted by the hardship associated with sustaining it in a world where moral ambiguity is common. Much like McDonald's fries discovered under the car seat several hours after the meal, our children's character may be hardened and unrecognizable because there is no place for it in a world that challenges rather than fosters what they have learned. It has been argued that character is dead because the social and cultural conditions necessary to sustain it are nonexistent.[65] I seek to advance this argument by adding that the McDonaldized models we are using to instill character may also ultimately contribute to its demise.

Character educators have brought us to an important place. They have clearly stressed both the complexity of character and the importance of moral grappling[66] as an essential element of moral development. They are able to describe for us various aspects of effective systems for providing character. These features are complex, and they require ongoing collaboration between school, home, and community. My key concern is that as character education shifts from the hidden curriculum to a federally funded agenda item, this acknowledged complexity will be disregarded because of our cultural tendency toward efficiency. We must recognize that the development of character will never be amenable to McDonaldized standards. The provision of funding for character education in No Child Left Behind with its emphasis on scientific methodology suggests that we are beginning to treat character as another educational outcome to be measured. The McDonaldization of the *process* by which we provide character education may detrimentally affect the *product*.

As there are solutions to avoid McDonaldization in everyday life,[67] there are also ways to prevent it from invading the processes by which we instill character. This "new and improved" version of character education will not, however, be efficient. It will emphasize deep and long-lasting changes in behavior that will not easily be quantified or tracked. There will be no immediate answers as to the effectiveness of educators' strategies, and in the short-term, the news may even be bad given that the development of character is likely not a linear process. Similarly, we will need to emphasize less predictable outcomes, and focus more on understanding the qualitative, real life experiences of students who receive school-based character education. Providing students with opportunities to try, fail, and learn from their mistakes may likely be an important aspect of character development that is lost in systems that only reward compliance. Finally, and perhaps with great difficulty, schools will need to relinquish some control because creating and sustaining character will need to be a collaborative venture, equally involving school, family, and community. Before we serve "billions and billions," we must improve our understanding of the long-term effects of formalized character instruction.

Thinking Critically

◆◆◆

1. Should morality be McDonaldized?

2. Should morality in already highly McDonaldized public schools be McDonaldized?

3. Does federal government involvement, wherever it occurs, lead to greater McDonaldization?

4. In what ways is the McDonaldization of character education an example of the irrationality of rationality?

5. How can we prevent the McDonaldization of morality? of character education?

NOTES

1. Material related to the definition and history of character education is taken from B. Edward McClellan, *Moral Education in America* (New York: Teachers College Press, 1999); Marcia McKenzie, "Seeing the Spectrum: New Approaches to Emotional Social and Moral Education," *The Educational Forum* 69, no. 1 (2004): 79–90; and Esther F. Schaeffer, "Character Education Makes a Big Difference," *Principal* 82, no. 3 (2003): 36–39.

2. "The 26th Annual Phi Delta Kappan/Gallup Poll of the Public's Attitude Toward the Public Schools," *Phi Delta Kappan*, 76, no. 1 (1994): 41–57.

3. Teacher perspectives on character education are considered in Carla Mathison, "How Teachers Feel About Character Education: A Descriptive Study," *Action in Teacher Education* 20, no. 4 (1998): 29–38; Andrew J. Milson and Lisa M. Mehlig, "Elementary School Teachers' Sense of Efficacy for Character Education," *The Journal of Elementary Research* 96, no. 1 (2002): 47–55.

4. Robert W. Howard, Marvin W. Berkowitz, and Esther F. Schaeffer, "Politics of Character Education," *Educational Policy* 18, no. 1 (2004): 188–215.

5. Michael Davis, "What's Wrong With Character Education?" *American Journal of Education* 110, no. 1 (2003): 32.

6. Brian Wilson, "College Urged to Better Define Academic Integrity and to Stress Its Importance," *Chronicle of Higher Education* 46, no. 8 (1999): A18.

7. Many experts have argued that character is a complex concept to measure. For a general overview see Marvin W. Berkowitz and Melinda C. Bier, "Research-Based Character Education," *Annals of the American Academy of Political and Social Science* 591 (2004): 72–85.

8. This definition of "McMorals" was first published in Suzanne S. Hudd, "Character Education in Contemporary America: McMorals?" *Taboo* 8, no. 2 (2005): 113–124.

9. These trends in youth behavior have been reported by Josephson Institute of Ethics, *2002 Report Card: The Ethics of American Youth*, www.josephsoninstitute.org/survey2002/; and Thomas Likona, *Educating for Character* (New York: Bantam Books, 1991).

10. Terri Demmon et al., "Moral and Character Development in Public Education" (1996): ERIC Document No. 409251.

11. James Coleman, "Schools and the Communities They Serve," *Phi Delta Kappan* (April 1985): 530.

12. Likona, *Educating for Character*.

13. These principles of effective character education are described in Schaeffer, "Character Education Makes a Big Difference," 36–39; and Berkowitz and Bier, "Research-Based Character Education," 72–85.

14. Direct and indirect methods of teaching character education are described by Jacques Benninga, "Moral and Character Education in the Elementary School: An Introduction," in Jacques S. Benninga, ed., *Moral, Character and Civic Education in the Elementary School* (New York: Teachers College Press, 1991); and Barbara Duncan, "Character Education: Reclaiming the Social," *Educational Theory* 47, no. 1 (1997): 119–125.

15. Schaeffer, "Character Education Makes a Big Difference," 38.

16. Berkowitz and Bier, "Research-Based Character Education," 72–85.

17. Eric Schaps, Esther F. Schaeffer, and Sanford N. McDonnell, "What's Right and Wrong in Character Education Today," *Education Week* 21, no. 2 (2001): 40.

18. Alfie Kohn, "The Trouble With Character Education," *The Yearbook of the National Society of Education* 96 (1997): 155.

19. James Davison Hunter, *The Death of Character* (New York: Basic Books, 2000).

20. Information on state legislation related to character education is taken from the Education Commission of the States, *Recent State Policies/Actions: Character Education* (2005), available at www.ecs.org/ecscat.nsf/.

21. The reference to efficient "prepackaged curricula" is taken from Timothy Rusnack and Frank Ribich, "The Death of Character," *Educational Horizons* 76 (1997): 10–13.

22. George Ritzer, *The McDonaldization of Society, Revised New Century Edition* (Thousand Oaks, CA: Pine Forge, 2004), 44, 154.

23. Davis, "What's Wrong With Character Education?" 32–57.

24. Willem L. Wardekker, "Schools and Moral Education: Conformism or Autonomy?" *Journal of the Philosophy of Education* 35, no. 1 (2001): 101–114.

25. Howard et al., "Politics of Character Education," 188–215.

26. See, for example, Schaeffer in "Character Education Makes a Big Difference," 36–39.

27. The Character Counts! Web site can be found at www.charactercounts.org.

28. Howard et al., "Politics of Character Education," 205.

29. This emphasis on quantitative research in the evaluation of character education programs was noted in a presentation given by Marvin W. Berkowitz and Melinda C. Bier, *What Works in Character Education* at the Annual Meeting of the Character Education Partnership on October 23, 2003, in Washington, D.C.

30. Ritzer, *The McDonaldization of Society*, 91.

31. Mathison, "How Teachers Feel About Character Education: A Descriptive Study," 29–30.

32. Report of the House Subcommittee on Early Childhood, Youth and Families, *The Role of Character Education in America's Schools* (Washington, DC: Government Printing Office, March 1, 2000).

33. Information related to the Character Education Partnership can be found at www.character.org.

34. Alfie Kohn, *What to Look for in a Classroom and Other Essays* (San Francisco: Jossey-Bass, 1998); and Ivor Pritchard, "Character Education: Research Prospects and Problems," *American Journal of Education* 96, no. 4 (1988): 469–495.

35. Schaps et al., "What's Right and Wrong in Character Education Today," 40, 44.

36. Kohn, "The Trouble With Character Education," 154–162.

37. Davis, "What's Wrong With Character Education?" 32–57.

38. Data on the effectiveness of Character Counts! can be reviewed at www.charactercounts.org.

39. James G. March and Herbert A. Simon, *Organizations* (Hoboken, NJ: Wiley, 1958).

40. The analogy of character education to school busing was offered by David Elkind in "Character Education: An Ineffective Luxury?" *Child Care Information Exchange* 124 (1998): 6–9.

41. Hunter, *The Death of Character*.

42. Ritzer, *The McDonaldization of Society*; and George Ritzer, *Enchanting a Disenchanted World: Revolutionizing the Means of Consumption* (Thousand Oaks, CA: Pine Forge, 1999).

43. Katherine G. Simon, *Moral Questions in the Classroom* (New Haven, CT: Yale University Press, 2001), 16.

44. Charles Perrow, "A Society of Organizations," *Theory and Society* 20 (1991): 753.

45. These examples are taken from the evaluation of character education programs using Character Counts! which can be found at www.charactercounts.org.

46. Ritzer, *The McDonaldization of Society*; and Ritzer, *Enchanting a Disenchanted World: Revolutionizing the Means of Consumption*.

47. Michael Romanowski, "Through the Eyes of Students: High School Students' Perspectives on Character Education," *American Secondary Education* 32, no. 1 (2003): 3–20.

48. See, for example, Julie Henry, "More Schools Found Guilty of Cheating," *The New York Times Educational Supplement* (November 23, 2001): 4; Barbara

Kantorowitz and Daniel McGinn, "When Teachers Are Cheaters," *Newsweek* (June 19, 2000): 48; and Brian A. Jacob and Steven D. Levitt, *Catching Cheating Teachers: The Results of an Unusual Experiment in Implementing Theory*, Working Paper No. 9414, National Bureau of Economic Research.

49. Ritzer, *The McDonaldization of Society*.

50. Information on Character Counts! can be obtained at www.character counts.org.

51. James Traub, "No Child Left Behind: Does It Work?" *New York Times Education Life Supplement* (November 10, 2002): Section 4A, Column 1: 24.

52. Kristin Fink and Linda McKay, *Making Character Education a Standard Part of Education* (Washington, DC: Character Education Partnership, 2003).

53. Ritzer, *The McDonaldization of Society*.

54. Rusnack and Ribich, "The Death of Character," 10–13.

55. The practice of administering rewards for demonstrating good character is critiqued by Kohn in *What to Look for in a Classroom: And Other Essays*.

56. Marvin W. Berkowitz in "Obstacles to Teacher Training in Character Education," *Action in Teacher Education* 20, no. 4 (1998): 1–10. See also Mathison, "How Teachers Feel About Character Education: A Descriptive Study," 29–38.

57. Ritzer, *The McDonaldization of Society*.

58. See, for example, Berkowitz and Bier, "Research-Based Character Education," 72–85.

59. Andrew Wilson, "Livin' on the Edge: A Look at the Need for Moral Education" (May 10, 1995): ERIC Document No. 388549.

60. Hunter, *The Death of Character*.

61. Jerome Kagan, "The Moral Function of the School," *Deadalus* 110, no. 3 (1981): 151–165.

62. George Ritzer, "Islands of the Living Dead: The Social Geography of McDonaldization," *The American Behavioral Scientist* 47, no. 2 (2003): 119–127.

63. A number of researchers have outlined trends in academic integrity at the college level including: Donald McCabe and Linda Klebe Trevino, "Honesty and Honor Codes," *Academe* 88, no. 1 (2002): 37–41; Kevin Bushweller, "Student Cheating: A Morality Moratorium?" *The Education Digest* 65, no. 3 (1999): 4–11; Donald McCabe and Patrick Drinan, "Toward a Culture of Academic Integrity," *The Chronicle of Higher Education* 8, no. 46 (1999): B7.

64. Marvin W. Berkowitz, "The Science of Character Education," in William Damon, ed., *Bringing in a New Era of Character Education* (Stanford, CA: Hoover Institution Press, 2002).

65. Hunter, *The Death of Character*.

66. Theodore R. Sizer and Nancy Faust Sizer, *The Students are Watching* (Boston: Beacon Press, 1999).

67. Ritzer, *The McDonaldization of Society*.

The Internet is a fascinating arena in which to examine the process of McDonaldization. Alan Neustadtl and Meyer Kestnbaum focus on the standardization of production and consumption processes (the McDonaldization of tools) and the homogenization of individual experiences (the McDonaldization of users' perception and use) on the Internet.

While there is some measure of standardization of the Internet, several developments are leading to an increase, not a decrease, of diversity on the Web. First, the standardization of production tools makes it possible for casual users, not just sophisticated programmers, to produce Web content. The programmers must then distinguish themselves from casual users by developing new standards and Web content which, in turn, leads to a further expansion of what casual users may produce. Second, there is increasing diversity on the Web because corporations can earn greater profits by improving quality and creating an ever-wider range of offerings. Finally, the different modes of communication over the Internet (e.g., text, audio, video) can be combined in many different ways to produce still greater diversity on the Web.

In spite of increasing diversity on the Web, the user's experience of the Internet has grown increasingly homogenized in various ways. First, regardless of the browser used, surfers go to the same sites and view the same content. Second, the predominance of two browsers—Netscape (about 13% of users) and especially Internet Explorer (a whopping 86% of users)—creates enormous homogeneity of experience on the Web. On the other side, however, all this standardization allows users to "actively shape their experience, determining not only what to view but also the timing and sequence of consumption, as well as the context within which content is viewed."

Is the Internet McDonaldized? From the perspective of the standardization of the tools of production and consumption on the Web and their control by a small number of corporations, the Internet is McDonaldized. The issue is more complex when we examine the Internet from the perspective of the user. On the one hand, the predominance of a small number of sites (Yahoo, E-Bay, Amazon.com) makes for homogeneity of experience. On the other, the standardization of tools puts the possibility of production in the hands of everyday users, and this leads to greater diversity, not homogeneity.

Thus, there is no simple answer to the question of whether or not the Internet is McDonaldized. However, it is clear that the Web is McDonaldized to some degree, and there is the danger that it will become even more McDonaldized in the future if an ever-smaller number of corporations come to control it and standards evolve that limit the ability of users to create their own content.

16

The McDonaldization of the Internet

Alan Neustadtl and Meyer Kestnbaum

◆◆◆————————————————————————————————

I s there anything not McDonaldized in modern society?. . .

Some have hailed the Internet as a revolutionary means of communication and interaction, while others have argued that the Internet is no more extraordinary than other powerful and transformative technologies such as the steam engine, telephony, or television. Regardless, for large numbers of North Americans and Northern Europeans, using the Internet has become a relatively common and routine experience. And the number of users in developing countries is growing as well. The birth of the Internet, the nascence of its general acceptance and diffusion, is often given as 1995—a scant 10 years ago. Enterprises such as McDonald's have had decades to develop or

Author's Note: Grateful acknowledgment is given to the National Science Foundation, Office of Science and Technology for support through grants NSF01523184 and NSF0086143.

Editor's Note: This chapter was written for the first edition of *McDonaldization: The Reader* (2002).

evolve to their present McDonaldized state, but what about less mature entities? So we raise the question, to what degree is the current Internet McDonaldized? And to the extent that the Internet is McDonaldized, how does it differ from other aspects of society characterized as McDonaldized?

ANALYTIC DISTINCTIONS: McDONALDIZATION AND THE INTERNET

The four precepts of McDonaldization—efficiency, calculability, predictability, and nonhuman control—are linked to each other because to varying degrees they are associated with a common outcome, the standardization and homogenization of production processes and experience, respectively. We propose to reduce these four dimensions of McDonaldization to one—standardization/homogenization—and to examine the Internet in these. By this means, standardization and homogenization become the benchmarks against which we can assess the extent to which the Internet is McDonaldized.

In distinction, *standardization* refers to the McDonaldization of the *tools* of production and consumption. *Homogenization* refers to the McDonaldization of *experience*. Tools can be standardized (e.g., nuts and bolts, assembly-line processes); experience can be homogenized. Tools and production processes may adhere to standards. If they do, then workers may have relatively homogeneous production experiences.

Homogenization of experience is applicable whether production or consumption is examined. Scientific management, for example, provides one basis for understanding the standardization and homogenization of production, turning largely craft and skilled labor into routinized, unskilled labor by transferring control and knowledge of the skills, tools, and processes of production from workers to managers and owners. Here, production is standardized, and the workers' experiences are homogenized.

Ritzer nicely details the standardization and homogenization of both production and consumption, using fast-food enterprises as exemplars. Similar to scientific management, owners and managers have transferred significant control and knowledge of the food production process from the workers to the owners using standardization. Production and consumption are closely related, and significant control of the consumption process rests with the owners and managers, not with customers who are made to do much of the work of fast-food production. Furthermore, customers experience fast-food consumption relatively homogeneously.

What distinguishes these forms of standardization and homogenization is who controls the processes associated with McDonaldization. For the most part, managers, owners, corporations—people or institutions other than the direct producer—control production processes. The consumption experience, while shaped by these same people and institutions, is somewhat less directly under their sway, although insofar as what is produced is, limited, then so too are consumption options. Again, considering fast food, consumers arguably retain more control than producers because they may make the final decision to avoid fast food completely, even if it is personally costly to them.

This lies in contrast to the Internet and World Wide Web where production processes are controlled by myriad actors that include corporations, professional programmers, organizations large and small, as well as large numbers of individuals motivated by the simple desire to communicate with others. Production is diffuse, controlled solely by managers and owners. We argue that this form of production counteracts the tendency toward McDonaldization but in a particular way. Because the tools used to produce Web content have been McDonaldized, the required skills to publish Web pages have been diminished. At the same time, the control of these tools does not lie solely with corporations and managers. Paradoxically, then, as the tools have become McDonaldized, this has allowed greater diversity in content by allowing more people to communicate using the Web.

INTERNET AND WORLD WIDE WEB TOOLS

For present purposes, the Internet is the collection of hardware and software used to connect discrete computers to exchange data. Layered on top of this is the World Wide Web (WWW), or simply the Web. The Web is also composed of hardware and software and is unique because it is possible for large numbers of actors *to be both producers and consumers of Internet content*.

It is possible to apply the analytic tools of McDonaldization to these areas, understanding that the process of McDonaldization might be different for production and consumption of the Web and may have different outcomes, both in the degree of standardization and homogenization and in the costs and benefits.

Fundamental to all that is the Internet is hardware. Leaving aside the development of personal computers, it was linking these computers together that created the Internet. Pre-Internet, people used computers as tools to work alone. "Each person who used a computer sat alone in front of a keyboard and screen." But this has changed as computers became connected so that "being at a computer is synonymous with being connected to the Internet. As a result HCI [human computer interaction] has become socialized."

Note that the production and consumption of Internet content is distinct producing and consuming the hardware and software required to create and maintain the physical basis of the Internet. We choose to examine issues surrounding the former, leaving to others the analysis of the latter, even though such analyses have merit. Consider that hardware constrains and facilitates certain kinds and amounts of data transfers and therefore has an effect on the production and consumption of Internet content.

We also defer discussion of the hardware of consumption to simplify our analysis, even though such an analysis also has merit. Personal computers are routinely equipped with sound cards and speakers, television and radio receivers, and ports to transfer multimedia data to a host of electronic devices (eg., ipods). The presence or absence of such hardware, as well as the quality of hardware, significantly affects Web users' experiences.

Although our focus is mostly on software, we assert that the interconnection of hardware forming a network that allows software to direct the flow of data from computer to computer or device to device requires a substantial degree of standardization.

Tools for the Production of Internet Content

The production of Web pages or content requires tools—software application tools. In the early days of the Web, these tools were mostly simple text editors used to create hypertext markup language (HTML) files that provided consistent consumption results on current browsers.

. . . Still, Web page production lay largely with computer professionals; the production of personal Web pages was not widely diffused because the necessary skills were also not widely diffused.

. . . The desire to communicate, however, provided significant motivation for people to acquire Web production skills and to produce content available to friends, family, and anyone who cared to look. The expansion of the number of people interested in creating Web content created a market that spurred the development of production tools.

The range of production tools has expanded greatly, driven by changes in HTML standards. . . . This has had the effect of lessening the competitive advantage of professional programmers. As often as not, these tools are given away freely or created as shareware and so are available at low cost.

Tools for the Consumption of Internet Content

For most Web users, all these production concerns are mostly not transparent because knowledge of the production of Internet content is not required for consumption. For our purposes, consumption refers to the activities of Web surfers. Primarily, this is the reception of textual, hyper-textual, audio, and graphical data from Web content producers via the Internet. The earliest consumption was quite single-minded—making nuclear physics data available to research colleagues. Now, however, there is enormously varied amount of content available that ranges from serious activities, such as many government functions, to frivolous Web pages dedicated to, say, a goldfish, with myriad kinds of content in between.

The key software application for Internet consumption is a Web browser. Browsers, typically through a personal computer, communicate with other computers, requesting information, and then format and display this information in their windows. Early browsers, like early editors, were text based. Web pages were collections of words, some of which might be "hyperlinks" to other Internet content. Graphics could not be displayed in the browsers because their formats fell outside of the then-current HTML standards.

Much has changed. Current browsers resemble a filter; this filter can deal with multiple kinds of information, including text, graphics, sound, and video. Data available on the Internet (the content) are delivered to the filter (the browser) where, according to current HTML standards, the content is formatted for presentation in the browser window.

Web browsers are analogous to windows that exist in places where people dwell (e.g., homes, businesses, and libraries) providing views not of the outside world, but of the Web. Early browsers were poor windows, providing limited views. Current browsers are substantially less limited and allow surfers to experience color, motion, and sound, if the hardware allows. Both the producers and the consumers of Internet content have the expectation that the browser will faithfully render the content as intended by the producer. This expectation is generally met if the producers adhere to current HTML production standards.

Given the large percentage of Web surfers who use Internet Explorer, in itself a fairly rigid form of standardization, it is almost superfluous to consider standardization across browsers. But it is instructive to look at software standardization across different types of applications. Developers creating software for the Windows operating systems often follow a set of design guidelines called common user access (CUA). The CUA interface was originally based on IBM's Common User Access (CUA) guidelines, but most developers now use Microsoft's *The Windows Interface: An Application Design Guide*. The idea behind CUA is to locate software functions in the same locations, using the same process access across applications. For example, the "File/Save" dialogue in Microsoft Word (word processing) is the same as the dialogue in Microsoft Excel (spreadsheet), as well as in Corel's WordPerfect (word processing). Because of CUA, if consumers are comfortable using one Windows application, they will probably find other applications easy to use. The same can be said for users of the Macintosh operating system. From its introduction, Apple Computers made standardization of the Macintosh interface across applications a priority. The consistency with which Apple's operating system interface has been implemented in a uniform fashion by software developers is largely responsible for the Macintosh's reputation of offering substantial ease of use.

Internet Content and the Outcomes of McDonaldization

To consume Internet content, surfers rely on standardization of the tools of consumption—how browsers format and deliver content as well as interface standardization (i.e., CUA). The effect of all of these forms of standardization is to limit a Web surfer's options, even if the range of Web content seems relatively large. And . . . to experience all Web content requires that developers strictly adhere to current HTML standards and that, simultaneously, Web browser developers adhere to the same standards. This imposes a "lowest common denominator" form of standardization. Users cannot view video or listen to audio as long as these types of content are outside the standards of Web content.

This, of course, is one kind of outcome associated with McDonaldization—constraining patterns and kinds of consumption—and is problematic as long as the standards either stop evolving or pushing limits or standards evolve in such a way as to further constrain consumption options. We argue that in the case of fast foods, production standards have evolved in ways that have homogenized the consumption experience but that Web standards have evolved in ways that have increased the range of consumption experiences. We return to this point later.

There is, however, an entirely different dimension where content or Web surfing can be homogenized, and that is the range of Web sites visited. Consider a hypothetical Web where only 10 Web sites are available. Arguably, there would be experiential homogeneity for Web surfers, given the limited choice of Web sites. A similar situation could exist if, in the face of hundreds of thousands of available Web sites, only a handful were normally surfed. That is, either because of surfers, explicit choices or because of the structure of hyperlinks, there is inequality in the Web sites that surfers visit. On a Web with perfect equality, every Web site would receive the same number of unique surfers. On a Web with perfect inequality, one site would receive all of the Web surfers, and the remainder of the sites none. Clearly, neither of these extreme situations exists in (virtual) reality. Yet they illustrate a way in which Web surfers' consumption experiences may be homogenized. Web oligopoly, the relative inequality of Web sites surfed, is yet another dimension of the McDonaldization of the Web.

THE PROS AND CONS OF
McDONALDIZATION: THE PRODUCTION SIDE

Although we have chosen to restrict most of our discussion to the examination of software, it is clear that without hardware standards the Internet as we experience it today could not exist. The majority of the Internet is hardwired, not wireless, and so relies on the ability to physically connect a large range of computers to each other, and that requires standardization. Proprietary standards, while allowing hardware connectivity, increase the possibility that McDonaldization will have negative effects by situating enormous decision-making power with a few people or organizations. Alternatively, without standards, as producers attempt to push their standard to the forefront of computer technology, the potential for chaos exists and tends to limit the hardware that can interconnect. Open standards are a compromise that require some minimum degree of hardware compatibility and provide for significant standardization, thereby maintaining the ability to connect different computers and to permit communication among them.

The situation with software is similar. Once computers have been connected or wired together, software facilitates how they can exchange data. The standard, or protocol, used by software to provide the flue that holds the Internet together as a Web is transmission control protocol/Internet protocol (TCP/IP). Without the ability to exchange data, the Web could not exist. Fundamentally, McDonaldization leads to standardization and is essential for the existence of the Web as a communication medium.

The standards associated with hardware and software provide the basis for the existence of the Internet and the WWW. The data that populate or are distributed on the Web make up the content that surfers experience. Content production requires production tools, and as detailed earlier, these tools range from the simple to the complicated. One role of computer scientists and programmers is to produce tools that automate production based on common standards. The more complicated production tools, HTML editors, make the production of complex content easy and available to a wide range of producers. HTML editors include many formatting functions, such as tables; frames; cascading style sheets; Web "themes"; bold, underlined, and italicized text; and others.

This leads to several interesting outcomes; the most fundamental is that the barriers to becoming a Web content producer have been lowered.

Knowledge of arcane HTML tags is not required for content production. Any computer user who has something to communicate and is comfortable with basic word processing functions, particularly those that adhere to CUA, can create Web content with little training. Practically, this means that anybody who wants to publish content has a relatively easy means to reach interested (and even uninterested) consumers. The McDonaldization of the tools of production has significantly moved control of the production of Web content from computer programmers and specialists to any interested person and provides a number of ways of communicating (e.g., text, graphics, audio, and video).

We believe that this shift in control in the production process is a liberating factor, fueling creativity and increasing the range of Web content available to surfers. People are free to share information about their hobbies (poems, Little League scores, photographs, etc.), work (accomplishments, resume, etc.), personal beliefs (politics, religion, etc.), and anything else they desire to communicate. In this situation, McDonaldization has a positive effect, leading to more diverse Web content, increasing what people can find on the Web, and making the Web surfing experience less homogeneous.

The standards that allow the flowering of diverse Web content, alternatively, constrain or limit what people can produce and consume—not everything that can be imagined can be distributed on the Web. Before audio standards were established, for example, idiosyncratic methods of receiving audio content were available only to experienced computer specialists and hobbyists; average Web surfers were unable to experience audio content.

These constraints, however, can be quite broad. If the standards regulating production are static, unchanging, or changing slowly, then McDonaldization of production reduces content options and constrains consumption. Several forces, however, have been pushing the evolution of production standards associated with more diverse content.

First, the standardization of production tools transfers significant Web production skills from dedicated programmers to more casual computer users. This de-skilling process is substantially different from the de-skilling associated with scientific management. Control of the tools of production is not restricted to entities with significant capital; because costs of production are low, almost anyone can own sophisticated production tools and make content available. By providing the possibility for more people to produce sophisticated Web content, the standardization of production tools provides the basis for greater diversity of content to be produced, as we have discussed.

At the same time, the associated de-skilling of professional programmers creates pressure on them to seek new frontiers of Web content. Professional programmers and Web developers are led to distinguish themselves from casual Web producers by developing new data formats that may lead to new standards. Upon introduction, these standards require greater than average skills to implement. This stretching and evolving of standards then stimulates the creation of new standardized tools, feeding back into content production generally by further expanding the range and complexity of what may be produced by even casual Web content producers.

Second, there are considerable financial incentives to increase the range of Web content. While casual Web producers may wish to use the Web to share their home videos with family members and others, the driving force to improve standards for audio and video content comes from corporations that envision the Web as a relatively inexpensive and flexible means of distributing this content commercially. As long as the standards are relatively open, and the standards can be influenced by large numbers of producers, content diversity will be encouraged. Again, McDonaldization in this context has positive effects by decreasing the homogeneity of Web experiences.

Finally, the current standards are sufficiently robust and support a large number of communication media (e.g., text, audio, video, graphics, interaction, etc.). Because these different modes of communication may be combined in various ways, the possible forms of unique Web communication are great and, currently, have not been fully exploited for communication.

THE PROS AND CONS OF McDONALDIZATION: THE CONSUMPTION SIDE

Standardization of the Tools of Consumption

To consume Web content requires a tool, a Web browser. Web browsers serve the common function of formatting and displaying Web content—to allow content to be consumed. Three factors are important when considering browsing tools.

First, as Web browsers have evolved, the Web surfing experience has become more homogenized in some ways. As HTML standards and the ability of browsers to interpret content produced within these standards have evolved, Web surfers are more likely to have similar experiences. Regardless of the browser used, surfers visiting the same Web sites will mostly see the same content. Moreover, as standards have become more comprehensive and producers have acquired skill in using those standards to create complex content, it is increasingly likely that what is viewed by a consumer will be what is intended by the producer. Although interpretations may differ, and therefore experiences may differ, at some level, browsing experiences are more homogeneous than in the early days of the Web.

Second, despite the diversity of browsers, nearly all Web surfers use either Internet Explorer (86%) or Netscape (13%). The concentration of Web surfers using one browsing tool is in itself an interesting homogenizing experience. This form of McDonaldization is potentially harmful because if Microsoft decides to break the standards in their browser, a huge percentage of Web surfers could be affected. However, as long as alternative browsers are easy to find and install, and more closely adhere to current standards, surfers could easily switch from Microsoft Internet Explorer to an alternative browser. To the extent that people are unlikely to switch to another browser, Web browser oligopoly may present a real problem, but currently, there are numerous alternatives.

Last, the standardization of the browser produces a third important effect. Despite the homogenization of experience that comes from content being presented in a single manner and the sameness of the window through which that content may be viewed, standardization permits Internet consumers to produce much of their own experience. Standardization permits the act of browsing itself, which in turn allows individuals to actively shape their experience, determining not only what to view but also the timing and sequence of consumption, as well as the context within which content is viewed. These selection, timing, sequence, and context issues, then, allow for substantial differentiation in the experiences of Web content consumers.

Oligopoly and the McDonaldization of Web Content

As discussed earlier, homogeneity in Web browsing experiences may occur to the extent that Web surfers tend to limit their browsing to a small section of the Web. This produces what we have called inequality in Web consumption patterns. As inequality increases, so does homogeneity of experience.

The primary force driving inequality in Web consumption patterns is financial. Commercial Web sites face pressure to capture the largest share of Web site visits possible. Historically, two major strategies have been used to produce Internet-generated income. The first is to charge commercial concerns for advertising on a Web site, based on the number of unique visitors a Web site receives. The second is to provide content that Web surfers are willing to pay for. These strategies may be used in combination.

The pressure to attract and retain the largest number of Web visitors possible produces conflicting pressures to homogenize Web surfing experiences but at the same time provide varied content. Commercial Web sites try to attract visitors and advertising dollars by providing powerful reasons to visit, either by offering special features or by being all things to all people.

Insofar as these efforts work and the Web site becomes commercially successful, there is an increasing likelihood that one business or set of businesses may be dominated by a small number of large enterprises. From the perspective of McDonaldization, the concern is that as Web surfers travel to fewer Web sites for consumption, Web surfing becomes a more homogenized experience. Not only are surfers not going elsewhere, exploring alternatives, but they are also browsing within a single site, within the confines of a more or less uniform interface, and are exposed only to content provided by the site. Insofar as this is the case, the rich diversity of life on the Web becomes muted, with more difficulty in experiencing Web content that does not conform to the standards of highly traveled Web sites. However, unless or until well-traveled sites, notably Web portals, prevent surfers from leaving their content-laden sites, there is a diverse Web to be explored, partially due to McDonaldization of the tools of production.

The question of alternative sites to visit brings us squarely, then, to the process used to explore the Web; Web surfers still have to find content. Search engines employ their own means for collecting and processing information on available Web sites and their own proprietary algorithms for prioritizing search results for users. As a result, they act as a kind of filter. Insofar as Web searches are dominated by a small number of different search engines, then we have concerns akin to those associated with other Web oligopolies. Web users are presented with a relatively small number of Web destinations, and thus, their surfing experience may be somewhat homogenized. However, this concern may not be particularly grave, given just how much of the Web search engines index and make available.

More problematic is the potential for search engines to introduce biases into their search results that may increase the likelihood of oligopoly on the Web. Consider the search strategy employed by Google (www.google.com), one of the more popular search sites. Google uses a technology they call PageRank. In their words,

> PageRank relies on the uniquely democratic nature of the web by using its vast link structure as an indicator of an individual page's value. In essence, Google interprets a link from page A to page B as a vote, by page A, for page B. But, Google looks at more than the sheer volume of votes, or links a page receives; it also analyzes the page that casts the vote. Votes cast by pages that are themselves "important" weigh more heavily and help to make other pages "important."

Although this appears to produce "democratic" search results, it is biased by increasing the likelihood that often-linked sites are (a) deemed to be inherently more valuable, and as a result, it (b) potentially increases Web traffic to these sites. Tautologically, this ranking scheme increases the probability that those same Web sites rated as being popular remain so, and may even increase in popularity, at the expense of those rated less popular. In short, the design strategy used by search sites may structure or lead to oligopoly by directing Web traffic, increasing inequality, and therefore increasing homogenization.

IS THE INTERNET McDONALDIZED?

Let us return to the questions with which we began. The answer to the question "Is the Internet McDonaldized?" as well as its subsidiary question, "Is this problematic?" depends on what exactly is being examined. If we look at the tools of production and consumption of Internet content, then we can say, emphatically, Yes, the Internet is McDonaldized. The tools have become standardized to an extraordinary degree. This standardization is constraining, certainly, because it limits both what may be produced and what may be consumed. However, this standardization of tools is precisely what makes the Internet itself *possible*. Standardization allows communication; indeed, it is the necessary precondition of communication, without which there would be no Internet, no Web, and in particular, no ability to draw from the Web and to construct one's own experience from different sources of content.

Standardization of the tools of Internet production and consumption becomes problematic only when those tools or the standards they encode come under the control of relatively small groups of people, either single organizations or firms. There are two scenarios in which this may arise. The first may occur when standards-forming bodies become insulated from the communities of users and developers they serve. Insofar as this occurs, standards may become less responsive to emerging needs of Web producers and consumers, retarding the evolution of standards that facilitate broad-based enhancements of Internet communication. Furthermore, they may be captured by special interests, placing the profits of one firm ahead of the demands of the medium itself. The second may occur when one tool becomes so dominant it becomes a *de facto* standard, as in the case of Microsoft Internet Explorer. In that instance, one firm owns the standard itself, and may use its ownership of the standard to favor its own economic position at the expense of the production and consumption of Internet content generally. Either way, when standards become unresponsive to the wide pool of users and developers, the Internet is impoverished and its potential to facilitate both the production and consumption of rich and varied content is reduced.

When we turn to the question of human experience, we arrive at two different pictures. The economics of the Web and the design of search engines have so far produced substantial inequality in the Web, spurring the formation of oligopoly in particular businesses, such as Amazon or E-Bay; particular Web service and content providers, such as AOL; and particular portals, such as YAHOO!, MSN, and Google. Where oligopolies form, the experience of consumers tends to become homogenized. This is the case because these sites impose a single, more or less uniform order on the experience of those visiting. If Web surfers go to a small number of such sites *rather than others*, not only are their own experiences while there homogeneous, but they are largely the same as the experiences of all those others who visit that destination instead of an alternative. In this sense, the Web is McDonaldized, and that outcome is potentially problematic.

However, at the very same time as the Web produces oligopoly, homogenizing experience, it also creates a solution to this same problem. The standardization of tools lowers the barriers to entry for the production and consumption of Internet content. By placing the capacity to produce content more or less as they wish in the hands of individuals, the diversity of content potentially available online substantially increases. Not only is the experience of those producing content likely to be less homogeneous, reflecting personal control over production, but the diversity of content produced means that the experiences of those surfing the Web is likely to be substantially less homogeneous as well. In this sense, the Web is not McDonaldized, with positive effects for those who both produce and consume content on the Web.

Taken together, the potential for oligopoly and the potential to produce diverse content may be seen as countervailing forces. Where oligopoly threatens to homogenize experience, diversity of production undercuts that threat. By the latter part of 2001, there were few data and little other evidence that would permit us to evaluate which force has advanced further or whether one may even be able to eclipse the other. Developing good measures will greatly increase our ability to assess, as well as to predict. However, we can say with confidence that the very ability of the Internet to undercut the homogenization of experience depends on the thoroughgoing McDonaldization of the tools of production and consumption. But even these will lose some of their ability to act as a countervailing force if the standards around which the Internet are built become unresponsive to the demands of open online communication. For those inclined to resist the McDonaldization of the Internet, we suggest going forth and producing content!

Thinking Critically

◆◆◆

1. In what ways has the Internet grown more McDonaldized?

2. In what ways has the Internet grown more deMcDonaldized?

3. What problems associated with the Internet would be ameliorated by greater McDonaldization?

4. What advantages associated with the Internet would be reduced or eliminated by greater McDonaldization?

5. Is a deMcDonaldized Internet possible?

Work had been highly rationalized long before the advent of McDonald's and McDonaldization, but the latter led to new heights in the rationalization of work, especially in the service sector, and to the creation of a new term to describe work in that sector—"McJobs." The paradigm of rationalized work for the first half of the 20th century was assembly-line work, especially in the automobile industry. During that period, virtually all the work in the service sector was performed rather haphazardly and had undergone comparatively little rationalization. All of that began to change with the beginning of the McDonald's chain in 1955 and the steady decline in manufacturing work in general, and assembly-line work in particular, in the United States in the last half of the 20th century. During that time, McDonald's and its clones, in and out of the fast-food industry, grew into megacorporations employing millions of people and spread across numerous settings throughout the United States and much of the world. To manage such far-flung operations, especially the work that takes place in them, these corporations were led to McDonaldize them. In fact, they relied on many of the ideas and principles behind the rationalization of assembly-line work, and indeed, at least some of the work in McDonaldized service settings closely resembled work on the assembly line. For instance, hamburgers are assembled in much the same way that automobiles are. Of course, assembling a hamburger takes far fewer steps and is much simpler. In that sense, such work is far more rationalized than that on the automobile assembly line.

My essay describes the increasing ubiquity of McJobs in the United States and analyzes them from the point of view of the four dimensions of McDonaldization, as well as examining the irrationality of rationality. Although they resemble assembly-line work in many ways, one of the distinctive aspects of McJobs is that they McDonaldize not only what people do but also what they say. This is accomplished through the use of scripts that dictate what people in McJobs are to say under various circumstances. This leads to new depths in de-skilling; lost is the ability to speak and interact with people on one's own.

Another revolutionary aspect of McDonaldized settings, at least as far as work is concerned, is the turning of customers into part-time, unpaid employees. We now all do many tasks (carry our own food and dispose of the debris afterward) that, in the past, were performed by paid employees. Thus, McDonaldized settings, at least in the realm of consumption, exploit both employees and consumers. In fact, in some ways (e.g., a lack of guaranteed work hours), those who hold McJobs are even more exploited than those who work on the assembly line.

Although work in McDonaldized settings is often dissatisfying, even alienating (both are reflected in the high turnover rates in the fast-food industry), many employees may not feel this way or even be conscious of the negative effects caused by the nature of their work. This may be traceable, in part, to the fact that people now live much of their daily lives in a McDonaldized world and therefore awareness of the McDonaldization of work and its negative effects are muted, as is the desire to rebel against it.

McJobs are clearly linked to class, with those in the lower classes far more likely to hold such positions. This leads to the point that although more and more work is being McDonaldized, a whole other sector of the economy, the postindustrial sector, offers well-paid, highly skilled, non-McDonaldized jobs (e.g., computer programmers). Thus, we are increasingly moving to a two-tiered occupational system differentiated between the postindustrial work of the middle and upper classes and the McDonaldized work of the lower classes.

17

McJobs

McDonaldization and Its Relationship to the Labor Process

George Ritzer

◆◆◆ ────────────────────────────────

I n recent years the spread of McDonaldized systems has led to the creation of an enormous number of jobs. Unfortunately, the majority of them can be thought of as McDonaldized jobs, or "McJobs." While we usually associate these types of positions with fast-food restaurants, and in fact there are many such jobs in that setting, McJobs have spread throughout much of the economy. . . .

It is worth outlining some of the basic realities of employment in the fast-food industry in the United States since those jobs serve as a model for employment in other McDonaldized settings. The large number of people employed in fast-food restaurants accounts for over 40 percent of the approximately 6 million people employed in restaurants of all types. Fast-food restaurants rely heavily on teenage employees—almost 70 percent of their employees are 20 years of

Editor's Note: From Ritzer, G. (1998). McJobs: McDonaldization and its Relationship to the Labour Process. In *The McDonaldization Thesis*. Copyright © 1998, George Ritzer, reprinted with permission of Sage Publications, Ltd.

age or younger. For many, the fast-food restaurant is likely to be their first employer. It is estimated that the first job for one of every 15 workers was at McDonald's; one out of every eight Americans has worked at McDonald's at some time in his or her life. The vast majority of employees are part-time workers; the average workweek in the fast-food industry is 29.5 hours. There is a high turnover rate: Only slightly more than half the employees remain on the job for a year or more. Minorities are overrepresented in these jobs—almost two-thirds of employees are women and nearly a quarter are non-white. These are low-paid occupations, with many earning the minimum wage or slightly more. As a result, these jobs are greatly affected by changes in the minimum wage: An upward revision has an important effect on the income of these workers. However, there is a real danger that many workers would lose their positions as a result of such increases, especially in economically marginal fast-food restaurants. . . .

McJobs are characterized by the . . . dimensions of McDonaldization. The jobs tend to involve a series of simple tasks in which the emphasis is on performing each as efficiently as possible. Second, the time associated with many of the tasks is carefully calculated and the emphasis on the quantity of time a task should take tends to diminish the quality of the work from the point of view of the worker. That is, tasks are so simplified and streamlined that they provide little or no meaning to the worker. Third, the work is predictable; employees do and say essentially the same things hour after hour, day after day. Fourth, many nonhuman technologies are employed to control workers and reduce them to robot-like actions. Some technologies are in place, and others are in development, that will lead to the eventual replacement of many of these "human robots" with computerized robots. Finally, the rationalized McJobs lead to a variety of irrationalities, especially the dehumanization of work. The result is the extraordinarily high turnover rate described above and difficulty in maintaining an adequate supply of replacements.

The claim is usually made by spokespeople for McDonaldized systems that they are offering a large number of entry-level positions that help give employees basic skills they will need in order to move up the occupational ladder within such systems (and many of them do). This is likely to be true in the instances in which the middle-level jobs to which they move—for example, shift leader in or assistant manager or manager of a fast-food restaurant—are also routinized and scripted. . . . However, the skills acquired in McJobs are not likely to prepare one for, help one to acquire, or help one to function well in, the far more desirable postindustrial occupations which are highly complex and require high levels of skill and education. Experience in routinized actions and scripted interactions do not help much when occupations require thought and creativity. . . .

McJobs are not simply the de-skilled jobs of our industrial past in new settings; they are jobs that have a variety of new and distinctive characteristics. . . . There have also emerged many distinctive aspects of the control of these workers. Industrial and McDonaldized jobs both tend to be highly routinized in terms of what people do on the job. However, one of the things that is distinctive about McDonaldized jobs, especially since so many of them involve work that requires interaction and communication, especially with consumers, is that what people say on the job is also highly routinized. To put this another way, McDonaldized jobs are tightly scripted: They are characterized by *both* routinized actions . . . and scripted interactions (examples include "May I help you?"; "Would you like a dessert to go with your meal?"; and "Have a nice day!"). Scripts are crucial because many of the workers in McDonaldized systems are interactive service workers. This means that they not only produce goods and provide services, but they often do so in interaction with customers.

The scripting of interaction leads to new depths in the de-skilling of workers. Not only have employee actions been de-skilled; employees' ability to speak and interact with customers is now being limited and controlled. There are not only scripts to handle general situations but also a range of subscripts to deal with a variety of contingencies. Verbal and interactive skills are being taken away from employees and built into the scripts in much the same way that manual skills were taken and built into various technologies. At one time distrusted in their ability to *do* the right thing, workers now find themselves no longer trusted to *say* the right thing. Once able to create distinctive interactive styles, and to adjust them to different circumstances, employees are now asked to follow scripts as mindlessly as possible. . . .

An analysis of Combined Insurance found that this company went even further and sought to transform and thereby control its employees' selves. This is consistent with the discovery that airlines sought to manage the emotions of their employees . . . . What we have evidence of here is a series of unprecedented efforts to control employees. It is not simply what people do and say on the job that many organizations now seek to control but also how they view themselves and how they feel.

However, Combined Insurance is not a good example of a McDonaldized firm, and such findings cannot be extended to most such settings. The fact is that McDonaldized systems have little interest in how their mainly part-time, short-time employees feel about and see themselves. These systems are merely interested in controlling their employees' overt behavior for as long as they work in such a system.

One very important, but rarely noted, aspect of the labor process in the fast-food restaurant and other McDonaldized systems is the extent to which customers are being led, perhaps even almost required, to perform a number of tasks without pay that were formerly performed by paid employees. For example, in the modern gasoline station the driver now does various things for free (pumps gas, cleans windows, checks oil, and even pays through a computerized credit card system built into the pump) that were formerly done by paid attendants. In these and many other settings, McDonaldization has brought the customer *into* the labor process: The customer *is* the laborer! This has several advantages for employers, such as lower (even nonexistent) labor costs, the need for fewer employers, and less trouble with personnel problems: Customers are far less likely to complain about a few seconds or minutes of tedious work than employees who devote a full work-day to such tasks. Because of its advantages, as well as because customers are growing accustomed to and accepting of it, I think customers are likely to become even more involved in the labor process.

This is the most revolutionary development, at least as far as the labor process is concerned, associated with McDonaldization. . . . The analysis of the labor process must be extended to what customers do in McDonaldized systems. The distinction between customer and employee is eroding, or in postmodern terms "imploding," and one can envision more and more work settings in which customers are asked to do an increasing amount of "work." More dramatically, it is also likely that we will see more work settings in which there are no employees at all! In such settings, customers, in interaction with non-human technologies, will *do* all of the human labor. A widespread example is the ATM in which customers (and the technology) do all of the work formerly done by bank tellers. More strikingly, we are beginning to see automated loan machines which dispense loans as high as $10,000. Again, customers and technologies do the work and, in the process, many loan-officer positions are eliminated. Similarly, the new automated gasoline pumps allow (or force) customers to do all of the required tasks; in some cases and at certain times (late at night) no employees at all are present.

In a sense, a key to the success of McDonaldized systems is that they have been able to supplement the exploitation of employees with the exploitation of customers. . . . In Marxian theory, the capitalists are seen as simply paying workers less than the value produced by the workers and as keeping the rest for themselves. This dynamic continues in contemporary society, but capitalists have learned that they can ratchet up the level of exploitation not only by exploiting workers more but also by exploiting a whole new group of people— consumers. In Marxian terms, customers create value in the tasks they perform for McDonaldized systems. And they are not simply paid less than the value they produce, they are paid *nothing at all*. In this way, customers are exploited to an even greater degree than workers. As is true of the exploitation of workers, owners are unaware of the fact that they are exploiting customers. But knowledge of exploitation is not a prerequisite to its practice.

While we have been focusing on the exploitation of customers in McDonaldized systems, this is not to say that employers have lost sight of the need to exploit workers. Beyond the usual exploitation of being paid less than the value of what they produce, McDonald's employees are often not guaranteed that they will work the number of hours they are supposed to on a given day. If business is slow, they may be sent home early in order that the employer can economize on labor costs: This reduces their take-home pay. As a result, employees often find it hard to count on a given level of income, meager as it might be, each week. In this way, and many others, employees of McDonaldized systems are even more exploited than their industrial counterparts.

This discussion brings together the two great theories in the history of sociology—Weber's theory of rationalization and Marx's theory of capitalist expansion and exploitation. Rationalization is a process that serves the interest of capitalists. They push it forward (largely unconsciously) because it heightens the level of exploitation of workers, allows new agents (e.g., customers) to be exploited and brings with it greater surplus value and higher profits. . . . We can see here how rationalization not only enhances control but also heightens the level and expands the reach of exploitation.

In various ways, McDonaldization is imposed on employees and even customers. They often have no choice but to conform, even if they would prefer things to be done in other ways. However, it would be a mistake to look at McDonaldization as simply being imposed on workers and customers. As discussed above, the basic ideas associated with McDonaldization are part of the value system: Many workers and customers have internalized them and conform to them of their own accord.

Furthermore, through their actions both workers and customers can be seen as actively "manufacturing" or "subjectifying" McDonaldization. By acceding to the constraints placed on them, by creating new and idiosyncratic ways of McDonaldizing their actions and interactions, and by extending McDonaldization to other aspects of their lives, workers and customers can be seen as actively involved in the manufacture, the social construction, of McDonaldization. This is another aspect of the way in which McDonaldization is not simply imposed on people. Workers and customers both often buy into McDonaldization and are actively involved in its creation.

The emphasis on the McDonaldization of work (like that on de-skilling) tends to emphasize only one side of the dialectic between structural changes, especially those imposed by management, and the significance of the responses of employees, which are consistently downplayed. But . . . the employees of McDonaldized systems often exhibit a considerable amount of independence, perhaps even creativity, on the job. . . . Also, . . . in our rush to condemn, we must not ignore the advantages to both employees and customers of the routinization, even the scripting, of work. . . .

There is also a dialectic between living one's life in a McDonaldized society and working in a McDonaldized job. These are mutually reinforcing, and the net result is that if most of one's life is spent in one McDonaldized system or another, then one is less likely to feel dissatisfied with either one's life or one's job. This helps to account for . . . [the] finding that McDonald's workers do not evidence a high level of dissatisfaction with their work. This, perhaps, is one of the most disturbing implications of the McDonaldization thesis. If most of one's life is spent in McDonaldized systems, then there is little or no basis for rebellion against one's McDonaldized job since one lacks a standard against which to compare, and to judge, such a job. More generally, there is little or no basis for rebelling against the system or for seeking out alternative, non-McDonaldized systems. McDonaldization then becomes the kind of iron cage described by Weber from which there is no escape and, worse, not even any interest in escaping.

This also undermines one of Marx's fundamental assumptions that when all is said and done workers remain at odds with the kind of work that is being imposed on them and are a threat to those who are imposing the work. To Marx, there is a creative core (species being, for example) lying just below the surface that is ever-ready to protest, or rebel against, the rationalized and exploitative character of work. However, can that creative core survive intact, or even at all, in the face of growing up in a McDonaldized world, being bombarded by media messages from McDonaldized systems, and being socialized by and educated in McDonaldized schools?

It has been argued that the kinds of trends discussed above and in Marx's work are occurring not only among the lower layers in the occupational hierarchy but also among the middle layers. McDonaldization is something that those at the top of any hierarchy seek to avoid for themselves but are willing and eager to impose on those who rank below them in the system. Initially, it is the lowest level employees who have their work McDonaldized, but it . . . eventually creeps into those middle layers.

While guilty of exploiting and controlling employees, franchise operators are, in turn, controlled and exploited by franchise companies. Many franchise operators have done well, even becoming multimillionaires controlling perhaps hundreds of franchises, but many others have staggered or failed as a result of high start-up costs and continuing fees to the franchise companies. (The inducement to the franchisor to open as many outlets as possible threatens the profitability and even the continued existence of extant franchise owners.) The operators take much of the financial risk, while the franchise companies sit back and (often) rake in the profits. In addition, the franchise companies frequently have detailed rules, regulations, and even inspectors that they use to control the operators.

While no class within society is immune to McDonaldization, the lower classes are the most affected. They are the ones who are most likely to go to McDonaldized schools; live in inexpensive, mass-produced tract houses; and work in McDonaldized jobs. Those in the upper classes have much more of a chance of sending their children to non-McDonaldized schools, living in custom-built homes, and working in occupations in which they impose McDonaldization on others while avoiding it to a large degree themselves.

Also related to the social class issue is the fact that the McDonaldization of a significant portion of the labor force does not mean that all, or even most, of the labor force is undergoing this process. In fact, the McDonaldization of some of the labor force is occurring at the same time that another large segment is moving in a postindustrial, that is, more highly skilled, direction. Being created in this sector of society are relatively high-status, well-paid occupations requiring high levels of education and training. In the main, these are far from McJobs and lack most, or all, of the dimensions discussed at the beginning of this chapter. The growth of such postindustrial occupations parallels the concern in the labor process literature with flexible specialization occurring side by side with the de-skilling of many other jobs. This points to a bifurcation in the class system. In spite of appearances, there is no contradiction here; McDonaldization and postindustrialization tend to occur in different sectors of the labor market. However, the spread of McJobs leads us to be dubious of the idea that we have moved into a new post-industrial era and have left behind the kind of de-skilled jobs we associated with industrial society.

It could be argued, as many have, that the focus in modern capitalism has shifted from the control and exploitation of production to the control and exploitation of consumption. While that may well be true, the fact is that capitalists do not, and will not, ignore the realm of production. . . . The nature of work is changing and capitalists are fully involved in finding new ways of controlling and exploiting workers. Further, they have discovered that they can even replace paid employees not only with machines, temporary workers, and so on but also with customers who are seemingly glad to do the work for nothing! Here, clearly, is a new gift to the capitalist. Surplus value is now not only to be derived from the labor time of the employee but also from the leisure time of the customer. McDonaldization is helping to open a whole new world of exploitation and growth to the contemporary capitalist.

Thinking Critically

1. Are McJobs an inevitable consequence of McDonaldization?

2. Would you be able to work in a McJob for most or all of your career?

3. If you wouldn't, do you think there are people who would/should? Who are they?

4. In what ways are high-status jobs—doctor, college professor, for example—becoming McJobs?

5. How would you cope with working in a McJob?

In an excerpt from Working for McDonald's in Europe: The Unequal Struggle? *Tony Royle looks at the nature of McJobs in a number of European nations. What he finds, not surprisingly, is a work situation very similar to that in American fast-food restaurants. Despite the tight control exerted over them, Europeans who work in those settings (like their American counterparts) do find shortcuts, and in some cases, they may rebel against, even sabotage, activities within the restaurant. However, managerial and organizational control is not easy to evade. Royle also discusses several reasons why workers are unlikely to resist managerial control, including that they are in a weak position and fear losing their jobs, that younger workers have nothing to which to compare the work, and that they do not intend to make that work a career so are not as upset about current working conditions. Overall, Royle concludes that McDonald's manages its employment relationship "across societal borders in a remarkably similar way through exceptionally rigid and detailed rules and procedures, a paternalistic management style and an 'acquiescent workforce.'" In other words, McDonald's has managed to McDonaldize its relationship with employees not only throughout the United States but also in Europe (and undoubtedly much of the rest of the world, as well).*

18

McWork in Europe

Tony Royle

◆◆◆ ───

V irtually all aspects of the [fast-food] business are highly standardized
and rigorously monitored. . . .

The modern ketchup dispensers are little changed from the McDonald
brothers' days: They squirt a measured amount of ketchup on each burger.
Workers learn a routinized job in 1 day. For example, to prepare and bag
French fries, workers follow 19 carefully calculated steps; the French fry
scoop enables workers to fill a bag and set it down in one continuous motion
and helps them to gauge the proper serving size. All the jobs can be learned
with no previous experience or with the minimum of training. Operations
are monitored and controlled using the *Operations and Training Manual* or
the "bible" as some McDonald's managers call it. It is some 600 pages in
length and extremely comprehensive; it includes full-color photographs,
which, among other things, illustrate the correct placement for ketchup and
mustard in the preferred five-point "flower" pattern, and it determines the
correct size of pickles to be placed on each type of hamburger. Rules and

Editor's Note: Excerpts from *Working for McDonald's in Europe: The Unequal
Struggle?* by Tony Royle, pp. 58–70, 72–75, 82–83. Copyright © 2000 by
Routledge Press, London. Used with permission.

procedures cover everything, eliminating decision making for workers and, as one respondent put it, make the job "virtually idiot-proof." One German floor manager stated, "Anyone can learn this job. There's no challenge for workers, only speed and exactitude." When the assembly-line output of burgers slackens because the restaurant is quiet, it does not mean that the workers are allowed to take a break. Ray Kroc was obsessed with cleanliness; he insisted that his staff should be constantly cleaning areas that no one else would even think about, with the cleaning cloth becoming an essential tool for every crew member. As Kroc frequently reminded his staff, "If you've got time to lean, you've got time to clean." So, although the work can be easily learned, it would be a mistake to think that it was easy.

. . .

The majority of workers in most countries in this study work part-time, so some may only do one full (8-hour) shift per week. However, if the restaurant is busy or short-staffed, workers are frequently asked to stay and work longer hours. In some cases, employees may end up working 10 hours or more; in fact, it can be much longer. Some full-time Finnish workers reported that they often worked a 14-hour day, and in one 2-week period they had worked 110 hours. Some workers may be quite happy to take the extra hours; in other cases, managers may tell workers that if they refuse they may not get work on other occasions. . . .

Although there are rules and tight procedures for everything and managers usually working alongside closely monitor the work, workers do sometimes find shortcuts. The research revealed that in several countries workers sometimes cheat on the system. They find shortcuts when the restaurant is busy and when working within the system cannot cope with demand. In the UK, some employees were referred to as "cowboys"; these workers would find shortcuts in exactly the same way as assembly-line workers in other industries in order to create some porosity in an otherwise hectic schedule. . . . In addition, some workers have reported on more deviant forms of behavior, which might be akin to physical sabotage. One example was what some young male employees called "sweating competitions." The hot kitchen conditions were used to see who could sweat the most over the products, apparently as a way of relieving the frustration or boredom, or as a way of seeking revenge on unpopular managers or the customer. Nor is this the only example; one worker reported that he purposely did not wash his hands after a visit to the toilet, whereas others would apply their nasal fluid onto the products as a way of getting back at customers and managers.

Sometimes, mustard and ketchup dispensers clog up and then too little or no sauce is placed on the burger, pickles are missed, or food falls on the floor (and, if the manager isn't watching, it sometimes ends up with the customer). Buns, burgers, and fries are taken out before the buzzer has buzzed; sometimes fries are kept longer than the regulation 7 minutes. . . . In some cases, it appears that managers adopt an "indulgency pattern"; when restaurants are short-staffed, managers may turn a blind eye to some of these behaviors, providing that customer demand is met.

. . .

The detailed analysis of the German and UK workforces, and that of the other European countries, suggest that McDonald's workers in most European countries are unlikely to resist management control. First, because of their weak labor market position and possible career aspirations, those who really need these jobs are unlikely to put their jobs on the line by complaining about company policy. Second, young workers who have very little or no previous work experience have little else with which to compare their working conditions. In any case, the majority do not intend to stay with the corporation. Like second-income earners, who often have family responsibilities, young workers still in education are less likely to be financially dependent on the company as they often live with others who support them. As one UK student (training squad) stated,

> I think full-time workers are exploited here. I don't know how they stick to it so long, if it was my career I would kick up a fuss, but it's not worth the hassle because I'm not staying with the company after my degree. I'm only a part-timer.

It is argued that in any employment relationship there is always a dynamic balance among control, consent, and resistance. McDonald's appears to manage this relationship across societal borders in a remarkably similar way through exceptionally rigid and detailed rules and procedures, a paternalistic management style, and an "acquiescent" workforce.

Thinking Critically

◆◆◆

1. Are you surprised that there are McJobs in Europe?

As *Andrew Knight* shows in the following chapter, written especially for this volume, both industrial agriculture and meat processing have grown increasingly McDonaldized. All sorts of trends are associated with the McDonaldization of agriculture including the growing size of farms, their increasing specialization (monoculture), their increased reliance on chemicals and biotechnology, crop simplification, increased productivity, greater precision, more predictable products, more perfect products (at least in terms of their appearance to the consumer), and even efforts to control the weather to make it more predictable (e.g., more rain, less hail). Perhaps the strongest examples of McDonaldization in agriculture relate to bioengineered seeds that farmers must purchase from large corporations each year rather than saving their own seeds. There are even plans for so-called terminator seeds that automatically become sterile after a year so that the farmer must purchase new ones from the biotechnology company.

Although agriculture is increasingly McDonaldized, or more likely because of it, there are increasing irrationalities associated with it. These include enormous pollution, waste of great quantities of water in a highly water-intensive industry and in a society in which water is in increasingly short supply, physical dangers to those who work in the industry, high costs and marginal profitability often traceable to the McDonaldization of farming, and an overabundance of relatively inexpensive food (leading to problems such as overconsumption and obesity).

Meat processing has been McDonaldized to at least the same, if not a greater, degree. Large feedlots, assembly-line disassembling of steers, massive chicken and hog farms, and the like all reflect and exemplify this trend toward increasing McDonaldization. Many irrationalities are associated with this including animal cruelty, increased resistance (among animals and the humans who eat parts of these disease-resistant animals and therefore ingest the traces of antibiotics that exist in their meat) to antibiotics, and an increased risk of food poisoning.

19

Supersizing Farms

The McDonaldization of Agriculture

Andrew J. Knight

◆◆◆———————————————————————————

With the introduction and advancement of chemicals, machinery, and breeding, industrial agriculture and meat processing have been bought into the McDonaldization process. Today, the agriculture industry is driven to become more efficient, calculable, predictable, and to control humans and nature through technological means. This chapter details how McDonaldization relates to industrial agriculture and describes the irrationalities that this system has produced. The first section of this chapter focuses on the McDonaldization of agriculture, followed by how the meat processing industry has applied the McDonaldization process. The next section discusses how the organic movement developed as an alternative to the industrial model. Questions surrounding the future of the McDonaldization of agriculture are raised in the final section.

Editor's Note: This chapter written for this volume.

THE McDONALDIZATION OF AGRICULTURE

For many farmers today there is only one way of farming—get big or get out. Large farms have dominated the agricultural landscape for more than 40 years and are thought to be more efficient than their smaller counterparts. Although the acreage of farmland only decreased modestly from 1945 to 1998, farm size has increased dramatically over this period. The average farm size in 1940, for example, was 135 acres; in 1998, it was 435 acres. At the same time, the number of farms has declined from approximately 6.1 million in 1940 to 2.2 million in 1998.

Farming techniques and practices began to change dramatically after World War II. Modern farms tend to specialize in one cash crop, whether it be corn, cotton, rice, soybeans, tobacco, wheat, beef, chicken, dairy, or pork. Monoculture farming, where the same crop is grown year after year in the same field, or very simple rotations are used, is deemed more efficient because specialized large farms enable the farmer to use machinery, which allows farmers to harvest more crops in less time and to specialize in a single cash crop.

Without chemical inputs, monoculture farming would be impractical. Fertilizers add nutrients to the soil to aid crops grow faster and replenish the soil so that land can be used annually for growing crops. Traditional methods of leaving land out of production to allow land to replenish itself or of rotating crops became obsolete, and land is better used for production purposes. Pesticides allow the farmer to control insects and, thus, enhance efficiency by reducing crop damage. They also enhance efficiency by saving time because other methods of pest control, such as organic or integrated pest management, require more time, knowledge, and management.

The biotechnology revolution also enhances farm efficiency by streamlining the process. Today many food crops in the United States and Canada have undergone some sort of genetic modification. According to Pew Initiatives on Food and Biotechnology, 85% of soybeans, 45% of corn, and 76% of cotton grown in the United States in 2004 were genetically modified. An estimated 54% of all canola and 50% of all papayas grown in 2001 were genetically modified. Other genetically modified crops currently grown in the United States include squash, sugar beets, potatoes, and sweet corn, although these crops have not been as widely adopted.

The large majority of these engineered crops are what can be termed "first wave" bioengineered agricultural products, where specific traits are added or enhanced in plants to increase yields through making plants pest and disease resistant, hardier, and less energy intensive. These plants are marketed as having many advantages over traditional plants such as increasing yields, reducing capital inputs, and saving time and energy, which in turn increases farm profitability. They also allow land previously deemed marginal for agricultural purposes to be used.

Several "second wave" bioengineered agricultural products are now available. These products are referred to as "nutraceuticals" or "functional foods," where specific traits are added or enhanced in plants to increase nutrients or taste in food crops. They are being marketed as providing healthier and better tasting food to consumers. For example, tomatoes are designed to produce more lycopene to lower cholesterol levels, golden rice was designed purportedly to enhance the level of vitamin A in rice to reduce the risk of blindness, and research is being conducted to reduce the bitterness in citrus fruits.

"Third wave" bioengineered agricultural products comprise crops that are grown for nonfood purposes such as plants grown for pharmaceutical, cosmetic, and industrial by-products that will then be harvested and processed into drugs, chemical compounds, and plastics. Often referred to as "plant molecular farming," these plants will produce vaccines, antibodies, or other pharmaceuticals or industrial enzymes or bioplastics in greater quantity and at lower costs than traditional methods.

Advances in science and technology increase efficiency by simplifying the product. Although grocery stores or supermarkets may provide an illusion of variety, a further examination of produce sections quickly reveals the lack of choice. Only a few varieties of lettuce, tomatoes, cucumbers, apples, and oranges are available for purchase. On closer inspection, much of what is presented as variety by food companies is mostly clever packaging of similar products. With the advent of machinery, it became more efficient to grow crops that are hardier and travel better. As Jim Hightower, a former Texas Agriculture Commissioner, would lament, "hard tomatoes" rule the grocery shelves at the expense of their more tasty heirloom varieties. Today, many consumers do not understand how their food is produced and lack knowledge about modern agricultural practices. Although the fast-food industry continuously strives for efficiency to reduce or replace labor, farms rely primarily on technology to replace labor as consumers are cut off from the farm process.

Specialization is more difficult on farms than food processing plants because the farmer must be involved in almost every aspect of farm life from purchasing seeds and chemical inputs to crop management to harvesting, storage, selling, and transportation of products. Also, land on farms may be unsuitable or marginal for agricultural production. Although biotechnology may ease these production concerns by developing less intensive and hardier plants, second and third wave biotechnology crops will likely add more variety and value-added products, which may increase the complexity and management of crops.

With advances in agricultural technology, agriculture has been able to calculate many aspects of farm life. The "hay days" of farming would be the late 1960s and 1970s when the United States focused on production for the export market, partially as a result of the need to feed Europe after World War II and the world thereafter. For the first time ever, the focus was on agricultural productivity and globalization rather than on emphasizing meeting regional consumers' demands. Maximum production policies have succeeded in increasing agricultural productivity growth. From 1948 to the mid 1990s, for instance, agricultural productivity growth has increased approximately 2.5 times.

The emphasis on productivity or—to be consistent with the process of McDonaldization—quantity is a major factor behind the specialization or monoculture of farms, increased size of farms, and the decline in variety of crops. Although some agricultural pundits fear that agricultural production has stagnated and will begin to decline, proponents of biotechnology see genetic engineering as a method to heighten agricultural productivity. In the controversial case of rBGH, for example, the genetically engineered synthetic version of the natural bovine growth hormone was designed to increase milk yields by 10% to 20%. By injecting cattle with rBGH, they are able to produce a greater amount of milk in a shorter time period.

The use of rBGH is a classic example of quantity over quality because there was no milk shortage before the advent of rBGH, and the demand for milk has been relatively stagnant. Also, the quality of milk has not increased. Critics claim that rBGH may pose health hazards, particularly to children and to cattle, and that farmers will bear the cost of the hormone, the inconvenience of administering daily injections to dairy cattle, and the economic implications of increased milk production. Despite these concerns, rBGH was approved for commercial use by the Food and Drug Administration in 1994.

With increased technology has also come more precise measurement of time, products, and processes. Precision farming allows farmers to use global positioning satellite (GPS) technology to manage soil and land quality at increasingly finer scales. This technology enables farmers to break down their fields into small plots, monitor yields, and apply chemicals as needed to these particular plots. For instance, with chemicals, precision farming should enable a farmer to conduct soil tests on a small plot of land, perhaps a 2.5- or 3.3-acre grid cell, and apply chemicals in the dosage necessary to that plot instead of applying chemicals to an entire field. Critics are concerned that precision farming is only another method to increase farmer dependence on off-farm suppliers and purchasers of farm products, as they provide the means for agribusiness to become integrated into field and farm-level production activities.

Predictability is relevant to the actual farming process. Industrial farms use the same practices and growing methods, and contract farming forces farmers to adopt similar methods. Industrial farming urges monoculture crops to be planted, irrigated, sprayed with chemicals, and machines to be used to harvest crops. One cotton, soybean, or rice field appears to be identical to another.

Another aspect of predictability is creating predictable products and processes. Ideally, fruits, vegetables, dairy and meat products would look the same, have the same shape, the same nutritional content, and the same taste. A pear, for instance, grown on one farm would be identical to another pear grown on another farm. Clearly, this ideal is not realistic as each pear is likely to vary in some way from other pears. Still, this ideal is approached particularly through breeding and the use of chemicals. Traditional breeding techniques have been relatively unsuccessful in achieving entirely predictable results, although the idea has been to work with limited varieties to come closer to this goal. The real hope for predictability lies with biotechnology. Biotechnology optimists portray a future where plants produce uniform crops. As well, cloning is hyped as a method to insure that animals will have similar traits, and to insure that each animal exhibits the best traits.

A final element of predictability is to minimize danger and unpleasantness. Although biotechnology optimists suggest bioengineered foods will be safer, tastier, and better for us, other methods have also been used (e.g., pesticides, irradiation) to protect the consumer. Pesticides are not only used to prevent loss of crops, but also limit pests from damaging fruits and vegetables aesthetically. Consumers will often search the produce bin for the perfect look- ing fruit or vegetable, and leave behind blemished ones. Scarecrows are used not only to scare away birds from eating produce but also to prevent them from damaging crops. The increased consumer distance from farm production has only exacerbated consumer desire for aesthetically pleasing foods.

Irradiation has been proposed as a method to not only insure the pleas- ant appearance of fruits and vegetables, but also prevent spoilage. The consumption of spoiled food is a leading cause of food-borne illnesses. As well, the irradiation of meat kills potentially dangerous bacteria such as *Salmonella* and *E. coli* in meats. Another benefit of irradiation is less regu- lation of meat and produce industries because unsanitary practices in meat processing plants or on farms would not affect human safety. Costly recalls would be a thing of the past.

Farming remains unpredictable because it is heavily dependent on the whims of nature. Drought, wind, rain, the amount of sunshine, soil differ- ences, and acts of God can all make farming unpredictable from one season to the next. Humans, however, appear to be endeavoring to make the weather more predictable. A quick search on weather modification on Yahoo.com yields various weather modification companies and projects in the United States. A popular method appears to be cloud seeding to suppress hail and enhance rain. According to William Cotton, funding for weather modification peaked in the 1970s, but weather modification programs exist in approximately 22 countries worldwide and in any given year, there may be as many as 40 operational seeding projects in the United States.

Throughout history, humans have attempted to control nature and their surrounding environment through the use of technology. The only difference today from that of our forbearers is the extent to which we can and plan to control nature through technological advancements. At its core, industrial agriculture requires human transformation and control of nature, which is only feasible if certain elements of nature can be controlled.

Traditional farming methods required rotating crops and fallowing to allow soils to replenish. One reason monoculture farming was impracticable was because plots of land used to grow one crop decrease soil quality. Under the industrial model, fertilizers are added to the soil to replenish nutrients and keep land in production.

Livestock and crops require water to survive and grow. Large farms, particularly ones located on marginal agricultural lands, require vast irrigation systems to water livestock and crops. Once again, nature is controlled or altered in order that livestock and crops have a steady and predictable supply of water.

Biotechnology methods increase control over nature and farmers to a much greater extent than traditional breeding methods because individual genes can be manipulated to be less vulnerable to the whims of nature. Cloning increases control of nature as we continue to develop methods to clone specific characteristics of animals or enhance nature through the addition of selected genes. (One of the major arguments for cloning animals is to reduce disease.)

Bioengineered seeds allow agribusiness more control over farmers by forcing farmers to sign license agreements to use their seeds. Often these seed agreements prevent farmers from saving seeds and reusing them the following year and place limits on how the seeds can be used. Because the seeds are formulated to be resistant to certain chemicals, farmers must also purchase pesticides from the same seed company. Monsanto Roundup Ready seeds, for instance, require that Roundup pesticides be applied because these plants are only resistant to Roundup.

Another aspect of controlling the farmer with biotechnology seeds is that the farmer loses the ability to choose seed characteristics and may have to pay a higher price for characteristics he does not want. Take the case of a farmer whose farm is located next to a lake with prevailing winds that act as a control mechanism for pests. This farmer, because of a more moderate climate, only seeks a hardier corn plant. However, the bioengineered seed is hardier and resistant to particular pesticides. The farmer must purchase this seed from the company that owns that specific patent and pay a premium for a characteristic he does not want or need.

Perhaps the most controversial method to control farmers by agribusiness was the development of the terminator seed, which is genetically engineered to prevent germination after a specific period of time and eliminate any option of seed saving. These seeds become sterile so that leftover seeds cannot be planted the following year. In March 1998, the U.S. Department of Agriculture and Delta & Pine Land Co. developed and patented these seeds to prevent unauthorized seed saving by farmers to protect patented seed technologies. The terminator seed patent was acquired by seed giant Monsanto in May 1998 when it purchased Delta & Pine. Terminator seeds, however, have not been marketable because of fierce opposition by numerous special interest groups and nongovernmental organizations.

Consumers are also controlled because biotechnology-derived products are considered similar to those created by traditional methods, making them exempt from labeling. Thus, consumers cannot distinguish between genetically modified foods (GMFs) and non-GMF products. Only by purchasing certified organic products are consumers able to limit purchases of bioengineered foods.

Agriculture is in many ways an irrational system and attempts to rationalize it are likely to produce irrational results. This section demonstrates how the negative effects or irrationalities of industrial agriculture may lead to its eventual decline. Perhaps the most irrational aspects of industrial agriculture are environmental because industrial agriculture is one of the most, if not the most, pollution-generating industries. An agricultural system based on monoculture is heavily dependent on chemicals, which have been linked to many negative effects. Although the effects of pesticides on humans is contested, some pesticides have been linked to groundwater contamination and numerous health problems, including birth defects, nerve damage, and cancer. Pesticide resistance has led to the development of even more potent pesticides, and genetically modified pesticide-resistant crops have not as of yet significantly decreased chemical use.

There is evidence that soils are degraded, and some suggest that productivity will decline as topsoil is continually eroded.

Over-irrigation and fertilization of land has resulted in the salinization of soil and eutrophication, a process where bodies of water receive excess nutrients that stimulate excessive algae and plant growth. The Gulf of Mexico, for instance, has an increasing dead zone as nitrogen from fertilizer and soil run-off chokes out aquatic life through oxygen depletion.

Agriculture is the second most water-intensive industry in the United States. As water becomes an evermore precious commodity, it is likely that conflict between farmers and residents will increase as demonstrated in several recent events. In Maine, cottage owners accused the blueberry industry of lowering lake levels. In Lakefield, Michigan, residents banded together against farms because their wells are going dry. In the Southwest, some farmers with water rights sell them to cities at an enormous profit, although their agricultural land remains fallow.

Industrial agriculture is extremely resource intensive, particularly relying on nonrenewable energy sources, such as fossil fuels. The reliance on monoculture farming, mechanization, and chemicals has also decreased biodiversity and affected wildlife negatively.

Technological advances have also been detrimental to farmers, farmworkers, and consumers. Not only has machinery reduced the need for many farm laborers, but farming and meat processing jobs are two of the most dangerous and low paying jobs in the United States. According to the Alabama Cooperative Extension System, more than 700 deaths occurred in farm-related activities in 2003, and another 150,000 agricultural workers suffered disabling work-related injuries. It is estimated that the number of deaths per 100,000 workers in agriculture has remained near 50 for the past 20 years. Approximately 68% of these farm-related deaths can be traced to machinery.

The case of rBGH may serve as an example of what is to come for farmers who adopt biotechnology. Although some farmers have experienced milk-yield increases, those farms have not become more profitable. As bioengineered foods become more commonplace, so have debates surrounding the ethicalness of biotechnology and its impact on biodiversity, wildlife, animal, and human health. Even some farmers are beginning to question biotechnology as evidenced by farmer opposition to genetically modified wheat in Canada. As contract farming has increased, critics argue that it has diminished knowledge and independence to the point where farmers have become wage laborers. Often, so-called technological advances require more management from farmers and are more capital intensive than traditional means. Still, the solution to all of these ills is more technology. This solution itself appears to be tautological and irrational as any technology is likely to spur additional side effects.

The cost of chemicals and capital inputs, such as machinery, has made farming an expensive business, and these costs have hindered the profitability of farms. Farming by nature is a risky business. Weather can affect crops, and productivity varies year by year. Farmers must also compete on world markets where prices fluctuate. In the late 1990s, more than half of all farms were in good financial health, but 45% of the small, noncommercial farms were financially vulnerable. U.S. Department of Agriculture data reveal that the farm debt-to-asset ratio is increasing, although it is still much lower than in the early 1980s during the farm crisis. Although the average annual income of farm households in 1997 was $52,300, approximately 89% of the average farm operator's income came from off-farm sources. Although the motto "Get Big or Get Out" applies, getting big does not guarantee farm survival, but may hasten or only delay the inevitable failure of many farms.

As a consequence of these trends, the federal government passed the largest farm bill in U.S. history in 2002 totalling $246.8 billion over the next decade. Farm subsidies have averaged more than $20 billion a year since 1999 with most of these funds benefiting the largest and wealthiest farms and agribusinesses. Eighty percent of the farm subsidies between 1998 and 2000 were to offset low prices, primarily to corn, cotton, rice, soybean, and wheat farmers.

As cities expand, farmland is threatened by development. Aside from agricultural values and practices conflicting, increased land values are a death knell for farmers, and it becomes unfeasible economically to leave the farm to their children in their wills. Perhaps because of this, the capital intensive nature of industrial agriculture, and the risky nature of agriculture, fewer students are enrolling in agricultural colleges.

Another irrationality of industrial agriculture is that it has led to an overabundance of food. According to Marion Nestle, the United States supplies a daily average of 3,800 calories per capita, nearly twice the amount needed to meet the energy requirements of most women, one-third more than needed by most men, and much higher than that needed by babies, young children, and the sedentary elderly. The overproduction of food results in waste and is a contributor to obesity. The American choice of a meat-laden diet also increases the amount of waste, as animal carcasses must be destroyed, and requires more energy to produce than a nonmeat diet.

A final irrationality of industrial agriculture is the belief that large monoculture farms are more efficient and productive than small farms. Despite the concentration of agribusinesses and the growth of large farms, small farms still constitute about 60% of all farms, although the larger farms are responsible for most of the agricultural output. Numerous studies have shown that smaller farms are more efficient at using resources than larger farms, and if total output per unit area is used instead of total yield as a measure of productivity, small farms are more productive than larger farms. There is also evidence that small farms are more beneficial for communities than large farms, and adopt more innovative marketing strategies. The trends of larger farms and concentration of ownership in agriculture have also been shown to be detrimental to rural economies.

McDONALDIZATION OF MEAT PROCESSING

In the processing of beef, cattle are corralled in overcrowded supersized lots close to the slaughterhouse, where large numbers of cattle are herded together in pens to maximize space. This housing method is much more efficient than conventional ranching styles, where cattle roam on the plains eating grass. This process also eliminates waste, because instead of putting dairy cattle that are beyond their milking days out to pasture, they are slaughtered for human consumption, and space is made for younger dairy cattle.

Cattle ready to be processed enter the slaughterhouse on conveyor belts, and on entry, are quickly killed by workers with the sole responsibility of cutting their throats. As the carcasses continue on the assembly line, each worker is responsible for one task in the disassembly process. Waste is reduced through the use of machines that attempt to take every morsel of meat from the carcass. This factory assembly-line approach is also used in the hog and poultry industries.

Contract farming has increased the need for calculability. In this system, processors outsource animals to farmers who are contracted to raise them for a specific period of time. Although only approximately 12% of farmers sell their products through production contracts, there has been an increase in contract farming in the United States. Almost all broiler chickens are raised under contract. Although cattle and hog industries are less integrated into the contract system, contract farming in the hog industry is becoming increasingly common.

In the chicken industry, processors drop off chicks on a farm close to the poultry processing plant to lower transportation costs. Farmers then raise the chickens for a specified period of time and according to the terms provided in the contract. This system places a focus on calculability because farmers are paid a specified number of cents per pound and provided incentives and penalties related to performance and quality standards. Typically, growers receive day-old chicks from the processors that can mature to four or five pounds in seven to eight weeks. Growers are only paid for live chickens. Similarly, beef and hog growers are also paid by weight gained.

Farm contracts with Tyson illustrate how farmers are controlled by agribusinesses. Farmers usually sign a four-year contract with Tyson (or other similar regional firms) that makes Tyson the sole provider of the chicks to be raised, the feed, and veterinary services. The company is also the sole determiner of the number, frequency, and type of chicks provided. Tyson then collects the mature birds after seven weeks, at a date and time of their own determination, providing the scales on which the birds are weighed, and the trucks take them away. The farmer provides the labor, the buildings in which the chicks are raised, and the land on which the buildings stand. The detailed control of inputs and farming practices are entirely in the hands of Tyson. Moreover, the farmer must adhere to the Company's "Broiler Growing Guide" and a failure to do so puts the farmer into "Intensified Management" status under the direct supervision of the Company's "Broiler Management and Technical Advisor."

Contract farming has been linked to the growth of larger farm size and fewer farms. In the hog industry, for example, the number of hog farms in the United States has decreased dramatically, although the number of hogs sold has increased. In particular, the fastest growth of hog farms is from super hog farms (50,000 to 500,000 hogs per year) and mega hog farms (greater than 500,000 hogs per year).

Farmers are controlled and are increasingly becoming more dependent on a few agribusinesses that sell inputs to farmers and then purchase their crops or livestock. This oligopoly of agricultural chemical companies and food processors determines the price of farm crops and controls the cost of seeds and chemicals. At the same time, vertical integration among processors has increased to the point where only a few companies control the food supply. ConAgra provides an example of the extent of both horizontal and vertical integration by agribusiness. ConAgra is one of the largest distributors of agricultural chemicals and fertilizers in North America, and has developed partnerships with seed companies. It is the largest turkey producer and second largest broiler producer in the United States, manufactures poultry and livestock feeds, owns and operates hatcheries, and processes foods. From farm to table, a significant proportion of the food system is owned and controlled by ConAgra.

Attempts to rationalize the meat processing industry have led to numerous irrationalities. Large feedlots have come under greater scrutiny for environmental, aesthetic, and health reasons. Animal-rights groups, such as People for the Ethical Treatment of Animals, have launched public relations campaigns against fast-food giants, such as McDonald's, on the issue of animal cruelty in food processing plants. Political conflicts between neighboring residents and large feedlots and meat processing plants have increased as residents concerned about air quality, waste, and property values attempt to shut down, relocate, or prevent the construction of large feedlots and meat processing plants.

A problem of large feedlots is the health of animals. In the case of beef, in order for large feedlots to be viable, cattle are fed grain instead of grass. This diet allows cattle to gain weight much faster than a traditional grass diet, and corn is often sold to meat processors below market value. The problem is that cattle's digestive systems are not designed to digest grains. Also, the concentration of cattle in a small area poses health problems as cattle eat and live where they defecate. To control the rate of disease infection, grain feed often contains antibiotics. This process has been linked to increased antibiotic resistant illness in humans.

Although the Department of Agriculture reassures the public that the U.S. food system is one of the safest in the world, the industrialization of food processing has heightened the risk of food contamination, particularly by bacteria such as *Salmonella, E. coli,* and *Listeria.* Although feeding livestock ruminants animal parts was banned in 1997 in response to the outbreak of Mad Cow disease in Europe, the recent discovery of a case in the United States highlights this irrational inefficient process. Still, the food processing industry is primarily responsible for regulating itself. Although contract farming provides guaranteed pricing, contract farming does not appear to be a system that enriches farmers. Few contract farmers are able to eliminate debt, and that concentration of ownership within the industry has created a financial crisis among growers.

REBELLING AGAINST THE McDONALDIZATION OF AGRICULTURE

The most vocal opponent of industrial agriculture is the organic movement. As people have become increasingly concerned about the environmental and health tolls of industrial agriculture, the organic industry has undergone massive growth. In 2001, organic foods represented a $5 billion industry, and by some industry estimates, sales have increased by 20% annually since 1990. Still, organic products represent only 2% of all food sales. Organic agriculture is in many ways the complete opposite of industrial agriculture. According to the U.S. Department of Agriculture, organic production systems emphasize the use of renewable resources and the conservation of soil and water to enhance environmental quality for future generations. Animals that are raised organically are not given antibiotics or artificial growth hormones. Organic food is produced without the use of most conventional pesticides, synthetic fertilizers, biotechnology, and irradiation. Organic farmers, handlers, and food processors must be inspected by government-approved certifiers to insure that all organic standards are met.

The organic movement is more than just an agricultural production system, however. One slogan of the organic movement is food with a face, a taste, and a place. It strives to be a fully integrated food system that connects farmers, local communities, and consumers, particularly through farmer's markets and community-supported agriculture. The organic movement shares many agrarian values as it espouses values of self-empowerment, social justice, economic gain, environmental health, creativity, autonomy, individualism, localism, and smallness. The challenge for organic agriculture, however, is whether these values can be maintained with growth, particularly as agribusinesses turn their attention to the growing organic industry.

THE FUTURE OF THE McDONALDIZATION OF AGRICULTURE

This chapter has demonstrated that, with a few exceptions, industrial agriculture is becoming increasingly McDonaldized, in that it seeks to make agriculture more efficient, calculable, and predictable, particularly through the use of nonhuman technologies, even though agriculture remains to a great extent an irrational industry. The analysis, however, has focused only on the production side of agriculture. Ritzer correctly points out that the McDonaldization process does have advantages, particularly for consumers. One advantage of industrial agriculture has been the production of an abundance of cheap food. Today's consumers, compared to previous generations, spend little of their disposable income on food. However, if one includes subsidies and the costs of the irrationalities of industrial agricultural production in the price of products, the actual price of food is much higher. And, it remains to be seen whether industrial agriculture can sustain the current level of productivity in the future. Another advantage of industrial agriculture and the globalization of food is the availability of products year round. Consumers are no longer tied to local and seasonal availability of foods.

Jean Kinsey noted several trends driving U.S. food demands, some of which favor the McDonaldization process and some of which may favor alternative methods of food production. Consumers demand more variety, homogeneous products worldwide, convenience, services from the public sector, environmentally friendly foods, and healthier foods. It remains to be seen whether the industrial model, particularly through the use of biotechnology, can make some of these demands become a reality or whether alternate food production systems, such as organic farming will become mainstream.

The trend toward the McDonaldization of agriculture is not limited to the United States. Like other industries, agriculture is becoming increasingly international. Just how far can the reach of McDonaldization be extended? In the case of agriculture, the answer to this question will likely be determined by the success or failure of biotechnology, and how well the ever-increasing irrationalities caused by the McDonaldization of agriculture can be addressed. The future of industrial agriculture seems to be putting all of its future eggs into one basket. Could it be that the long arm of McDonaldization may be reaching too far?

Thinking Critically

1. What are the advantages of McDonaldizing farms?

2. What are the disadvantages of McDonaldizing farms?

3. If you were a farmer, would you prefer to work on and/or own a McDonaldized or a non-McDonaldized farm?

4. If you were a farm animal, would you prefer to exist on a McDonaldized or a non-McDonaldized farm?

5. On balance, is McDonaldization good or bad for the consumer of U.S. farm products?

This chapter contains a recent essay in which John Drane extends the arguments of The McDonaldization of Society. *Drane concludes that the church is indeed highly McDonaldized and that this is one of the key sources of the crisis facing the church today. In fact, the church has a history of increasing rationalization that predates the advent of the fast-food restaurant by centuries; it is traceable to the earliest history of the church. A good example of the McDonaldization of the church, and an indicator of its current crisis, is the mega-church movement. Indeed, the church and McDonald's are seen as growing in tandem with one another and more alike over the last few decades. The culmination of this was the opening in 2001 of the first McDonald's franchise in a church—naturally, a mega-church. More generally, instead of offering spirituality and liberation, the church is seen as processing churchgoers in much the same way that fast-food restaurants process customers or hamburgers. Ironically, what is ostensibly the most human of social institutions has, like many other institutions, grown increasingly dehumanized.*

20

From Creeds to Burgers

Religious Control, Spiritual Search, and the Future of the World

John Drane

When I first read George Ritzer's pioneering work *The McDonaldization of Society*, I was—like many others—struck by the way in which his iconic notion of 'McDonaldization' captures so poignantly the sense of anxiety and futurelessness felt by people who struggle with life in an increasingly rationalized world, and it seemed an obvious step to speculate as to whether his insights could also add to our understanding of the predicament of the church in post-modern society. It soon became evident that McDonaldization, with its fourfold foundation of efficiency, calculability, predictability, and control, did indeed describe the way that many people experience the church, even if they are not values that all church leaders would self-consciously espouse as their guiding principles. Ritzer's description of the dehumanizing effects of McDonaldization expressed what many people who

Editor's Note: From Drane, J. (2005). From Creeds to Burgers. In J. A. Beckford & J. Wallis (Eds.). *Theorising Religion: Classical and Contemporary Debates.* Copyright © 2005, reprinted with permission from Ashgate Publishing.

abandon the church—and not a few who remain in it—complain about: 'Human beings, equipped with a wide array of skills and abilities, are asked to perform a limited number of highly simplified tasks over and over . . . forced to deny their humanity and act in a robot-like manner.'

More recently, Alan Jamieson's study of people who leave the church has provided empirical confirmation of what for me was originally no more than an informed guess. He reports countless conversations with leavers for whom the McDonaldized nature of church had been a significant catalyst—if not the major underlying reason—in their decision to abandon the institution, many of them claiming that this was a necessary part of their spiritual growth and development because, just as the fast-food industry had apparently devalued the experience of eating, so the church had become an unhelpful distraction in their desire to live out the Christian faith with integrity. One of Jamieson's interviewees (a former church minister) expressed this sense of spiritual frustration in terms that are almost a textbook summary of Ritzer's analysis of the angst felt by so many in relation to society at large:

> The person last night was essentially saying that their spirituality had dried up, and they wanted to get out of the church. They were saying they go through this rote every week. They come to church twice on Sundays, sing the songs and listen to the messages but their spirituality has dried up. They want to get out and get to something, not just another church, but something that brings their spirituality alive again. That really means something to them, with a deep conviction. It is not just a routine you go through . . .

I was not taken aback by this, because I had already argued that Ritzer's four marks of McDonaldization were present in the structures and attitudes of most churches. What did surprise me, however, was Ritzer's own surprise when he included my analysis in the first edition of *McDonaldization: The Reader* and posed the rhetorical question, 'Who would ever have thought that the church . . . could have been thought of as McDonaldized?' Though my original study highlighted the detail of everyday life in the average church—things like the conduct of worship, the collection of statistics, marketing strategies, the presentation of beliefs, and so on—there are many other aspects of contemporary church life that connect very directly with both the philosophical concepts behind McDonaldization and also the pragmatism of the fast-food industry which provided the source of the model. I shall suggest below that the cultural strands which together constitute the fabric of a McDonaldized society are in fact much older and more deeply rooted in western civilization than has generally been acknowledged, while recognizing that some of the most striking examples of the McDonaldization of the church have developed in parallel with ostensibly 'secular' trends, specifically that entrepreneurial mindset which has characterized the can-do culture of southern California since the 1950s and 1960s. The growth of the fast-food industry during that period has a number of uncanny parallels with the history of the church in the same time frame, including some overtly religious overtones to the way in which fast food has been packaged and promoted, as well as the adoption of McDonaldized marketing strategies by some churches.

One of the most noticeable developments in church life over the past fifty years has been the emergence of large churches with thousands of members and attenders (the so-called 'mega-church'). It is largely an American phenomenon, though one that is increasingly admired, if not copied, by churches in other parts of the world. The period of rapid growth of such churches during the 1990s matches the development of the fast food industry, which is unlikely to be a coincidence as they both tend to develop following the same formulaic pattern: entrepreneurial mavericks step outside the box of cultural conformity to imagine new ways of doing things, which then become rationalized in such a thoroughgoing way that the organization actually inhibits the kind of free thinking that led to its emergence in the first place. According to Charisma News Service (www.charisma.com) in 1970 there were only ten such mega-churches in the US, rising to 250 by 1990, and not far short of 800 by 2004 with many more aspiring to such status. The early promotion of the McDonald's restaurant chain incorporated so many echoes of both the language and underlying ideology of the church, particularly in its American free-market version, that it is hard to think that founder Ray Kroc was not consciously modeling his business on the religious attitudes which were familiar from the cultural matrix in which he operated. Like the founder of a new faith, he often insisted that franchisees sever ties with other business enterprises, and offered them a restaurant well away from their homes so as to encourage them to leave behind other commitments and be single-minded in their devotion. In his memoirs, Kroc invokes overtly religious language to describe the processes of food preparation, so that cooking fries becomes 'a ritual to be followed religiously.' Even the golden arches apparently convey a quasi-spiritual nurturing message as a portrayal of 'mother McDonald's breasts,' while a cartoon character on the McDonald's Web site in 1998 told children that Ronald McDonald, like God, was 'the ultimate authority in everything.' It was therefore almost inevitable that sooner or later church and McDonald's would come together, the only surprise being that it took until 2001 before what was hailed as the world's first McDonald's franchise to be situated within a church complex opened at Brentwood Baptist Church in Houston, Texas—itself a mega-church.

The irony of such a development has not passed unnoticed. James L. Evans is a Baptist leader whose vision of Christian faith is clearly somewhat different from that offered at Brentwood:

It's a development rich in irony. Christianity began as a home-based religious movement. Now the faith boasts of mega-churches that actually draw people out of their homes and into buildings called "family life centers," or in Brentwood's case, "community life centers." Christianity began as a movement of hope symbolized by the sharing of a simple fellowship meal of wine and bread. Now the faith has become a complex corporate-like affair, with such heavy demands on members that fast food must be provided so everyone can get to their meetings.

Moreover, he proposes that there is something intrinsically incompatible between this and what he regards as authentic Christian values: 'If we are where we eat, we are alone, watching without touching other diners as we all we all hurry off to our next meeting. It's sad if we think about it. The meal used to be the meeting.' In other words, McDonaldization and church do not mix: to embrace the one, the other is forced to deny its core values.

This is the same criticism that is increasingly now leveled at the fast-food industry itself. While the advertising images depict happy families spending quality time together, there is a growing recognition that the reality for many is uncontrollable obesity and declining health, if not an early death—something that even the food companies are now taking seriously, with a switch to menus offering 'healthier' portions and even vegetarian options. But the application of an ideology based on efficiency, calculability, predictability and control is by no means restricted to fast food. On the contrary, it is virtually ubiquitous throughout Western culture, and the more it spreads the more dangerous the world becomes. This is not the time or place for it, but in due course it will be interesting to apply this thesis to the events surrounding the toppling of Saddam Hussein from power in Iraq in 2003, or for that matter to the concerns about asylum-seekers that have dominated the domestic British headlines throughout the early years of this century. Difference and diversity are no longer regarded as a cause for celebration—nor even for natural curiosity about other people's ways of being—but traits to be ironed out and replaced by the bland canvas of homogeneity. Schlosser puts into words what many intuitively feel when he comments that 'An economic system promising freedom has too often become a means of denying it, as the narrow dictates of the market gain precedence over more important democratic values.'

If we were to substitute 'religious' for 'economic,' 'institution' for 'market,' and 'gospel' for 'democratic,' we would have a statement which for many people encapsulates the predicament in which the church now finds itself. For those who prefer to be 'spiritual' rather than 'religious,' the church—like much in contemporary Western culture—appears to have denied its own core values, and has ended up processing people rather than liberating them, even imprisoning God in prescriptive propositional formulas rather than recognizing that, whoever or whatever 'God' might be, it is certainly a contradiction in terms to conceive of him or her in terms of anything that is remotely connected to the four marks of McDonaldization. Like the prevailing culture, the church is still to a remarkable degree in a state of denial about this reality. Contemporary hymn books are full of songs declaring that Christians are 'taking ground' and 'claiming the land' and happy-clappy worshipers sing them with gusto—while their churches are dying on their feet! This is the same kind of self-delusion as restaurant owners who manage to ignore the true cost of their practices by refusing to contemplate the environmental and human cost of the farming and employment methods that they have encouraged over recent decades. Even a sympathetic observer like Peter Brierley, commenting on the declining level of church involvement in England, paints a bleak picture: 'I am a statistician, not a theologian. The numbers in this book show a haemorrhage akin to a burst artery. The country is littered with people who used to go to church but no longer do. We could well bleed to death. The tide is running out. At the present rate of change we are one generation from extinction.'

The ease with which what are increasingly perceived as dehumanizing trends in the marketplace can be paralleled within the churches is a major challenge for those Christians who believe they have a contribution to make to the future well-being of the planet and its people. To put it simply, if the church merely offers more of the same McDonaldized way of being, then why would any reasonable person want to connect with it? Not all Christians think about these questions, of course, but among some who do there is a tendency to imagine that the problems now being encountered have come about as a result of what they like to label the 'secularization' of the church, by which they generally mean its adoption of values and attitudes that in some way are intrinsically 'un-Christian,' usually identified with 'the Enlightenment.' Not only is 'the Enlightenment' itself a disputed category, but we also need to take seriously the insights of Weber and the likelihood that the tendency toward rationalization (of which McDonaldization is just a particular, exaggerated form) derives, at least in part, from the legacy of the Protestant Reformation, particularly in its Calvinist manifestation (Weber 1930). That being the case, if the church is to escape the effects of McDonaldization, it will be required to engage in a more far-reaching self-examination. For if, in some measure, the church has contributed to the store of raw materials out of which the iron cage has been constructed, it was probably inevitable that sooner or later it would come to be regarded not as part of the solution, but as part of the problem.

Because of the neat fit between McDonaldization and cultural trends since the 1960s, it is often assumed that these tendencies emerged only in the second half of the 20th century or, at most, were the natural outcome of the assembly-line mentality associated with Fordism a few decades earlier. . . .

. . . The signs of McDonaldization are not hard to find more or less throughout the history of the church. The ideology of the British empire owed a good deal to the memory of Christendom, which in turn had been modeled on the Roman empire and from which it took its philosophical and technological inspiration. When viewed within this frame of reference, enterprises such as the Crusades can be understood as a manifestation of the same organizational tendencies so neatly encapsulated in Ritzer's emphasis on efficiency, calculability, predictability and control. Even further back, one might use the same perspective to understand the many internal ecclesiastical battles that took place between the second and the fourth centuries, leading to the definition of a clear canon of sacred scripture, centralization of power in the hands of bishops, and eventually the formalized statements of Christian belief known as the creeds—all of which put together had the effect of creating a monolithic, McDonaldized institution with clear definitions of who could do what, and how and when. Though Ritzer is surely correct in proposing that in its present form McDonaldization would not have emerged without the development of scientific technology, in terms of the impact that an imposed rationalization has on the human spirit, it might plausibly be argued that these episodes in the life of the church promoted a McDonaldized spirituality in a more extreme form than anything we have witnessed in recent decades. In more ancient times, all roads led to Rome, which also means they led from Rome and facilitated the dissemination of such a one-world ideology. McDonald's Hamburger University in Oak Brook, Illinois, is only a pale reflection of the educational powerhouse of ancient Rome.

Thinking Critically

1. Assuming you are a religious person, would the McDonaldization of the church attract or repel you?

2. Why should we not be surprised that the church has McDonaldized?

3. What might a non-McDonaldized church look like? Are there any examples?

4. What religious goals are facilitated by McDonaldization?

5. What religious goals are impeded by McDonaldization?

Politics occupies our attention in Chapter 21. Bryan Turner discusses the ways in which McDonaldization leads to "thin"/"cool" politics: that is, political activity that is thin—"superficial, transient, and simple" and cool—the opposite of hot politics that involve "hysteria, effervescence, mystical trances, and spiritual possession" (see Chapter 25, "Jihad vs. McWorld," in Part III). Modern hot loyalty and thick solidarity are associated with the kinds of ethnic political conflicts that we associate with Northern Ireland, Kosovo, Afghanistan and now, Iraq. Most modern societies, however, are characterized by "cooler modes of identification and thinner forms of solidarity." The latter might be described as "drive-in democracy" with cool assumptions about how committed people should be to political causes. Turner also associates the latter with "ironic liberalism." Ironic liberals refuse to be committed to grand political visions and ambitious efforts at social reform. They are opposed to inflicting pain in the name of a political cause. Their political detachment is related to Turner's notion of "drive-in democracy."

Given this argument, Turner points to the positive side of McDonaldization, at least in the political sphere. That is, he views hot loyalty and thick homogeneity in politics as hazardous in the contemporary world. They are likely to lead to dangerous conflagrations at the local level that have the potential to become much wider conflicts. Instead, Turner urges that we turn to McDonald's for our political models. A McDonaldized model of politics would lead to "cool cosmopolitans with ironic vocabularies" who would not only be averse to actions that might lead to political conflagration but would in fact serve as preventives to such conflagrations. Thus, Turner comes down, at least ironically, on the side of "global McCitizenship."

21

McCitizens

Risk, Coolness, and Irony in Contemporary Politics

Bryan S. Turner

◆◆◆ ───

While Ritzer's position is [not] overtly political, I want to suggest . . . that his approach to McDonaldization might present us with a fruitful and important perspective on the requirements of citizenship (as a form of cultural lifestyle) in globalized social systems. . . .

I want therefore to suggest a more interesting reading of Ritzer by an examination of eating styles in McDonald's as a metaphor for political commitments in a global and multicultural environment. There is obviously an important difference between eating and its social role in modern societies by contrast with traditional societies. In presenting this difference between a continuum that ranges from the orgy to a McDonald's snack, I draw upon . . . the emergence of the reflexive self with the growth of consumerism, because the modern self is produced through the notion of unlimited

Editor's Note: Excerpts from "McCitizens" by Bryan S. Turner, pp. 83–100, in *Resisting McDonaldization*, edited by Barry Smarr. Copyright © 1999 by Sage Ltd., London. Used with permission.

consumption. The consuming self with its insatiable desires is elaborated through and by the consumer industry. Changing patterns of food consumption are an important part of this evolving self. In traditional societies, the self was closely bound into the rituals of social solidarity, associated with festival. The ritual meal sacrifice in the Abrahamic religions was the basis of the bond between God and humans and between people. Eating together was a fundamental basis of social order in which the exchange of gifts (especially food) took place. In Christianity, the bread and wine are exchanged as symbols of the sacred gift of body and blood.

If we treat McDonaldization as a secularization of religious patterns of friendship and familiarity associated with sacred meals, then the McDonald's snack represents a privatized and individualistic pattern of consumption which does not aim to build bonds of belonging. Brand loyalty does not lead to the creation of societies. McDonaldization involves a limited menu, precise measurements of food, the standardization of taste, and the elimination of surprises; it stands at the opposite end of a continuum from ritualized orgy.

I wish to argue that ... we can compare and contrast these traditional and religious patterns of eating with the modern fast-food restaurant in terms of two dichotomies: thick/thin solidarity and hot/cool commitments. Traditional religious festivals generate a thick solidarity, characterized by its intensity, duration, and complexity; ritualized meals take place within and produce patterns of social solidarity such as brotherhoods, tribes, and communities. The social solidarity of eating in McDonald's is superficial, transient, and simple. McDonaldization produces global identities and images (the Big M), but these create thin communities. At the same time, the commitments of tribal festivals are hot; they involve hysteria, effervescence, mystical trances, and spiritual possession.

Eating in McDonald's requires the participants to be cool. Customers form short queues and assemble quickly to give their orders, they retire to their tables in well-regulated movements, and they sit quietly eating their standardized and predictable meals. There are no expectations that the meal will receive an applause. The regulated patterns and general silence are punctuated only by the occasional children's birthday parties where party uniforms are issued to small groups of children. These social forms are thin and cool. In terms of conventional sociology, participation in McDonald's outlets has many of the features ... of "role distance," where social actors learn techniques of subjective neutrality. University professors out with their children for Saturday lunch at McDonald's learn to show to others that they are not really there. These patterns of coolness of commitment and thin solidarity offer a model of social interaction which perfectly conforms to the emerging patterns of global citizenship.

We can briefly trace the development of Western citizenship through four broad historical stages. In medieval society, the status of citizen in the city-state was more or less equivalent to denizen. It involved minimal privileges of immunity and a limited range of obligations. Although there was considerable pride in civility within the city walls, there was little notion of city identity and membership (cool commitments and identity). There was, however, a density of social involvement within the narrow confines of the city (in the guilds, for example) which resulted in thick membership. Modern citizenship as we know it really started with the nation-state, which through doctrines of nationalism in the 19th century encouraged hot nationalist commitment in order to create a homogeneous community as the base of the state. The nation-state attempted to overcome internal divisions within civil society (religion, ethnicity, and regional membership) to forge patterns of thick solidarity. These patterns of involvement were threatened by class divisions, but under welfare capitalism the welfare state functioned to reduce class divisions and to enhance commitment to the state. Finally, with the growth of a world economy and the globalization of cultures, the increase in migration, trade, and tourism creates a more diverse culture and multiple political loyalties. For example, there is an increase in dual citizenship. With globalization, the traditional forms of hot loyalty and thick solidarity become irrelevant to modern citizenship forms; indeed, hot loyalties of a national or local variety can often become dangerous in a world system which needs tolerance as a functional basis of political interaction. The ethnic conflicts of Eastern Europe, Russia, and Northern Ireland can be understood in terms of the negative consequences of hot nationalist loyalties in societies which require cooler modes of identification and thinner forms of solidarity. Global citizenship, organized around high levels of labor migration, might form a cultural pattern which is parallel to McDonald's—political loyalties should be formed on the assumption of high mobility in which citizens would enjoy the privileges of a drive-in democracy, which in turn had cool assumptions about the level of political commitment.

These assumptions also fit the . . . view of "private irony and liberal hope." An ironist is a person who believes that his or her "final vocabulary" is always open to criticism and revision. Ironists are nominalists and historicists, and as a result they do not believe there is a natural order to which language approximates. An ironist is skeptical about the legitimacy of "grand narratives" and hence there is a similarity between varieties of postmodernism and language theory. In political terms, the latter is also minimalistic—liberals support "bourgeois freedoms" as a basic level for social consensus not because liberalism is true but simply because it offers opportunities for self-creation and personal liberties. Ironic liberals do not commit themselves to a grand vision of history and social reform. Their basic assumption is that the worst thing we can do to another person is to inflict pain by an act of intentional cruelty. In short, ironists are cool about their commitment to political systems, they do not feel that thick solidarity is necessarily helpful in the realization of personal freedoms, and their detachment from traditional ideologies (especially nationalism) has an elective affinity with the concept of a drive-in McDemocracy.

. . .

The quest for community has been particularly powerful in the imagination of political philosophers where the legacy of a small Greek democracy continues to haunt the debate about democratic participation. Now Greek democracy, like Protestant sects, requires hot commitments and thick solidarities; modern democracy, as we know, presupposes large nation-states, mass audiences, ethnic pluralism, mass migrations, and globalized systems of communication. Hot democratic identities are probably dangerous in such an environment; where, to continue with this metaphor, nationalist fervor can fan the coals of ethnic hatred and difference. Bosnia, Cambodia, and Algeria are contemporary examples of the quest for thick homogeneity and hot loyalty in societies which are in fact subject to forces of global diversification. If we were to seek out a metaphor for modern citizenship, we may be better to look neither to Athens nor Jerusalem . . . but to McDonald's for our political models of association. Modern societies probably need cool cosmopolitans with ironic vocabularies if they are to avoid the conflagration of nationalistic versions of political authenticity and membership.

Thinking Critically

1. In what ways is the world threatened by non-McDonaldized politics?

2. In what ways is the world threatened by McDonaldized politics?

3. What are the links between McDonaldized/non-McDonaldized politics and 9/11?

4. If we are moving toward a drive-in democracy, what does that auger for the future of democracy in the US?

5. Can you envision a world in which the major division is between those governments that are McDonaldized and those that are not?

The issue of consumption in general, and as it relates to McDonaldization, is closely tied to production and work in many ways (e.g., the earlier discussion of consumers as workers). However, it is important to keep these topics distinct, especially because of the increasing importance of consumption in the contemporary world and because the idea of McDonaldization has such strong roots in the world of consumption. This chapter offers an excerpt from my 2005 book, Enchanting a Disenchanted World: Revolutionizing the Means of Consumption. *Means of consumption (also called "cathedrals of consumption") are settings or places that allow people to consume goods and services. The focus is on the "new" means of consumption, those created in the United States in the half century after the close of World War II. Of course, the chains of fast-food restaurants (1955) are one of the new means, as are fully enclosed shopping malls (1956), megamalls (1981), superstores (e.g., Toys 'R Us, 1957), theme parks (1955), cruise ships (1966), and casino-hotels (1946). One central point is that all the cathedrals of consumption, not just the fast-food restaurants, are highly McDonaldized (or rationalized), and they all produce a variety of irrationalities of rationality.*

What is new here is the discussion of the link between these McDonaldized systems and disenchantment. That is, rationalized systems seek to remove all magic, mystery, and enchantment from their operations. For example, to operate efficiently, McDonaldized systems seek to eliminate any form of enchantment that impedes the efficient operation of the system. Or predictability is anathema to any sense of enchantment that, almost by definition, must be unpredictable.

Interestingly, although McDonaldization leads to disenchantment, there is a sense in which McDonaldization can be enchanting. For example, the efficiency of McDonald's or FedEx can seem quite magical as consumers marvel over how quickly their meals arrive or packages are delivered. On the FedEx Web site, one can see the various stops a package makes en route to its destination and find out the precise time of its arrival. Consumers can be similarly amazed that the Big Mac they ate in New York today is identical to the one they had in Tokyo the day before. Perhaps no aspect of McDonaldization is more seemingly magical than the nonhuman technologies. Thus, the modern cruise ship appears to be a technological marvel encompassing so many different things and so many passengers and crew that it is a wonder it can even float, let alone provide so many different types of entertainment (and so much food) to so many people.

22

Cathedrals of Consumption

Rationalization, Enchantment, and Disenchantment

George Ritzer

◆◆◆ ─────────────────────────────────────

O ne of the concepts used to describe the settings of concern . . . is *means of consumption*. These settings, as means, allow us to consume a wide range of goods and services. . . . These places do more than simply permit us to consume things; they are structured to lead and even coerce us into consumption. . . .

The *new means of consumption* are, in the main, settings that have come into existence or taken new forms since the end of World War II and that, building on but going beyond earlier settings, have dramatically transformed the nature of consumption. Because of important continuities, it is not always easy to clearly distinguish between new and older means of consumption.

The concept . . . *cathedrals of consumption* . . . points up the quasi-religious, "enchanted" nature of these new settings. They have become locales to which we make "pilgrimages" in order to practice our consumer religion. . . .

Editor's Note: Excerpts from *Enchanting a Disenchanted World: Revolutionizing the Means of Consumption*, 2nd ed. by George Ritzer. Copyright © 2005 by Pine Forge Press, Thousand Oaks, CA. Used with permission.

This . . . chapter is divided into two sections. First, I will link rationalization (McDonaldization) to the disenchantment of these settings. Second, I will deal with the degree to which rationalized systems can, themselves, be enchanting. Overarching all of this is the problem of continuing to attract, control, and exploit customers. Rationalization is needed to accomplish these objectives on a large scale, but the resultant disenchantment can have the opposite effect. . . .

LINKING RATIONALIZATION TO DISENCHANTMENT

. . . The process of rationalization leads, by definition, to the disenchantment of the settings in which it occurs. The term clearly implies the loss of a quality—enchantment—that was at one time very important to people. Although we undoubtedly have gained much from the rationalization of society in general, and the means of consumption in particular, we also have lost something of great, if hard to define, value.

Efficient systems have no room for anything smacking of enchantment and systematically seek to root it out of all aspects of their operation. Anything that is magical, mysterious, fantastic, dreamy, and so on is apt to be inefficient. Enchanted systems typically involve highly convoluted means to whatever end is involved. Furthermore, enchanted worlds may well exist without any obvious goals at all. Efficient systems, also by definition, do not permit such meanderings, and designers and implementers will do whatever is necessary to eliminate them. The elimination of meanderings and aimlessness is one of the reasons that rationalized systems were, for Weber, disenchanted systems.

. . . One major aspect of efficiency is using the customer as an unpaid worker. It is worth noting that all of the mystery associated with an operation is removed when consumers perform it themselves; after all, they know exactly what they did. Mystery is far more likely when others perform such tasks, and consumers are unable to see precisely what they do. What transpires in the closed kitchen of a gourmet restaurant is far more mysterious than the "cooking" that takes place in the open kitchen of a fast-food restaurant, to say nothing of the tasks consumers perform in such settings.

The same point applies to employees of rationalized systems. Their work is broken down into a series of steps, the best way to perform each step is discovered, and then all workers are taught to perform each step in that way. There is no mystery in any of this for the employee, who more or less unthinkingly follows the dictates of the organization. There is little or no room for any creative problem solving on the job, much less any sense of enchantment.

With regard to *calculability*, in the main, enchantment has far more to do with quality than quantity. Magic, fantasies, dreams, and the like relate more to the inherent nature of an experience and the qualitative aspects of that experience than, for example, to the number of such experiences one has. An emphasis on producing and participating in a large number of experiences tends to diminish the magical quality of each of them. Put another way, it is difficult to imagine the mass production of magic, fantasy, and dreams. Such mass production may be common in the movies, but magic is more difficult, if not impossible, to produce in settings designed to deliver large numbers of goods and services frequently and over great geographic spaces. The mass production of such things is virtually guaranteed to undermine their enchanted qualities. This is a fundamental dilemma facing the new means of consumption.

Take, for example, the shows that are put on over and over by the various new means of consumption—the "Beauty and the Beast" show at Disney World, the sea battle in front of the Treasure Island casino-hotel in Las Vegas, or the night club shows on cruise ships. The fact that they must be performed over and over tends to turn them into highly mechanical performances in which whatever "magic" they produce stems from the size of the spectacle and the technologies associated with them rather than the quality of the performers and their performances.

. . .

No characteristic of rationalization is more inimical to enchantment than *predictability*. Magical, fantastic, or dream-like experiences are almost by definition unpredictable. Nothing would destroy an enchanted experience more easily than having it become predictable.

The Disney theme parks sought to eliminate the unpredictability of the midway at an old-fashioned amusement park such as Coney Island with its milling crowds, disorder, and debris. Instead, Disney World built a setting defined by cleanliness, orderliness, predictability, and—some would say—sterility. Disney has successfully destroyed the old form of enchantment and in its place created a new, highly predictable form of entertainment. As the many fans of Disney World will attest, there is enchantment there, but it is a very different, mass-produced, assembly-line form, consciously fabricated and routinely produced over and over rather than emerging spontaneously from the interaction among visitors, employees, and the park itself.

. . .

Both *control* and the *nonhuman technologies* that produce it tend to be inimical to enchantment. As a general rule, fantasy, magic, and dreams cannot be subjected to external controls; indeed, autonomy is much of what gives them their enchanted quality. Fantastic experiences can go anywhere; anything can happen. Such unpredictability clearly is not possible in a tightly controlled environment. It is possible that tight and total control can be a fantasy, but for many it would be more a nightmare than a dream. Much the same can be said of nonhuman technologies. Such cold, mechanical systems are usually the antitheses of the dream worlds associated with enchantment. Again, it is true that there are fantasies associated with nonhuman technologies, but they too tend to be more nightmarish than dream-like.

An interesting example of the replacement of human with nonhuman technology is currently taking place in Las Vegas. Shows in the old casino-hotels used to feature major stars such as Frank Sinatra and Elvis Presley. One could argue that such stars had charisma; they had an enchanted relationship with their fans. Now the emphasis has shifted to huge, tightly choreographed (i.e., predictable) extravaganzas without individual stars. For example, the Rio Hotel and Casino features "ballet dancers who bounce, toes pointed, from bungee cords, hooked to the casino ceiling . . . [and] a mechanical dolphin that dives from aloft with a rider playing Lady Godiva." The focus is on the nonhuman technology (which controls the performers) and not on the individuals performing the acts. The performers in such extravaganzas are easily replaceable; they are interchangeable parts.

The point of this section has been to argue that increasing rationalization is related to, if not inextricably intertwined with, disenchantment. However, as we shall see, there are aspects of rationalization that actually heighten enchantment.

RATIONALIZATION AS ENCHANTMENT

There is no question that although rationalized systems lead in various ways to disenchantment, they paradoxically and simultaneously serve to create their own kinds of enchantment. We should bear in mind that this enchantment varies in terms of time and place. Because these settings are now commonplace to most of the readers of this book, few of them (especially fast-food restaurants) are likely to be thought of as enchanting. However, it should be remembered that they still enchant children, as they did us for some time (and, in many cases, may still); it is certainly the case that they enchanted our parents and grandparents; and they are found enchanting in other societies to which they are newly exported. It is also worth remembering that there are degrees of enchantment; Disney World and Las Vegas are undoubtedly seen by most as more enchanting than Wal-Mart and the Sears catalog.

Reflect for a moment on the highly rationalized, and therefore presumably disenchanted, setting of Sam's Club and other warehouse stores. What could be more disenchanting than stores built to look like warehouses—comparatively cold, spare, and inelegant? Compare them to the "dream worlds" of early department stores like Bon Marché. Great effort was made to make the latter warm, well-appointed, and elegant settings that helped enflame the consumer's fantasies—in a word, enchanting. Sam's Club has gone to great lengths in the opposite direction; it seems to have sought to create as rationalized and disenchanted a setting as possible. It comes strikingly close, in the realm of retailing, to Weber's image of the rational cage.

Yet this disenchanted structure produces another kind of fantasy—that of finding oneself set loose in a warehouse piled to the ceiling with goods that, if they are not free, are made out to be great bargains. It is a cold, utilitarian fantasy, but a fantasy nonetheless. As a general rule, disenchanted structures have not eliminated fantasies but, rather, replaced older fantasies with more contemporary ones. The new, rationalized fantasies involve getting a lot of things at low prices rather than the fantasies associated with the older department stores that might involve imagining what it would be like to wear elegant clothing or to surround one's self with luxurious home furnishings.

. . .

Perhaps the ultimate in the capacity of the rationalization of the new means of consumption to enchant us comes from their advanced *technologies*. Although at one time enchantment stemmed from human wizards or magicians, it now stems from the wizardry of modern robotic and computerized technology. Ultimately, it is the technology of the modern cruise line, the Las Vegas casino, and Disney World that astounds us, not the humans who happen to work in these settings or the things they do. Our amazement can stem from the technologies themselves or from what they produce. We can, for example, marvel over how McDonald's French fries always look and taste the same. Or we can be impressed by the fact that Wal-Mart's shelves are always so well-stocked.

. . .

Are the contemporary fantasies associated with rational systems as satisfying as those conjured up in the past? This is a complex and highly controversial issue. Clearly, the huge number of people who flock to the new means of consumption find them quite magical. However, it is fair to wonder whether rationally produced enchantment is truly enchanting or whether it is as enchanting as the less rational, more human, forms of enchantment that it tends to squeeze out. We might ask whether one of the *irrational* consequences of all of this is that these contemporary fantasies come closer to nightmares than did their predecessors. After all, it is far harder to think of a nightmare associated with an elegant department store than with a warehouse. In any case, it is clear that rationally produced enchantment is deemed [by many to be] insufficient. . . .

Thinking Critically

1. Can you think of places like shopping malls as cathedrals?

2. Can you conceive of consumption as a kind of religious activity?

3. Do you find the cathedrals of consumption enchanting? In what ways?

4. What devices do those cathedrals employ to make themselves seem enchanted?

5. Do you find rationalization/McDonaldization enchanting? In what ways?

Next, Steven Miles deals with the relationship between primarily youthful consumers and what he calls the global sports store (one of the new means, or cathedrals, of consumption discussed earlier). On the one hand, Miles sees many elements of McDonaldization in these settings. For example, the sports store he studied is part of an international chain of about 5,000 such stores, and the corporation seeks to present the shop in a standardized way that makes the setup of each store quite predictable to those who have visited other stores in the chain. Similar uniformity and predictability is found among the sales staff, who must abide by a dress code—everyone must wear the prescribed uniform. Scripts exist to make sure that employees say just what they are supposed to say.

The main thrust of Miles's essay, however, is to take the McDonaldization thesis to task for ignoring the way in which consumers experience, negotiate, and use the sports store. In other words, they are not merely controlled by the McDonaldized structure of the store, they actively create meaning for themselves within such settings. Rather than being controlled by McDonaldization, young consumers use its well-established parameters to create their sense of individuality with little risk posed to them. To put it in academic terms, McDonaldized structures do not simply constrain consumers (and others), but they also enable them to do things they otherwise would not be able to do. While the world outside may seem risky (few jobs, family life that is difficult to negotiate), the world inside the McDonaldized sports store seems much safer (i.e., predictable). Thus, Miles sees McDonaldization as beneficial in this sense (and perhaps many others), whereas he sees my work as focusing on its negative aspects.

23

McDonaldization and the Global Sports Store

Constructing Consumer Meanings in a Rationalized Society

Steven Miles

◆◆◆

THE SPORTS STORE AS "SELLING MACHINE"?

... The store in which I worked was efficient in the sense that though it was not located in an actual mall, it was in a prime location: a pedestrianized collection of high-order stores in the center of a northern English industrial town. Indeed, it is worth pointing out at this point that British shopping centers are extremely predictable and uniform, perhaps even more so than their North American counterparts. The town in which my research was located is overwhelmingly dominated by the ubiquitous chain store. This, as Ritzer points out, has the advantage of predictability, inasmuch as during a shopping excursion the consumer knows what to expect and where to expect it. However, the converse effect is that both the shopping center and the

Editor's Note: Excerpts from "McDonaldization and the Global Sports Store: Constructing Consumer Meanings in a Rationalized Society" by Steven Miles, pp. 53–65 in *McDonaldization Revisited* by Mark Alfino et al. Copyright © 1998 by Greenwood Press, Westport, CT. Used with permission.

individual consumer using that center lose the opportunity to impact a certain degree of spontaneity and creativity into the shopping experience.

The convenience of predictability is reemphasized within the actual setting of the sports store itself. . . . The customer should not be surprised if he or she were to enter one branch of the store in North America and another on his or her vacation in Great Britain, only to find the same items on sale in the same replicated layout.

The predictability of the shopping experience is personified by the actual sales assistants themselves. Local color and flavor simply do not fit into the rationalized world of the sports store sales assistant. The store concerned abides by a very strict dress or uniform code, the nature of which is determined by the Head Office. Uniforms are provided by the company, and there is a definite determination on their part to portray a common image throughout its stores. There is no room for any display of individuality in this context.

As for the actual stock, this too displays some of the characteristics Ritzer associates with rationalization. The manager of the branch in which I worked has limited control over the stock coming into his store. The company as a whole has a universal stocking policy within which there is little room for flexibility. . . .

Once new stock does arrive and once the consumer sits down to try on a new pair of training shoes, he or she is not encouraged to hang around. Reminiscent of the uncomfortable seats that Ritzer argues are characteristic of the "get 'em in and get 'em out" mentality of McDonald's, the sports store offers its customers an extremely uninviting bench which discourages any intention to loiter, thereby maximizing the efficiency of the "selling machine."

This notion of predictability is further emphasized when you consider the atmosphere that the management actively seeks to promote in its stores. All branches of the sports store concerned are dominated by a large TV monitor overlooking the shop floor. This acts as a magnet for passing customers. . . . And this helps to create a relatively straightforward means of perpetuating a superficial feeling, on the part of the customer, of personal familiarity with what it is to experience in this particular store.

In many respects then, it could be argued that the foundations of rationalization, and in particular, predictability, are crucial to the sports store experience. . . .

The company concerned adopted an unwritten law that all customers should be "greeted" (or should that read "controlled"?) within three minutes of entering the store. In this sense, the shopping experience is a predictable one, though the fact that assistants are encouraged to embellish such predictability with a personal edge is clearly intended to convince the consumer otherwise. Sales assistants receive a large amount of customer-service training and are told that under no circumstances should they approach a customer and say "How can I help you?" The managerial preference is that they ask something like "Hi, how are you doing today?" altering their tack according to circumstances and, more important, according to the "needs" of the customer concerned.

THE SPORTS STORE AS "MEANING MACHINE"?

. . . I want to argue that . . . the McDonaldization thesis is, in fact, misleading, in that though at a superficial level the experience of the sports store may appear to be McDonaldized, the actual relationships young consumers have with that store and the products it offers are far more subjective than Ritzer is prepared to concede. I would suggest, in fact, that young consumers are at least partially aware of the rationalized nature of the consuming experience and actually use that experience to their own personal and communal advantage. McDonaldized experience is negotiated in the sense that young people use the goods available on the marketplace (which, in turn, are often produced, at least partly, as a reaction to what is acceptable to consumers "on the street") as a means of constructing their own sense of everyday stability. McDonaldized consumption offers producers the profits they aspire to, while serving a pragmatic function for the consumers they are targeting.

An overriding theme that emerged throughout my research was the way in which young people appear to deny the existence of any pressure to buy particular models of training shoe for their fashion value and yet readily become involved in the craze to buy them. This might be seen to reflect the standardized nature of contemporary forms of consumption, but what I want to argue is that, in fact, in this respect, McDonaldization is positively *embraced* by young people. Far from wanting to express their individuality through sports goods *per se*—thereby being ensnared by the standardized nature of the goods and the services provided for them—young people are more concerned with establishing their individuality according to youth cultural parameters that are already well established and therefore involve minimal risk on their part. They actively embrace the predictable nature of the consuming experience, and the actual process of consumption, because it gives them a sense of *control*. Young people gain benefit from their consumption experiences precisely *because* such experiences are rationalized. As I [next] explain, . . . such an argument can be further developed in the context of debates regarding the existence of a "risk society.". . .

The argument that consumers are experiencing an increasingly unpredictable social life appears, at first glance, to directly contradict Ritzer's vision of a highly predictable rationalized world. My argument is that the trends that Ritzer actually describes are far more psychosocially beneficial than he is willing to admit. In effect, as I suggested earlier, Ritzer underestimates the ways in which structures of McDonaldization can be actively negotiated. The structures of McDonaldization are, in this sense, enabling equally as much as they are constraining. In fact, the individual is constituted in an increasingly global culture which appears to offer a greater diversity of lifestyle choices. McDonaldization amounts to a means by which consumers can begin to assert some sense of control over the *diversity* of modern life.

By immersing themselves in consumer-led experiences, young people appear to be able to forget about the stresses inherent in the prospects of a dilapidated labor market, divided families, and limited resources. Consumption, which is made possible through part-time employment and parental pocket money, appears to offer some form of an escape, an idea that . . . is equally applicable to the more specific enjoyment children experience in a visit to a McDonald's. But the use of the word "escape" should not imply that young people are simply leaving that risk behind. In viewing it in this way consumption could be perceived to be an easy option, a means of avoiding the harsh realities characteristic of an identity crisis. This, I believe, is an oversimplification. More than simply opting out of a risky lifestyle, consumption actually appears to provide young people with a sense of control, a means of offsetting risk. But the irony here is that the risks inherent in social pressures to consume are potentially riskier than everyday experience itself. Young people find themselves in a predicament where, to a large extent, they *have* to consume in particular ways. Ultimately, this does not simply mean that they are controlled but, rather, that they choose to trade a sense of individuality for the sense of stability that is offered to them through their consumption habits.

As far as young people are concerned then, the McDonaldization of the sports store can, therefore, actually be perceived to be liberating. Upon entering the sports store the young people I observed were able to forget, indeed, escape from, their everyday concerns. They became immersed in another culture, a culture symbolized by the street life portrayed by MTV. In a world characterized by insecurity and uncertainty as to the future, as well as the present, young people can open this "window of stability" and enter a whole new world—a world in which, regardless of family background or work prospects, they can be treated as equals, in the sense that they have equal access, depending upon resources, to the cultural capital of consumption.

Thinking Critically

1. In what ways do you go about creating meaning in a setting like a global sports store (e.g., Nike)?

2. Do you find the predictability of these settings attractive?

3. In what ways does their predictability inhibit you from creating meaning in them?

4. Are you aware, or do you even care, that your local sports store may be highly McDonaldized?

5. Do you care that sports stores and all the other cathedrals of consumption use McDonaldization to become selling machines; to sell you more than you might want to buy?

Remaining within the realm of consumption, the final essay of Part II is an excerpt from another of my books, Expressing America: A Critique of the Global Credit Card Society *(1995). I analyze one of the keys to the modern consumer society, the credit card, from the point of view of the McDonaldization thesis. The credit card has McDonaldized the consumer loan business and it, in turn, has led to the rationalization of other types of loans, such as automobile and home equity loans. More generally, it has played a central role in McDonaldizing the entire banking business with, for example, a nonhuman technology, the ATM, progressively replacing human tellers as a source of cash. The bulk of this excerpt is concerned with analyzing the credit card from the perspective of each dimension of McDonaldization, as well as from the vantage point of the irrationality of rationality.*

24

Credit Cards, Fast-Food Restaurants, and Rationalization

George Ritzer

◆◆◆ ───

The credit card, like the fast-food restaurant, is not only a part of this process of rationalization but is also a significant force in the development and spread of rationalization. Just as McDonald's rationalized the delivery of prepared food, the credit card rationalized (or "McDonaldized") the consumer loan business. Prior to credit cards, the process of obtaining loans was slow, cumbersome, and nonrationalized. But obtaining a modern credit card (which can be thought of as a collateralized consumer loan) is now a very efficient process, often requiring little more than filling out a short questionnaire. With credit bureaus and computerization, credit records can be checked and applications approved (or disapproved) very rapidly. Furthermore, the unpredictability of loan approval has been greatly reduced

Editor's Note: Excerpts from "Credit Cards, Fast-Food Restaurants, and Rationalization" by George Ritzer, pp. 129–156, in *Expressing America: A Critique of the Global Credit Card Society* by George Ritzer. Copyright © 1995 by Pine Forge Press, Thousand Oaks, CA. Used with permission.

and, in the case of preapproved credit cards, completely eliminated. The decision to offer a preapproved card, or to approve an application for a card, is increasingly left to a nonhuman technology—the computer. Computerized scoring systems exert control over credit card company employees by, for example, preventing them from approving an application if the score falls below the agreed-on standard. And these scoring systems are, by definition, calculable, relying on quantitative measures rather than qualitative judgments about things like the applicant's "character." Thus, credit card loans, like fast-food hamburgers, are now being served up in a highly rationalized, assembly-line fashion. As a result, a variety of irrationalities of rationality, especially dehumanization, have come to be associated with both.

It is worth noting that the rationalization of credit card loans has played a central role in fostering the rationalization of other types of loans, such as automobile and home equity loans. Automobile loan approvals used to take days, but now a loan can be approved, and one can drive off in a new car, in a matter of hours, if not minutes. Similarly, home equity loans can now be obtained much more quickly and easily than was the case in the past. Such loans rely on many of the same technologies and procedures, such as scoring systems, that are used in decision making involving credit cards. Thus, just as the process of rationalization in society as a whole has been spearheaded by the fast-food industry, it is reverberating across the banking and loan business led by the credit card industry. We can anticipate that over time other types of loans, involving larger and larger sums of money (mortgages and business loans, for example), will be increasingly rationalized. Virtually every facet of banking and finance will be moving in that direction.

. . .

CALCULABILITY: THE ALL-IMPORTANT CREDIT REPORT

. . . A particularly revealing example of quantification in the credit card industry is the use of "credit scoring" in determining whether an applicant should be issued a credit card (or receive other kinds of credit). Of course, in the end the majority of applicants are approved by one credit card firm or another because the profits from the credit card business are extraordinarily high. Credit card firms can afford to have a small proportion of cardholders who are delinquent in paying their bills or even who default on them. Nonetheless, it is obviously in the interest of the card companies to weed out those who will not be able to pay their bills.

Credit scoring is usually a two-step process. First, the application itself is scored by the credit card company. For example, a homeowner might get more points than a person who rents. If an application scores a sufficient number of points, the lender then buys a credit report on the applicant from a credit bureau. The score on the credit report is key to the decision to issue a card. Said a vice president of a company in the business of designing scoring models for lenders: "You can have an application that's good as gold, but if you've got a lousy credit report, you'll get turned down every time." In other words, it is the numbers, not qualitative factors, that are ultimately decisive.

Scoring models vary from one locale to another and are updated to reflect changing conditions. Despite great variation from report to report, the following items usually receive the most weight:

- ◆ Possession of a number of credit and charge cards. . . .
- ◆ Record of paying off accumulated charges. . . .
- ◆ Suits, judgments, and bankruptcies involving the applicant. . . .
- ◆ Measures of stability. . . .
- ◆ Income. . . .
- ◆ Occupation and employer. . . .
- ◆ Age. . . .
- ◆ Possession of savings and checking accounts. . . .
- ◆ Homeownership. . . .

Scoring systems clearly quantify the decision-making process. In doing so, they reduce human qualities to abstract quantities. That is, they reduce the individual quality of creditworthiness to a simple, single number that "decides" whether or not an applicant is, in fact, worthy of credit. The more human judgment of an official of a credit card firm is then considered unnecessary. One banking consultant claims that "the character of an individual is much more important than [a credit score]. You can't decide who to lend to by using a computer." However, with a crush of applicants brought in large part by active recruiting efforts, credit card firms are increasingly relying on computerized scoring systems and paying more attention to quantifiable scores.

. . .

EFFICIENCY: THE FASTER THE BETTER

. . . The credit card is a highly efficient method for obtaining, granting, and expending loans. Applicants need do little more than fill out a brief application, and in the case of preapproved credit cards, even that requirement may be waived. In most cases, the customer is granted a line of credit, which is accessed and expended quickly and easily each time the card is used. Assuming a good credit record, as the credit limit is approached it will be increased automatically, thereby effortlessly increasing the potential total loan amount.

Furthermore, the credit card tends to greatly enhance the efficiency of virtually all kinds of shopping. Instead of carrying unwieldy amounts of cash, all one needs is a thin piece of plastic. There is no need to plan for purchases by going to the bank to obtain cash, no need to carry burdensome checkbooks and the identification needed to get checks approved. With their credit cards, consumers are no longer even required to know how to count out the needed amount of currency or to make sure the change is correct.

Credit (and debit) cards are also more efficient from the merchant's point of view. . . . Although it might be a tad slower than cash at the checkout counter, a card transaction is ultimately far more efficient than a cash deal because it requires little from the merchant except the initial electronic transmission of the charge. Handling cash is, as one supermarket electronic banking services executive points out, "labor intensive. From the time it leaves the customer's hands to the time it hits the bank, cash may get handled six to eight different times, both at the store and at the bank level." All these steps are eliminated in a charge (or debit) transaction.

. . .

PREDICTABILITY: AVOIDING THOSE PAINFUL LULLS

. . . The credit card has made the process of obtaining a loan quite predictable as well. Consumers have grown accustomed to routine steps (filling out the questionnaire, for example) that lead to the appearance of a new card in the mail. After all, many people have gone through these same steps many times. In the case of preapproved credit cards, the few remaining unpredictabilities have been eliminated because offer and acceptance arrive in the very same letter.

. . .

The credit card also serves to make consumption in general more predictable. Before credit cards, people had to spend more slowly, or even stop consuming altogether, when cash on hand or in the bank dipped too low. This unpredictability at the individual level was mirrored at the societal level by general slowdown in consumption during recessionary periods. But the credit card frees consumers, at least to some degree, from the unpredictabilities associated with cash-flow and the absence of cash on hand. It even frees them, at least for a time, from the limitations of depleted checking and savings accounts. Overall, the credit card has a smoothing effect on consumption. We are now better able to avoid "painful" lulls when we are unable to participate in the economy because of a lack of ready cash. Most generally, the credit card even allows people to consume, at least to some degree, during recessionary periods. For the purveyors of goods and services, the availability of credit cards makes the world more predictable by helping to ensure a steadier stream of customers during bad times as well as good ones.

NONHUMAN FOR HUMAN TECHNOLOGY: NO VISITORS, NO STAFF

. . . The credit card is itself a kind of nonhuman technology. More important, it has given birth to technologies that intervene between buyer and seller and serve to constrain both. Most notable is the vast computerized system that "decides" whether to authorize a new credit card and whether to authorize a given purchase. Shopkeeper and customer may both want to consummate a deal, but if the computer system says no (because, for example, the consumer's card is over its credit limit), then there is likely to be no sale. Similarly, an employee of a credit card firm may want to approve a sale but be loath, and perhaps forbidden, to do so if the computer indicates that the sale should be disapproved. The general trend within rationalized societies is to take decision-making power away from people (customers, shopkeepers, and credit card company employees alike) and give it to nonhuman technologies.

With the advent of smart cards, the card itself will "decide" whether a sale is to be consummated. Embedded in the card's computer chip will be such information as spending limits, so the card itself will be able to reject a purchase that is over the limit.

Not only do some aspects of our credit card society take decision making away from human beings, but other of its elements eliminate people altogether. Thus, widespread distribution of the smart card may eliminate many of the people who now operate the credit card companies' extensive computer systems. Today, ATMs have been increasingly replacing bank tellers. A bank vice president is quite explicit about the substitution of ATMs for human beings: "This might sound funny, but if we can keep people out of our branches, we don't have to hire staff to handle peaktime booms and the like. That drives down costs." A similar point can be made about debit cards, which involve far less human labor than do the checks that they are designed to replace. The growth of debit cards has undoubtedly led to the loss of many bank positions involved in clearing checks. Similarly, because credit cards are designed to be used in place of cash, the increasing use of such cards has led to the loss of positions involved in a cash economy (for example, bank tellers needed to dole out cash).

. . .

IRRATIONALITY OF RATIONALITY: CAUGHT IN THE HEAVY MACHINERY

The irrationality of rationality takes several forms . . . . Credit cards are supposed to offer greater efficiency but sometimes are quite inefficient. Take, for example, the Discover Card's program to allow its cardholders access to Sprint's long-distance service. To make a long-distance call with the card, "all you need do is dial Sprint's 11-digit access number. Then 0. Then a 10-digit phone number. Then the 16-digit account number from your Discover Card. Then a four-digit 'Personal Access Code.'" A highly inefficient string of 42 digits must be entered just to make one long-distance telephone call. To take another example, the credit card companies are supposed to function highly predictably. Thus, for example, our bills should be error free. However, billing errors do find their way into monthly statements. For example, there may be charges that we did not make or the amount entered may be incorrect.

. . . The credit card world is also highly dehumanized because people generally interact with nonhuman technologies, with such products as bills or overdue notices, or with people whose actions or decisions are constrained if not determined by nonhuman technologies. Horror stories abound of people caught in the "heavy machinery" of the credit card companies. Pity the poor consumers who get charged for things they did not buy or who are sent a series of computer letters with escalating threats because the computer erroneously considers them to be delinquent in their payments. Then there are the many complaints of people who get turned down for credit because erroneous information has crept into their credit reports. Trying to get satisfaction from the technologies, or from their often robot-like representatives, is perhaps the ultimate in the dehumanization associated with a rationalizing society.

. . . Computerized credit approval is associated with a greater likelihood of delinquency and default than when financial institutions employ more traditional methods. Credit card companies are willing to accept these risks because of the relatively small amounts involved in credit card loans and the fact that credit cards in general are so profitable. Such losses are hardly noticeable.

. . .

Perhaps the most persistent and reprehensible activities of the credit card companies . . . are their efforts to keep interest rates high even when interest rates in general are low or declining. Of course, there are many other irrationalities of the rationalized credit card industry . . . the tendency of credit card companies to engage in practices that lead people to spend recklessly, the secrecy of many aspects of the credit card business, the invasion of the privacy of cardholders, and the fraudulent activities engaged in by various players in the credit card world. . . .

Thinking Critically

1. In what ways have credit cards, and the McDonaldization process that stands at their base, improved your life?

2. In what ways has your life been adversely affected by credit cards and their McDonaldization?

3. How do you feel when you "interact" with an ATM?

4. Why do the credit card companies charge interest rates several times the rate that is charged for other loans (mortgage, car)? Is such a rate defensible?

5. Do you pay off your credit card balance in full in each month? If not, should you?

Part II

1. How do the elements of McDonaldization operate in the legal justice system? Draw parallels to its effects in the education and health systems in the United States.

2. What does the McDonaldization of social services mean for ethnic, religious, and racial minority groups in the society? How does the irrationality of rationality affect the daily practices of these minority groups?

3. Think about the dialectical relationship of agency and McDonaldization. Does the power of individual agency increase or decrease in a McDonaldized system? Does it lead to ever-increasing alienation in the society?

4. If you have computer access, visit the Web sites of the political parties in the United States. Examine their agendas on social issues. To what extent are their solutions McDonaldized?

5. Not only is the Internet changing the way people think about politics, but it is one more way to motivate them to get involved in politics. Discuss the ways in which McDonaldization turns the Internet into the foremost political medium.

6. In your experience, have you noted the effects of McDonaldization on your sex life? Do you find the emphasis on the standardization of sex life oppressive? If so, in what ways?

7. Given the high rate of divorce in the United States, would it be more appropriate to view divorce as the irrationality of rationality?

8. Discuss the advantages and disadvantages of McDonaldization on your Internet use. How does McDonaldization of production affect Internet content? Does it generate homogeneity?

9. How are the customers involved in the labor process? What are the advantages/disadvantages of this trend for the customer and the corporations? Does it generate surplus value in a Marxian sense?

10. How does McDonaldization affect ecology? Discuss its effects on the ecosystem with reference to monoculture farming, genetically engineered seeds, chemicals, and mechanization.

11. Is McDonaldization only applicable to Christianity? Are other world religions McDonaldized as well? How does McDonaldization change the beliefs, rituals, and experiences of those faiths?

12. Would McDonaldized politics lead to public alienation about social problems? How does it adjust public involvement in gender, environmental, and class politics?

13. Discuss the notions of political commitment and global citizenship in supranational political organizations such as the UN, G-8, and NATO. Does modern democracy necessarily require "hot" commitment?

14. How does McDonaldization relate to the enchantment and disenchantment of the modern world? What is the relationship between rationalization and disenchantment?

15. Are credit cards really helpful in periods of economic recession? Do they inflate the economy artificially?

PART III

Cross-Cultural Analysis, Social
Movements, and Social Change

In Part III of the book, we deal with a wide range of subjects that relate McDonaldization to cross-cultural developments and social change, including an issue—Jihad—that is very much in the headlines as I write, along with the hotly debated topic of globalization (see Part IV).

The first essay in Part III is a now-famous, and extraordinarily prescient (it was published in 1992), article by Benjamin Barber titled "Jihad vs. McWorld." Barber developed his idea of McWorld independently of my concept of McDonaldization, but there are obvious similarities between them (including the use of McDonald's as a model), and for the purposes of this book, they will be treated as being essentially the same idea. Barber treats McWorld as one of the dominant processes in the world, but his work is unique (he is a political scientist, not a sociologist) in that he juxtaposes it to another important process throughout much of the world—Jihad. The term "Jihad" (literally "struggle") is derived from Islam (where it is seen as battles against those who threaten the faith), but it is clear that Barber is not restricting it to the Islamic world; he discusses many different nations that are experiencing Jihad-like movements (e.g., Spain and even Switzerland). What is so prescient about Barber's work, however, is that it seemed to anticipate the cataclysmic events of September 11, 2001; the U.S. attacks on the Taliban in Afghanistan; the war against the terrorist organization Al Qaeda; and the declaration of a Jihad against the United States by the leadership of the Taliban and Al Qaeda. In the early 21st century, we are involved in a struggle that is well described as Jihad versus McWorld.

Barber looks at what he considers a clash between two global forces. One, McWorld, is quite clear to us, at least to the degree that it overlaps with McDonaldization. The other, however, needs clarification. Here is the way Barber defines "Jihad":

> subnational factions in permanent rebellion against uniformity and integration . . . they are cultures, not countries; parts not wholes; sects, not religions; rebellious factions and dissenting minorities at war not just with globalism but with the traditional nation-state . . . people without countries, inhabiting nations not their own, seeking smaller worlds within borders that will seal them off from modernity.

While McWorld seems to have most of the advantages (the fruits of McDonaldization, especially a massive number and diversity of military weapons), the passion behind Jihad makes it a formidable and dangerous opponent.

25

Jihad vs. McWorld

Benjamin R. Barber

◆◆◆ ————————————————————————————

*The two axial principles of our age—tribalism and globalism—
clash at every point except one: they may both be threatening to
democracy.*

Just beyond the horizon of current events lie two possible political
futures—both bleak, neither democratic. The first is a retribalization
of large swaths of humankind by war and bloodshed: a threatened
Lebanonization of national states in which culture is pitted against culture,
people against people, tribe against tribe—a Jihad in the name of a hundred
narrowly conceived faiths against every kind of interdependence, every kind
of artificial social cooperation and civic mutuality. The second is being borne
in on us by the onrush of economic and ecological forces that demand integration and uniformity and that mesmerize the world with fast music, fast
computers, and fast food—with MTV, Macintosh, and McDonald's, pressing
nations into one commercially homogenous global network: one McWorld

---

Editor's Note: Excerpts of an article published originally in *The Atlantic Monthly*,
March 1992, as an introduction to *Jihad vs. McWorld* (1996), a volume that
discusses and extends the themes of the original article.

tied together by technology, ecology, communications, and commerce. The planet is falling precipitantly apart *and* coming reluctantly together at the very same moment. . .

The tendencies of what I am here calling the forces of Jihad and the forces of McWorld operate with equal strength in opposite directions, the one driven by parochial hatreds, the other by universalizing markets, the one re-creating ancient subnational and ethnic borders from within, the other making national borders porous from without. They have one thing in common: neither offers much hope to citizens looking for practical ways to govern themselves democratically. If the global future is to pit Jihad's centrifugal whirlwind against McWorld's centripetal black hole, the outcome is unlikely to be democratic—or so I will argue.

McWORLD, OR THE GLOBALIZATION OF POLITICS

Four imperatives make up the dynamic of McWorld: a market imperative, a resource imperative, an information-technology imperative, and an ecological imperative. By shrinking the world and diminishing the salience of national borders, these imperatives have in combination achieved a considerable victory over factiousness and particularism, and not least of all over their most virulent traditional form—nationalism. . . .

The Market Imperative . . . All national economies are now vulnerable to the inroads of larger, transnational markets within which trade is free, currencies are convertible, access to banking is open, and contracts are enforceable under law. In Europe, Asia, Africa, the South Pacific, and the Americas such markets are eroding national sovereignty and giving rise to entities— international banks, trade associations, transnational lobbies like OPEC and Greenpeace, world news services like CNN and the BBC, and multinational corporations that increasingly lack a meaningful national identity—that neither reflect nor respect nationhood as an organizing or regulative principle.

The market imperative has also reinforced the quest for international peace and stability, requisites of an efficient international economy. Markets are enemies of parochialism, isolation, factiousness, war. Market psychology attenuates the psychology of ideological and religious cleavages and assumes a concord among producers and consumers—categories that ill fit narrowly conceived national or religious cultures. Shopping has little tolerance for blue laws, whether dictated by pub-closing British paternalism, Sabbath-observing Jewish Orthodox fundamentalism, or no-Sunday-liquor-sales Massachusetts puritanism. In the context of common markets, international law ceases to be a vision of justice and becomes a workaday framework for getting things done—enforcing contracts, ensuring that governments abide by deals, regulating trade and currency relations, and so forth.

Common markets demand a common language, as well as a common currency, and they produce common behaviors of the kind bred by cosmopolitan city life everywhere. Commercial pilots, computer programmers, international bankers, media specialists, oil riggers. entertainment celebrities, ecology experts, demographers, accountants, professors, athletes—these compose a new breed of men and women for whom religion, culture, and nationality can seem only marginal elements in a working identity. Although sociologists of everyday life will no doubt continue to distinguish a Japanese from an American mode, shopping has a common signature throughout the world. Cynics might even say that some of the recent revolutions in Eastern Europe have had as their true goal not liberty and the right to vote but well-paying jobs and the right to shop (although the vote is proving easier to acquire than consumer goods). The market imperative is, then, plenty powerful; but, notwithstanding some of the claims made for "democratic capitalism," it is not identical with the democratic imperative.

The Resource Imperative. Democrats once dreamed of societies whose political autonomy rested firmly on economic independence. . . .

But the rapid depletion of resources even in a country like ours, where they once seemed inexhaustible, and the maldistribution of arable soil and mineral resources on the planet, leave even the wealthiest societies ever more resource-dependent and many other nationals in permanently desperate straits.

Every nation, it turns out, needs something another nation has; some nations have almost nothing they need.

The Information-Technology Imperative. Enlightenment science and the technologies derived from it are inherently universalizing. They entail a quest for descriptive principles of general application, a search for universal solutions to particular problems, and an unswerving embrace of objectivity and impartiality.

Scientific progress embodies and depends on open communication, a common discourse rooted in rationality, collaboration, and an easy and regular flow and exchange of information. Such ideals can be hypocritical covers for power-mongering by elites, and they may be shown to be wanting in many other ways; but they are entailed by the very idea of science and they make science and globalization practical allies.

Business, banking, and commerce all depend on information flow and are facilitated by new communication technologies. The hardware of these technologies tends to be systemic and integrated—computer, television, cable, satellite, laser, fiber-optic, and microchip technologies combining to create a vast interactive communications and information network that can potentially give every person on earth access to every other person, and make every datum, every byte, available to every set of eyes. If . . . electronic telecommunication and information systems are an ideology at 186,000 miles per second—[that] makes for a very small planet in a very big hurry. Individual cultures speak particular languages; commerce and science increasingly speak English; the whole world speaks logarithms and binary mathematics.

Moreover, the pursuit of science and technology asks for, even compels, open societies. Satellite footprints do not respect national borders; telephone wires penetrate the most closed societies. . . . In their social requisites, secrecy and science are enemies.

The new technology's software is perhaps even more globalizing than its hardware. The information arm of international commerce's sprawling body reaches out and touches distinct nationals and parochial cultures, and gives them a common face chiseled in Hollywood, on Madison Avenue, and in Silicon Valley. . . . This kind of software supremacy may in the long term be far more important than hardware superiority, because culture has become more potent than armaments. What is the power of the Pentagon compared with Disneyland? Can the Sixth Fleet keep up with CNN? McDonald's in Moscow and Coke in China will do more to create a global culture than military colonization ever could. It is less the goods than the brand names that do the work, for they convey lifestyle images that alter perception and challenge behavior. They make up the seductive software of McWorld's common (at times much too common) soul.

Yet in all this high-tech commercial world there is nothing that looks particularly democratic. It lends itself to surveillance as well as liberty, to new forms of manipulation and covert control as well as new kinds of participation, to skewed, unjust market outcomes as well as greater productivity. The consumer society and the open society are not quite synonymous. Capitalism and democracy have a relationship, but it is something less than a marriage. An efficient free market after all requires that consumers be free to vote their dollars on competing goods, not that citizens be free to vote their values and beliefs on competing political candidates and programs. The free market flourished in junta-run Chile, in military-governed Taiwan and Korea, and, earlier, in a variety of autocratic European empires as well as their colonial possessions.

The Ecological Imperative. The impact of globalization on ecology is a cliché even to world leaders who ignore it. We know well enough that the

German forests can be destroyed by Swiss and Italians driving gas-guzzlers fueled by leaded gas. We also know that the planet can be asphyxiated by greenhouse gases because Brazilian farmers want to be part of the twentieth century and are burning down tropical rain forests to clear a little land to plough, and because Indonesians make a living out of converting their lush jungle into toothpicks for fastidious Japanese diners, upsetting the delicate oxygen balance and in effect puncturing our global lungs. Yet this ecological consciousness has meant not only greater awareness but also greater inequality, as modernized nations try to slam the door behind them, saying to developing nations, "The world cannot afford *your* modernization; ours has wrung it dry!"

Each of the four imperatives just cited is transnational, transideological, and transcultural. Each applies impartially to Catholics, Jews, Muslims, Hindus, and Buddhists; to democrats and totalitarians; to capitalists and socialists. The Enlightenment dream of a universal rational society has to a remarkable degree been realized—but in a form that is commercialized, homogenized, depoliticized, bureaucratized, and, of course, radically incomplete, for the movement toward McWorld is in competition with forces of global breakdown, national dissolution, and centrifugal corruption. These forces, working in the opposite direction, are the essence of what I call Jihad.

JIHAD, OR THE LEBANONIZATION OF THE WORLD

OPEC, the World Bank, the United Nations, the International Red Cross, the multinational corporation. . .there are scores of institutions that reflect globalization. But they often appear as ineffective reactors to the world's real actors: national states and, to an ever greater degree, subnational factions in permanent rebellion against uniformity and integration—even the kind represented by universal law and justice. The headlines feature these players regularly: they are cultures, not countries; parts, not wholes; sects, not religions; rebellious factions and dissenting minorities at war not just with globalism but with the traditional nation-state. Kurds, Basques, Puerto Ricans, Ossetians, East Timoreans, Quebecois, the Catholics of Northern Ireland, Abkhasians, Kurile Islander Japanese, the Zulus of Inkatha, Catalonians, Tamils, and, of course, Palestinians—people without countries, inhabiting nations not their own, seeking smaller worlds within borders that will seal them off from modernity.

A powerful irony is at work here. Nationalism was once a force of integration and unification, a movement aimed at bringing together disparate clans, tribes, and cultural fragments under new, assimiliationist flags. But as Ortega y Gasset noted more than sixty years ago, having won its victories, nationalism changed its strategy. In the 1920s, and again today, it is more often a reactionary and divisive force, pulverizing the very nations it once helped cement together. The force that creates nationals is "inclusive," Ortega wrote in *The Revolt of the Masses*. "In periods of consolidation, nationalism has a positive value, and is a lofty standard. But in Europe everything is more than consolidated, and nationalism is nothing but a mania. . . ."

This mania has left the post-Cold War smoldering with hot wars; the international scene is little more unified than it was at the end of the Great War, in Ortega's own time. There were more than thirty wars in progress last year, most of them ethnic, racial, tribal, or religious in character, and the list of unsafe regions doesn't seem to be getting any shorter. Some new world order!

The aim of many of these small-scale wars is to redraw boundaries, to implode states and resecure parochial identities: to escape McWorld's dully insistent imperatives. The mood is that of Jihad: war not as an instrument of policy but as an emblem of identity, an expression of community, an end in itself. Even where there is no shooting war, there is fractiousness, secession, and the quest for ever smaller communities. Add to the list of dangerous countries those at risk: In Switzerland and Spain, Jurassian and Basque separatists still argue the virtues of ancient identities, sometimes in the language of bombs. Hyperdisintegration in the former Soviet Union may well continue unabated— not just a Ukraine independent from the Soviet Union but a Bessarabian Ukraine independent from the Ukrainian republic; not just Russia severed from the defunct union but Tatarstan severed from Russia. Yugoslavia makes even the disunited, ex-Soviet, nonsocialist republics that were once the Soviet Union look integrated, its sectarian fatherlands springing up within factional motherlands like weeds within weeds within weeds. Kurdish independence would threaten the territorial integrity of four Middle Eastern nations. Well before the current cataclysm Soviet Georgia made a claim for autonomy from the Soviet Union, only to be faced with its Ossetians (164,000 in a republic of 5.5 million) demanding their own self-determination within Georgia. The Abkhasian minority in Georgia has followed suit. Even the good will established by Canada's once promising Meech Lake protocols is in danger, with Francophone Quebec again threatening the dissolution of the federation. In South Africa the emergence from apartheid was hardly achieved when friction between Inkatha's Zulus and the African National Congress's tribally identified members threatened to replace Europeans' racism with an indigenous tribal war. After thirty years of attempted integration using the colonial language (English) as a unifier, Nigeria is now playing with the idea of linguistic multiculturalism—which could mean the cultural breakup of the nation into hundreds of tribal fragments. . . .

The passing of communism has torn away the thin veneer of internationalism (workers of the world unite!) to reveal ethnic prejudices that are not only ugly and deep-seated but increasingly murderous. Europe's old scourge, anti-Semitism, is back with a vengeance, but it is only one of many antagonisms. It appears all too easy to throw the historical gears into reverse and pass from a Communist dictatorship back into a tribal state.

Among the tribes, religion is also a battlefield. ("Jihad" is a rich word whose generic meaning is "struggle"—usually the struggle of the soul to avert evil. Strictly applied to religious war, it is used only in reference to battles where the faith is under assault, or battles against a government that denies the practice of Islam. My use here is rhetorical, but does follow both journalistic practice and history.) Remember the Thirty Years War? Whatever forms of Enlightenment universalism might once have come to grace such historically related forms of monotheism as Judaism, Christianity, and Islam, in many of their modern incarnations they are parochial rather than cosmopolitan, angry rather than loving, proselytizing rather than ecumenical, zealous rather than rationalist, sectarian rather than deistic, ethnocentric rather than universalizing. As a result, like the new forms of hypernationalism, the new expressions of religious fundamentalism are fractious and pulverizing, never integrating. This is religion as the Crusaders knew it, a battle to the death for souls that if not saved will be forever lost.

The atmospherics of Jihad have resulted in a breakdown of civility in the name of identity, of comity in the name of community. International relations have sometimes taken on the aspect of gang war—cultural turf battles featuring tribal factions that were supposed to be sublimated as integral parts of large national, economic, postcolonial, and constitutional entities.

Thinking Critically

1. Is there such a thing as McWorld?

2. Is there such a thing as Jihad?

3. Are you afraid of McWorld?

4. Are you afraid of Jihad?

5. Are you afraid of what might happen if the tensions between McWorld and Jihad increase?

The potential for danger discussed by Barber came to fruition on September 11, 2001. In the next essay, I deal with the relationship between the spread of fast-food restaurants, credit cards, and the cathedrals of consumption, and the kind of terrorism that occurred that day. I am certainly not arguing that the worldwide expansion of these phenomena caused these events. Nor am I condoning the acts of September 11 (they cannot be condoned) or condemning the United States. However, we do have to recognize that the attacks were aimed at national symbols, and the World Trade Center was a dramatic symbol of America's worldwide economic power. While America's economic power takes many forms, it is most visible to many people around the world in the realm of consumption. Thus, it could be argued that the attack on the World Trade Center was, in part, an attack on a symbol that stood for the incursions of symbols of the American economy, including those associated with consumption, into the lives of many people around the world.

The main thrust of this essay is to argue that fast-food restaurants, credit cards, and cathedrals of consumption bring with them American ways of doing business, American ways of consuming, and powerful American icons (such as the "golden arches" of McDonald's). Let us be absolutely clear: The vast majority of people in most nations welcome these incursions. However, others are, to varying degrees, offended by them. They have their own ways of doing business and of consuming, and American ways may be seen not only as different but also as offensive. In addition, for those who resent these things, there are the seemingly omnipresent symbols of the icons of these incursions, such as those of McDonald's, Visa, and Wal-Mart. They serve as highly visible and constant reminders of these American ways of doing things and of the perceived insults to indigenous practices. They also serve as a backdrop for a wide range of expressions of outrage against the United States.

The clearest support for this argument involves the case of "Carlos the Jackal," a terrorist linked to a variety of skyjackings, bombings, and machine-gun attacks. A Venezuelan, Carlos was reported to have worked for a number of Islamic leaders. Carlos was eventually captured and convicted of murder in France. He is serving a life sentence for his crimes. In his closing speech before sentencing, Carlos spoke of "world war, war to the death, the war that humanity must win against McDonaldization."

26

September 11, 2001

Mass Murder and Its Roots in the Symbolism of American Consumer Culture

George Ritzer

◆◆◆ ————————————————————————————————

O n September 11, 2001, the terrorists not only killed thousands of innocent people and destroyed buildings of various sorts, they also sought to destroy (and in one case succeeded) major symbols of America's preeminent position in the globalization process: The World Trade Center was a symbol of America's global hegemony in the economic realm, and the Pentagon is obviously the icon of its military preeminence around the world. In addition, there is a widespread belief that the fourth plane, the one that crashed in Pennsylvania, was headed for the symbol of American political power—the White House. Obviously, the common element in all these targets is that they are, among other things, cultural icons, with the result that the terrorist attacks can be seen as assaults on American culture. (This is not, of course, to deny the very material effects on people, buildings, the economy, and so on.) Furthermore, although symbols, jobs, businesses, and lives were crippled or destroyed, the main objective was symbolic—the demonstration

---

Editor's Note: This chapter was written for *McDonaldization: The Reader* (2002).

that the most important symbols of American culture were not only vulnerable but could be, and were, badly hurt or destroyed. The goal was to show the world that the United States was not an invulnerable superpower but that it could be assaulted successfully by a small number of terrorists. One implication was that if such important symbols could be attacked successfully, nothing in the United States (as well as in U.S. interests around the world) was safe from the wrath of terrorists. Thus, we are talking about an assault on, among other things, culture—an assault designed to have a wide-ranging impact throughout the United States and the world.

In emphasizing culture, I am not implying that economic, political, and military issues (to say nothing of the loss of life) are less important. Indeed, these domains are encompassed, at least in part, under the broad heading of culture and attacks on cultural icons. Clearly, many throughout the world are angered by a variety of things about the United States, especially its enormous economic, political, and military influence and power. In fact, this essay will focus on one aspect of the economy—consumption—and its role in producing hostility to the United States. . . .

By focusing on America's role in consumption and its impact around the world, I am not condoning the terrorist attacks (they are among the most heinous of acts in human history) or blaming the United States for those attacks. Rather, my objective is to discuss one set of reasons that people in many different countries loathe (while a far larger number of people love) the United States. Indeed, it is a truism that, often, love and hate coexist in the same people. However, needless to say, those involved in these terrorist acts had nothing but hatred for the United States.

CONSUMPTION

American hegemony throughout the world is most visible and, arguably, of greatest significance, in economic and cultural terms, in the realm of consumption. On a day-to-day basis in much of the world, people are far more likely to be confronted by American imperialism in the realm of consumption than they are in other economic domains (American factories and companies are far less obvious than the consumer products they offer for sale throughout the world), the military (U.S. troops and advisers are far less visible throughout the world than they used to be and certainly less than Nike shoes or McDonald's hamburgers), and the polity (American political influence is most likely to be covert in terms of its impact within the governments of most nations around the world). While the firing of American cruise missiles into sovereign nations such as Somalia may have provoked occasional demonstrations and intense outbursts of anger, the ubiquitousness of American consumption sites (e.g., McDonald's restaurants) and products (Nike shoes) is likely to be, at least for some, a long-running provocation that leads in the end to great animosity toward the United States and its intrusion into the everyday life of many cultures (of course, to many others they are irresistible attractions). In other words, we need to pay at least as much attention to everyday perceptions (in the realm of consumption and elsewhere) of provocations and insults as we do to the far more dramatic, but distant and intermittent, economic, political, and military actions.

Rather than focus on consumption in general, I will discuss three of its aspects of greatest concern to me: fast-food restaurants, credit cards, and "cathedrals of consumption" (for example, discounters such as Wal-Mart). Before getting to these, it is important to point out that they, and many other components of our consumer culture, are not only physical presences throughout the world, they are media presences by way of television, movies, the Internet, and so on. Furthermore, even in those countries where these phenomena are not yet material realities, they are already media presences. As a result, their impact is felt even though they have not yet entered a particular country, and in those countries where they already exist, their impact is increased because they are also media presences.

I want to focus on the ways in which, from the perspective of those in other nations and cultures, fast-food restaurants, credit cards, and cathedrals of consumption bring with them (a) an American way of doing business, (b) an American way of consuming, and (c) American cultural icons. I will examine why some may react negatively to one, two, or all three of these things. However, it is important to remember that the vast majority of those in most, if not all, nations throughout the world not only welcome these forms of Americana but actively seek them out and work hard to make them part of their country. In fact, the majority of people in nations that lack some or all of these (and who are aware of them) feel deprived by their absence and are eager to do what is necessary to bring them to their country. Again, in our focus on problems and negative effects and perceptions, we must never lose sight of the advantages and the great attraction to most people everywhere of these and many other aspects of our consumer culture.

FAST-FOOD RESTAURANTS

Let us begin with fast-food restaurants, particularly the paradigmatic chain of fast-food restaurants, McDonald's. . . .

As it moves into each new nation, it brings with it a variety of American ways of doing business. In fact, in more recent years, the impact of its ways of doing business were surely felt long before the restaurant chain itself became a physical presence. McDonald's has been such a resounding success, and has offered so many important business innovations, that business leaders in other nations were undoubtedly incorporating many of its ideas almost from the inception of the chain. Of course, the major business innovation here is the franchise system. Although the franchise system predated McDonald's by many years (Singer Sewing Machine was involved in franchising prior to the Civil War, retailers such as Rexall and IGA were franchising by the 1930s, and in the fast-food industry A&W Root Beer was the pioneer in 1924), the franchise system came of age with the development of the McDonald's chain. Kroc made a number of innovations in franchising (he retained centralized control by refusing to grant blocs of regional franchises to entrepreneurs, and he based the corporation's income not on high initial fees but on a relatively large and continuing percentage of all sales; McDonald's also owned the real estate on which its restaurants were built and continued to earn rent as well as having the advantage of the increasing value of its real estate holdings that served to make it a far more successful system. The central point, given the interests of this essay, is that this system has been adopted, adapted, and modified by all sorts of businesses not only in the United States but throughout the world. In the case of franchise systems in other nations, they are doing business in a way that is similar to, if not identical with, comparable American franchises.

The fact that indigenous businesses (e.g., Russkoye Bistro in Russia, Nirulas in India) are conducting their business based, at least to a large degree, on an American business model is not visible to most people. However, they are affected in innumerable ways by the ways in which these franchises operate. Thus, day-to-day behaviors are influenced by all this, even if consumers are unaware of these effects.

What is far more obvious, even to consumers, is that people are increasingly consuming like Americans. This is clear not only in American chains in other countries but in indigenous clones of those chains. In terms of the former, in Japan, to take one example, McDonald's has altered long-standing traditions about how people are expected to eat. Thus, although eating while standing has long been taboo, in McDonald's restaurants, many Japanese eat just that way. Similarly, long expected not to touch food with their hands or drink directly from containers, many Japanese are doing just that in McDonald's and elsewhere. Much the same kind of thing is happening in indigenous clones of American fast-food restaurants in Japan such as Mos Burger.

These and many other changes in the way people consume are obvious, and they affect the way people live their lives on a daily basis. Just as many Japanese may resent these incursions into, and changes in, the ways in which they have traditionally conducted their everyday lives, those in many other cultures are likely to have their own wide-ranging set of resentments.

However, these changes involve much more than transformations in the way people eat. . . . Almost no sector of society is immune from McDonaldization, and this means that innumerable aspects of people's everyday lives are transformed by it.

Finally, the spread of McDonald's and other fast-food chains around the world has brought with it a range of American cultural icons. Of course, McDonald's itself has become such an icon, as has its "golden arches," Ronald McDonald, and many of its products—Big Mac, Egg McMuffin, and so on. Other fast-food chains have brought with them their own icons—Burger King's Whopper, Colonel Sanders of Kentucky Fried Chicken, and so on. These icons are accepted, even embraced, by most, but others are likely to be angered by them. For example, traditional Japanese foods such as sushi and rice are being replaced, at least for some, by Big Macs and large order of French fried potatoes. Because food is such a central part of any culture, such a transformation is likely to enrage some. More important, perhaps, is the ubiquity of the McDonald's restaurant, especially its golden arches, throughout so many nations of the world. To many in other societies, these are not only important symbols in themselves but have become symbols of the United States and, in some cases, even more important than more traditional symbols (such as the American embassy and the flag). In fact, there have been a number of incidents in recent years in which protests against the United States and its actions have taken the form of actions against the local McDonald's restaurants. To some, a McDonald's restaurant, especially when it is placed in some traditionally important locale, represents an affront, a "thumb in the eye," to the society and its culture. It is also perceived as a kind of "Trojan Horse," and the view is that hidden within its bright and attractive wrappings and trappings are all manner of potential threats to local culture. Insulted by, and fearful of, such "foreign" entities, a few react by striking out at them and the American culture and business world that stands behind them.

CREDIT CARDS

The modern, "universal" credit card (Chapter 24) can be used in a variety of settings throughout the United States and, increasingly, the rest of the world. This is another American invention (circa 1950), although it was preceded by many years by various other forms of credit and even specific credit cards that could be used in department stores and gasoline stations. It took a decade or two for the credit card to take off in the United States, but in the last three decades, its use has skyrocketed as has the number of cards in existence, the amount of credit card expenditures, and the total credit card debt.

Credit cards were slower to gain acceptance in other parts of the world, but in more recent years, credit card use has exploded in many countries. Even Germany, long seen as averse to credit instruments, has in the last few years embraced the credit card. Although credit cards are issued by innumerable local banks throughout the United States and the world, they almost always issue American cards, especially Visa and MasterCard. A few other cards are available (e.g., JCB in Japan), but the world market for credit cards is dominated by American brands and credit card companies. With the American market for credit cards approaching saturation levels, those companies have shifted much of their attention to obtaining the new business available through the exportation of their cards to the rest of the world.

The credit card represents an American way of doing business, especially a reliance on the extension of credit to maintain and to increase sales. Many nations have been dominated, and some still are, by "cash-and-carry" business. Businesses have typically been loathe to grant credit, and when they do, it has usually not been for large amounts of money. When credit was granted, strong collateral was required. This is in great contrast to the credit card industry, which has granted billions of dollars in credit with little or no collateral. In these and many other ways, traditional methods of doing business are being threatened and eroded by the incursion of the credit card.

Once again, although the business side of this transformation is not obvious to most people, its flip side in the realm of consumption is abundantly clear. That is, increasing numbers of people have been, and are, changing the way they consume from cash to credit card transactions. They are aware of this not only on a day-to-day basis as they consume but also quite pointedly (and sometimes alarmingly) at the end of each month when they must confront their credit card bills and, possibly, accumulating interest charges. As in the United States, those in other nations who can pay their bills in full each month are quite happy with their credit cards and the many advantages they offer. However, those who cannot pay those bills and must wrestle with large balances and exorbitant interest charges are apt to become increasingly discomforted by credit cards. Given this state of discomfiture, when they look at their bills and their cards what they see are the names and the logos of the American credit card companies that can easily be blamed for their plight. After all, it is easier to blame credit card companies than oneself. It is not a great leap from blaming the American credit card firms to blaming America itself.

But there is a more important issue here, one that will be also dealt with later. That is, credit cards are perceived as playing a key role in the development and expansion of consumer culture, a role characterized by hyperconsumption. Although many are overjoyed to be deeply immersed in consumer culture and others would dearly love to be so involved, still others are deeply worried by it on various grounds. One of the concerns, felt not only in the United States but perhaps even more elsewhere in the world, is the degree to which immersion in the seeming superficialities of consumption and fashion represents a threat, if not an affront, to deep-seated cultural and religious values. For example, many have viewed modern consumption as a kind of religion, and I have described malls and other consumption settings as cathedrals of consumption. As such, they can be seen as alternatives, and threats, to conventional religions in many parts of the world. At the minimum, the myriad attractions of consumption and a day at the mall serve as powerful alternatives to visiting one's church, mosque, or synagogue.

Finally, credit cards in general, to say nothing of the major brands—Visa and MasterCard (as well as the "charge card" and its dominant brand, American Express)—are seen as major icons of American culture. While these icons are similar to, say, McDonald's and its golden arches, there is something quite unique and powerful about credit cards. Although one who lives outside the United States may encounter a McDonald's and its arches every day, or maybe every few days, a Visa credit card, for example, is *always* with those who have one. It is always there in one's wallet, and it is probably a constant subconscious reality. Furthermore, one is continually reminded of it every time one passes a consumption site, especially one that has the logo of the credit card on its door or display window. Even without the latter, the mere presence of a shop and its goods is a reminder that one possesses a credit card and that the shop can be entered and goods can be purchased. The credit card is a uniquely powerful cultural icon because it is with cardholders all the time and they are likely to be reminded of it continually.

CATHEDRALS OF CONSUMPTION

Cathedrals of consumption, many of which are also American innovations, are increasing presences elsewhere in the world. There is a long list of these cathedrals of consumption (see Chapter 22), but let us focus on two—shopping malls and discounters, especially Wal-Mart. American-style fully enclosed shopping malls are springing up all over the world (a good example is the abundance of such malls on Orchard Road in Singapore). Most of these are indigenous developments, but the model is the American mall. Discount stores are experiencing a similar proliferation, but this is taking the form of indigenous versions as well as the exportation of American representatives such as Wal-Mart to many parts of the world.

These, of course, represent American ways of doing business. In the case of the mall, this involves the concentration of businesses in a single setting devoted to them. In the case of discounters, it represents the much greater propensity of American businesses (in comparison with their peers around the world) to compete on a price basis and to offer consumers deep discounts. Although appealing to many people, resentment may develop not only because these represent American rather than indigenous business practices but because they pose threats to local businesses. As in the United States, still more resentment is likely to be generated because small local shops are likely to be driven out of business by the development of a mall or the opening of a Wal-Mart on the outskirts of town.

Again, more obvious is the way consumers are led to alter their behaviors as a result of these developments. For example, instead of walking or bicycling to local shops, increasing numbers are more likely to drive to the new and very attractive malls and discounters. This can also lead to movement toward the increasing American reality that such trips are not just about shopping; such settings have become *destinations* where people spend many hours wandering from shop to shop, having lunch, and even seeing a movie or having a drink. Consumption sites have become places to while away days, and as such, they pose threats to alternative public sites, such as parks, zoos, and museums. In the end, malls and discounters are additional and very important contributors to the development of hyperconsumption and all the advantages and problems associated with it. Settings such as a massive shopping mall with a huge adjacent parking lot and a large Wal-Mart with its parking lot are abundantly obvious to people, as are the changes they help to create in the way natives consume.

Settings such as these are perceived as American cultural icons. Wal-Mart may be second only to McDonald's in terms of the association of consumption sites with things American, and the suburban mall is certainly broadly perceived in a similar way. Furthermore, malls are likely to house a number of other cultural icons, such as McDonald's, the Gap, and so on. And still further, the latter are selling yet other icons in the form of products such as Big Macs, blue jeans, Nike shoes, and so on. Many of those icons will be taken from the malls and eaten, worn, and otherwise displayed in public. Their impact is amplified because their well-known logos and names are likely to be plastered all over these products. Again, there is an "in-your-face" quality to all of this, and although many will be led to want these things, others will react negatively to the ubiquity of these emblems of America and its consumer culture and that these emblems tend to supplant indigenous symbols.

The argument here is that the recent terrorist attacks can be seen as assaults on American cultural icons—specifically the World Trade Center (business and consumption), the Pentagon (military), and potentially, the White House (political). That cultural icons were the target is further reflected by the closing of Disney theme parks, the restrictions put in place around Las Vegas casinos, the enormous loss of business for cruise lines, the suspension of major league baseball for a week, the cancellation of National Football League games for the week, and so on. Now, of course, there are pragmatic factors involved here; all of these involve large numbers of people in a single location, but beyond that, they were perceived as potential targets because of their symbolic importance.

Although I have focused on three American cultural icons in this essay and their worldwide proliferation, in vast portions of the world they are of minimal importance or completely nonexistent. Even where they are not physical presences, however, they are known through movies, television, magazines, and newspapers, and even by word of mouth. Thus, their influence throughout the world far exceeds their material presence in the world.

Their media presence leads to another problem. When those in most other countries get a glimpse of American consumer culture in the media, it is usually one that underscores that no matter how far (or little) their own consumer culture has advanced, it lags far behind that in the United States. Specifically, there are far more fast-food restaurants, credit cards, and cathedrals of consumption and the consumer products they offer for sale in the United States than anywhere else in the world. This is likely to be especially galling to those in nations that offer little more than a subsistence economy, if that. Media images of American affluence—sparkling fast-food restaurants, people with credit cards in hand rushing about in the Mall of America, the incredible sites of Las Vegas and gamblers betting more on one roll of the dice than people in many nations in the world will earn in their lifetimes—anger some in impoverished nations who may not know where their next meal will come from. Thus, the phenomena discussed in this essay do not even have to exist in a given nation for there to be a great deal of hostility toward them and the American society that is their source and center.

Although there is clearly a link between the phenomena just discussed and hostile reactions around the world (this is evident in several of the essays that follow in this volume), what is the case for relating them to events such as those of September 11? Afghanistan had no McDonald's restaurants, and Osama Bin Laden has never been quoted (to my knowledge) as expressing anger over credit cards, fast-food restaurants, or Wal-Mart. In fact, some of those involved in the September 11 attacks used credit cards to finance some of their actions and were known to frequent McDonaldized settings. Bin Laden, Al Qaeda, and the Taliban are Islamic fundamentalists who are hostile to the United States (and other nations) because of the threat it poses to basic Islamic beliefs and modes of life. In terms of our interests here, they see no place for fundamentalist Islam in fast-food restaurants and, more generally, in a world dominated by indebtedness and consumerism made possible and incited by credit cards and cathedrals of consumption.

Islamic fundamentalists such as Bin Laden are mainly motivated by animus to the presence of American political and military might in Islamic nations, by the leadership of Saudi Arabia (which permits tens of thousands of non-Muslims to live there, to say nothing of accepting an American military presence), and by Israel (which, interestingly, one observer views as "like a giant McDonald's franchise in the Middle East") and its relationship to the Palestinians. However, the kinds of concerns discussed in this essay are linked to, and are everyday reminders of, American influence in the Islamic world. Thus, in the wake of the American war on the Taliban in Afghanistan, and its effort to hunt down Bin Laden and Al Qaeda, Islamic protests broke out in various parts of the world. For example, in Indonesia, the world's largest Muslim nation, the protesters bombed a Kentucky Fried Chicken restaurant and shook their fists at the golden arches of a McDonald's restaurant in Jakarta situated close to the American embassy. Whenever a protest approached, employees of the restaurant responded by raising a banner saying "This store is owned by a Muslim."

However, the clearest example for the link being made in this essay involves "Carlos the Jackal," a terrorist linked to a variety of skyjackings, bombings, and machine gun attacks. Carlos (a Venezuelan) was reported to have worked for a number of Islamic leaders, including Mohammar Qaddafi (Libya), Saddam Hussein (Iraq), Hafez Assad (Syria), and George Habash (Popular Front for the Liberation of Palestine). Carlos was eventually captured and convicted of murder in France. He is serving a life sentence for his crimes. In his closing speech before sentencing, Carlos spoke of "world war, war to the death, the war that humanity must win against McDonaldization." More generally, the argument being made here is that there are many around the world, including a number within the Islamic world, who are waging war against McDonaldization and American-style consumerism.

RESPONDING TO THE CRISIS

It is interesting to note that some notable responses to the crisis of September 11 occurred in the realm of consumption. The mayor of New York, Rudolph Giuliani, was quickly heard and seen urging the citizens of the city, as well all of America, to get back to their normal routine, especially by going shopping. Similar calls soon came from President Bush. A quick reaction to these calls came from former Secretary of Labor Robert Reich, who penned an essay on the front page of the *Washington Post's* Outlook section titled, "How Did Spending Become Our Patriotic Duty?"

The answer to Reich's rhetorical question is that the demand that we spend and shop has been with us for some time, and it has been growing more powerful. One measure of this is the increasing attention and importance given to data associated with consumption, especially the index of consumer confidence. In the past, production data were of greatest importance to the stock market, but more recently, it seems that consumption-related data have become as important, if not more important. Declines in consumption, as well as consumer confidence, are viewed as harbingers of big trouble to corporations and their profits, as well as increases in unemployment rates. With traditional production industries (steel, autos, textiles) declining or even disappearing in the United States, it is little wonder that consumption is gaining ascendancy. Furthermore, the nation's economy as a whole is increasingly tied to consumption, and a recession seems to be increasingly tied, at least in part, to recalcitrant consumers. Thus, to Americans, it *has* come to seem that they have a duty to the nation, the economy, corporations, and their fellow workers to spend and consume.

Another interesting aspect of the aftermath of September 11 is the sense that Americans can protect themselves from various threats by buying the right product. The answer to the threat of some form of gas being released into the environment is to buy gas masks, even though one is unlikely to have one at hand if such an attack were to occur, let alone even know that gas has been released. The answer to the mini-outbreak of anthrax was the antibiotic Cipro, with the result that many called their doctors, or exploited other less legal methods, to get a supply on hand *in case* they contracted the disease. As other crises emerge, other consumables will emerge as solutions.

Not only are such actions unnecessary in almost all cases, but they also support the widespread view throughout the world that Americans are the world's most affluent consumers. In many nations in the world, there is not enough to eat or there are few, if any, medications, even for those who are already quite ill and likely to die without them. The latter cannot obtain Cipro even if it could be of help, and it is certainly too costly for the vast majority of other people in less developed countries. In those nations, as well as among the disenchanted within developed nations where hostility to America and its affluence already exists, we are likely to see an exacerbation of that hostility as people watch Americans endeavoring to spend their way into some measure of safety from both real and imagined dangers. The great capacity of Americans to spend and consume is *both* a great source of national strength *and* the nation's Achilles heel in that it has helped to create a hostility that found expression on September 11 and beyond and may well find other ways of expressing itself in the years to come.

CONCLUSION

Wars are always about culture, at least to some degree, but the one we have embarked on seems to reek with cultural symbolism. We live in an era—the era of globalization—in which not only cultural products and the businesses that sell them but also the symbols that go to their essence are known throughout the world. In fact, some—Nike and Tommy Hilfiger come to mind—are *nothing but symbols*; they manufacture nothing (except symbols). Although we deeply mourn the loss of life, the terrorists were after more. Surely, they wanted to kill people, but mainly because their deaths represented symbolically the fact that America could be made to bleed. But they also wanted to destroy some of the American symbols best known throughout the world; in destroying them, they were, they thought, symbolically destroying the United States. Interestingly, the initial response from the United States was largely symbolic—American flags were displayed everywhere; the sounds of the national anthem wafted through the air on a regular basis; red, white, and blue ribbons were wrapped around trees and telephone poles; and so on. Of course, the response soon went beyond symbols: Missiles have been launched and bombs dropped, special forces are in action, and people are dying. However, should the mastermind of the terrorist acts—Osama Bin Laden—be caught or killed, he will quickly become an even greater cultural icon than he is at the moment (his likeness already adorns T-shirts in Pakistan and elsewhere). Destroying his body may be satisfying to some, but it may well create a greater cultural problem for the United States, one that might translate into still more American citizens killed and structures destroyed.

Returning to my central point, the emphasis here has been on the peculiar power of consumption and the icons associated with it to arouse both admiration and hatred in many parts of the world. The symbols of our business, political, and military influence throughout the world are likely to be half-hidden, and when they become clear, it is usually only on an intermittent basis and for a short period of time. They are not highly involved, at least in any way that is apparent to most, with the day-to-day lives of most people around the world. Certainly, their impact is often indirect and quite powerful, but people on a daily basis are at best only half-conscious of that impact and power. It is quite a different matter in the realm of consumption, particularly in terms of the phenomena of concern here—fast-food restaurants, credit cards, and cathedrals of consumption. In the many nations of the world in which they have become prominent, their impact is clear for all to see, continuous, and long lasting. They are obvious both to those who long for them and those who hate them. They surround these people, and they are on their person—T-shirts, Nike shoes, jeans with a Visa card in the wallets in their pockets.

Of course, such representatives of American consumer culture have long been objects of antiglobalization forces. For example, McDonald's restaurants have been boycotted and picketed, had manure dumped in front of them, and have been destroyed. Nike and its sweatshops in Southeast Asia and elsewhere have also been favorite targets. The terrorists of September 11, 2001, however, were after even bigger symbolic game. McDonald's is a major symbol, but it is dispersed across more than 30,000 settings throughout the world. Aiming a plane at one McDonald's restaurant, or even at one corporation (say, McDonald's headquarters outside Chicago), is not likely to have the impact of crashing planes into twin towers that represent not only such businesses but many others as well. I am not equating the forces opposed to globalization with the terrorists, but they do share the goal of symbolic assault.

In conclusion, the focus of this chapter on key symbols of American consumer culture is not to denigrate the importance of other symbols, much less that of the material realities associated not only with that culture but with the United States as a whole. Furthermore, a focus on consumption is not to deny the importance of other economic symbols and material realities or those associated with politics, the military, and the polity. The symbols, as well as American consumer culture in general, are important not only in themselves but also because of their very distinctive capacity to influence the day-to-day lives of people throughout the world. Many welcome this influence, even want more of it, but a few are enraged by it (and many other things associated with the United States) and want to destroy it and its source—the United States. This certainly does not excuse the heinous acts of September 11, 2001, but it does help us to analyze at least one of the root causes of such terrorism.

Thinking Critically

1. Is there a global war against McDonaldization?

2. Was 9/11 part of it?

3. Are American consumption patterns offensive to those in other nations?

4. Are they objectionable within an American context?

5. Is spending and consumption our national duty?

The next three essays deal with several examples of collective behavior/social movements in various parts of the world (especially Great Britain, France, and Italy) that target McDonald's as well as the larger process of McDonaldization. In Chapter 27, the McSpotlight group offers a summary of the now infamous McLibel trial. This is a one-sided perspective on the trial, but it is presented here because it represents the viewpoint of the social movement against McDonald's that emerged from the trial. The facts are that McDonald's sued two activists involved in London Greenpeace for passing out a leaflet critical of McDonald's on a variety of grounds. The trial began in 1994 and ultimately became the longest running trial in British history. While McDonald's "won" the case (although the judge found for the defendants on several grounds), it was a public relations disaster for the company. The case continues on with a series of appeals undertaken by the defendants.

The trial and its history are important in themselves, but of greatest interest to us here is the formation of the group known as McSpotlight, which now is in the forefront not only of anti-McDonald's activity but also in opposition to many different multinational corporations. Of greatest importance is its Web site, which has become the international center for communicating, and finding out, about activities being mounted against McDonald's and other corporations around the world. The McSpotlight group is a social movement as well as a spur to other such movements.

27

The McLibel Trial Story

McSpotlight

◆◆◆ ──

Handing out leaflets on the streets was one of the main activities of the small activist group London Greenpeace, who'd been campaigning on a variety of environmental and social justice issues since the early 1970s. (The group predates the more well known Greenpeace International and the two organizations are unconnected.)

In 1978, local postman Dave Morris worked alongside London Greenpeace activists in protests against nuclear power. By 1982 he had started attending the group's meetings.

London Greenpeace campaigned on a wide range of issues from nuclear power and third world debt to anti-traffic actions and the Miners Strike. In the mid 1980s, the group began a campaign focusing on McDonald's as a high-profile organization symbolizing everything they considered wrong with the prevailing corporate mentality. In 1985, they launched the International Day of Action Against McDonald's, which has been held on October 16 ever since. In 1986, they produced a 6-sided fact sheet called "What's Wrong With McDonald's? Everything They Don't Want You to Know." The leaflet

─────────────

Editor's Note: Excerpts from "The McLibel Trial Story" available online from McSpotlight (www.mcspotlight.org/case/trial/story.html).

attacked almost all aspects of the corporation's business, accusing them of exploiting children with advertising, promoting an unhealthy diet, exploiting their staff, and being responsible for environmental damage and ill treatment of animals.

But the group also continued with other campaigns, and in 1987, 21-year-old gardener Helen Steel went along to meetings to get involved with protests in support of Aboriginal land rights at the time of the reenactment of the First Fleet sailing to Australia.

Meanwhile, McDonald's were busily suing (or threatening to sue) almost everyone who criticized them—from the BBC and *The Guardian* to student unions and green groups. . . .

In 1989, as the campaign grew and was taken up by more and more groups around the world, McDonald's produced their own "McFact cards" detailing their position on many of the accusations made in the leaflet. They also decided to take extreme action against London Greenpeace.

McDonald's hired two firms of private investigators and instructed them to infiltrate the group in order to find out how they operated, who did what and, most importantly, who was responsible for the production and distribution of the leaflet.

Since London Greenpeace was an unincorporated association, if McDonald's wanted to bring legal action to stop the campaign it would have to be against named individuals—which meant the company needed to find out people's names and addresses. Seven spies in total infiltrated the group. They followed people home, took letters sent to the group, got fully involved in the activities (including giving out anti-McDonald's leaflets), and invented spurious reasons to find out people's addresses. One spy (Michelle Hooker) even had a 6-month love affair with one of the activists. Another, Allan Claire, broke into the office of London Greenpeace and took a series of photographs.

At some London Greenpeace meetings there were as many spies as campaigners present and, as McDonald's didn't tell each agency about the other, the spies were busily spying on each other (the court later heard how Allan Claire had noted the behavior of Brian Bishop, another spy, as "suspicious").

Not all the spies were unaffected by the experience: Fran Tiller "felt very uncomfortable" doing the job and "disliked the deception, spying on people and interfering with their lives." She later gave evidence for the defendants in the trial, stating "I didn't think there was anything wrong with what the group was doing" and "I believe people are entitled to their views."

In 1990, McDonald's served libel writs on five volunteers in the group over the "What's Wrong With McDonald's?" leaflet. They offered a stark choice: retract the allegations made in the leaflet and apologize or go to court.

There is no legal aid (public money) for libel cases, but the five did get two hours' free legal advice, which boiled down to: the legal procedures in libel are extremely complex and weighted against defendants, you'll incur huge costs, with no money or legal experience you'll have no chance against McDonald's legal team, you probably won't even get past the legal obstacles before the full trial. In short: back out and apologize while you've got the chance. One of the barristers that they met at this time, Keir Starmer, said that if they decided to fight he would back them up for free.

Three of the five took the advice and reluctantly apologized. Which left Helen Steel and Dave Morris. Dave's partner and his very young son had a bad accident and he was nursing them single-handed (he and his partner later split up and Dave became a full-time single father). He said he would go along with whatever Helen decided.

"It just really stuck in the throat to apologize to McDonald's. I thought it was them that should have been apologizing to us—well not us specifically, but to society for the damage they do to society and the environment"—Helen Steel.

Unlike anyone McDonald's had ever sued for libel before, Helen and Dave decided that they would stand up to the burger giants in court. They knew each other well from their involvement in community-based campaigns in their local North London neighborhood and felt that although the odds were stacked against them, people would rally round to ensure that McDonald's wouldn't succeed in silencing their critics.

Long before you get to trial, there are an enormous number of preliminary hearings and procedures that have to be completed. First, Helen and Dave had to prepare their Defense—a detailed response to McDonald's Statement of Claim. Then there were several rounds of "Further and Better Particulars of Justification and Fair Comment" to complete.

Meanwhile, the McLibel Support Campaign was set up to generate solidarity and financial support for Helen and Dave. Over the next few years they would raise more than £35,000 to pay for witness airfares, court costs, expenses, and so on—every penny coming from donations from the public. Helen and Dave would only claim some travel and administration expenses (photocopying, phone calls to witnesses, etc.)—they were determined that they would never take a penny for themselves.

In 1991, the defendants took the British government to the European Court of Human Rights to demand the right to legal aid or the simplification of libel procedures. Paradoxically, the court ruled that, as the defendants had put up a "tenacious defense," they could not say they were being denied access to justice. They lost the application.

Meanwhile, back in the UK High Court, legal battles were raging between the two sides over McDonald's refusal to disclose all the relevant documents in its possession. McDonald's barrister argued that the defense case was very weak, that Helen and Dave would not be able to produce evidence to support it, so large parts of it should be dismissed and therefore there was no need for McDonald's to hand over the documents. The judge overturned normal procedures (whereby documents are disclosed before exchange of witness statements) and ruled that the defendants had three weeks to produce witness statements.

To everyone's surprise, Helen and Dave came back with 65 statements. McDonald's then took the unusual step of bringing in a top lawyer at this pretrial stage: employing Richard Rampton QC, one of Britain's top libel lawyers for a reputed fee of £2,000 a day plus a 6-figure briefing fee. Their legal team now comprised Rampton, his junior barrister, solicitor Patti Brinley-Codd, at least five solicitors and assistants from [the] leading city law firm Barlow, Lyde, and Gilbert, and even someone to carry Rampton's files. Helen and Dave were representing themselves, with occasional backup from Keir Starmer. At this time, Mr. Justice Bell, who ultimately presided over the full McLibel trial, took over the pretrial hearings. . . .

In late 1993, Richard Rampton started to prove why he is paid so much money. He applied for the trial to be heard by a judge only, arguing that the scientific evidence necessary to examine the links between diet and disease are too complicated for the ordinary people of a jury to understand. This was despite the obvious fact that the defendants themselves were ordinary people with no scientific training.

The judge ruled in favor of McDonald's, saying that it would be too complex for lay people to adjudicate some of the issues, and it could be tried more "conveniently" without a jury. The trial would now be heard by a single judge: a major blow to the defendants as it was very likely that a jury would be more sympathetic. They may even have been outraged that the case was ever brought at all.

McDonald's also applied for an order striking out certain parts of the defense on the grounds that the witness statements gathered by the defendants did not sufficiently support those areas of the defense. The judge agreed to strike out the entire rainforest section and many of the pleadings relating to trade union disputes in other countries around the world.

Dave Morris and Helen Steel applied unsuccessfully to the Court of Appeal and the House of Lords to reinstate the jury. However, in a landmark legal decision, the Court of Appeal restored all parts of the defense struck out by the judge, on the basis that the defendants are entitled to rely on not only their own witnesses' statements but also those from McDonald's witnesses, the future discovery of McDonald's documents, and what they might reasonably expect to discover under cross-examination of the company's witnesses.

Steel and Morris prepared to prove that the statements in the allegedly libelous leaflet were true or fair comment. Defendants are required under British libel law to provide "primary sources" of evidence to substantiate their case. This means witness statements and documentary proof rather than press reports, common knowledge, or even scientific journals.

Just before the trial proper was due to start, in March 1994, McDonald's produced 300,000 copies of a leaflet to distribute to their customers via their burger outlets. The leaflet stated that "This action is not about freedom of speech; it is about the right to stop people telling lies." The company also issued press releases in a similar vein. In a neat legal move, Helen and Dave issued a counterclaim against McDonald's over the accusation that the company's critics (including them) are liars. This meant that, as well as the defendants having to prove that the criticisms made in the "What's Wrong With McDonald's?" leaflet are true, McDonald's would now have to prove they are false (and that the defendants knew they were false) if they wanted to win the counterclaim. As it turned out, however, the judge did not run the trial in this way.

June 28, 1994, and the full libel trial finally started in Court 35 of the Royal Courts of Justice, London. It was presided over by Mr. Justice Bell, a new judge with almost no experience of libel.

The contested allegations made in the leaflet can be divided into seven broad categories: nutrition, rainforests, recycling and waste, employment, food poisoning, animals, and publication (i.e., did Steel and Morris publish the leaflet?). . . .

Meanwhile, questions were being asked in the UK parliament. Labor MP Jeremy Corbyn sponsored two Early Day Motions called "McDonald's and Censorship" in which he said that "this House opposes the routine use of libel writs as a form of censorship" and that "apologies and damages have been obtained under false pretences after McDonald's lied about their practices." Serious stuff.

The nutrition section of the case got off to a flying start with a contrast between McDonald's internal company memo—"We can't really address or defend nutrition. We don't sell nutrition and people don't come to McDonald's for nutrition"—and one of their public leaflets—"Every time you eat at McDonald's, you'll eat good, nutritious food." Defense witness Tim Lobstein testified that McDonald's concept of a balanced diet is "meaningless." "You could eat a roll of cellotape as part of a balanced diet," he said.

Classic Court Moment Number 1 came on September 12, 1994, when McDonald's expert witness on cancer, Dr. Sydney Arnott, inadvertently admitted that one of the most contentious statements made in the leaflet was a "very reasonable thing to say."

Around this time the defendants received a most unexpected message: McDonald's wanted to meet them to discuss a settlement. . . . McDonald's said they would drop the suit and pay a substantial sum to a third party if the defendants agreed never to publicly criticize McDonald's again. Helen and Dave said they wanted an undertaking from McDonald's not to sue anyone for making similar criticisms again and for the company to apologize to those they've sued in the past. No deal, so back to court.

By Autumn 1994, the court was listening to evidence on McDonald's advertising techniques, and part of their confidential *Operation Manual* was read out in court: "Ronald loves McDonald's and McDonald's food. And so do children, because they love Ronald. Remember, children exert a phenomenal influence when it comes to restaurant selection. This means you should do everything you can to appeal to children's love for Ronald and McDonald's."

On Day 102 in court—March 13, 1995—McLibel became the longest ever UK libel trial. . . .

Around this time an Australian documentary team received a leaked confidential McDonald's Australia memo, which detailed their strategy for dealing with media interest in the McLibel case. It included such gems as "we could worsen the controversy by adding our opinion" and "we want to keep it at arm's length—not become guilty by association."

Meanwhile, McDonald's shareholders were getting upset. At the annual general meeting in Chicago, Michael Quinlan, Chair and Chief Executive, said the case would be "coming to a wrap soon." It actually lasted two more years.

June 28, 1995, and the trial celebrated its first anniversary, with a birthday cake and picket outside the court.

Before the trial started, McDonald's had made an agreement with the judge and with Helen and Dave to pay for daily transcripts of the trial to be made, and to give copies to all parties. In July 1995, they said that they were withdrawing this agreement unless the defendants agreed to stop giving quotes to the press. Helen and Dave considered this to be a crude attempt by McDonald's to stop the swell of negative publicity based on quotes from the transcripts—especially admissions obtained during their cross-examination of McDonald's witnesses. McDonald's said that it was to stop Helen and Dave distorting what their witnesses had said. The McLibel Support Campaign launched an appeal to raise the £35,000 needed to pay for transcripts for the remainder of the trial (£425 per day). . . .

In June 1995, at McDonald's request, the two sides met again for more settlement negotiations. . . . McDonald's repeated that they can't possibly agree to never sue anyone again. Helen and Dave repeated that they couldn't possibly agree not to criticize McDonald's anymore. The talks failed, and the trial continued.

By October 1995, the court was listening to evidence on McDonald's employment practices—over 30 ex-employees and trade union officials and activists from around the world would be called. Media highlights included allegations of racism, cooking in a kitchen flooded with sewage, watering down products, illegal hours worked, underage staff employed, fiddling of time cards, and obsessive anti-union practices. . . .

McLibel notched up another one for the record books on December 11, 1995, as it became the longest civil case (as opposed to criminal case) in British history.

The greatest moment of the whole case, campaign, and possibly the history of the planet came on February 16, 1996, when Helen and Dave launch the McSpotlight Internet site from a laptop connected to the Internet via a mobile phone outside a McDonald's store in Central London. The Web site was accessed more than a million times in its first month, of which 2,700 were from a computer called "mcdonalds.com."

Between February and April of that year the court heard evidence on one of the most controversial allegations in the leaflet: that McDonald's were responsible for the destruction of rainforests in Central and South America to make way for cattle pasture. Witness Sue Brandford, appearing for the Defense, testified that she visited one of the particular areas in Brazil under contention 20 years ago and that it was rainforest then. The judge said that it was the most important evidence heard so far on this issue.

The defendants were by now completely exhausted but were refused an adjournment for rest.

Around this time, the judge denied the defendants leave to appeal his decision to allow McDonald's to change their Statement of Claim (original case against Morris and Steel) regarding the issues of nutrition and animal welfare. The Court of Appeal also refused them leave to appeal.

After rainforests came publication. Did Helen and Dave produce or distribute the fact sheet? If McDonald's did not manage to prove this, then their whole case would fall apart.

The majority of McDonald's case on publication relied on the spies who had been paid to infiltrate the London Greenpeace meetings in the 1980s. Four of them came to give evidence for McDonald's. But, in one of the great twists of the trial, another one, Fran Tiller, appeared on behalf of Helen and Dave. She testified that she "did not think there was anything wrong with what the group was doing." Three of the spies admitted distributing the leaflet, and so the defendants claimed McDonald's had consented to its publication.

In June, the trial celebrated its second anniversary with a Ronald McDonald cake outside court.

On July 17, 1996, the court closed with all the evidence completed. Each side now had just three months to write their closing speeches—analyzing

40,000 pages of documentary evidence, 20,000 pages of transcript testimony, and dealing with many complex legal arguments and submissions—in order to present their final case. . . .

In fact, the corporation was receiving increasingly bad publicity now, and as the trial progressed, campaigners were stepping up their protests against McDonald's worldwide. In particular, "What's Wrong With McDonald's?" leaflets were becoming probably the most famous and widely distributed protest leaflets in history.

The two sides returned to court in October to start the closing speeches. The judge turned down the defendants' request either for more time to prepare or for McDonald's to go first with the closing speeches. The defendants argued that they were unprepared and couldn't hope to analyze even half the testimony in the time available. They also argued that they had no experience in what should be included and since McDonald's were represented by experienced lawyers they should go first. The judge said no, and a few weeks later, the Court of Appeal refused to give the defendants leave to appeal against the judge's ruling.

Helen and Dave started their closing speeches on October 21 and carried on for a massive 6 weeks. This surely had to be one of the longest speeches ever made in history, not least because . . . two weeks later, on November 1, 1996 (Court Day 292), McLibel became the longest trial of any kind in English history. . . . The *Guinness Book of Records* took note.

Richard Rampton QC, for McDonald's, decided to present his closing speech in written form and handed his 5-volume document to the judge on November 28, 1996. All that remained was a few days of legal arguments. The defendants argued that the UK libel laws are oppressive and unfair, particularly (in this case) the denial of legal aid and a jury trial and that multinational corporations should no longer be allowed to sue their critics in order to silence them over issues of public interest. They cited European and U.S. laws which would debar such a case and also recent developments in UK law debarring governmental bodies from suing for libel. It was further argued that the McLibel case was beyond all precedent, was an abuse of procedure and of public rights, and that there was "an overriding imperative for decisions to be made to protect the public interest."

December 13, 1996, was the last day of final submissions. Mr. Justice Bell said, "I will say now that I propose to reserve any judgment. It will take me some time to write it. I don't mean to be difficult when I say I don't know when I will deliver it because I don't know." He denied newspaper reports that his ruling would come at the beginning of 1997 or early 1997, adding "It will take me longer than that."

The media frenzy continued as the judge deliberated, with Channel 4 TV news stating that the McLibel case was considered to be "the biggest corporate PR disaster in history.". . .

But things were going well for the corporation too: In April, they announced that "systemwide sales exceeded $30 billion for the first time, and net income crossed the $1.5 billion threshold."

Despite the build-up in the preceding weeks, no one had any inkling of the scale of the media attention on Judgment Day—June 19, 1997. . . .

Mr. Justice Bell took two hours to read his summary to a packed courtroom. He ruled that Helen and Dave had not proved the allegations against McDonald's on rainforest destruction, heart disease and cancer, food poisoning, starvation in the third world, and bad working conditions. But they had proved that McDonald's "exploits children" with their advertising, falsely advertise their food as nutritious, risk the health of their most regular, long-term customers, are "culpably responsible" for cruelty to animals, are "strongly antipathetic" to unions, and pay their workers low wages.

. . . "Not proved" does not mean that the allegations against McDonald's are not true, just that the judge felt that Helen and Dave did not bring sufficient evidence to prove the meanings he had attributed to the leaflet. The judge ruled that Helen and Dave had libeled McDonald's, but as they had proved many of the allegations, they would only owe half of the claimed damages: £60,000.

Helen eloquently summarized the defendants' response: "McDonald's don't deserve a penny and in any event we haven't got any money." McDonald's had 4 weeks to decide whether they were going to pursue their costs and the injunction which they had originally set out to obtain back in September 1990.

Press interest was at a peak around the day of the verdict. McSpotlight was accessed 2.2 million times. . . .

Two days after the verdict Helen and Dave were leafleting outside McDonald's again, in defiance of any injunction McDonald's may serve. They weren't alone: Over 400,000 leaflets were distributed outside 500 of McDonald's 750 UK stores, and solidarity protests were held in over a dozen countries. . . .

McDonald's dropped their claim for damages as well as their intention of getting an injunction (meaning that if Helen and Dave continued to distribute the leaflets it would be contempt of court, for which they could be jailed). Although this was a sensible move, PR-wise (as the defendants had already stated that they would defy any injunction) it signaled a clear admission of defeat. The securing of damages and an injunction had been the corporation's two aims in starting proceedings. . . . They are now claiming that they were only interested in establishing the truth (for example, that they exploit children).

Two months after the verdict, the defendants' appeal was safely lodged. Helen and Dave argued that the trial was unfair and the libel laws oppressive, that the defense evidence on all of the issues was overwhelming, and that in any case Mr. Justice Bell's findings against the corporation were so damaging to McDonald's reputation that the case should have been found in the defendants' favor overall.

After a short break to recover from the stress of the trial, the defendants would have to start extensive preparation anew.

Meanwhile, the global protests and the distribution of London Greenpeace leaflets continued to grow—including a week of action around Anti-McDonald's Day in October 1997.

Pre-appeal hearings—and legal arguments and disputes—took place throughout 1998 in front of three Lord Justices. The appeal itself finally started on January 12, 1999, ending on March 21, 1999. . . . The defendants represented themselves, opposed by the usual McSuspects on the other side of the room. . . .

McDonald's on the other hand, did not appeal against any of the rulings made against them. In fact, they had conceded in writing on January 5, 1999, that the trial judge had been "correct in his conclusions.". . .

On March 31, 1999, Lord Justices Pill, May, and Keane announced their verdict on 309 pages. The controversy continued as they added to the findings already made against McDonald's. They ruled that it was a fact that McDonald's food was linked to a greater risk of heart disease and that it was fair comment to say McDonald's workers worldwide suffer poor pay and conditions.

The defendants felt that, although the battle with McDonald's was now largely won, it was important to continue to push for an outright victory and for changes in the libel laws. On July 31, 1999, they lodged a 43-point petition to the House of Lords for Leave to Appeal further. Should this petition fail they were planning to take the British government to the European Court of Human Rights While the legal dispute continued, opposition to McDonald's did likewise—during 1999 . . . dramatic protests by local residents, French farmers, and the first unionization of a McStore in North America. On October 16, 1999, there were protests in 345 towns in 23 countries. . . . After the House of Lords, the defendants plan to take their fight to the European Court of Human Rights, where they will argue that, because they had to represent themselves and there was no jury, the whole trial was unfair and the verdict should be overturned.*

---

* In February, 2005, the court ruled that Morris and Steel had been denied their human rights; they should have been given legal aid to pay for appropriate representation.

Thinking Critically

1. What was the McLibel trial all about?

2. Was it a victory or loss for McDonald's?

3. Would you have persevered the way Dave Morris and Helen Steel did?

4. Do you think, as the judge did, that McDonald's exploits children?

5. Is the global opposition to McDonald's a good thing? A bad thing?

Chapter 28 offers some insight into the efforts in the late 1990s of French farmer José Bové and his compatriots to protest American and World Trade Organization (WTO) policies by attacking McDonald's (or "MacDo" as it is called by some in France) sites in a variety of ways (dumping three tons of manure on a restaurant floor, occupying a McDonald's with fowl of various types). Bové was eventually tried and convicted for being involved (with nine others) in wrecking a McDonald's construction site by driving tractors through it. Bové and his efforts attracted a great deal of media attention and won many adherents to his cause. Bové himself became an international celebrity. He has also been involved in anti-WTO protests, which represent another form of collective behavior/social movement aimed, at least in part, against McDonald's.

28

Striking the Golden Arches

French Farmers Protest McD's Globalization

David Morse

◆◆◆ —————————————————————————————

José Bové . . . and nine other peasants from the Confédération Paysanne, the farmer's union which he co-founded, had driven their tractors through the half-completed McDonald's outlet to protest the punitive tariffs enacted by the U.S. a month earlier on foie gras and Roquefort cheese and other European farm products. The tariffs, sanctioned by the World Trade Organization, were in retaliation for the European Union's refusal to accept American hormone-treated beef.

Farmers like Bové are caught in the middle, their livelihoods threatened by the machinations of huge corporations operating through the WTO and other bureaucracies established to promote global trade. But the farmers' agenda goes well beyond economic self-interest, to fundamental issues of culture and democratic choice within the global economy.

José Bové is not only a sheep farmer, of course; he is a committed trade unionist and environmental activist with a sophisticated sense of symbolism. . . .

Editor's Note: Excerpts from "Striking the Golden Arches: French Farmers Protest McD's Globalization" by David Morse online (www.populist.com/00.14.morse.html).

But it has been the recent and well-publicized attacks on McDonald's—or "MacDo," as it is known in France—that have captured headlines in the French press and elevated the pipe-smoking Bové to the status of a pop icon. The attacks have been non-violent but trenchant in their symbolism—consisting in one case of his dumping three tons of manure on a McDonald's floor. On another occasion, farmers protested by occupying a McDonald's with the chickens, geese, turkeys, and ducks that figure prominently in local indigenous agriculture. Another McDonald's outlet was filled with apples. In Seattle last November, Bové joined the WTO protest by destroying a cask of his own Roquefort cheese in front of a McDonald's.

Why target McDonald's? . . . As Bové puts it, the struggle is between two ways of farming and eating: "real food and real farmers," as opposed to "industrial agriculture and corporate control."

"Look," Bové said, "cooking is culture. All over the world. Every nation, every region, has its own food cultures. Food and farming define people. We cannot let it all go, to be replaced with hamburgers. People will not let it happen."

Bové's choice of McDonald's as his . . . target forged in an implicit link between the fast-food giant and these larger issues of local control. The McDonald's presence in France touches a nerve that goes well beyond the golden arches. With 804 outlets in France at last count, McDonald's is the most visible embodiment of the larger process of McDonaldization that threatens more than French food.

Sociologist George Ritzer, in his book *The McDonaldization of Society*, applies the term to a wide variety of enterprises, from Toys 'R Us to Home Depot, that are replicated identically in the interests of efficiency and absolute predictability. "Efficiency, predictability, calculability, and control through nonhuman technology can be thought of as the basic components of a rational system," he observes. "However, rational systems inevitably spawn irrationalities." Ritzer cites as one example the degree of control over employees required to produce identical experiences for customers.

This enforcement of uniformity was brought home last March when Remi Millet, a 23-year-old cashier at a McDonald's outlet in the south of France, was fired for giving five cheeseburgers to a homeless woman. Millet contends he was giving away his own food; the cheeseburgers were earned through a McDonald's "point" system designed to reward employees for taking unpopular shifts or performing special services. But he was fired anyway for breaking the company's rigid work rules.

The incident made a splash in France, confirming people's worst suspicions about the inhumanity of U.S.-style capitalism. Millet was widely interviewed on television. He was contacted by José Bové and invited to appear at the forthcoming meeting of the EU parliament. Now he is working in

Paris with a group organizing fast-food workers. He is also among those lobbying for a subsidy of traditional cuisine that would allow young diners—from ages 5 to 21—to eat for 50 francs at a good (two-star, in Paris) restaurant.

Since all the flap, Millet told this writer that MacDo has done its best to vilify him. An official letter from his old boss enumerated 30 complaints, including drug dealing—which Millet says is a complete fabrication. Denis Hennequin, Chairman of McDonald's France, a subsidiary of McDonald's Corporation, has reportedly brought pressure to get the EU to cancel the invitation and has written letters to mayors all around France in an effort to discredit the fired cashier.

In April, a month after Millet's firing, McDonald's was on French television again, this time in Brittany, when an unidentified bomber rigged three pounds of dynamite to a kitchen timer set to go off at night outside the drive-through of a McDonald's. The timer failed, and an employee who showed up for the breakfast shift was killed. Investigations have focused on a separatist group, the Breton Revolutionary Army.

José Bové was quick at the time to decry the violence of the Brittany attack. He called it misguided and "imbecilic."

However, the prosecutor at the present trial in Millau has tried to link Bové to the attack indirectly, suggesting that by turning McDonald's into a symbolic target Bové may have contributed to an atmosphere in which violent or unstable individuals might follow his lead. The accusation was roundly booed by observers in the courtroom and by the thousands of Bové supporters outside once they were informed.

Eyewitnesses report that when Bové came to the courthouse window and asked for quiet, so that the windows in the stuffy building could be kept open, the huge but orderly crowd fell into an impressive silence.

. . . The trial continues to serve as a forum for energetic debate. Whether the larger symbolism will be appreciated or even understood in our own country—where McDonaldization is the rule, and McNews is king—remains to be seen.

Thinking Critically

◆◆◆

1. What do you think of the protests of French farmers against McDonald's?

2. Was it fair for them to single out McDonald's?

3. Should José Bové have gone to jail?

4. In what ways is food culture?

Mara Miele and Jonathan Murdoch deal with a third social movement that targets fast-food restaurants and McDonaldization—the Italian-based Slow Food movement that is rapidly setting up outposts throughout the world. Slow Food began in 1986 because of a concern for the impact of McDonald's on local food and was given impetus by protests (unsuccessful) against the opening of the first McDonald's in Rome at the famous Piazza di Spagna (Spanish Steps). In its early years, the movement focused on protecting local products and cuisines, but in recent years it has extended its reach to include the protection of local products that are threatened with extinction. Over the years, Slow Food has created a "culinary network" that stands in opposition to McDonald's much larger and powerful network. Thus, McDonaldization has stimulated strong countermovements that include not only Slow Food but also McLibel and José Bové and his supporters. Miele and Murdoch point out, however, that it would be wrong to draw a sharp distinction between those who go to McDonald's and those who are sympathetic to such countermovements. It is possible to eat at McDonald's for lunch because one is in a hurry and then seek out a traditional restaurant or prepare a traditional meal at home.

29

Slow Food

Mara Miele and Jonathan Murdoch

◆◆◆──

> [T]he degree of slowness is directly proportional to the intensity
> of memory; the degree of speed is directly proportional to the
> intensity of forgetting.
>
> *Milan Kundera*, Slowness

S low Food was established in Bra, a small town in the Piedmont region
in the North of Italy, in 1986 by a group of food writers and chefs. The
immediate motivation was growing concern about the potential impact of
McDonald's on food cultures in Italy. The first Italian McDonald's had
opened the previous year in Trentino Alto Adige, a region in the North East

---

of Italy. It was quickly followed by a second in Rome. This latter restaurant, because of its location in the famous Piazza di Spagna, gave rise to a series of protests. These protests provided the spur for the founding of Slow Food.

In the beginning, the movement's founders were concerned that the arrival of McDonald's would threaten not the growing upmarket restaurants frequented by the middle/upper-class city dwellers but local *osterie* and *trattorie*, the kinds of places that serve local dishes and which have traditionally been frequented by people of all classes. Because, in the Italian context, traditional eateries retain a close connection to local food production systems, Slow Food argued that their protection required the general promotion of local food cultures. As the Slow Food Manifesto put it, the aim of the movement is to promulgate a new "philosophy of taste" where the guiding principles should be "conviviality and the right to taste and pleasure." Other key objectives include disseminating and stimulating knowledge of "material culture" (e.g., every product reflects its place of origin and production techniques), preserving the agroindustrial heritage (e.g., defending the biodiversity of crops, craft-based food production, and traditions), and protecting the historical, artistic, and environmental heritage of traditional foods (e.g., cafés, cake shops, inns, craft workshops, and so on) (see www.slowfood.com). In short, the movement sought to develop new forms of "gastronomic associationalism" that link the cultural life of food to biodiverse production spaces.

Slow Food was established on the basis of a local structure, coordinated by a central headquarters in Bra. The local branches effectively engage in a range of activities aimed at strengthening local cuisines (see below). These branches were initially established in all the Italian regions (and were called *condotte*) but soon began to spread to other European countries and then further afield (outside Italy the branches are called *convivia*). In 1989, Slow Food was formally launched as an international movement. In that year representatives from 20 countries attended a meeting in Paris and agreed to both an international structure and a manifesto. The manifesto asserted "a firm defense of quiet material pleasure" and stated "Our aim is to rediscover the richness and aromas of local cuisines to fight the standardization of Fast Food." It went on to say "Our defense should begin at the table. . . . Let us rediscover the flavors and savors of regional cooking and banish the degrading effects of Fast Food . . . That is what real culture is all about: developing taste rather than demeaning it." The movement thus began to establish itself outside Italy, and at the time of writing, convivia exist in 40 countries and the movement has around 70,000 members.

In outlining how Slow Food has developed, we describe below the changing character of its activities. In general, the main focus of the movement has been the diffusion of knowledge about typical products and local cuisines to consumers. However, more recently, another complementary set of activities has been added. The new activities are aimed at rescuing from "extinction" the typical products that are facing a dramatic decline in their market. These are long-term projects that require the cooperation of a large number of actors—farmers, food processors, retailers, local institutions, and so forth. We document here the broadening nature of the movement and show it has come to extend the notion of "gastronomic association" from consumers to producers.

In articulating a response to the spread of McDonald's throughout Italy, Slow Food first began to disseminate information about local food cultures and the challenges they face. In so doing, it effectively became a "clearing house" for knowledge of local foods, initially in Italy but latterly more globally. The main means by which knowledge about local and typical cuisines is disseminated is the publishing company, established in 1990. Slow Food Editore publishes a range of guides in order to lead consumers to the food products available in a whole variety of local areas. In the main, these refer to Italian cuisines. Thus, alongside the *Vini d'Italia* wine guide, published in collaboration with the *Gambero Rosso* food monthly, Slow Food publishes *Osterie d'Italia*, a guide to the traditional cuisine of the Italian regions. However, as the movement has internationalized, so its publications have begun to focus upon typical foods found outside Italy. It recently published the *Guida ai Vini del Mondo*, a world wine guide describing as many as 1,900 cellars in 30 countries, and *Fromaggi d'Europa*, a "fact sheet" on the 127 European DOP cheeses in 1997. The movement's quarterly magazine *Slow* is produced in five languages and carries articles on foods from around the world.

The dissemination of knowledge also takes place through the local members. Every Slow Food group is encouraged to organize periodic theme dinners, food and wine tours, and tasting courses. The collaboration of the groups underpins national and international initiatives. The following are the most noteworthy: *Excellentia*, a three-day event involving 5,000 people all over Italy in twice-yearly blind tastings of international and Italian wines; "Taste Week" (*La Settimana del Gusto*), which sets out to familiarize young people with quality catering; "Friendship Tables" (*Le Tavole Fraterne*), which finance charity initiatives (such as the installation of a canteen in a hospital for Amazonian Indians, the rebuilding of a school in Sarajevo, and the restructuring of an Umbrian dairy damaged by the 1997 earthquake); and the "Hall of Taste," a food fair held every two years in Turin (this is a large, prestigious event that, in 1998, recorded over 120,000 visitors).

In its publications, tastings, talks, conventions, etc., Slow Food frames regional and local foods in ways that partially isolate them from their surrounding contexts but which retain strong ecological and cultural connections.

It readily recognizes that one of the reasons many local and regional food products are disappearing is because they are too embedded in local food cultures and ecologies; they are not easily extracted and sold into modern food markets (there has been little technological or organizational innovation around them, and they often cannot travel the long distances, either for cultural or ecological reasons, covered by McDonald's burgers). So Slow Food attempts to bring modern consumers to these traditional products and the restaurants in which they are served by stressing their symbolic value. In short, it attempts to bring the products to new markets (or, more accurately, bring new markets to the products).

The activities outlined above are aimed at consumers. However, since it began to identify the importance of local cuisines in maintaining food diversity, Slow Food has also become aware of the problems faced by the producers and processors of the products which compose local cuisines. It has therefore begun to play a more direct role in the protection and promotion of such products. The first of these initiatives was the "Ark of Taste," launched in 1996, which aims to "save from extinction" such typical foods as tiny production of cured meats (e.g., *lardo di colonnata*), artisan cheeses, local varieties of cereals and vegetables, and local breeds. To assist this activity, an Advisory Commission (composed of researchers, journalists, and other food "experts") was formed in order to evaluate products proposed for inclusion in the "Ark." The Commission was charged with gathering information on the processing, cultivation, or breeding techniques and commercial potential of the products, and also with developing intervention strategies to facilitate their "rescue." As part of this project. Slow Food has begun a major "census" of quality small-scale agroindustrial production and has encouraged Slow Food *osterie* and *trattorie* (i.e., those listed in *Osterie d'Italia*) to include the products in their dishes. The Ark project thus aims to enlarge the market for these lesser known products.

Slow Food is now broadening the range of these producer-oriented initiatives. It recently established local groups (*Praesidia*) in order to provide practical assistance to small producers of typical products (e.g., organizing commercial workshops, identifying new marketing channels). Another initiative targeted at producers, and aimed at protecting biodiversity, is the "Slow Food Award." The first award was given in October 2000 in Bologna (the European City of Culture) to biologists, fishermen, and small-scale entrepreneurs whose work helps defend the world's biodiversity. And, in a conscious emulation of McDonald's, Slow Food is about to establish a "Slow University" which aims to spread good practice in relation to the growing, processing, preparation, and consumption of typical products.

This second set of initiatives indicates that the Slow Food movement has entered a new stage in its development. As we have seen, it arose as a response to the arrival of McDonald's in Italy and claimed to be concerned for local *trattorie* and *osterie*. Since that time, its goals have broadened and the organization has become more complex. Thus, after spending the early years developing the capacity to disseminate knowledge about local cuisines and typical products to middle-class consumers, Slow Food has now started to engage more directly with producers and processors in order to strengthen the local base of typical production. In so doing, it has shifted its attention from the marketing of typical foods to the full range of activities that lie between producer and consumer. In this respect, the movement stands as an example of a sophisticated reaction to the spread of fast food: It extends from the local to global but seeks to put in place sets of gastronomic relations which effectively promote diversity in food as an intrinsic part of cultural and environmental diversity. In this sense, Slow Food stands in direct opposition to McDonald's.

Thinking Critically

1. What does the Slow Food movement stand for?

2. What do you think of it?

3. Do you think it's elitist?

4. Do you agree that it is possible to both eat in McDonald's and support Slow Food?

Part III

PEDAGOGICAL QUESTIONS

1. Benjamin Barber suggests that the four imperatives of the McWorld theory replace the premises of the nation-states that are based on territory and political sovereignty. Are these four imperatives as influential as the theory suggests? Evaluate the standpoints of world leaders on issues such as Middle Eastern politics, global warming, and AIDS.

2. To what extent are science and technology impartial? Do science and technology that provide the means for a greater public voice necessarily compel global actors to better reflect the public interest? Are innovations in technology substitutes for real change in the economic and power structures of the global world?

3. Do you think limiting McDonaldization is necessary to secure our environmental future? Why or why not?

4. To what extent does McDonaldization correlate with Americanization? Are they really distinct processes? What are their common features?

5. Is the omnipresence of U.S. consumer products, images, and sounds around the world supported by U.S. corporate, political, or military power? How discrete are their agendas? Think about the recent overseas interventions by the United States and the reconstruction efforts in these countries.

6. In what ways have credit cards changed your and your family's consumption patterns? Give examples of the irrationalities of rationality in your consumption patterns caused by the introduction of credit cards.

7. Does the replacement of a local restaurant with a McDonald's restaurant imply a greater political and economic transformation? Why or why not?

8. What does the domination of credit cards by U.S. brands and credit card companies indicate in terms of the global economy? How does individual consumption affect global economic dependence and interdependence?

9. Could the spread of consumer culture be perceived as a reflection of neo-imperialism?

10. What is the relationship between terrorism and national and global economies? Analyze the ever-growing national security industry. Do antiterrorism measures maintain local industries that serve government goals on national security?

11. Is it likely that the Slow Food Movement can resist McDonaldization? Can it be successful? Does it necessarily lead to de-McDonaldization?

12. Keeping in mind that movements such as Slow Food might be restricted to a limited group of people who have higher income levels, how realistic do you think such anti-McDonaldization efforts are?

13. Modern agribusiness uses high-tech farming methods that involve new hybrid seeds, advanced irrigation methods, chemical fertilizers, and pesticides for insect control to raise agricultural yields in poor nations. Given the fact that global agribusiness is controlled by developed countries, discuss the role of those countries in global economic development.

14. Does the authority of multinational corporations over global agricultural production replicate colonial-style patterns? Is there a possibility for poor nations to develop industries of their own and also to trade with one another? Does McDonaldization block paths to development for poor countries?

PART IV

The Debate Over the
Relationship Between
McDonaldization and Globalization

Jan Nederveen Pieterse identified three major paradigms in theorizing the cultural aspects of globalization, specifically on the centrally important issue of whether cultures around the globe are eternally different, converging, or creating new hybrid forms out of the unique combination of global and local cultures.

Cultural Differentialism. Those who adopt this paradigm argue that there are lasting differences among cultures that are largely unaffected by globalization. This is not to say that culture is unaffected by globalization, but that at its core, a culture remains much as it has always been. In this perspective, globalization only occurs on the surface with the deep structure of cultures largely, if not totally, unaffected by it. In one image, the world is envisioned as a mosaic of largely separate cultures. More menacing is a billiard ball image, with billiard balls (representing cultures) bouncing off others (representing other cultures). This is more menacing because it indicates the possibility of dangerous and potentially catastrophic collisions among and between world cultures.

Cultural Convergence. This paradigm is based on the idea of globalization leading to increasing sameness throughout the world. Those who support this perspective see cultures changing, sometimes radically, as a result of globalization. The cultures of the world are seen as growing increasingly similar, at least to some degree and in some ways. There is a tendency to see global assimilation moving in the direction of dominant groups and societies in the world. Those who operate from this perspective focus on such things as cultural imperialism, Americanization, and McDonaldization. At a global level, McDonaldization can be seen, at least in part, as a force in cultural convergence.

Cultural Hybridization. The third paradigm emphasizes the mixing of cultures as a result of globalization and the production, out of the integration of the global and the local, of new and unique hybrid cultures that are not reducible to either the local or the global culture. From this perspective, McDonaldization may be taking place, but it leads to largely superficial changes. Much more important is the integration of McDonaldization with various local realities to produce new and distinctive hybrid forms that indicate continued heterogenization rather than homogenization. Hybridization is a very positive, even romantic, view of globalization as a profoundly creative process out of which emerges new cultural realities and continuing, if not increasing, heterogeneity in many different locales.

30

Globalization and Culture

Three Paradigms

Jan Nederveen Pieterse

◆◆◆ ──

This is a . . . reflection on cultural difference that argues that there are three, and only three, perspectives on cultural difference: cultural differentialism or lasting difference, cultural convergence or growing sameness, and cultural hybridization or ongoing mixing. Each of these positions involves particular theoretical precepts and as such they are paradigms. Each represents a particular politics *of difference*—as lasting and immutable, as erasable and being erased, and as mixing and in the process generating new translocal forms of difference. Each involves different subjectivities and larger perspectives. The first view, according to which cultural difference is immutable, may be the oldest perspective on cultural difference. The second, the thesis of cultural convergence, is as old as the earliest forms of universalism, as in the world religions. Both have been revived and renewed as varieties of modernism, respectively in its romantic and Enlightenment versions, while the third perspective, hybridization, refers to a postmodern sensibility of traveling culture. . . . Arguably there may be other takes on cultural difference, such as indifference, but none have the scope and depth of the three perspectives outlined here.

CLASH OF CIVILIZATIONS

In 1993 Samuel Huntington . . . published a controversial paper in which he argued that "a crucial, indeed a central, aspect of what global politics is likely to be in the coming years . . . will be the clash of civilizations. . . . With the end of the Cold War, international politics moves out of its Western phase, and its centerpiece becomes the interaction between the West and non-Western civilizations and among non-Western civilizations."

The imagery is that of civilizational spheres as tectonic plates at whose fault lines conflict, no longer subsumed under ideology, is increasingly likely. The argument centers on Islam: the "centuries-old military interaction between the West and Islam is unlikely to decline." "Islam has bloody borders." The fault lines include Islam's borders in Europe (as in former Yugoslavia), Africa (animist or Christian cultures to the south and west), and Asia (India, China). Huntington warns against a "Confucian-Islamic military connection" that has come into being in the form of arms flows between East Asia and the Middle East. Thus "the paramount axis of world politics will be the relations between 'the West and the Rest'" and "a central focus of conflict for the immediate future will be between the West and several Islamic-Confucian states." He therefore recommends greater cooperation and unity in the West, between Europe and North America; the inclusion of Eastern Europe and Latin America in the West; cooperative relations with Russia and Japan; exploiting differences and conflicts among Confucian and Islamic states; and for the West to maintain its economic and military power to protect its interests . . .

McDONALDIZATION

The McDonaldization thesis is a version of the recent idea of the worldwide homogenization of societies through the impact of multinational corporations.

McDonaldization is a variation on a theme: on the classical theme of universalism and its modern forms of modernization and the global spread of capitalist relations. Diffusionism, if cultural diffusion is taken as emanating from a single center (e.g., Egypt), has been a general form of this line of thinking. From the 1950s, this has been held to take the form of Americanizations. Since the 1960s, multinational corporations have been viewed as harbingers of American modernization. In Latin America in the 1970s, this effect was known as Coca-colonization. These are variations on the theme of cultural imperialism, in the form of consumerist universalism or global media influence. This line of thinking has been prominent in media studies according to which the influence of American media makes for global cultural synchronization.

Modernization and Americanization are the latest versions of westernization. If colonialism delivered Europeanization, neocolonialism under U.S. hegemony delivers Americanization. Common to both is the modernization thesis, of which Marx and Weber have been the most influential proponents. Marx's thesis was the worldwide spread of capitalism. World-system theory is a current version of this perspective. With Weber, the emphasis is on rationalization, in the form of bureaucratization and other rational social technologies. Both perspectives fall within the general framework of evolutionism, a single-track universal process of evolution through which all societies, some faster than others, are progressing—a vision of universal progress such as befits an imperial world. . . .

HYBRIDIZATION: THE RHIZOME OF CULTURE

Mixing has been perennial as a process but new as an imaginary. As a perspective, it differs fundamentally from the previous two paradigms. It does not build on an older theorem but opens new windows. It is fundamentally excluded from the other two paradigms.

Hybridization . . . takes as its point of departure precisely those experiences that have been banished, marginalized, tabooed in cultural differentialism. It subverts nationalism because it privileges border-crossing. It subverts identity politics such as ethnic or other claims to purity and authenticity because it starts out from the fuzziness of boundaries. If modernity stands for an ethos of order and neat separation by tight boundaries, hybridization reflects a postmodern sensibility of cut 'n' mix, transgression, subversion. It represents, in Foucault's terms, a "resurrection of subjugated knowledges" because it foregrounds those effects and experiences which modern cosmologies, whether rationalist or romantic, would not tolerate.

Hybridization goes under various aliases such as syncretism, creolization, métissage, mestizaje, crossover. Related notions are global ecumene, global localization, and local globalization. . . . Hybridization may conceal the asymmetry and unevenness in the process and the elements of mixing. Distinctions need to be made between different times, patterns, types, and styles of mixing; besides mixing carries different meanings in different cultural settings.

Hybridization occurs of course also among cultural elements and spheres *within* societies. . . .

Intercultural mingling itself is a deeply creative process not only in the present phase of accelerated globalization but stretching far back in time. Cees Hamelink notes: "The richest cultural traditions emerged at the actual meeting point of markedly different cultures, such as Sudan, Athens, the Indus Valley, and Mexico." . . .

A schematic précis of the three paradigms of cultural difference is in Table 30.1.

FUTURES

The futures evoked by these three paradigms are dramatically different. McDonaldization evokes both a triumphalist Americanism and a gloomy picture of a global "iron cage" and global cultural disenchantment. The clash of civilizations likewise offers a horizon of a world of iron, a deeply pessimistic politics of cultural division as a curse that dooms humanity to lasting conflict and rivalry; the world as an archipelago of incommunicable differences, the human dialogue as a dialogue of war, and the global ecumene as an everlasting battlefield. The political scientist Benjamin Barber in *Jihad vs. McWorld* (Chapter 25) presents the clash between these two perspectives without giving a sense of the third option, mixing. Mixing or hybridization is open-ended in terms of experience as well as in a theoretical sense. Its newness means that its ramifications over time are not predictable because it doesn't fit an existing matrix or established paradigm but itself signifies a paradigm shift.

Each paradigm represents a different politics of *multiculturalism*. Cultural differentialism translates into a policy of closure and apartheid. If outsiders are let in at all, they are preferably kept at arm's length in ghettos, reservations, or concentration zones. Cultural communities are best kept separate, as in colonial "plural society" in which communities are not supposed to mix except in the marketplace, or as in gated communities that keep themselves apart. Cultural convergence translates into a politics of assimilation with the dominant group as the cultural center of gravity. Cultural mixing refers to a politics of integration without the need to give up cultural identity while cohabitation is expected to yield new cross-cultural patterns of difference. This is a future of ongoing mixing, ever-generating new commonalities and new differences.

Each paradigm involves a different take on *globalization*. According to cultural differentialism, globalization is a surface phenomenon only: the real dynamic is regionalization, or the formation of regional blocs, which tend to correspond with civilizational clusters. Therefore, the future of globalization is interregional rivalry. According to the convergence principle, contemporary globalization is westernization or Americanization writ large, a fulfillment in installments of the classical imperial and the modernization theses. According to the mixing approach, the outcome of globalization processes is

Table 30.1   Three Ways of Seeing Cultural Difference

Dimensions	Differentialism	Convergence	Mixing
Cosmologies	Purity	Emanation	Synthesis
Analytics	Territorial culture	Cultural centers and diffusion	Translocal culture
Lineages	Differences in language, religion, region. Caste.	Imperial and religious universalisms. Ancient "centrisms."	Cultural mixing of technologies, languages, religions
Modern times	Romantic differentialism. Race thinking, chauvinism. Cultural relativism.	Rationalist universalism. Evolutionism. Modernization. Coca-colonization.	Métissage, hybridization, creolization, syncretism.
Present	"Clash of civilizations." Ethnic cleansing. Ethnodevelopment.	McDonaldization, Disneyfication, Barbiefication, Homogenization.	Postmodern views of culture, cultural flows, crossover, cut 'n' mix
Futures	A mosaic of immutably different cultures and civilizations	Global cultural homogeneity	Open-ended ongoing mixing

open-ended and current globalization is as much a process of easternization as of westernization, as well as of many interstitial influences.

Thinking Critically

◆◆◆

1. In what ways are cultures of the world growing increasingly different?

2. In what ways are cultures of the world growing increasingly the same?

3. Can cultures be simultaneously growing increasingly similar and different?

4. What are cultural hybrids and are you familiar with any? If so, can you describe them?

5. Would you rather live in a world characterized by cultural differentiation, convergence, or hybridity? Why?

Malcolm Waters is a key contributor to the literature on globalization, and from that perspective, he takes issue in Chapter 31 with the idea of McDonaldization (and Americanization). First, Waters contends that I argue that globalization must be seen as homogenization. This is not true. I argue that McDonaldization implies a large degree of homogenization, but I do not equate globalization with McDonaldization. I understand that McDonaldization can be seen as a subtype of globalization and that the latter is the broader concept that encompasses, among others, both McDonaldization and Americanization (as well as Jihad). However, Water's second point is more interesting and provocative. He argues that although McDonaldization may have homogenizing effects, it also can be used in local communities in ways that are unanticipated by the forces that push it. That is, it may be used in ways that further heterogeneity rather than homogeneity.

31

McDonaldization and the Global Culture of Consumption

Malcolm Waters

◆◆◆ ————————————————————————————————

On the face of it ..., Ritzer offers a persuasive case that McDonaldization is an influential globalizing flow. The imperatives of the rationalization of consumption appear to drive McDonald's and like enterprises into every corner of the globe so that all localities are assimilated. The imperatives of such rationalization are expressed neatly:

> [C]onsumption is work, it takes time and it competes with itself since choosing, hauling, maintaining and repairing the things we buy is so time-consuming that we are forced to save time on eating, drinking, sex, dressing, sleeping, exercising and relaxing. The result is that Americans have taught us to eat standing, walking, running and driving—and, above all, never to finish a meal in favour of the endless snack ... we can now pizza, burger, fry and coffee ourselves as quickly as we can gas our autos.

Editor's Note: Excerpts from Waters, M. (1996). "McDonaldization and the Global Culture of Consumption." *Sociale Wetenshappen, 39,* 17–28. Used with permission.

. . . The globalization of "McTopia," a paradise of effortless and instantaneous consumption, is also underpinned by its democratizing effect. It democratizes by de-skilling, but not merely by de-skilling McWorkers but also by de-skilling family domestic labor. The kitchen is invaded by frozen food and microwaves so that domestic cooks, usually women, can provide McDonaldized fare at home. In the process, non-cooks, usually men and children, can share the cooking. Meals can become "de-familized" (i.e., de-differentiated) insofar as all members can cook, purchase, and consume the same fatty, starchy, sugary foods. Consequently, while "America is the only country in the world where the rich eat as badly as the poor," the appeal of such "gastronomic leveling" can serve as a magnet for others elsewhere.

However, we can put in perspective the alarmist in Ritzer's neo-Weberian suggestions that globalization will lead to a homogenized common culture of consumption if we expose them to the full gamut of globalization theory. Globalization theory normally specifies that a globalized culture is chaotic rather than orderly—it is integrated and connected so that the meanings of its components are "relativized" to one another but it is not unified or central-ized. The absolute globalization of culture would involve the creation of a common but hyperdifferentiated field of value, taste, and style opportunities, accessible by each individual without constraint for purposes either of self-expression or consumption. Under a globalized cultural regime, Islam would not be linked to particular territorially based communities in the Middle East, North Africa, and Asia but would be universally available across the planet and with varying degrees of "orthodoxy." Similarly, in the sphere of the polit-ical ideology, the apparently opposed political values of private property and power sharing might be combined to establish new ideologies of economic enterprise. In the sphere of consumption, cardboard hamburgers would be available not only in Pasadena but anywhere in the world, just as classical French cuisine would be available not only in Escoffier's in Paris but any-where. A globalized culture thus admits a continuous flow of ideas, informa-tion, commitment, values, and tastes mediated through mobile individuals, symbolic tokens, and electronic simulations. Its key feature is to suggest that the world is one place not because it is homogenized but because it accepts only social differentiation and not spatial or geographical differentiation.

These flows give a globalized culture a particular shape. First, it links together previously encapsulated and formerly homogeneous cultural niches. Local devel-opments and preferences are ineluctably shaped by similar patterns occurring in very distant locations. Second, it allows for the development of genuinely transna-tional cultures not linked to any particular nation-state-society, which may be either novel or syncretistic. Appadurai's increasingly influential argument about the global cultural economy identifies several of the important fields in which these developments take place. The fields are identified by the suffix "-scape";

that is, they are globalized mental pictures of the social world perceived from the flows of cultural objects. The flows include ethnoscapes, the distribution of mobile individuals (tourists, migrants, refugees, etc.); technoscapes, the distribution of technology; finanscapes, the distribution of capital; mediascapes, the distribution of information; and ideoscapes, the distribution of political ideas and values (e.g., freedom, democracy, human rights).

McDonaldization infiltrates several of these flows, including ethnoscapes, technoscapes, finanscapes, and ideoscapes. However, its effects are by no means universally homogenizing. The dynamics that are at work center on processes of relativization, reflexivity, and localization that operate against the assumed capacity of McDonaldization to regiment consumer behavior into uniform patterns. The return of agency that many authors have identified is not simply a series of isolated and individualized coping reactions of the type advocated by Ritzer in *McDonaldization* but a generalized feature of contemporary society that arises from the intersection of these globalizing flows. Indeed, such developments might be called the dysfunctions of McDonaldization in much the way that post-Weberian organizational theorists wrote of the dysfunctions of bureaucracy . . .

The term "relativization" . . . implies that globalizing flows do not simply swamp local differences. Rather, it implies that the inhabitants of local contexts must now make sense of their lifeworlds not only by reference to embedded traditions and practices but by reference to events occurring in distant places. McDonaldization is such an intrusive, neonistic development that it implies decisions about whether to accept its modernizing and rationalizing potential or to reject it in favor of a reassertion of local products and traditions. In some instances, this may involve a reorganization of local practices to meet the challenge. If we remain at the mundane level of hamburgers to find our examples, there is a story about the introduction of McDonald's in the Philippines that can illustrate the point:

> Originally, Filipino hamburger chains marketed their product on the basis of its "Americanness." However, when McDonald's entered the field and, as it were, monopolized the symbols of "Americanness," the indigenous chains began to market their product on the basis of local taste.

The relativization effect of McDonaldization goes of course much further than this because it involves the global diffusion not only of particular products but of icons of American capitalist culture. Relativizing reactions can therefore encompass highly generalized responses to that culture, whether positive or negative.

As people increasingly become implicated in global cultural flows they also become more reflexive. . . . Participation in a global system means that one's lifeworld is determined by impersonal flows of money and expertise that are beyond one's personal or even organizational control. If European governments cannot even control the values of their currencies against speculation, then individual lifeworlds must be highly vulnerable. Aware of such risk, people constantly watch, seek information about, and consider the value of money and the validity of expertise. Modern society is therefore specifically reflexive in character. Social activity is constantly informed by flows of information and analysis that subject it to continuous revision and thereby constitute and reproduce it. "Knowing what to do" in modern society, even in such resolutely traditional contexts as kinship or child rearing, almost always involves acquiring knowledge about how to do it from books, or television programs, or expert consultations, rather than relying on habit, mimesis, or authoritative direction from elders. McDonaldization is implicated in this process precisely because it challenges the validity of habit and tradition by introducing expertly rationalized systems, especially insofar as its capacity to commercialize and to commodify has never been in doubt.

The concept of localization is connected with the notions of relativization and reflexivity. The latter imply that the residents of a local area will increasingly come to want to make conscious decisions about which values and amenities they want to stress in their communities and that these decisions will increasingly be referenced against global scapes. Localization implies a reflexive reconstruction of community in the face of the dehumanizing implications of such rationalizing and commodifying forces as McDonaldization. The activist middle classes who mobilize civic initiatives and heritage preservation associations often stand in direct opposition to the expansion of McDonaldized outlets and hark back to an often merely imagined prior golden age.

Returning to more abstract issues, these three processes can assure us that a globalized world will not be a McWorld. It is a world with the potential for the displacement of local homogeneity not by global homogeneity but by global diversity. Three developments can confirm this hopeful prognosis.

First, one of the features of Fordist mass-production systems, of which McDonaldization might be the ultimate example, is that they sought to standardize at the levels of both production and consumption. Ultimately, they failed not only because they refused to recognize that responsible and committed workers would produce more in quantity and quality than controlled and alienated ones but because markets for standardized products became saturated. The succeeding paradigm of "flexible specialization" involved flexibly contracted workers using multiple skills and computerized machinery to dovetail products to rapidly shifting market demand. So consumer products took on a new form and function. Taste became the only determinant of their utility, so it became ephemeral and subject to whim. Product demand is determined by fashion, and unfashionable products are disposable. Moreover, taste and fashion became linked to social standing as product-based classes appeared as central features of social organization.

The outcome has been a restless search by producers for niche-marketing strategies in which they can multiply product variation in order to match market demand. In many instances, this has forced a downscaling of enterprises that can maximize market sensitivity. Correspondingly, affluent consumers engage in a restless search for authenticity. The intersection of these trends implies a multiplication of products and production styles. The world is becoming an enormous bazaar as much as a consumption factory. One of the most impressive examples of consumer and producer resistance to rationalization is the French bread industry, which is as non-McDonaldized as can be. . . . Consumers and producers struggled collectively against invasions by industrialized bakers, the former to preserve the authenticity of their food, the latter to maintain independent enterprises. Bread-baking is an artisanal form of production that reproduces peasant domestic traditions. About 80 percent of baking (Ritzer's *Croissanteries* notwithstanding) is still done in small firms. The product, of course, is the envy of global, middleclass consumers.

This diversification is accelerated by an aestheticization of production. As is well known, the history of modern society involves an increasing production of mass-cultural items. For most of this century, this production has been Fordist in character, an obvious example being broadcasting by large-scale private or state TV networks to closed markets. Three key features in the current period are the deregulation of markets by the introduction of direct-satellite and broadband fiber-optic technology; the vertical disintegration of aesthetic production to produce "a transaction-rich nexus of markets linking small firms, often of one self-employed person"; and the tendency of de-differentiation of producer and consumer within emerging multimedia technologies associated with the Internet and interactive television. The implication is that a very rapidly increasing proportion of consumption is aesthetic in character, that aesthetic production is taking place within an increasingly perfectionalized market, and that these aesthetic products are decreasingly susceptible to McDonaldization. An enormous range of individualized, unpredictable, inefficient, and irrational products can be inspected simply by surfing the Internet.

The last development that can disconfirm the thesis of a homogenized global culture is the way in which globalization has released opposing forces of opinion, commitment, and interest that many observers find threatening to the fabric of society and indeed to global security. One of these is the widespread religious revivalism that is often expressed as fundamentalism. Globalization carries the discontents of modernization and postmodernization (including McDonaldization) to religious traditions that might previously have remained encapsulated. . . . Religious systems are obliged to relativize themselves to these global postmodernizing trends. This relativization can involve an embracement of postmodernizing patterns, an abstract and humanistic ecumenism, but it can also take the form of a rejective search for original traditions. It is this latter that has given rise to both Islamic fundamentalism and . . . the New Christian Right.

Globalization equally contributes to ethnic diversity. It pluralizes the world by recognizing the value of cultural niches and local abilities. Importantly, it weakens the putative nexis between nation and state releasing absorbed ethnic minorities and allowing the reconstitution of nations across former state boundaries. This is especially important in the context of states that are confederations of minorities. It can actually alter the mix of ethnic identities in any nation-state by virtue of the flow of economic migrants from relatively disadvantaged sectors of the globe to relatively advantaged ones. Previously homogeneous nation-states have, as a consequence, moved in the direction of multiculturalism.

CONCLUSION

The paradox of McDonaldization is that in seeking to control consumers it recognizes that human individuals potentially are autonomous, a feature that is notoriously lacking in "cultural dupe" or "couch potato" theories of the spread of consumer culture. As dire as they may be, fast-food restaurants only take money in return for modestly nutritious and palatable fare. They do not seek to run the lives of their customers, although they might seek to run their diets. They attract rather than coerce so that one can always choose not to enter. Indeed, advertising gives consumers the message, however dubious, that they are exercising choice.

It might therefore be argued, *contra* Ritzer, that consumer culture is the source of the increased cultural effectivity that is often argued to accompany globalization and postmodernization. Insofar as we have a consumer culture, the individual is expected to exercise choice. Under such a culture, political issues and work can equally become items of consumption. A liberal-democratic political system might only be possible where there is a culture of consumption precisely because it offers the possibility of election—even if such a democracy itself tends to become McDonaldized, as leaders become the mass-mediated images of photo opportunities and juicy one-liners, and issues are drawn in starkly simplistic packages. Equally, work can no longer be expected to be a duty or a calling or even a means of creative self-expression. Choice of occupation, indeed choice of whether to work at all, can be expected increasingly to become a matter of status affiliation rather than of material advantage.

Ritzer is about right when he suggests that McDonaldization is an extension, perhaps the ultimate extension, of Fordism. However, the implication is that just as one now has a better chance of finding a Fordist factory in Russia or India than in Detroit, it should not surprise us to find that McDonaldization is penetrating the furthest corners of the globe, and there is some indication that, as far as the restaurant goes, there is stagnation if not yet decline in the homeland. McDonaldization faces post-Fordist limits and part of the crisis that these limits imply involves a transformation to a chaotic, taste- and value-driven, irrational, and possibly threatening global society. It will not be harmonious, but the price of harmony would be to accept the predominance of Christendom, or Communism, or Fordism, or McDonaldism.

This chapter, then, takes issue with the position taken by Ritzer. . . . First, there is a single globalization-localization process in which local sensibilities are aroused and exacerbated in fundamentalist forms by such modernizing flows as McDonaldization. Even in the fast-food realm, McDonaldization promotes demands for authenticity, even to the extent of the fundamentalism of vegetarianism. Second, the emerging global culture is likely to exhibit a rich level of diversity that arises out of this intersection. Globalization exposes each locality to numerous global flows so that any such locality can accommodate, to use food examples once again, not only burgers but a kaleidoscope of ethnically diverse possibilities hierarchically ordered by price and thus by the extent to which the meal has been crafted as opposed to manufactured. Thus while it is not possible to escape the ubiquity of McDonald's in one sense, the golden arches are indeed everywhere, in another it certainly is, one can simply drive by and buy either finger food from a market stall or haute cuisine at a high priced restaurant. Ritzer is not wrong then to argue that McDonaldization is a significant component of globalization. Rather, he is mistaken in assuming first that globalization must be understood as homogenization and second that McDonaldization only has homogenizing effects.

Thinking Critically

◆◆◆

1. What is the relationship between McDonaldization and Americanization?

2. What is the relationship between McDonaldization and globalization?

3. In what ways can McDonaldization foster heterogenization?

4. What do you think of the case being made in this essay for globalization leading to increasing heterogenization?

5. Are people around the world "cultural dupes"? Have you ever been duped?

James Watson draws a number of conclusions that tend to support Waters's position and the critique of McDonaldization. Although Watson recognizes that "McDonald's has effected small but influential changes in East Asian dietary patterns," his overriding conclusion is that "East Asian consumers have quietly, and in some cases stubbornly, transformed their neighborhood McDonald's into local institutions." In other words, McDonald's is not a force, or at least a successful force, for cultural imperialism.

One of Watson's most interesting contentions is that East Asian cities are being reinvented so rapidly that it is hard to even differentiate between what is local and what is global (or foreign). That is, the global is adopted and adapted so rapidly that it becomes part of the local. Thus, many Japanese children are likely to think that Ronald McDonald is Japanese.

Watson also does not see McDonald's as a typical transnational corporation with headquarters in the first world. Rather, to him, McDonald's is more like "a federation of semiautonomous enterprises" with the result that local McDonald's are empowered to go in their own separate directions, at least to some degree. Thus, Watson offers examples of the ways in which McDonald's adapts its menu to local tastes, although he also recognizes that its basic menu remains largely the same everywhere in the world. In the same way, locals have accepted some of McDonald's "standard operating procedures," but they have also modified or rejected others. McDonald's undergoes a process of localization whereby the locals, especially young people, no longer see it as a "foreign" entity.

While Watson takes this process of localization as a positive development, I find it more worrisome from the point of view of the concern with the growing McDonaldization of the world. If McDonaldization remains a foreign presence, it is easy to identify and oppose, at least for those concerned about it. However, if it worms its way into the local culture and comes to be perceived as a local phenomenon, it becomes virtually impossible to identify and to oppose.

32

Transnationalism, Localization, and Fast Foods in East Asia

James L. Watson

◆◆◆————————————————————————————————

D oes the spread of fast food undermine the integrity of indigenous cuisines? Are food chains helping to create a homogenous, global culture better suited to the needs of a capitalist world order?

. . .We do not celebrate McDonald's as a paragon of capitalist virtue, nor do we condemn the corporation as an evil empire. Our goal is to produce ethnographic accounts of McDonald's social, political, and economic impact on five local cultures. These are not small-scale cultures under imminent threat of extinction; we are dealing with economically resilient, technologically advanced societies noted for their haute cuisines. If McDonald's can make inroads in these societies, one might be tempted to conclude, it may indeed be an irresistible force for world culinary change. But isn't another scenario possible? Have people in East Asia conspired to change

Editor's Note: Excerpts from the introduction "Transnationalism, Localization, and Fast Foods in East Asia" by James L. Watson in *Golden Arches East: McDonald's in East Asia* edited by James L. Watson, 1997, Stanford University Press. Copyright © 1997 by Stanford University Press, Stanford, CA. Used with permission.

McDonald's, modifying this seemingly monolithic institution to fit local conditions?

. . . The interaction process works both ways. McDonald's *has* effected small but influential changes in East Asian dietary patterns. Until the introduction of McDonald's, for example, Japanese consumers rarely, *if* ever, ate with their hands; . . . this is now an acceptable mode of dining. In Hong Kong, McDonald's has replaced traditional teahouses and street stalls as the most popular breakfast venue. And among Taiwanese youth, French fries have become a dietary staple, owing almost entirely to the influence of McDonald's.

At the same time, however, East Asian consumers have quietly, and in some cases stubbornly, transformed their neighborhood McDonald's into a local institution. In the United States, fast food may indeed imply fast consumption, but this is certainly not the case everywhere. In Beijing, Seoul, and Taipei, for instance, McDonald's restaurants are treated as leisure centers, where people can retreat from the stresses of urban life. In Hong Kong, middle school students often sit in McDonald's for hours—studying, gossiping, and picking over snacks; for them, the restaurants are the equivalent of youth clubs. . . . Suffice it to note here that McDonald's does not always call the shots.

GLOBALISM AND LOCAL CULTURES

. . .The operative term is "local culture," shorthand for the experience of everyday life as lived by ordinary people in specific localities. In using it, we attempt to capture the feelings of appropriateness, comfort, and correctness that govern the construction of personal preferences, or "tastes." Dietary patterns, attitudes toward food, and notions of what constitutes a proper meal . . . are central to the experience of everyday life and hence are integral to the maintenance of local cultures.

Readers will note . . . class, gender, and status differences, especially in relation to consumption practices. One surprise was the discovery that many McDonald's restaurants in East Asia have become sanctuaries for women who wish to avoid male-dominated settings. In Beijing and Seoul, new categories of yuppies treat McDonald's as an arena for conspicuous consumption. Anthropologists who work in such settings must pay close attention to rapid changes in consumer preferences. Twenty years ago, McDonald's catered to the children of Hong Kong's wealthy elite; the current generation of Hong Kong hyperconsumers has long since abandoned the golden arches and moved upmarket to more expensive watering holes (e.g., Planet Hollywood). Meanwhile, McDonald's has become a mainstay for working-class people, who are attracted by its low cost, convenience, and predictability.

One of our conclusions . . . is that societies in East Asia are changing as fast as cuisines—there is nothing immutable or primordial about cultural systems. In Hong Kong, for instance, it would be impossible to isolate what is specifically "local" about the cuisine, given the propensity of Hong Kong people to adopt new foods. . . . Hong Kong's cuisine, and with it Hong Kong's local culture, is a moving target. Hong Kong is the quintessential postmodern environment, where the boundaries of status, style, and taste dissolve almost as fast as they are formed. What is "in" today is "out" tomorrow.

TRANSNATIONALISM AND THE MULTILOCAL CORPORATION

It has become an academic cliché to argue that people are constantly reinventing themselves. Nevertheless, the speed of that reinvention process in places like Hong Kong, Taipei, and Seoul is so rapid that it defies description. In the realm of popular culture, it is no longer possible to distinguish between what is "local" and what is "foreign." Who is to say that Mickey Mouse is not Japanese, or that Ronald McDonald is not Chinese? To millions of children who watch Chinese television, "Uncle McDonald" (alias Ronald) is probably more familiar than the mythical characters of Chinese folklore.

We have entered here the realm of the transnational, a new field of study that focuses on the "deterritorialization" of popular culture. . . . The world economy can no longer be understood by assuming that the original producers of a commodity necessarily control its consumption. A good example is the spread of "Asian" martial arts to North and South America, fostered by Hollywood and the Hong Kong film industry. Transnationalism describes a condition by which people, commodities, and ideas literally cross—transgress—national boundaries and are not identified with a single place of origin. One of the leading theorists of this new field argues that transnational phenomena are best perceived as the building blocks of "third cultures," which are "oriented beyond national boundaries."

Transnational corporations are popularly regarded as the clearest expressions of this new adaptation, given that business operations, manufacturing, and marketing are often spread around the globe to dozens of societies.

At first glance, McDonald's would appear to be the quintessential transnational. On closer inspection, however, the company does not conform to expectations; it resembles a federation of semiautonomous enterprises. James Cantalupo, former President of McDonald's International, claims that the goal of McDonald's is to "become as much a part of the local culture as possible." He objects when "[p]eople call us a multinational. I like to call us *multilocal*," meaning that McDonald's goes to great lengths to find local suppliers and local partners whenever new branches are opened.

... McDonald's International retains at least a 50 percent stake in its East Asian enterprises; the other half is owned by local operators.

MODIFIED MENUS AND LOCAL SENSITIVITIES: McDONALD'S ADAPTS

The key to McDonald's worldwide success is that people everywhere know what to expect when they pass through the Golden Arches. This does not mean, however, that the corporation has resisted change or refused to adapt when local customs require flexibility. . . . McDonald's restaurants in India serve Vegetable McNuggets and a mutton-based Maharaja Mac, innovations that are necessary in a country where Hindus do not eat beef, Muslims do not eat pork, and Jains (among others) do not eat meat of any type. In Malaysia and Singapore, McDonald's underwent rigorous inspections by Muslim clerics to ensure ritual cleanliness; the chain was rewarded with a *halal* ("clean," "acceptable") certificate, indicating the total absence of pork products.

Variations on McDonald's original, American-style menu exist in many parts of the world: chilled yogurt drinks (*ayran*) in Turkey, espresso and cold pasta in Italy, teriyaki burgers in Japan (also in Taiwan and Hong Kong), vegetarian burgers in the Netherlands, McSpagetti in the Philippines, McLaks (grilled salmon sandwich) in Norway, frankfurters and beer in Germany, McHuevo (poached egg hamburger) in Uruguay. . . .

Irrespective of local variations (espresso, McLaks) and recent additions (carrot sticks), the structure of the McDonald's menu remains essentially uniform the world over: main course burger/sandwich, fries, and a drink—overwhelmingly Coca-Cola. The keystone of this winning combination is *not*, as most observers might assume, the Big Mac or even the generic hamburger. It is the fries. The main course may vary widely (fish sandwiches in Hong Kong, vegetable burgers in Amsterdam), but the signature innovation of McDonald's—thin, elongated fries cut from russet potatoes—is ever-present and consumed with great gusto by Muslims, Jews, Christians, Buddhists, Hindus, vegetarians (now that vegetable oil is used), communists, Tories, marathoners, and armchair athletes. . . .

CONCLUSION: McDONALDIZATION VERSUS LOCALIZATION

McDonald's has become such a powerful symbol of the standardization and routinization of modern life that it has inspired a new vocabulary: McThink, McMyth, McJobs, McSpiritually, and, of course, McDonaldization. George Ritzer, author of a popular book titled *The McDonaldization of Society*

. . . treats McDonald's as the "paradigm case" of social regimentation and argues that "McDonaldization has shown every sign of being an inexorable process as it sweeps through seemingly impervious institutions and parts of the world."

Is McDonald's in fact the revolutionary, disruptive institution that theorists of cultural imperialism deem it to be? Evidence . . . could be marshaled in support of such a view but only at the risk of ignoring historical process. There is indeed an initial, "intrusive" encounter when McDonald's enters a new market—especially in an environment where American-style fast food is largely unknown to the ordinary consumer. In five cases, . . . McDonald's was treated as an exotic import—a taste of Americana—during its first few years of operation. Indeed, the company drew on this association to establish itself in foreign markets. But this initial euphoria cannot sustain a mature business.

Unlike Coca-Cola and Spam, for instance, McDonald's standard fare (the burger-and-fries combo) could not be absorbed into the preexisting cuisines of East Asia. . . . Spam quickly became an integral feature of Korean cooking in the aftermath of the Korean War; it was a recognizable form of meat that required no special preparation. Coca-Cola, too, was a relatively neutral import when first introduced to Chinese consumers. During the 1960s, villagers in rural Hong Kong treated Coke as a special beverage, reserved primarily for medicinal use. It was served most frequently as *bo ho la*, Cantonese for "boiled Cola," a tangy blend of fresh ginger and herbs served in piping hot Coke—an excellent remedy for colds. Only later was the beverage consumed by itself, first at banquets (mixed with brandy) and later for special events such as a visit by relatives. There was nothing particularly revolutionary about Coca-Cola or Spam; both products were quickly adapted to suit local needs and did not require any radical adjustments on the part of consumers.

McDonald's is something altogether different. Eating at the Golden Arches is a total experience, one that takes people out of their ordinary routines. One "goes to" a McDonald's; it does not come to the consumer, nor is it taken home. . .

From this vantage point it would appear that McDonald's may indeed have been an intrusive force, undermining the integrity of East Asian cuisines. On closer inspection, however, it is clear that consumers are not the automatons many analysts would have us believe they are. The initial encounter soon begins to fade as McDonald's loses its exotic appeal and gradually gains acceptance (or rejection) as ordinary food for busy consumers. The hamburger-fries combo becomes simply another alternative among many types of ready-made food.

The process of localization is a two-way street: It implies changes in the local culture as well as modifications in the company's standard operating procedures. Key elements of McDonald's industrialized system—queuing, self-provisioning, self-seating—have been accepted by consumers throughout East Asia. Other aspects of the industrial model have been rejected, notably those relating to time and space. In many parts of East Asia, consumers have turned their local McDonald's into leisure centers and after school clubs. The meaning of "fast" has been subverted in these settings: It refers to the *delivery* of food, not to its consumption. Resident managers have had little choice but to embrace these consumer trends and make virtues of them: "Students create a good atmosphere which is good for our business," one Hong Kong manager told me as he surveyed a sea of young people chatting, studying, and snacking in his restaurant.

The process of localization correlates closely with the maturation of a generation of local people who grew up eating at the Golden Arches. By the time the children of these original consumers enter the scene, McDonald's is no longer perceived as a foreign enterprise. Parents see it as a haven of cleanliness and predictability. For children, McDonald's represents fun, familiarity, and a place where they can choose their own food—something that may not be permitted at home.

. . . Localization is not a unilinear process that ends the same everywhere. McDonald's has become a routine, unremarkable feature of the urban landscape in Japan and Hong Kong. It is so local that many younger consumers do not know of the company's foreign origins. The process of localization has hardly begun in China, where McDonald's outlets are still treated as exotic outposts, selling a cultural experience rather than food. At this writing, it is unclear what will happen to expansion efforts in Korea; the political environment there is such that many citizens will continue to treat the Golden Arches as a symbol of American imperialism. In Taiwan, the confused, and exhilarating, pace of identity politics may well rebound on American corporations in ways as yet unseen. Irrespective of these imponderables, McDonald's is no longer dependent on the United States market for its future development. . . .

As McDonald's enters the 21st century, its multilocal strategy, like its famous double-arches logo, is being pirated by a vast array of corporations eager to emulate its success. In the end, however, McDonald's is likely to prove difficult to clone.

Thinking Critically

◆◆◆

1. In what ways can locals transform McDonald's into local institutions?

2. In what ways is McDonaldization unaffected by local actions?

3. In what ways can localization be worrisome to those who fear McDonaldization?

4. Have you or anyone you know eaten in McDonald's in East Asia (or anywhere else in the world)? If so, in what ways was it and was it not different from eating in McDonald's in the U.S.?

Bryan Turner surveys the ways in which McDonald's has modified itself in order to fit into various regions of the world—Russia, Australia, Asia, and the Middle East. He demonstrates the global power and reach of McDonald's and McDonaldization. He focuses on the food and concludes that McDonald's has made major modifications in its menu in many locales. He sees this as compromising the basic McDonald's model—burgers and fries—at least as far as food is concerned. Turner's limited perspective is shaped by his view that: "At the end of the day, McDonald's simply is a burger joint." If this book has demonstrated anything, it is that McDonald's, and the process of McDonaldization that it played a key role in spawning, is far more than a burger joint. Rather, it is a structure that has served as a model for the restructuring of a wide range of social structures and social institutions in the United States and throughout the world.

33

The McDonald's Mosaic

Glocalization and Diversity

Bryan S. Turner

◆◆◆ ──

There is considerable ethnographic evidence that McDonald's outlets have adjusted to local circumstances by incorporating local cuisines and values into their customer services. The success of global McDonald's has been to organize and present itself as a local company, where it specifically aims to incorporate local taste and local dishes—the curry potato pie from Hong Kong, the Singapore Loveburger (grilled chicken, honey, and mustard sauce), and the Teriyaki burger (sausage patty) and the Tukbul burger with cheese for the Korean market. Let us take the Russian example. The Russian experience of Western culture in the last decade has been intensely ambiguous. The obvious seduction of Western consumerism that had begun in the 1970s continued into the early 1990s, and young people in particular rushed to embrace the latest Western consumer goods and habits. Yet unsurprisingly, the promise of a widespread democratic consumer culture has not been fulfilled. Among older Russians, there has been a growing nostalgia for

Editor's Note: From Turner, B. (2003). The McDonaldization Mosaic: Globalization and Diversity. In *American Behavioral Scientist*, 47(2). Copyright © 2003, reprinted with permission of Sage Publications, Inc.

a putative Russian "way of doing things" and a concomitant suspicion of Western cultural institutions.

In this context of disappointed ambitions and expectations, one would expect McDonald's to be an obvious target of Russian hostility. Even in Western countries themselves, McDonald's is often seen as representative of the detrimental, exploitative, and pervasive reach of global capitalism. For many critics, McDonald's exploits and poisons workers. Its culture of fast and unimaginative food is symbolic of the worst aspects of consumerism. From a Russian perspective, the characteristics of McDonald's, including its style—such as its particular forms of graphic design and its presentation of food—its emphasis on customer service and training, and its standardized global presence are decidedly Western. Russia is a society in which, as a result of its communist legacy, personal service, friendliness, and helpfulness are still corrupt bourgeois customs.

Of interest, however, Russians have a decidedly ambivalent view of McDonald's, in part because they are pragmatic in their responses to Western influences. Seventy years of Soviet rule has taught them to be judicious in their use of principle because they have learned to live with inconsistency and contradiction. McDonald's offers a surfeit of cultural contradiction because, notwithstanding the overtly Western style of McDonald's, there are also numerous forms of convergence with Russian habits and values.

First, there is the compatibility of the Fordist labor process, food process, and purchasing protocols in McDonald's with those that were developed during the Soviet period in Russia and that have continued under postcommunism. These processes and protocols, although often different in content, are consistently Fordist in form and structure. In both a McDonald's and postcommunist setting, there are clear expectations of standardized and predictable products, delivery of products, staff and their uniform dress, and consumer protocols. In both settings, production and social interaction are rule driven and steered through authoritarian decision-making processes.

Second, the formal standardized structure and method of operation of a McDonald's restaurant is underpinned by an egalitarian ethos. In particular, the egalitarian ethos in Russia has been manifested in disdain for the external trappings of a service culture (as a sign of inequality) and is currently manifested in popular contempt for the ostentatious consumption of "the new Russians." McDonald's presents its food as sustenance for the "common people." In addition, the way of eating the food, using hands rather than knives and forks, appeals to ordinary people in a country where haute cuisine has been seen as, and continues to be defined as, a form of cultural pretension. The service culture of McDonald's is based on a commitment to a formal equality between customer and service assistant.

Finally, the actual content of McDonald's food has a definite appeal to Russian taste. For example, McDonald's food, such as the buns, sauces, and even the meat, tends to be sweeter than the average European or Asian cuisine.

Desserts are generally based on dairy produce and include exceedingly sweet sauces. Potato chips and fried chicken appeal to the Russian preference for food fried in saturated fat rather than food that is grilled or uncooked. Thus, although McDonald's might be seen as a harbinger of the worst of Western cultural imperialism, the pragmatic Russian will usually be prepared to frequent McDonald's restaurants because of the quality and compatibility of the food with Russian taste and the familiarity of the setting and delivery process. However, the cost of McDonald's food in Russia is prohibitive and for many is a luxury item for which the average family must save.

In Australia, by contrast, McDonald's culture is highly compatible with a society that has embraced egalitarianism to such an extent that cultural distinction is explicitly rejected in such popular expressions such as "to cut down tall poppies" and by the emphasis on mateship. Historically, the Australian food consumption has contained a high level of meat, especially lamb and beef. Dietary innovations such as replacing lard by canola resulted in a 50% cut in sales in Sydney stores. McDonald's has been particularly successful down under, where it is claimed by the *Weekend Australian* that a million Australians consume more than $4.8 million burgers, fries, and drinks at the 683 McDonald's stores each day. McDonald's arrived in Australia in 1971, opening 118 stores in its first year. The company had an important impact on services in Australia, where it led the way in modernizing work practices, corporate culture, and philanthropy. Their business strategy involved the development of community and educational links through Rotary clubs and churches. McDonald's successfully survived much local criticism against American cultural imperialism and developed educational programs that have been addressed to kindergartens and schools. McDonald's built playgrounds and distributed toys. Through the development of McHappy Day, it donates generously to hospitals and charities. It also developed Ronald McDonald House Charities that in 2001 raised $2.4 million for charity. Ray Kroc's four commandments—quality, service, cleanliness, and value—have been adopted as core elements in a two-unit educational diploma that can be taken in certain Australian high schools as components of their educational experience.

Although it has been a significant commercial success and now controls 42% of the fast-food market, the high-water mark was achieved in the mid-1990s when 145 stores were opened in the space of 2 years. Sales figures have become static, customer satisfaction is declining, and McDonald's has been the subject of public criticism. McDonald's suffered economically when the Liberal Government of John Howard introduced the GST (General Sales Tax) and McDonald's hamburgers were not exempt. The result was 10% decline in sales, and they failed to achieve their target of 900 stores by the year 2000. McDonald's has responded to this decline in several ways, including the diversification of their products into McCafes and by moving up-market into Mexican-style restaurants and sandwich bars.

In Asia, McDonald's outlets have been successful in penetrating local markets. In the process, however, McDonald's products have been changing. The doctrine that societies that are connected by trade do not go to war is being tested in the case of China and Taiwan. For example, Taiwan has 341 and the People's Republic of China has 326 McDonald's restaurants. The new Chinese elite in its drive to industrialize and modernize society has accepted McDonald's outlets because McDonald's is seen to epitomize healthy food based on nutritious ingredients and scientific cooking. Although the Party is still in control and formally promotes communist ideals of loyalty and dedication, young people have adopted the Ronald McDonald backpack as a sign of modernist consumerism. McDonald's entered Taiwan in 1984, where it now sells 92 million hamburgers and 60 million McNuggets to a population of 22.2 million. McDonald's has become ubiquitous partly by adding corn soup to its regular menu once it was realized that no meal is complete without soup. McDonald's in Taiwan also abandoned its antiloitering policy once it accepted the fact that students saw the air-conditioned McDonald's as an attractive and cool venue for study. Other changes in this densely populated society followed, such as building three-storey outlets that can seat more than 250 people at a time.

South Korea is another society that enthusiastically embraced McDonald's. The first outlet was opened in Apkujong-dong in Seoul during the 1988 Olympic Games and expanded rapidly to become the second largest fast-food service retailer after Lotteria. The World Cup provided important marketing opportunities for McDonald's, and the company sought to increase its outlets, adding another 100 restaurants. The company initiated a "Player Escort" scheme to select Korean children to participate by escorting soccer players to the football dome. The current McDonald's president Kim Hyung-soo has adopted the sociological expression "glocalization" to describe the customization of McDonald's menus to satisfy the demands of local customers by developing Korean-style burgers such as Bulgogi Burger and Kimchi Burger. Another promotional strategy has been to make Internet available in its restaurants located in famous hang-out places for Korean youth, such as the ASEM mall and Shinohon.

The market in Asia is also diversifying as further Westernized commodities and lifestyles are imported. . . . The growing demand for coffee in Asia, where it is now beginning to challenge the cultural hegemony of tea. . . . in the last 5 years, Starbucks has become as widespread as McDonald's. . . .

McDonald's has responded by creating McSnack. . . . It offers chicken and beef curry rice, bagels and English muffin sandwiches, and waffles. It also offers nine different hot and cold coffee drinks. The important feature of the coffee craze is that Korean customers expect to loiter in the outlets, which are used as meeting places and spaces for study. McDonald's staff tolerate customers who sit for hours inside the restaurant or on chairs outside hardly buying anything. During their university examinations period, students are packed into McSnack and so actual customers often find it difficult to secure a seat. Customers also bring food into McSnack from other restaurants to eat at the nice, clean, air-conditioned outlets.

These national case studies show us how McDonald's fast-food outlets interact with local cultures. Perhaps the best illustration of these local tensions is in the Middle East, where 300 McDonald's have opened, mainly following the Gulf war. McDonald's has been successful in Saudi Arabia, where McDonald's has spread rapidly, despite periodic fundamentalist boycotts, and where its stores are closed five times a day for prayers. The company now intends to open McDonald's in Afghanistan. In Turkey, McDonald's started to open branches in the 1980s in Istanbul and Ankara. Although McDonald's has expanded to around 100 outlets, almost half of these are in Istanbul. There is a McDonald's in Kayseri, the center of the Islamist vote in Istanbul. The only remarkable protest against McDonald's was held at the Middle East Technical University when it tried to open a branch there in the 1990s, but this protest came from socialists not Islamic students. Ironically, Muslim couples often use McDonald's as a place to meet because they know that their traditionalist parents would not dine there. McDonald's in Turkey also has been sensitive to Islamic norms and it offers *iftar*, an evening meal served during the Ramadan. In Egypt, McDonald's has also become popular and serves sandwiches, Egyptian boulettes, and other local items. Although Egyptian intellectuals condemn Kentucky Fried Chicken and McDonald's as examples of Western corruption of local taste and cuisine, McDonald's now exists without conflict alongside street vendors and local cafes.

McDonald's outlets have paradoxically been popular in many Muslim societies, despite strong anti-American sentiments, because parents recognize them as places where alcohol will not be served. In addition, the mildly exotic Western taste of a burger and fries is an alternative to local fare. Indonesian youth use McDonald's in the same way that Western youth gravitate toward shopping malls. With temperatures consistently in the 30°C range (90°F) and humidity often more than 80%, McDonald's is simply a convenient, clean, and cool place to be. The company has once more adapted to local taste by introducing sweet iced tea, spicy burgers, and rice. The economic crisis in early 1998 forced McDonald's to experiment with a cheaper menu as the price of burgers exploded. McDonald's customers remained with the company to consume McTime, PaNas, and Paket Nasi. For many years, McDonald's has advertised its products as *halal*, reassuring its Muslim customers that its products are religiously clean. Similar to Egyptian McDonald's, in Indonesia, a postsunset meal is offered as a "special" during Ramadan. To avoid any criticism of Americanization,

McDonald's is a local business that is owned by a Muslim, whose advertising banners proclaim in Arabic that McDonald's Indonesia is fully owned by an indigenous Muslim. Proprietors also will proudly boast their Muslim status by the use of post-pilgrimage titles such as *Haji*.

CONCLUSIONS: CULTURAL LIQUIDITY

These local case studies show how the rational model of McDonald's adjusts to local cultural preferences, but the result is a diminution of the original McDonald's product (the burger and fries). In fact, the more the company adjusts to local conditions, the more the appeal of the specifically American product may be lost. At the end of the day, McDonald's simply is a burger joint. Therefore, . . . we need to distinguish between specific studies of McDonald's and macro-studies of McDonaldization as rationalization. . . . The global reach of McDonald's is hardly at issue, and I have attempted to illustrate some of the complexity of that reach through several vignettes of McDonald's in Russia, Australia, the Middle East, and Asia. The spread of McDonald's clearly illustrates the fact that McDonaldization has been a powerful force behind the administrative rationalism of modern societies. With globalization, rationalization has become a global dimension of the basic social processes of any modern society. In this sense, the McDonaldization thesis is also a potent defense of the continuing relevance of Weber's general sociology of modernity.

More fundamentally, the diversification of McDonald's through its interaction with local cultures has produced new management strategies, consumer cultures, and product range that depart radically from the Fordist linearity of the original model. McDonald's is slowly disappearing under the weight of its fragmentation, differentiation, and adaptation. . . . The unstoppable march of McDonald's through urban society has come to an end.

Thinking Critically

◆◆◆

1. Is McDonald's simply a "burger joint"?

2. Does the nature of the food served matter much from the point of view of McDonaldization?

3. What stresses and strains does McDonald's face in other national settings?

4. How do you account for the fact that McDonald's now appears to be more successful outside the U.S. than inside the U.S.?

5. Is McDonald's disappearing as a result of local adaptations?

Melissa Caldwell offers a detailed anthropological study of the ways in which McDonald's and its food have become part of local culture in Russia. On one level, Russians personalize McDonaldized public spaces (e.g., holding birthday parties in McDonald's). On another level, they bring aspects of McDonald's into their intimate, everyday lives; they "domesticate" them. Thus, they prepare foods at home that are modeled after those served in McDonald's. Caldwell sees this as evidence that Russia is not McDonaldized, but rather transforms what McDonald's brings to Russia into genuinely local products. This is localization in her view, not McDonaldization. In Pieterse terms, it is closer to cultural hybridization than cultural convergence. However, like Turner, Caldwell focuses largely on the food and not on the basic principles that lie at the base of McDonaldization.

34

Domesticating the French Fry

McDonald's and Consumerism in Moscow

Melissa L. Caldwell

◆◆◆ ───

During my yearly research trips to Moscow, I periodically visited my friend Veronika who lives in a small town several hours outside the city. Concerned that Moscow's metropolitan setting was sapping my energy and giving me an atypical view of Russian life, Veronika insisted that these visits and her home-cooked meals would both rejuvenate me and provide a more 'authentic' Russian experience. Shortly after I had arrived at Veronika's apartment in summer 2000, my hostess arranged a large bowl, electric mixer, fresh strawberries from her garden and vanilla ice cream on her kitchen table. She explained that an acquaintance had told her about the latest craze in Moscow: the 'milk cocktail' (*molochnyi kokteil*). More commonly known as 'milkshakes' to American consumers, these milk cocktails were introduced to Russia by McDonald's in the early 1990s. Given that I am an American and presumably experienced in such matters, Veronika

Editor's Note: From Caldwell, M. (2204). "Domesticating the French Fry: McDonald's and Consumerism in Moscow. *Journal of Consumer Culture,* 4(1), 5–26. Copyright © Sage Publications, Ltd. Reprinted with permission.

asked me to do the honors. When I was done mixing, my friend called her 85-year-old father, a decorated Second World War veteran, into the kitchen to have a sample. The older man skeptically took his glass and left the room. Within minutes, he returned with an empty glass and asked for a refill.

Today, with more than 75 outlets throughout Russia, McDonald's is a prominent feature in the local landscape. In Moscow, where the majority of restaurants are located, the physical topography of city streets and pedestrian walkways is shaped by large red signs with recognizable golden arches and arrows directing pedestrians and motorists to the nearest restaurant, and local residents use McDonald's restaurants as reference points when giving directions to friends from out of town. Political demonstrators use McDonald's restaurants as landmarks for staging and dispersal areas such as during an anti-government and anti-American demonstration in early October 1998, when marchers first assembled at the McDonald's store at Dobryninskaia metro station and were then joined by additional supporters when the procession went past the outlet at Tretiakovskaia station. Muscovite acquaintances who participated in the demonstration ate lunch beforehand at the McDonald's at Dobryninskaia metro station. Whereas school groups formerly took cultural excursions to sites such as Lenin's tomb, museums and factories, today these same groups take educational tours through McDonald's restaurants and the McComplex production facilities.

Muscovites' experiences of McDonald's offer an instructive intervention into theories about the nature of globalization and the local/global tensions that social scientists have ascribed to transnational movements. Specifically, Muscovites' efforts to incorporate McDonald's into their daily lives complicate the arguments proposed by Giddens, Ritzer, Tomlinson and others that the homogenizing effects of global movements such as McDonaldization elide meaning from daily life. Instead, Muscovites have publicly affirmed and embraced McDonald's and its products as significant and meaningful elements in their social worlds. More importantly, however, Muscovites have incorporated McDonald's into the more intimate and sentimental spaces of their personal lives: family celebrations, cuisine and discourses about what it means to be Russian today. In so doing, Muscovites have drawn McDonald's into the very processes by which local cultural forms are generated, authenticated and made meaningful. It is by passing through this process of domestication that McDonald's has become localized.

In this article, I am concerned with the ways in which Russian consumers' experiences with McDonald's depart from local/global paradigms that juxtapose 'the global' with an authentic and unquestionably indigenous 'local.' As I will describe, Russian consumers are blurring the boundaries between the global and the local, the new and the original, through a set of domesticating tactics grounded in flexible ideologies of trust, comfort and intimacy. Through the application of these principles, Russian consumers render McDonald's restaurants and food as locally constituted (and, more importantly, as locally meaningful) phenomena and not simply as transnational entities with local features or as local entities enmeshed in transnational forces. Ultimately, my task in this analysis is to explore how the 'local' itself is reinvented through processes of domestication.

This motif of 'domestication' calls attention to Russian practices of consumption that link ideas about home and intimacy with ideas about the nation. In Russia, after an initial period in the early and mid-1990s when foreign goods were valued precisely for their *foreignness*, Russian consumers have refocussed their attentions on the merits of domestically produced goods. When making selections in the marketplace, Russian shoppers consider such qualities as the cultural heritage and ethnic background of producers and their products. The appeal of the inherent *localness* of goods has only been heightened in the wake of Russia's August 1998 financial crisis, when the mass departure of transnational firms from the country not only created opportunities for domestic companies to meet market demands, but also prompted customers to support local industries for both patriotic and economic reasons. A nationwide 'Buy Russia' campaign that explicitly invoked the rhetorics of nationalism and insiderness associated with the segmentary system of *Nash* ('ours') appealed to Russian consumers to give priority to domestically produced goods.

Because the flexible discourse of Nash invokes claims of intimacy and familiarity, it incorporates both the imagined space of the nation, occasionally rendered as *otechesvennyi* (which means 'fatherland' and 'domestic industry,' also 'patriotic'), and the physical space of the home, usually rendered as *domashnii* (which means 'of the home'), or even more simply as *bytovoi* ('of daily life'). An approach that employs this dual sense of 'home' is critical for understanding the larger significance of McDonald's induction into Russian social life. At the same time that McDonald's and Muscovites' home lives intersect in intriguing and powerful ways, so that consumers are both taking McDonald's home with them and bringing their home lives to McDonald's, Russians' encounters with McDonald's also reflect their interest in nationally constituted local cultures.

More important, however, while the process of Nash typically evokes a sense of nationalist qualities, Russian consumers also use it more simply to demarcate feelings of intimacy that are not exclusively national. Specifically, the emphasis on sentimental familiarity, trust and comfort that is embodied in the Nash ideology transcends absolute distinctions between local and foreign and instead creates more abstract categories of insider and outsider.

As I describe later in this article, the flexible and inclusive nature of Nash emerges clearly when Russians apply it to indicate that their relationships with foreign persons and products are intimate, ordinary and meaningful. In this sense, a consideration of domestication as a form of Nashification approximates the process by which goods and values acquire a state whereby they seem natural and ordinary. . . .

To pursue this theme of domestication, I consider . . . the specific case of McDonald's and an examination of the processes by which the company and its products have been incorporated into Muscovites' daily lives. This discussion resonates with other accounts of how transnational food corporations have entered foreign markets by simultaneously responding to local practices and cultivating new local interests oriented to the company's goals. From this discussion, I address the processes by which Muscovite consumers have encouraged and shaped the company's efforts to 'go native' and what these efforts reveal about Russian social practice. . . .

LOCALITY, HOME AND MEANING IN GLOBALIZATION THEORIES

[In] the complexities of the local/global experience in Russia . . . the origins of specific goods and behaviors are often less important than the values that Russians attach to them. Even as local and foreign observers depict McDonald's as the ultimate symbol of cultural imperialism, many Russian consumers who support local businesses and commodities have transferred that support to McDonald's. As McDonald's has lost its strangeness and become familiar and comfortable, it has become, in very tangible ways, domesticated. Thus, an approach that focusses on the processes by which the local is invented and rendered familiar is more productive for understanding the case of McDonald's in Moscow. As Appadurai notes, the production of the local is a continuous process of creativity and adjustment. What this means is that although the social processes of localization may be culturally specific, the content of local culture is continually invented.

In the rest of this article, I explore the processes by which Muscovites and McDonald's have collaborated to achieve this domestication. This process of domestication is twofold and reflects the cooperative efforts of McDonald's and Russian consumers. The first section presents a more familiar narrative of how McDonald's interprets local interests and carefully responds to—or exploits—them. The second section, however, presents an alternative vision of the domestication of McDonald's in Russia. Specifically, by illustrating how Russian customers actively rework McDonald's to fit their own needs and values, this section emphasizes the agency and autonomy of Russian social actors as they engage with global processes.

FROM THE EXOTIC TO THE MUNDANE:
CULTIVATING FRIENDSHIP, INTIMACY, AND TRUST

Within consumption studies of postsocialist societies, McDonald's has emerged as a prime symbol of the processes and stakes at work in negotiations among local, regional, national and global forces. For the specific case of Russia, the foreign/local tension is particularly significant in light of McDonald's role among Russian institutions and its place within Russian culinary traditions. Throughout Russia's history, food has been both a celebrated aspect of Russian cultural, social and political life and an evocative symbol of national tastes and practices. This importance was heightened during the Soviet period when, as in other socialist states, control of the food services sector provided a key venue for articulating and implementing political philosophies and social control.

Soviet leaders linked their visions of an egalitarian communist society with the goals of producing and distributing sufficient food supplies for the population. To accomplish these tasks, authorities put the entire sphere of food services under state control; the culinary arts were standardized through the professionalization of food workers and the regulation of cuisine. Food production shifted from home kitchens and private restaurants to communal kitchens, state-owned cafeterias and food shops, workplace canteens and cafeterias run by consumers' societies. It was within this modernist vision of industrialized food services that privately owned transnational food corporations such as McDonald's first emerged.

After 14 years of negotiations with Soviet authorities, George Cohon, president of McDonald's Canada and *not* McDonald's USA—a distinction that Soviet leaders requested because of political tensions between the Soviet Union and the USA—opened Russia's first outlet in 1990. To attract new customers, the company quickly immersed itself in Russian daily life by highlighting not its novelty and foreignness, but its very ordinariness. Specifically, the company crafted itself as a place where ordinary people work and visit. . . .

More revealing, however, are McDonald's explicit efforts to position itself vis-à-vis Russians' cherished principle of Nash as a marker of trust, intimacy and sociality. First, McDonald's acknowledged the value that Russian consumers have historically placed on social networks and concepts of collective responsibility by situating itself as a responsive member of the local community. In addition to such activities as sponsoring athletic events and donating profits to a children's oncology program, the company has collaborated with local officials to develop fire safety programs in the city and established a Russian branch of the Ronald McDonald Children's Charity Fund. On a more individual level, McDonald's directly facilitates connections among consumers. In summer 2000, displays in several restaurants invited children to join a collectors' group to exchange toys and meet new people. Children treat the statue of Ronald McDonald that is invariably to be found in each restaurant as a friend with whom they sit and visit.

McDonald's officials next responded to local ideas about health and nutrition as essential qualities of Nash products. Russian consumers articulate food preferences through evaluations of the purity and healthiness of particular foods. Many Russians initially found the anonymity and technological regulation of McDonald's austere and sterile kitchen facilities, as well as the mass manufacture of foodstuffs, unnatural and disquieting. . . .

In contrast, Russians determine the healthiness and authenticity of foods according to where they are produced and by whom. More specifically, consumers privilege fruits and vegetables that are grown on farms in the Russian countryside or in gardens at private summer cottages (*dachas*) and then collected or prepared by friends or relatives. . . .

In their responses to these local preferences, McDonald's executives have joined other Russian companies in promoting the local origins of their produce. Using billboards, signs on the sides of freight trucks and tray liners, McDonald's advertises its contract with a Russian agricultural corporation whose name explicitly invokes the symbolic power of the Russian countryside and personal gardening, *Belaia dacha* ('white cottage'). McDonald's thus reassures customers not only that its produce is Russian-grown, but also that it meets 'the standards accepted by the Russian Federation' and that it uses 'only the highest quality meat without additives and fillers'. . . .

McDonald's efforts to cultivate a sense of trust among Moscow consumers emerged most visibly when the company explicitly appropriated the rhetoric of Nash. . . .

McDonald's had begun invoking the rhetoric of Nash in posters that reminded consumers that the company was 'Our McDonald's' (*Nash Makdonalds*). This move enabled McDonald's to position itself within the parameters of the imagined—and, more importantly, *trusted*—collectivity to which its Muscovite customers belonged. Moreover, McDonald's claimed status as a local entity by cultivating . . . the essential features of local culture. . . .

. . . Russians are autonomous social actors who themselves encourage, accept, shape and discipline this sense of familiarity and intimacy. . . . As the Russian McDonald's case illustrates, this process is one that Russian consumers are actively producing and fashioning. In the next section, I turn to a discussion of how Muscovites express their autonomy by creatively incorporating McDonald's into their most intimate and personal activities: their home lives.

FEELING AT HOME: McDONALD'S AS COMFORT FOOD

Initially, Muscovites' relationship with McDonald's was framed through themes of novelty and exoticness. . . .

... For many Muscovites, McDonald's has become so ordinary that it is no longer culturally marked. This shift to invisibility emerged vividly in conversations with schoolchildren and college students about what constituted Russian foods. Intriguingly, in their responses, students often included transnational foods such as McDonald's and Coca-Cola. When asked why they had included these items as 'Russian,' students typically replied that they simply took them for granted and did not contemplate their origins.

Another example that illustrates this process of domestication is the extent to which Russian consumers have accepted, and even facilitated, the inclusion of McDonald's foods in Russian cuisine. . . . Despite a long culinary history, however, Muscovites' food practices are changing as imported foods become more available. As one young woman observed: 'In Moscow it is impossible to distinguish between Russian and foreign foods because they are so mixed.' A specific example of these changes is evident in the 'milkshake craze' that my friend Veronika described when we prepared milkshakes at her home. By the end of the 1990s, milkshakes were available in both fast-food and high-end restaurants throughout Moscow as well as at temporary sidewalk food stalls. Even vendors in the lobbies of Moscow's finest theaters and opera houses had added fresh milkshakes to their more typical intermission offerings of elegant chocolates, open-faced sandwiches topped with smoked fish and caviar, and champagne. Russian restaurant owners now provide French fries with their main courses, and vendors at walk-up sidewalk stands include, among the usual assortment of candy bars, chips and nuts, Russian-made knock-offs named *Big mak* and *gamburgr roial* (as Quarterpounders are called in Russia).

Nevertheless, these examples point only to the spread of foods inspired by McDonald's throughout the commercial sphere. What is more intriguing is the extent to which Muscovites have incorporated McDonald's into their 'home cooking' (*domashchnaia pishcha*), a domain that Muscovites consider uniquely Russian. . . .

What was particularly instructive about . . . insistence that foods prepared at home are authentically Russian was that their repertoires of Russian cuisine included imitations of McDonald's foods. Like several middle-aged mothers I interviewed, my landlady Anya periodically attempts to make hamburgers at home to please her children and grandchildren, who want to eat at McDonald's, but are unable, owing to cost or time constraints, to do so. In some cases, cooks have resorted to highly creative culinary reinventions such as the meal described by one of my students. When the student's sister studied in Moscow, her host family offered to make McDonald's hamburgers at home. The promised meal turned out to be fried cabbage between two pieces of bread.

More revealing, however, were the responses I received from schoolchildren . . . four out of nine children independently depicted Russian-style fried potatoes (*zharennye kartoshki*), a staple in most families' meals, in recognizable McDonald's French fry boxes. In a similarly illuminating incident at a birthday party I attended, the guest of honor, a friend's four-year-old daughter who loved French fries, could barely contain her excitement at the news that we would have fried potatoes for dinner. When she was presented with the homemade French fries, however, she took one look at them and shrieked in horror: 'But they're not McDonald's!'

Collectively, these transformations in local food habits reveal that Muscovites have effectively turned the tables on McDonald's and transformed it not simply into something that is familiar and ordinary, but into something that is authentically indigenous as well as desirable and personally meaningful. More significantly, as the comments and actions of the schoolchildren whom I interviewed illustrate, McDonald's has become the local standard against which Russians' own food practices are measured. In this respect, as McDonald's has been more fully domesticated, it has lost its distinctiveness as something alien and visible and has instead become part of everyday life.

The routinization and habituation of McDonald's into the most ordinary and intimate aspects of Muscovites' daily lives are most vivid within the context of negotiations over the parameters of both domestic and domesticated space. As illustrated in the previous section, Muscovites are taking aspects of McDonald's into their homes. Yet, more and more, they are also taking their home lives into McDonald's, a practice that Muscovite employees facilitate by rarely limiting the amount of time that customers spend in the restaurants. For individuals without accommodation, such as visitors to the city and homeless persons, McDonald's serves as a surrogate home. I have frequently observed visitors using the bathrooms to bathe themselves and to wash out their clothes and dishes. Street children also find the restaurants to be safe havens. The store managers of a central Moscow McDonald's allow these children to sit at the tables and eat food that has been left on diners' trays. On one occasion, I watched as the store manager engaged several homeless children in friendly conversation and offered to help them with their problems. Even Muscovites who have apartments and jobs nearby elect to go to McDonald's to sit and enjoy their homemade lunches (and sometimes even a bottle of beer or two) that they have brought with them into the restaurant.

Other Muscovites have transferred their social lives to McDonald's. Instead of gathering for meals at someone's home, as was a more usual practice during Soviet days when meals in private kitchens were more cost-effective and safe from the prying eyes of others, friends, relatives and colleagues now meet at McDonald's to socialize or conduct business. . . . During interviews that I conducted with a group of schoolchildren who lived several hours away from Moscow (and the nearest McDonald's), the students excitedly described how frequently they traveled to the city with their friends simply to have dinner at McDonald's. Similarly, several college students confessed that before they had come to Moscow to study, they were unfamiliar with McDonald's. After spending a few months in the city, however, they had quickly begun congregating at McDonald's with their friends for late night meals and conversations.

Birthday parties, which Muscovites generally observe at home or at the family cottage, now represent the most obvious example of these efforts to refashion McDonald's as a domestic and socially significant space. Brightly colored posters and flyers invite children to celebrate their birthdays with a formal party organized and hosted by McDonald's staff. Such events occur regularly throughout the city and, on weekends, the restaurants are often busy with multiple parties taking place simultaneously. . . . Muscovites with more limited resources organize their own birthday parties at McDonald's. I sat near one such party and watched as a group of children chatted and played together at a table that their parents had decorated themselves. The parents first delivered their food orders from the counter and later divided a cake and other sweets that they had brought with them from home. . . .

As a place invested with meaning, value, delight and, more importantly, heightened sociality, McDonald's is an intrinsically and authentically local space.

THE DOMESTIC OTHER: CREATING THE NEW LOCAL

In many ways, Muscovites' experiences with McDonald's appear to resonate with the premises underlying the McDonaldization thesis: that the routinizing nature of McDonald's facilitates its insinuation into the organization and regulation of daily life and that McDonald's inherent rationality replaces indigenous, and hence more authentic, meaning with its own set of values and practices. At this point in time, however, it is impossible to predict whether complete McDonaldization will eventually be achieved in Russia. Yet preliminary comparison of McDonald's with other food transnationals in Moscow suggests that, as of now, McDonald's has not yet achieved the same degrees of rationality in Muscovites' everyday lives.

Specifically, we can look to the spread of coffee shops and sushi bars (sometimes coexisting in the same café) across Moscow during the past three years. There is an obvious sameness particularly among Russian coffee shops, as managers educate their clientele as to proper (i.e., American-style) coffee etiquette and tastes. The manager of one coffee shop boasted that his goal was to turn his Russian patrons into American coffee connoisseurs.

Muscovite consumers have visibly adapted themselves to these changes by substituting cappuccinos and espressos for their more usual afternoon teas or instant coffees and by learning to debate the subtleties of muffins, bagels and other American pastries. Most noticeable is the change in social relations that has accompanied these shifts: previously, afternoon tea was a social occasion when co-workers would stop working for a few moments to sit and socialize with each other. In Moscow's coffee shops, however, it is common to see individuals sitting alone and working on school or work projects while drinking a cup of coffee. In contrast, even as Muscovites treat coffee shops as impersonal and generic settings, they continue to approach McDonald's as a trusted social space where they gather with friends and relax. More importantly, Muscovites are actively manipulating McDonald's by refashioning the eating experience to reflect their own ideas of what constitutes private space and personally meaningful activities. Hence, at this stage, McDonald's has not yet reached the same degree of homogeneity as that pursued and promoted by its competitors.

I have grounded my analysis in an ethnographic perspective, that proposes that Muscovites are autonomous social agents—even when their choices are constrained by external forces. Thus, by focussing on Muscovite consumers as individuals who actively engage with the institutions and forces with which they coexist, I have drawn attention to the ways in which Muscovites produce and enact the domesticating process of Nash. Although Muscovites may in some ways be complicit partners with McDonald's in this process, it is ultimately these consumers who set the indigenous standards that McDonald's must exploit and satisfy. Finally, because my intent in this article was to highlight the ways in which Muscovites are finding and making meanings within new cultural systems, a focus on the domesticating process of Nash as a particular form of localization calls attention to the ways in which Muscovites do not simply appropriate and refashion foreign elements as familiar and special, as happens in processes of glocalization, but rather reorient their attitudes, feelings and affections in order to experience and know the foreign as something mundane and, hence, part of the local landscape. Despite the power of McDonald's to position itself as local, Muscovites are the final arbiters of this distinction.

In this article, I have suggested that the uniqueness of the McDonald's experience in Russia is evident in the ways that consumers affirm its place in local culture not simply by embracing it as just another part of the ordinary routines of daily life, but more accurately by taking it for granted. For many Muscovites, McDonald's has become . . . 'invisible.' Furthermore, at the same time as Muscovite consumers have accepted McDonald's as a local and personally meaningful experience, they have privileged it over other, more visibly foreign and uncomfortable, experiences. This quality of domestication emerged clearly when two Muscovite friends, a young middle-class married couple, recounted their driving vacation across the USA. Vera commented that because she and her husband were comfortable with the service and food at the McDonald's near their home in Moscow, they stopped at a McDonald's restaurant along an American interstate, but were surprised to find dirty facilities. They were even more astonished, she added, to discover that the food in the American McDonald's was not as tasty as that in Russia. Ultimately, Vera and her husband decided not to visit another McDonald's while they were on vacation, but to wait until they returned to Russia. As Vera noted, the McDonald's restaurants in Moscow were familiar and trustworthy and thus distinct from their North American prototypes.

By extending values of trust and intimacy to McDonald's, not only are Russian consumers reworking local understandings of such fundamental concepts as the private and the public, the domestic and the foreign, the personal and the popular, but they are also setting the standards that McDonald's must meet in order to flourish. McDonald's is more than a localized or a glocalized entity in Russia. By undergoing a specifically Russian process of localization—Nashification—it has become a locally meaningful, and hence domesticated, entity.

Thinking Critically

◆◆◆

1. From the point of view of McDonaldization, how do you interpret the tendency for Russians to have children's birthday parties at McDonald's?

2. From the point of view of McDonaldization, how do you interpret the tendency for Russians to prepare food (e.g., milkshakes) at home modeled after that at McDonald's?

3. Is all of this evidence of localization? Or a deeper level of McDonaldization?

4. How did fast food become "comfort food" for Russians?

5. Should critics of McDonaldization rejoice or be more fearful because of the fact that it has become "invisible" in Russia?

Although others focus on the food when they discuss McDonald's and McDonaldization, they miss the central point that both are really about systems for accomplishing various tasks and achieving various goals. Bryman understands this and applies it not only to McDonaldization but also to Disneyization. The key is the basic principles of McDonaldization (and Disneyization) that lie at the base of those systems. And those principles remain essentially the same whatever products and/or services are being proffered and wherever in the world they are on offer. This perspective reduces the import of the critiques offered by analysts like Waters, Watson, Turner, and Caldwell because their primary focus is largely limited to the foods and the ways in which they are adapted to different cultures.

35

Global Implications of McDonaldization and Disneyization

Alan Bryman

◆◆◆

O ne way in which Disneyization and McDonaldization can be viewed
as parallel processes is that both can legitimately be viewed as signals
of globalization. Ritzer makes this point in relation to McDonaldization
in his more recent work, and it is apparent that the dimensions of
Disneyization . . . are similarly spreading throughout the globe. But what is
striking about the two concepts is that they do not refer specifically to the
global diffusion of products. Much of the writing on globalization is full of
hyperbole about the global spread and recognizability of prominent brands:
Nike, Coca-Cola, Pepsi-Cola, Pizza Hut, KFC, Benetton, Body Shop, and
so on. And, of course, one could hardly disregard the golden arches of
McDonald's or Mickey's ears and Walt's signature as involved in the global
travels of brand names. But that is *not* what McDonaldization and

Editor's Note: From Bryman, A. (2003). Global Implications of McDonaldization
and Disneyization. *American Behavioral Scientist, 47*(2). Copyright © 2003,
reprinted with permission of Sage Publications, Inc.

Disneyization are about: They are concerned essentially with the diffusion of *modes of delivery* of goods and services. McDonaldization relates primarily to a mode of delivery in the sense of the *production* of goods and services. It is a means of providing an efficient and highly predictable product in a manner that would have appealed to people such as Ford and Taylor. It belongs to an era of mass consumption that is not disappearing but whose emphases are becoming less central to modern society with the passage of time. Disneyization is a mode of delivery in the sense of the *staging* of goods and services for consumption. It provides a context for increasing the allure of goods and services. Indeed, it may be that one of the reasons for the growing use of theming in the form of external narratives in some McDonald's restaurants has to do with the limitations of McDonaldization itself. McDonaldization's emphasis on standardization sits uneasily in an increasingly post-Fordist era of choice and variety. Theming becomes a means of reducing the sense of sameness and thereby enhancing the appeal of its products.

What is important about such a suggestion is that it is crucial to appreciate that McDonaldization and Disneyization are both *systems*, that is, they are ways of producing or presenting goods and services. One of the problems with tying the names of these systems to well-known icons of popular culture—McDonald's and Disney—is that it is easy to make the mistake of lapsing into a discussion of just McDonald's and Disney. This is an error because the two companies are merely emblems of the underlying processes associated with their respective systems.

By emphasizing processes associated with Disneyization and McDonaldization as systems, it is possible to get away from the shrill but not always revealing accounts of the global reach of prominent brands. It can hardly be doubted that there is a clutch of high-profile brands that have spread through much of the globe, but systems such as Disneyization and McDonaldization are in a sense more significant than that. For one thing, their presence is perhaps less immediately obvious than the arrival of McDonald's restaurants or the impending arrival of a new Disney theme park in Hong Kong. Focusing on the products obscures the more fundamental issue of the diffusion of underlying principles through which goods and services are produced and then put into people's mouths and homes. Although McDonald's restaurants have been the focus of anti-globalization campaigners and Disney was given a decidedly gallic cold shoulder among intellectuals in France when Disneyland Paris was in the planning stage, occasioning the famous "cultural Chernobyl" comment, the spread of the fundamental principles that can be divined from an examination of what McDonald's and the Disney theme parks exemplify is much less frequently, and perhaps less likely to be, a focus of comment.

When considered in this way, it is striking how poorly Disneyization and McDonaldization fit into Appadurai's influential delineation of different forms of "-scape," that is, contexts for the flow of goods, people, finance, and other items around the globe. Appadurai distinguished between five scapes; ethnoscapes (the movement of people), technoscapes (the movement of technology), financescapes (the movement of capital), mediascapes (the movement of information), and ideoscapes (the movement of ideas and ideals). Waters [Chapter 31] has argued that "McDonaldization infiltrates several of these flows." However, such a view does not do justice to the significance of McDonaldization and by implication Disneyization. In a sense, we need a new conceptual term for them, which we might call "system-scapes," to refer to the flow of contexts for the production and display of goods and services. Although they incorporate elements of the five scapes, as Waters suggests, McDonaldization and Disneyization are somewhat more than this. They represent important templates for the production of goods and services and their exhibition for sale.

Of course, we must give due consideration to the charge that we are subscribing here to a simplistic globalization or Americanization thesis that depicts icons of American culture spreading by design across the globe and riding roughshod over local conditions and practices. Research on McDonald's which can be treated as the *locus classicus* of McDonaldization, suggests that it is dangerous to think of a simple process of subsuming foreign cultures. Not only has McDonald's accommodated to local tastes and dietary requirements and preferences but it is also used in different ways in different cultures. It is sometimes regarded as a sophisticated eating environment for special occasions or dating couples, as a meeting place, as an area for study, and so on. Similar remarks can be made in relation to the Disney theme parks when they have been transported abroad. Raz observes in relation to Tokyo Disneyland that although it is invariably claimed to be a copy of the American original, it has in fact been Japanized. Thus, the Mystery Tour in the castle in Tokyo Disneyland is a Disney version of the Japanese ghost house. The Meet the World show is . . . as "a show about and for the Japanese." Similar adaptation can be seen in Disneyland Paris, where after a disappointing beginning, the company was forced to adapt the park to European tastes. The alcohol ban, in particular, had to be dropped. Such local adaptations and accommodations are frequently and quite rightly latched on to by the critics of a simple globalization thesis. They are also reassuring that the world is not becoming a single homogenized realm because there are signs of resistance even in the face of the momentum of two revered representatives of popular culture.

However, although reassuring, these indications of the continued relevance of the local for McDonald's and the Disney theme parks should not blind us to the fact that although McDonald's may be used differently in Tapei and that Tokyo Disneyland has adapted many attractions to the Japanese sensibility, this is not what McDonaldization and Disneyization are about. As previously argued, they are about *principles* to do with the production and delivery of goods and services. What the researchers who tell us about the different ways that McDonald's has adapted to or been differentially appropriated by diverse cultures is how McDonald's has been adapted to and appropriated, not McDonaldization as such. In a sense, Disneyization and McDonaldization are more worrying for the critics of globalization as a homogenizing force than the arrival of golden arches in far reaches of the globe or the transplanting of Disney theme parks abroad. They are more worrying because Disneyization and McDonaldization are potentially more insidious processes because they are far less visible and immediately obvious in their emergence than the appearance of golden arches or of magic kingdoms on nations' doorsteps. As Ritzer points out in relation to McDonald's, "The fundamental operating procedures remain essentially the same everywhere in the globe," a view that is largely endorsed by company representatives. Robert Kwan, at the time managing director of McDonald's in Singapore, is quoted by Watson as saying, "McDonald's sells . . . a system, not products" [Chapter 32]. In other words, finding adaptations to and local uses of McDonald's and Disney theme parks should not make us think that this means or even necessarily entails adaptations to and local uses of McDonaldization and Disneyization.

Turning more specifically to Disneyization, particularly in relation to McDonald's, none of what has been said previously should be taken to imply that there are likely to be no processes of local adaptation or resistance or culturally specific uses in relation to Disneyization. Emotional labor has been a particularly prominent site for resistance, as studies of the local reception of McDonald's demonstrate. Watson has observed that during the early period of the restaurant's arrival in Moscow, people standing in queues had to be given information about such things as how to order. In addition, they had to be told, "The employees inside will smile at you. This does not mean that they are laughing at you. We smile because we are happy to serve you." Watson also remarks on the basis of his fieldwork in Hong Kong that people who are overly congenial are regarded with suspicion, so that a smile is not necessarily regarded as a positive feature. Also, consumers did not display any interest in the displays or friendliness from crew personnel. It is not surprising, therefore, that the display of emotional labor is not a significant feature of the behavior and demeanor of counter staff in McDonald's in Hong Kong. Watson says, "Instead, they project qualities that are admired in the local culture: competence, directness, and unflappability. . . . Workers who smile on the job are assumed to be enjoying themselves at the consumer's (and the management's) expense."

A somewhat different slant is provided by Fantasia's account of the reception of McDonald's in France. There, the attraction of McDonald's for young people was what he calls the "American ambience." Insofar as the display of emotional labor is an ingredient of this ambience, it may be that it is not that the French enthusiasts respond positively to emotional labor per se but that in the context of McDonald's they respond positively to the total package, of which smiling counter staff is a component. In other words, as the writers who emphasize local adaptations to global processes point out, local consumers frequently make their own culturally bespoken uses of the forces of globalization.

Clearly, there are risks with the foregoing argument. At a time when writers on globalization prefer to emphasize "glocalization" or "creolization" as ways of coming to terms with the varied ways in which global forces have to run the gauntlet of local cultural conditions and preferences, it is unfashionable to suggest that impulses emanating from the United States are tramping over the globe. Indeed, as the previously cited evidence concerned with emotional labor implies, we do need to take into account the ways such global influences are working their way into and are being incorporated into local cultures. But Disneyization is a more invisible process than the arrival of brand names on foreign shores. It is designed to maximize consumers' willingness to purchase goods and services that in many cases they might not otherwise have been prompted to buy. Theming provides the consumer with a narrative that acts as a draw by providing an experience that lessens the sense of an economic transaction and increases the likelihood of purchasing merchandise. Dedifferentiation of consumption is meant to give the consumer as many opportunities as possible to make purchases and therefore to keep them as long as possible in the theme park, mall, or whatever. Emotional labor is the oil of the whole process in many ways: in differentiating otherwise identical goods and services, as an enactment of theming, and as a milieu for increasing the inclination to purchase merchandise. It may be that, as in Russia and Hong Kong, emotional labor is ignored or not effective. However, these are fairly small responses to the diffusion of these instruments of consumerism. And insofar as we can regard McDonald's as a Disneyized institution, the process of Disneyization has a high-profile partner that is likely to enhance the global spread of its underlying principles.

Thinking Critically

◆◆◆

1. What is the relationship between McDonaldization, Disneyization, and globalization?

2. What is the main focus of both McDonaldization and Disneyization?

3. How does Bryman's view on the relationship between McDonaldization (and Disneyization) and globalization differ from that of Caldwell, Watson, and others covered in this part?

4. How do McDonaldization, Disneyization, and globalization relate to Americanization?

Uri Ram offers an interesting case study of McDonald's in Israel. Although McDonald's has been successful, it has not destroyed the local falafel industry. Rather, part of that business has McDonaldized, while another has been "gourmetized." Depicted is a complex mix of the global and the local rather than one winning over the other. Ram puts this in the context of the debate between one-way (e.g., McDonaldization, although now that process is multidirectional and not just running from the United States to the rest of the world) and two-way (Appadurai's landscapes) models of globalization. Ram responds creatively that both approaches are correct but on different levels. Structurally (and this resembles Bryman's view on systems), he sees a one-way model predominate, but, symbolically, it is a two-way street. So, much of the falafel industry in Israel has been transformed structurally into an industrial-standardized system—a McDonaldized system. Symbolically, a two-way system is operant with the falafel and the McDonald's hamburger coexisting and mutually affecting one another. Thus, although Israel is characterized by a structural uniformity, symbolically, Israel remains different from other societies, including the United States. However, Ram seems to betray this perspective by arguing that Israeli differences have only "managed to linger on." Such phrasing seems to indicate that even to Ram, symbolic differences, like structural differences, are likely to disappear leading to increasing McDonaldization in both realms.

36

Glocommodification

How the Global Consumes the Local—McDonald's in Israel

Uri Ram

One of the more controversial aspects of globalization is its cultural implications: does globalization lead to universal cultural uniformity, or does it leave room for particularism and cultural diversity? The global-local encounter has spawned a complex polemic between 'homogenizers' and 'heterogenizers.' This article proposes to shift the ground of the debate from the homogeneous-heterogeneous dichotomy to a structural-symbolic construct. It is argued here that while both homogenization and hetero-genizations are dimensions of globalization, they take place at different societal levels: homogenization occurs at the structural-institutional level; heterogenization, at the expressive-symbolic. The proposed structural-symbolic model facilitates a realistic assessment of global-local relations. In

Editor's Note: From Ram, U. (2004). Glocommodification: How the Global Consumes the Local McDonald's in Israel. *Current Sociology, 52*(1), 11–31. Sage Publications, © International Sociological Association/ISA, 2004. Reprinted with permission.

this view, while global technological, organizational and commercial flows need not destroy local habits and customs, but, indeed, may preserve or even revive them, the global does tend to subsume and appropriate the local, or to consume it, so to say, sometimes to the extent that the seemingly local, symbolically, becomes a specimen of the global, structurally.

The starting point for this analysis is the McDonaldization of Israeli culture. McDonald's opened its first outlet in Israel in 1993. Since then, it has been involved in a variety of symbolic encounters . . . the encounter between McDonald's, as the epitome of global fast food, and the local version of fast food, namely the falafel . . . local idioms have thrived, though only symbolically. On the structural level, they have been subsumed and appropriated by global social relationships.

GLOBAL COMMERCE ENCOUNTERS THE LOCAL
EATING HABITUS: McDONALD'S AND THE FALAFEL

The industrialized hamburger first arrived on Israel's shores back in the late 1960s, although the chains involved at the time did not make much of an impression. In 1972, Burger Ranch (BR) opened a local hamburger joint that expanded into a chain only in the 1980s. It took the advent of McDonald's, however, for the 'great gluttony' of the fast hamburger to begin. McDonald's opened its first branch in October 1993. It was followed by Burger King (BK), the world's second largest hamburger chain, which opened its first branch in Israel in early 1994. Between McDonald's arrival and the year 2000, sales in the hamburger industry soared by 600 percent. By 2000, annual revenues from fast-food chains in Israel reached NIS 1 billion (about US$200 million according to the 2002 exchange rate). McDonald's is the leading chain in the industry, with 50 percent of the sales, followed by BR with 32 percent, and BK with 18 percent. In 2002 the three chains had a total of 250 branches in place: McDonald's, 100; BR, 94 and BK, 56.

McDonald's, like Coca-Cola—both flagship American brands— conquered front-line positions in the war over the Israeli consumer. The same is true of many other American styles and brands, such as jeans, T-shirts, Nike and Reebok footwear, as well as mega-stores, such as Home Center, Office Depot, Super-Pharm, etc. . . . As for eating habits, apart from the spread of fast-food chains, other Americanisms have found a growing niche in the Israeli market: frozen 'TV dinners,' whether in family or individual packs, and an upsurge in fast-food deliveries. These developments stem from the transformation of the familial lifestyle as an increasing number of women are no longer (or not only) housewives, the growth of singles households, and the rise in family incomes. All this, along with accelerated economic activity, has raised the demand for fast or easy-to-prepare foods. As has happened elsewhere, technological advancements and business interests have set the stage for changes in Israeli eating habits. Another typical development has been the mirror process that accompanies the expansion of standardized fast foods, namely, the proliferation of particularist cuisines and ethnic foods as evinced by the sprouting of restaurants that cater to the culinary curiosity and open purses of a new Yuppie class in Tel Aviv, Herzliya and elsewhere.

As in other countries, the 'arrival' of McDonald's in Israel raised questions and even concern about the survival of the local national culture. A common complaint against McDonald's is that it impinges on local cultures, as manifested primarily in the local eating habitus both actual and symbolic. If Israel ever had a distinct national equivalent to fast food, it was unquestionably the falafel—fried chick-pea balls served in a 'pocket' of pita bread with vegetable salad and tahini (sesame) sauce. The falafel, a Mediterranean delicacy of Egyptian origin, was adopted in Israel as its 'national food.' Although in the 1930s and 1940s the falafel was primarily eaten by the young and impecunious, in the 1950s and 1960s a family visit to the falafel stand for a fast, hot bite became common practice, much like the visit paid nowadays to McDonald's. The falafel even became an Israeli tourist symbol, served as a national dish at formal receptions of the Ministry of Foreign Affairs. Indeed, one kiosk in Tel Aviv advertises itself as a "'mighty' falafel for a mighty people."

Despite the falafel's fall from glory in the 1970s and 1980s vis-à-vis other fast foods, such as *shawarma* (lamb or turkey pieces on a spit), pizza and the early hamburger stands, and notwithstanding the unwholesome reputation it developed, an estimated 1200 falafel eateries currently operate in Israel. Altogether, they dish up about 200,000 portions a day to the 62 percent of Israelis who are self-confessed falafel eaters. The annual industry turnover is some NIS 600 million—not that far short of the hamburger industry. Thus, surprisingly enough, in the late 1990s, McDonald's presence, or rather the general McDonaldization of Israeli food habits, led to the falafel's renaissance, rather than to its demise.

The falafel's comeback, vintage 2000, is available in two forms: gourmet and fast-food. The clean, refined, gourmet Tel-Avivian specimen targets mainly yuppies and was launched in 1999—five years after McDonald's landed in the country—in a prestigious restaurant owned by two women, famed as Orna and Ella. Located in the financial district, which is swiftly being gentrified, it is known as 'The Falafel Queens'—a hip, ironic feminist version of the well-known 'Falafel King'—one of the most popular designations for Israeli falafel joints, which always take the masculine form. The new, 'improved' gourmet model comes in a variety of flavors. Apart from the traditional 'brown' variety, the Queens offer an original 'red' falafel, based on roasted peppers, as well as 'green' falafel, based on olive paste. Beverages are a mixed bag, including orange-Campari and grapefruit-arrack ice. Owner Ella Shein rightly notes that the falafel's revival reflects a composite global-local trend:

> We have opened up to the world culinarily speaking, we have been exposed to new raw materials, new techniques, a process that occurs simultaneously with a kind of return to one's origins, to one's roots.

Apart from its 'gourmetization,' the falafel has simultaneously undergone 'McDonaldized' standardization. The Israeli franchise of Domino's Pizza inaugurated a new falafel chain, setting itself a nationwide target of 60 branches. Furthermore, its reported intention is to 'take the tidings of Israeli fast-food abroad.' The falafel has thus been rescued from parochialism and upgraded to a world standard-bearer of 'Israeli fast food,' or, as one observer put it, it has been transformed from 'grub' into 'brand.' In fact, the Ma'oz chain already operates 12 falafel eateries in Amsterdam, Paris and Barcelona and, lately, also in Israel. The new chains have developed a 'concept' of 'clean, fresh, and healthy,' with global implications, because: 'if you are handed an inferior product at "Ma'oz" in Amsterdam, you won't set foot in the Paris branch' either. In contrast to the traditional falafel stand, which stands in the street and absorbs street fumes and filth, the new falafel is served indoors, at spruce, air-conditioned outlets, where portions are wrapped in designer bags and sauces flow out of stylized fountains. At Falafels, the balls are not moulded manually, but dispensed by a mechanical implement at the rate of 80 balls/minute. There are two kinds—the Syrian Zafur and the Turkish Baladi. And as befits an industrial commodity, the new falafel is 'engineered' by food technicians and subjected to tastings by focus groups.

Like any self-respecting post-Fordist commodity, the falafel of the new chains is not only a matter of matter but, as stated above, of concept or, more precisely, of fantasy, rendering the past as nostalgia or retro. Branches are designed in a nostalgic style—in order to evoke yearning within the primary target sector—and they carry, in the name of 'retro,' old-fashioned soda pops. This is the local Israeli habitus dusted off, 'branded' and 'designed' so as to be marketed as a mass standardized commodity. Another trendy aspect of the new falafel is its linkage to the new discourses on the environment or nutrition. The proprietor of Ma'oz notes that 'salads, tehini, and falafel are healthy foods, and we have taken the health issue further by offering also whole-wheat pita bread. The health issue is becoming so central that we are now considering establishing a falafel branch that would serve only organic vegetables.' To sum up, the distinction between the old falafel and the new, post-McDonald's falafel, is identified in a local newspaper report as follows:

If in the past every Falafel King took pride in the unique taste [of his own product, the secret of] which was sometimes passed down from father to son, and which acquired a reputation that attracted customers from far and wide, in the [new] chains, the taste would always be the same. Uniqueness and authenticity would be lost for the sake of quality and free market rules.

One major change is Israel's culinary habitus as a result of its McDonaldization, therefore, is the demise of the old 'authentic' falafel and the appearance of the new commodified 'falafel 2000.'

But McDonald's had to surmount another—no less challenging—culinary hurdle: the Israeli carnivorous palate. . . . Given this hankering for meat, especially of the grilled variety, the McDonald's hamburger appeared rather puny, and the Israeli consumer tended to favour the Burger King broiled product. In 1998, McDonald's bowed to the Israeli appetite, changing both the preparation and size of its hamburger. It shifted to a combined technique of fire and charcoal, and increased portion size by 25 percent. The Israeli customer now has the distinction of being served the largest hamburger (120 grams) marketed by McDonald's worldwide. But the most striking fast-food modification to the Israeli habitus is the 'Combina' (the Hebrew equivalent of 'combo'), launched in 2001 by Burger Ranch—a packaged meal for four eaters that taps into the local custom of 'sharing' and, to quote the marketing blurb, allows for 'a group experience while retaining individual dining expression.'

It may thus be concluded that the interrelations of McDonald's and the falafel are not simply a contrast between local decline and global rise. Rather, they are a complex mix, though certainly under the banner of the global. Indeed, the global (McDonald's) contributed somewhat to the revival of the local (the falafel). In the process, however, the global also transformed the nature and meaning of the local. The local, in turn, caused a slight modification in the taste and size of the global, while leaving its basic institutional patterns and organizational practices intact. The 'new falafel' is a component of both a mass-standardized consumer market, on the one hand, and a post-modern consumer market niche, on the other. This sort of relationship between McDonald's and the falafel, in which the global does not eliminate the local symbolically but rather restructures or appropriates it structurally, is typical of the global-local interrelations epitomized by McDonald's.

DISCUSSION I: 'ONE-WAY' OR 'TWO-WAY'?

Based on this case analysis, how, then, are we to conceive the relations between global commerce and local idioms?

The literature on relations between the global and the local presents a myriad of cases. Heuristically, the lessons from these may be condensed into two competing—contrasting, almost—approaches: the one gives more weight to globalization, which it regards as fostering cultural uniformity (or homogeneity); the other gives more weight to localization, which it regards as preserving cultural plurality, or cultural 'differences' (or heterogeneity). . . . the former is known also as cultural imperialism and McDonaldization, . . . The latter is known also as hybridization. . . . For the sake of simplicity we shall call the former the 'one-way' approach, i.e., seeing the effect as emanating from the global to the local; and the latter, as the 'two-way' approach, i.e., seeing the effect as an interchange between the global and the local.

The most prominent exponent of the one-way approach is George Ritzer, in his book *The McDonaldization of Society*. Ritzer, more than anyone else, is responsible for the term that describes the social process of McDonaldization. . . .

Contrary to this one-way approach . . . the literature offers another view, which we call here the two-way approach. This view considers globalization only a single vector in two-way traffic, the other vector being localization. The latter suspends, refines, or diffuses the intakes from the former, so that traditional and local cultures do not dissolve; they rather ingest global flows and reshape them in the digestion.

Arjun Appadurai, for one, asserts that it is impossible to think of the processes of cultural globalization in terms of mechanical flow from center to periphery. Their complexity and disjunctures allow for a chaotic contest between the global and the local that is never resolved. . . .

One typical significant omission of the two-way perspective is its disregard for imbalances of power. . . . Positing 'localization' as a counterbalance to globalization, rather than as an offshoot, some of the cultural studies literature is indeed rich in texture and subtlety when depicting the encounters of global commerce with local popular cultures and everyday life. This literature is at its best when acknowledging that its task is to 'twist the stick in the other direction,' from the top-down political-economic perspective to a bottom-up cultural perspective. It falters, however, when it attempts to replace, wholesale, the top-down approach with a bottom-up one, without weighting the relative power of the top and the bottom.

The latter move is evident in an ethnographic study of McDonaldization conducted in Southeast Asia by a team of anthropologists [Chapter 32]. They argue overall that even though McDonald's transformed local customs, customers were nonetheless able to transform McDonald's in their areas into local establishments; this led them to conclude that McDonald's does not always call the shots. They claim that, in the realm of popular culture, it is no longer possible to distinguish between the 'local' and the 'external.' Who, they protest, is to say whether or not Mickey Mouse is Japanese, or Ronald McDonald, Chinese; perhaps, this attests to a 'third culture' that belongs neither to one nationality nor the other, but constitutes rather a transnational culture.

This ethnographic discussion stresses the variety of supplemental dishes McDonald's has included on its menu in order to accommodate various local cultures. Applying this approach to our case study, the new falafel, for instance, can be considered a manifestation of . . . hybridization of McDonald's. The new falafel assimilated some of McDonald's practices, but accommodated them to local traditions and tastes.

The two-way approach to the global-local encounter is usually portrayed as critical and espoused by radical social scientists, because it 'empowers' the sustainability of local cultures and fosters local identities. . . .

DISCUSSION II: 'BOTH WAYS'

. . . To the question of homogenization vs heterogenization in global-local relationships, we suggest here the following resolution: (1) both perspectives are valid; (2) yet they apply to discrete societal levels; and (3) the one-way approach is restricted to one level of social reality, the structural-institutional level, i.e., patterns and practices which are inscribed into institutions and organizations; the two-way approach is restricted to the symbolic-expressive level of social reality, i.e., the level of explicit symbolization. Finally, (4) we suggest a global-local structural-symbolic model, in which the one-way structural homogenization process and the two-way symbolic heterogenization process are combined. Thus, heuristically speaking, our theoretical resolution is predicated on the distinction between two different levels, the structural-institutional level and the expressive-symbolic level.

While each of the rival perspectives on the global-local encounter is attuned to only one of these levels, we propose that globalization be seen as a process that is simultaneously one-sided and two-sided but in two distinct societal levels. In other words, on the structural level, globalization is a one-way street; but on the symbolic level, it is a two-way street. In Israel's case, for instance, this would mean that, symbolically, the falafel and McDonald's coexist side by side; structurally, however, the falafel is produced and consumed as if it were an industrialized-standardized (McDonaldized) hamburger, or as its artisan-made 'gourmet' counterpart. . . .

The two-way approach to globalization, which highlights the persistence of cultural 'difference,' contains more than a grain of empirical truth. On the symbolic level, it accounts for the diversity that does not succumb to homogeneity—in our case, the falafel once again steams from the pita; the Israeli hamburger is larger than other national McDonald's specimens (and kosher for Passover. . .). On the symbolic level, the 'difference' that renders the local distinctive has managed to linger on. At the same time, on the structural level, that great leveller of 'sameness' at all locales prevails: the falafel has become McDonaldized. . . .

A strong structuralist argument sees symbolic 'differences' not merely as tolerated but indeed as functional to structural 'sameness,' in that they are purported to conceal the structure's underlying uniformity and to promote niches of consumer identity. In other words, the variety of local cultural identities 'licensed' under global capitalist commercial expansion disguises the unified formula of capital, thereby fostering legitimacy and even sales.

. . . A variety of observers—all with the intention of 'giving voice' to the 'other' and the 'subaltern'—may unwittingly be achieving an opposite effect. . . . Exclusive attention to explicit symbolism may divert attention from implicit structures.

Transnational corporations are quick to take advantage of multiculturalism, postcolonialism and ethnography, and exploit genuine cultural concerns to their benefit. It is worth quoting at some length a former Coca-Cola marketing executive:

> We don't change the concept. What we do is maybe change the music, maybe change the execution, certainly change the casting, but in terms of what it sounds like and what it looks like and what it is selling, at a particular point in time, we have kept it more or less patterned. . . . [our activity] has been all keyed on a local basis, overlaid with an umbrella of the global strategy. We have been dealing with various ethnic demographic groups with an overall concept. Very recently . . . the company has moved to a more fragmented approach, based on the assumption that the media today is fragmented and that each of these groups that are targeted by that media core should be communicated to in their own way with their own message, with their own sound, with their own visualization. . . .

The case study presented here has shown a number of instances of the process whereby global commodities appropriate local traditions. To recap with the example of the 'new falafel,' McDonaldization did not bring about its demise, but, indeed, contributed to its revival, vindicating, as it were, the two-way perspective. The falafel's new lease on life, however, is modelled after McDonald's, that is, a standardized, mechanical, mass-commodified product, on the one hand; or responds to it in a commercial 'gourmetized' and 'ethnicitized' product, on the other hand. In both cases, global McDonaldization prevails structurally, while it may give a symbolic leeway to the local. . . . Indeed, from the end-user's or individual consumer's perspective, the particular explicit symbolic 'difference' may be a source of great emotional gratification; but from the perspective of the social structure, the system of production and consumption, what matters is the exact opposite—namely, the implicit structural homogenization.

Thus, the question of global homogenization vs. local heterogenization cannot be exhausted by invoking symbolic differences, as is attempted by the two-way approach. 'McDonaldization' is not merely or mainly about the manufactured objects—the hamburgers—but first and foremost about the deep-seated social relationships involved in their production and consumption—i.e., it is about commodification and instrumentalization. In its broadest sense here, McDonaldization represents a robust commodification and instrumentalization of social relations, production and consumption, and therefore an appropriation of local cultures by global flows. This study . . . proposes looking at the relations between the global and the local as a composite of the structural and symbolic levels, a composite in which the structural inherently appropriates the symbolic but without explicitly suppressing it. . . .

This is what is meant by glocommodification—global commodification combining structural uniformity with symbolic diversity.

Thinking Critically

1. In terms of fast food, in what ways has Israel grown more like the U.S.?

2. In terms of fast food, in what ways has Israel grown less like the U.S.?

3. Are whatever differences that remain in Israel, and elsewhere, merely "hanging on"?

4. Is McDonaldization a one-way or a two-way process?

5. Would a critic of McDonaldization be optimistic based on this analysis of the Israeli fast-food industry?

In this chapter, I address the relationship between McDonaldization and the ideas developed in a more recent book of mine, The Globalization of Nothing *(2004). In that work, I develop a theoretical model to help us grapple with the issues raised throughout this section. Many of the perspectives discussed earlier (e.g., hybridity) relate to the idea of glocalization, but I create the term "grobalization" to deal with the imposition of cultural forms on other societies (cultural convergence). From my point of view, McDonaldization is best thought of as a specific type of grobalization.*

In addition, I create the terms "nothing" (social forms that are centrally conceived, controlled, and lacking in distinctive content) and "something" (social forms that are locally conceived, controlled, and rich in distinctive content). Clearly, McDonald's, its products, and its systems are paradigmatic forms of nothing. (An example of something would be a local farmer's or craft market.) Although I discuss various permutations and combinations, it is clear that McDonaldization fits best under the heading of the grobalization of nothing. Further, it is so powerful that it threatens the other major forms of globalization, especially the glocalization of something.

37

Globalization and McDonaldization

Does It All Amount to . . . Nothing?

George Ritzer

◆◆◆ ───

GLOBALIZATION

[G]lobalization can be defined as "the worldwide diffusion of practices, expansion of relations across continents, organization of social life on a global scale, and growth of a shared global consciousness." It is clear that the world has been affected increasingly by globalization in general, as well as by the subdimensions of that process enumerated in this definition.

McDonaldization can be seen, at least in part, as one of a number of globalization processes. While it is important to remember that McDonaldization is *not* only a globalization process (for example, it is also revolutionizing life *within* the United States), it is clear that in at least some of its aspects, it can be considered under that heading. Let us look at the relationship between McDonaldization and each of the four aspects of globalization that make up the definition of that term as it was employed above.

Editor's Note: From Ritzer, G. (2004). *McDonaldization of Society, Revised New Century Edition.* Copyright © 2004, reprinted with permission of Sage Publications, Inc.

First, the *practices* (for example, putting customers to work, routinely eating meals quickly and on the run, using drive-through windows) developed by McDonald's (and other leaders of the fast-food industry) in the United States have been diffused to fast-food restaurants in many other countries around the world. More generally, a wide range of practices that define many different McDonaldized settings (for example, education, law enforcement) have similarly been disseminated globally. Thus, for example, universities in many parts of the world have been drawn toward the increasing use of large lecture-style classes, and police forces in many countries employ many of the efficient techniques for law enforcement and crowd control pioneered in the United States.

Second, many intercontinental *relationships* that did not exist before came into being as a result of the proliferation of McDonaldized systems. That is, the deep linkages among and between McDonaldized systems have necessitated a large number of such global relationships. For example, there are strong ties among the various restaurants around the world that are part of Yum! Brands, Inc. (for example, Kentucky Fried Chicken outlets in various geographic locales). Less formal, but no less important, are the relationships between law enforcement agencies or universities as they share knowledge of, and experiences with, the latest advances in the McDonaldization of their respective domains.

Third, the ensemble of these relationships has led to *new ways of organizing social life* throughout the world and across the globe. To put it most generally, the ways in which the social world is organized, even across great distances, have been McDonaldized. Thus, not only has the way people eat been restructured (for example, less in the home and more in fast-food restaurants) but so has the way higher education (fewer personal tutorials, more large lectures) and law enforcement (the increased use of "assembly line" justice) are structured. In innumerable ways, the organization of everyday life has been altered, sometimes dramatically, by the spread of McDonaldization across the globe.

Finally, McDonald's, to say nothing of the many other McDonaldized systems, has led to a new *global consciousness*. There are those who are well aware that they are part of an increasingly McDonaldized world and who revel in that knowledge. Thus, some people are more willing to travel to far-off locales because they know that their ability to adjust to those settings will be made easier by the existence of familiar McDonaldized settings. However, there are others with a similar (if not greater) level of awareness who abhor the process and what it is doing to their lives and the lives of many throughout the world. Such people may be disinclined to travel to at least some places because they know they have become so highly McDonaldized. Most generally, McDonald's and other McDonaldized businesses are such active and aggressive marketers that people can hardly avoid being conscious of them and the way they are changing their lives and the lives of many others throughout the world.

Globalization: Glocalization and Grobalization

. . . *Glocalization* can be defined as *the interpenetration of the global and the local, resulting in unique outcomes in different geographic areas.* That is, global forces, often associated with a tendency toward homogenization, run headlong into the local in any geographic location. Rather than either one overwhelming the other, the global and the local interpenetrate, producing unique outcomes in each location.

This emphasis on glocalization has a variety of implications for thinking about globalization in general. First, it leads to the view that the world is growing increasingly pluralistic. Glocalization theory is exceptionally sensitive to differences within and between areas of the world. Thus, the glocal realities in one part of the world are likely to be quite different from such realities in other parts of the world. Such a view of the world leads one to downplay many of the fears associated with globalization in general (and McDonaldization more specifically), especially the fear of increasing homogeneity throughout the world.

This absence of fear of the negative aspects of globalization is associated with a tendency on the part of those who emphasize glocalization to argue that individuals and local groups have great power to adapt, innovate, and maneuver within a glocalized world. Glocalization theory sees individuals and groups as important and creative agents. Thus, while they may be subject to globalizing processes, these powerful individuals and groups are not likely to be overwhelmed by, and subjugated to, them. Rather, they are likely to modify and adapt them to their own needs and interests. In other words, they are able to glocalize them.

Thus, social processes, especially those that relate to globalization, are seen as relational and contingent. That is, forces pushing globalization emanate from many sources, but they generally face counterforces in any given area of the world. Consequently, what develops in any area is a result of the relationship between these forces and counterforces. This also means that whether or not the forces of globalization overwhelm the local is contingent on the specific relationship between the forces and counterforces in any given locale. Where the counterforces are weak, globalizing forces may successfully impose themselves, but where they are strong (and to glocalization theorists, they appear strong in most areas), a glocal form is likely to emerge that uniquely integrates the global and the local. Thus, to fully understand globalization, we must deal with the specific and contingent relationships that exist in any given locale.

From the point of view of glocalization, the forces impelling globalization are *not* seen as (totally) coercive but, rather, as providing material to be used, in concert with the local, in individual and group creation of distinctive glocal realities. Thus, for example, the global mass media (say, CNN or

Al-Jazeera) are not seen as defining and controlling what people think and believe in a given locale but, rather, as providing them with additional inputs that are integrated with many other media inputs (especially those that are local) to create unique sets of ideas and viewpoints.

There is no question that glocalization is an important part of globalization, but it is far from the entire story. Furthermore, while, as we will see, some degree of glocalization occurs under the heading of McDonaldization, another side of globalization relates better to McDonaldization. That aspect of globalization is well described by the concept of grobalization, coined in my book *The Globalization of Nothing*, for the first time as a much-needed companion to the notion of glocalization. *Grobalization focuses on the imperialistic ambitions of nations, corporations, organizations, and the like and their desire, indeed need, to impose themselves on various geographic areas.* Their main interest is in seeing their power, influence, and in some cases profits *grow* (hence the term *grobalization*) throughout the world. Grobalization involves a variety of subprocesses, three of which—capitalism, Americanization, and McDonaldization—are not only central driving forces in grobalization but also of particular interest to the author. While all three were dealt with in *The Globalization of Nothing*, the focus below will naturally be on McDonaldization. That is, McDonaldization is both a major example of, and a key driving force in, grobalization.

Grobalization leads to a variety of ideas that are largely antithetical to the basic ideas associated with glocalization. Rather than emphasizing the great diversity among various glocalized locales, grobalization leads to the view that the world is growing increasingly similar. While it is recognized that there are differences within and between areas of the world, what is emphasized is their increasing similarity. Thus, grobalization theory is especially sensitive to the increasing number of similarities that characterize many areas of the world. This, of course, tends to heighten the fears of those who are concerned about the increasing homogenization associated with globalization.

In contrast to the view associated with glocalization, individuals and groups throughout the world are seen as having relatively little ability to adapt, innovate, and maneuver within a grobalized world. Grobalization theory sees larger structures and forces tending to overwhelm the ability of individuals and groups to create themselves and their worlds.

In yet another stark contrast, grobalization tends to see social processes as largely unidirectional and deterministic. That is, the forces flow from the global to the local, and there is little or no possibility of the local having any significant impact on the global. As a result, the global is generally seen as largely determining what transpires at the local level; the impact of the global is not seen as contingent on what transpires at the local level or on how the local reacts to the global. Thus, grobalization tends to overpower the local. It also limits the ability of the local to act and react, let alone to act back on the grobal.

Thus, from the perspective of grobalization, global forces *are* seen as largely determining what individual(s) and groups think and do throughout the world. For example, this view accords far more power to grobal media powers such as CNN and Al-Jazeera to influence people in any given geographic area than does the viewpoint that emphasizes glocalization.

McDONALDIZATION AND GROBALIZATION

In terms of globalization, the McDonaldization thesis contends that highly McDonaldized systems—and more important, the principles that lie at their base—have been exported from the United States to much of the rest of the world. Many nations throughout the world, and innumerable subsystems within each, are undergoing the process of McDonaldization. To put it another way, the influence of McDonaldization has been *growing* throughout much of the world, and this clearly places it under the heading of *gro*balization. The major driving force is economics—the ability of McDonaldized systems to increase profits continually is based on the need to steadily expand markets throughout the world. However, other factors help account for the growing global presence of McDonaldization, including a deep belief in the system by those who push it and a strong desire on the part of those who do not have it to obtain it.

McDonaldization is obviously a global perspective, especially a grobal one, but it is both less and more than a theory of globalization. On the one hand, McDonaldization does not involve anything approaching the full range of global processes. . . . On the other hand, McDonaldization involves much more than an analysis of its global impact. For example, much of it involves the manifold transformations taking place *within* the United States, the source and still the center of this process. . . . Thus, McDonaldization is not coterminous with globalization, nor is it solely a global process. Nonetheless, McDonaldization has global implications and can thus be a useful lens through which to examine changes taking place around the globe.

What is clear is that McDonaldization deserves a place in any thoroughgoing account of globalization, especially grobalization. There can be little doubt that the logic of McDonaldization generates a set of values and practices that have a competitive advantage over other models. It not only promises many specific advantages, it also reproduces itself more easily than other models of consumption (and in many other areas of society, as well). The success of McDonaldization in the United States over the past half century, coupled with the international ambitions of McDonald's and its ilk, as well as those of indigenous clones throughout the world, strongly suggests that McDonaldization will continue to make inroads into the global marketplace, not only through the efforts of existing corporations but also via the diffusion of the paradigm.

It should be noted, however, that the continued advance of McDonaldization, at least in its present form, is far from assured. In fact, there are even signs in the United States, as well as in other parts of the world, of what I have previously called *de-McDonaldization*. . . . Nonetheless, at the moment and for the foreseeable future, McDonaldization will continue to be an important force, and it is clearly and unequivocally not only a grobal process but also one that contributes mightily to the spread of "nothingness."

NOTHING-SOMETHING AND McDONALDIZATION

I have now discussed the ideas of glocalization-grobalization as they relate to McDonaldization, but a second set of ideas—nothing-something, also derived from *The Globalization of Nothing*—needs to be discussed here. As we will see, these ideas relate not only directly to McDonaldization but also to its relationship to globalization in general and grobalization-glocalization in particular.

Nothing can be defined as a *"social form that is generally centrally conceived, controlled and comparatively devoid of distinctive substantive content."* It should be abundantly clear that any McDonaldized system, with the fast-food restaurant being a prime example, would be a major form of nothing. However, it is important to point out that there are many other examples of nothing that have little or no direct relationship to McDonaldization.

Let us look at the example of a chain of fast-food restaurants from the point of view of the basic components of our definition of nothing. First, as parts of chains, fast-food restaurants are, virtually by definition, centrally conceived. That is, those who created the chain and are associated with its central offices conceived of the chain originally and are continually involved in its reconceptualization. For their part, owners and managers of local chain restaurants do little or no conceptualizing on their own. Indeed, they have bought the rights to the franchise, and continue to pay a percentage of their profits for it, because they want those with the demonstrated knowledge and expertise to do the conceptualizing. This relative absence of independent conceptualization at the level of the local franchise is one of the reasons we can think of the franchise as nothing.

We are led to a similar view when we turn to the second aspect of our definition of nothing—control. Just as those in the central office do the conceptualization for the local franchises, they also exert great control over them. Indeed, to some degree, such control is derived from the fact that conceptualization is in the hands of the central office; the act of conceptualizing and reconceptualizing the franchise yields a significant amount of control. However, control is exercised by the central office over the franchises in more direct ways as well. For example, it may get a percentage of a local franchise's profits, and if its cut is down because profits are down, the central office may put pressure on the local franchise to alter its procedures to increase profitability. The central office may also deploy inspectors to make periodic and unannounced visits to local franchises. Those franchises found not to be operating the way they are supposed to will come under pressure to bring their operations in line with company standards. Those that do not are likely to suffer adverse consequences, including the ultimate punishment of the loss of the franchise. Thus, local franchises can also be seen as nothing because they do not control their own destinies.

The third aspect of our definition of nothing is that it involves social forms largely lacking in distinctive content. This is essentially true by definition of chains of franchised fast-food restaurants. That is, the whole idea is to turn out restaurants that are virtual clones of one another. To put it another way, the goal is to produce restaurants that are as alike one another as possible—they generally look much the same from outside, they are structured similarly within, the same foods are served, workers act and interact in much the same way, and so on. There is little that distinguishes one outlet of a chain of fast-food restaurants from all the others.

Thus, there is a near perfect fit between the definition of nothing offered above and a chain of fast-food restaurants. However, this is a rather extreme view since, in a sense, "nothing is nothing." In other words, all social forms (including fast-food restaurants) have characteristics that deviate from the extreme form of nothing. That is, they involve some local conceptualization and control, and each one has at least some distinctive elements. To put this another way, all social forms have some elements of somethingness. Consequently, we need to think not only in terms of nothing but also in terms of something as well as a something-nothing continuum.

This leads us to a definition of something as *"a social form that is generally indigenously conceived, controlled, and comparatively rich in distinctive substantive content."* This makes it clear that neither nothing nor something exists independently of the other; *each makes sense only when paired with, and contrasted to, the other.*

If a fast-food restaurant is an example of nothing, then a meal cooked at home from scratch would be an example of something. The meal is conceived by the individual cook and not by a central office. Control rests in the hands of that cook. Finally, that which the cook prepares is rich in distinctive content and different from that prepared by other cooks, even those who prepare the same meals.

While nothing and something are presented as if they were a dichotomy, we really need to think in terms of a *continuum* from something to nothing, and that is precisely the way the concepts will be employed here—as the two poles of that continuum. Thus, while a fast-food restaurant falls toward the nothing end of the continuum, every fast-food restaurant has at least some elements that are different from all others; each has some elements of some-thingness associated with it. Conversely, while every home-cooked meal is distinctive, they are likely to have at least some elements in common (for example, they may rely on a common cookbook or recipe) and therefore have some elements of nothingness. Therefore, no social form exists at the extreme nothing or something pole of the continuum; they *all* fall somewhere between the two. However, it remains the case that some lie closer to the nothing end of the continuum, whereas others lie more toward the something end. In terms of our interests here, fast-food restaurants, and more generally all McDonaldized systems, fall toward the nothing end of the something-nothing continuum.

NOTHING-SOMETHING AND GROBALIZATION-GLOCALIZATION

I turn now to a discussion of the relationship between grobalization-glocalization and something-nothing and its implications for our under-standing of McDonaldization. Figure 37.1 offers the four basic possibilities that emerge when we crosscut the grobalization-glocalization and some-thing-nothing continua. It should be noted that while this yields four "ideal types," there are no hard-and-fast lines between them. This is reflected in the use of both dotted lines and multidirectional arrows in Figure 37.1.

Quadrants 1 and 4 in Figure 37.1 are of greatest importance, at least for the purposes of this analysis. They represent a key point of tension and con-flict in the world today. Clearly, there is great pressure to grobalize nothing (Quadrant 4) and often all that stands in its way in terms of achieving global hegemony is the glocalization of something (Quadrant 1). . . .

While the other two quadrants (2 and 3) are clearly residual in nature and of secondary importance, it is necessary to recognize that there is, at least to some degree, a glocalization of nothing (quadrant 2) and a grobal-ization of something (quadrant 3). However, whatever tensions may exist between them are of far less significance than those between the grobaliza-tion of nothing and the glocalization of something. A discussion of the glo-calization of nothing and the grobalization of something makes it clear that grobalization is not an unmitigated source of nothing (it can involve some-thing) and glocalization is not to be seen solely as a source of something (it can involve nothing). . . .

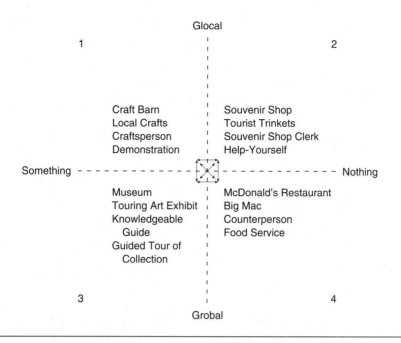

Figure 37.1   The Relationship Between Glocal-Grobal and Something-Nothing
With Examples

SOURCE: Adapted from George Ritzer. *The Globalization of Nothing.* Thousand Oaks, CA:
Pine Forge Press, 2004, p. 98.

The Grobalization of Nothing

The example of the grobalization of nothing in Figure 37.1 is a meal
at McDonald's. There is little or nothing distinctive about any given
McDonald's restaurant, the food served there, the people who work in these
settings, and the "services" they offer. And, of course, there has been a very
aggressive effort to expand the presence of McDonald's throughout much of
the world. Thus, the global expansion of McDonald's (and other fast-food
chains) is a near-perfect example of the grobalization of nothing.

The main reasons for the strong affinity between grobalization and
nothing are basically the inverse of the reasons for the lack of such affinity
between grobalization and something. For example:

1. Above all, there is a far greater demand throughout the world for nothing
    than something. This is the case because nothing tends (although not
    always) to be less expensive than something, with the result that more

people can afford the former than the latter (As we know, McDonald's places great emphasis on its low prices and "value meals").

2. Large numbers of people are also far more likely to want the various forms of nothing because their comparative simplicity and lack of distinctiveness appeals to a wider range of tastes (the food at McDonald's is famous for its simple and familiar—salty and sweet—taste).

3. In addition . . . that which is nothing, largely devoid of distinctive content, is far less likely to bother or offend those in other cultures (although it has aroused outrage in some cultures, McDonald's simple and basic foods have shown the ability to fit into many different cultures).

4. Finally, because of the far greater potential sales, much more money can be, and is, devoted to the advertising and marketing of nothing, thereby creating a still greater demand for it than for something (McDonald's spends huge sums on advertising and has been very successful at generating great demand for its fare).

Given the great demand, it is far easier to mass-produce and -distribute the empty forms of nothing than the substantively rich forms of something. Indeed, many forms of something lend themselves best to limited, if not one-of-a-kind, production. A skilled potter may produce a few dozen pieces of pottery and an artist a painting or two in, perhaps, a week, a month, or even a year(s). While these craft and art works may, over time, move from owner to owner in various parts of the world, this traffic barely registers in the total of all global trade and commerce. Of course, there are the rare masterpieces that may bring millions of dollars, but in the main, these one-of-a-kind works are small-ticket items. In contrast, thousands, even many millions, and sometimes billions of varieties of nothing are mass-produced and sold throughout the globe. Thus, the global sale of fast food like Big Macs, Whoppers, Kentucky Fried Chicken, as well as the myriad other forms of nothing, is a far greater factor in grobalization than the international sale of pieces of high art (for example, the art of Van Gogh) or of tickets to the Rolling Stones' most recent world tour.

Furthermore, the economics of the marketplace demands that the massive amount of nothing that is produced be marketed and sold on a grobal basis. For one thing, the economics of scale mean that the more that is produced and sold, the lower the price. This means that, almost inevitably, American producers of nothing (and they are, by far, the world leaders in this) must become dissatisfied with the American market, no matter how vast it is, and aggressively pursue a world market for their products. The greater the grobal market, the lower the price that can be charged (McDonald's can buy hamburger meat on the global market at rock-bottom prices because of the huge number of burgers it sells), and this, in turn, means that even greater numbers of nothing can be sold to far reaches of the globe in less-developed countries.

Another economic factor stems from the demand of the stock market that corporations that produce and sell nothing (indeed, all corporations) increase sales and profits from one year to the next. The stocks of those corporations (and McDonald's has recently been one of them) that simply meet the previous year's profitability, or experience a decline, are likely to be punished in the stock market and see their stock prices fall, sometimes precipitously. To increase profits continually, the corporation is forced, as Karl Marx understood long ago, to continue to search out new markets. One way of doing that is to constantly expand globally. In contrast, since something is less likely to be produced by corporations, certainly the large corporations listed in the stock market, there is far less pressure to expand the market for it. In any case, given the limited number of these things that can be produced by artisans, skilled chefs, artists, and so on, there are profound limits on such expansion. This, in turn, brings us back to the pricing issue and relates to the price advantage that nothing ordinarily has over something. As a general rule, the various types of nothing cost far less than something. The result, obviously, is that nothing can be marketed globally far more aggressively than something.

Also, nothing has an advantage in terms of transportation around the world. These are things that generally can be easily and efficiently packaged and moved, often over vast areas. The frozen hamburgers and french fries that are the basis of McDonald's business are prime examples of this. Clearly, it would be much harder to package and move fresh hamburgers and freshly sliced potatoes, especially over large distances. Furthermore, because the unit cost of such items is low, it is of comparatively little consequence if they go awry, are lost, or are stolen. In contrast, it is more difficult and expensive to package something—say, a piece of handmade pottery or an antique vase—and losing such things, having them stolen, or their being broken is a disaster. As a result, it is far more expensive to insure something than nothing, and this difference is another reason for the cost advantage that nothing has over something. These sorts of things serve to greatly limit the global trade in items that can be included under the heading of something.

. . .

THE CASE FOR McDONALDIZATION AS AN EXAMPLE OF THE GROBALIZATION OF NOTHING

. . . McDonaldized systems must be standardized. Thus, they cannot help but impose themselves (and their standardized products and systems), at least to some degree, on local markets throughout the world. Although McDonald's may adapt to local realities in various ways, its basic menu and the fundamental operating procedures remain essentially the same everywhere in the world. In this sense, McDonald's can be seen as the epitome of the grobalization of nothing. Thus, the "nothingness" of its standard fare and its basic operating principles tend to threaten, and in many cases replace, local fare and principles of operation.

The enormous expansion in the international arena of the giant fast-food chains that originated in the United States is one manifestation of the grobalization of nothing. In many ways, however, the mere existence of standard American chains in other countries is *not* the most important indicator of the grobalization of nothing in the form of the spread of McDonaldization; rather, it is the existence of indigenous clones of those McDonaldized enterprises in an increasing number of countries throughout the world. After all, the presence of American imports could simply be a manifestation of an invasion of isolated and superficial elements that represent no fundamental threat to, or change in, a local culture. But the emergence of native versions does reflect an underlying change in those societies, a genuine McDonaldization, and powerful evidence of the grobalization of nothing.

The following examples reflect the power of McDonald's to transform local restaurants. They are also manifestations of nothing in the sense that they are largely lacking in distinctive content and aping many standards developed by McDonald's and others of its ilk.

♦ The success of the many McDonald's in Russia led to the development of indigenous enterprises such as Russkoye Bistro. Said Russkoye Bistro's deputy director, "If McDonald's had not come to our country, then we probably wouldn't be here." Furthermore, "We need to create fast food here that fits our lifestyle and traditions. . . . We see McDonald's like an older brother . . . We have a lot to learn from them."

♦ In China, Ronghua Chicken and Xiangfei Roast Chicken emulate Kentucky Fried Chicken. The Beijing Fast Food Company has almost a thousand local restaurants and street stalls that sell local fare. Several of the company's executives are former employees of KFC or McDonald's, where they learned basic management techniques. Even "the most famous restaurant in Beijing—Quanjude Roast Duck Restaurant—sent its management staff to McDonald's in 1993 and then introduced its own 'roast duck fast food' in early 1994."

♦ In Japan, the strongest competitor to McDonald's is Mos Burger (with over 1,500 outlets), which serves "a sloppy-joe-style concoction of meat and chile sauce on a bun." The corporate parent also operates chains under other names such as Chirimentei, a chain of 161 Chinese noodle shops in Japan (and 2 more in the People's Republic of China), Nakau (rice and Japanese noodles) with 82 outlets, and Mikoshi, 4 Japanese noodle houses in California.

♦ In Seoul, competitors to McDonald's include Uncle Joe's Hamburger (the inventor of the *kimchi* burger, featuring an important local condiment made from spicy pickled cabbage) and Americana.

Beyond providing a model for local restaurants (and many other local institutions), McDonaldization poses a threat to the customs of society as a whole. This involves the grobalization of nothing to the degree that distinctive local customs are dropped and replaced by those that have their origins elsewhere and are lacking in distinction. For example,

- ♦ While their parents still call them "chips," British children now routinely ask for "french fries."
- ♦ In Korea (and Japan), the individualism of eating a meal at McDonald's threatens the commensality of eating rice, which is cooked in a common pot, and of sharing side dishes.
- ♦ As in the United States, McDonald's has helped to transform children into customers in Hong Kong (and in many other places).
- ♦ Immigrants to Hong Kong are given a tour that ends at McDonald's. If all cities did this, there would, at least in this case, be nothing to distinguish one city from another.
- ♦ In Japan, McDonald's is described as a new "local" phenomenon. A Japanese Boy Scout was surprised to find a McDonald's in Chicago; he thought it was a Japanese firm.

As local residents come to see McDonald's and McDonaldized systems as their own, the process of McDonaldization, and more generally the grobalization of nothing, will surely embed itself ever more deeply into the realities of cultures throughout the world. For example, the traditional and quite distinctive Japanese taboo against eating while standing has been undermined by the fast-food restaurant. Also subverted to some degree is the cultural sanction against drinking directly from a can or bottle. The norm against eating with one's hands is holding up better (the Japanese typically eat their burgers in the wrappers so that their hands do not touch the food directly). Nevertheless, the fact that deeply held norms are being transformed by McDonald's is evidence of the profound impact of McDonaldization. It reflects the grobalization of nothing in the sense that norms common in the United States and elsewhere (for example, eating while standing and drinking from a can) are now replacing norms distinctive to Japan (and many other nations).

McDonaldization and the globalization of nothing are powerful global, realities, but they do not affect all nations, nor do they affect nations to the same degree. For example, Korea, unlike other East Asian locales, has a long history of anti-Americanism (coexisting with pro-American feelings) and of fearing that Americanism will destroy Korean self-identity. Thus, one would anticipate more opposition there to McDonaldization than in most other nations.

Despite the negative effects of McDonaldization on local customs, we must not forget that McDonaldized systems bring with them many advances. For example, in Hong Kong (and in Taipei), McDonald's served as a catalyst for improving sanitary conditions at many other restaurants in the city.

In addition, McDonaldization has at times helped resuscitate local traditions. For example, although fast-food restaurants have boomed in Taipei, they have encouraged a revival of indigenous food traditions, such as the eating of betel nuts. More generally, Benjamin Barber (Chapter 25) argues that the spread of "McWorld" brings with it the development of local fundamentalist movements ("Jihads") deeply opposed to McDonaldization. However, in the end, Barber concludes that McWorld will win out over Jihad. To succeed on a large scale, he says fundamentalist movements must begin to use McDonaldized systems (such as e-mail, the Internet, television).

Thinking Critically

◆◆◆

1. Does McDonaldization in the end amount to nothing (as that term is defined here)?

2. Does globalization in the end amount to nothing (as that term is defined here)?

3. Make a case for the glocalization of something as the hope against McDonaldization and the spread of nothing.

4. Make a case for the grobalization of something as the hope against McDonaldization and the spread of nothing.

5. Which is the stronger hope, the glocalization or the grobalization of something? Why?

This chapter—an excerpt from Globaloney *by Michael Veseth—critically analyzes McDonaldization, the globalization of nothing, and their relationship to one another. Veseth sees rationalization, or McDonaldization, as the "ugly side" of globalization. But, he also wonders whether we really learn much about globalization through an analysis of the fast-food restaurant. However, in analyzing McDonaldization I am interested, as Veseth himself states, in much more than the fast-food restaurant, and there is little doubt that McDonaldization is at least one important global process. Given the rise of indigenous McDonaldized restaurants, as well as other organizations in other societies and their exportation to the United States, I also have my doubts about the association Veseth makes between Americanization and McDonaldization (although the latter certainly had its roots in the former).*

Veseth creates the interesting idea of "McNothing" to combine my ideas on McDonaldization and nothing. He clearly likes much about the idea of the globalization of nothing, but he also offers several critiques of it. However, most of the criticism results from a failure to understand and follow through on what I mean by nothing and something. In fact, he does understand my definitions but leaves them behind when it comes to critique. Most of his criticisms stem from a tendency, shared by many, to slide into thinking of nothing as relating to meaning rather than to structures that are centrally conceived, controlled, and lacking in distinctive content. Thus, to respond to his criticisms: Movies are meaningful to me, but they are still nothing from the point of view of this definition; McDonald's customers do manufacture meaning, but it is still within the context of nothing (the structure of the McDonald's restaurant and its menu); gourmet chefs do try to prepare dishes exactly the same way, but what they do is not centrally conceived, controlled, and lacking in distinctive content—it is something not nothing.

Veseth makes much of Starbucks and what he claims is my changed views on it. I did think in 1998, and still do, that Starbucks serves high-quality coffee. However, in now using it as an example of nothing, I am not contradicting the idea that the coffee is of high quality. As I take pains to point out in The Globalization of Nothing, *although nothing is usually associated with mediocre products, this need not necessarily be the case (and, conversely, something is not necessarily high in quality). Thus Starbucks coffee is* both *high in quality and nothing (centrally conceived, controlled, and lacking in distinctive content).*

38

Globaloney

Michael Veseth

◆◆◆ ─────────────────────────────────

RATIONALIZATION: THE UGLY GLOBALIZATION

Capitalism's tendency to reward and therefore promote efficiency is well known. It is the secret behind Adam Smith's pin factory and invisible hand. For Marx and Engels, it is the force that enables global capitalism to transform foreign countries, not simply penetrate them. Capitalism's drive for greater and greater efficiency causes it to do for society in general what it did for Adam Smith's pin factory in particular: break it down into basic components and reassemble it in the most starkly efficient fashion. There is not much harm done (and much benefit produced) when the division of labor is applied to the manufacture of pins. The stakes are higher when whole societies are involved, as some have suggested. This, not the superficial influence of advertising and electronic media, is the truly ugly side of globalization.

Efficiency, and the process of rational calculation that is necessary to achieve it, reaches its zenith inside a McDonald's restaurant. The American sociologist George Ritzer observed this fact in his 1993 book, *The McDonaldization of Society: An Investigation into the Changing Character of Social Life*. If you make even a casual study of a McDonald's restaurant you will see Ritzer's point. McDonald's makes efficiency the top-most goal and consciously organizes its assembly line accordingly. This is not news, of course, since the McDonald brothers began doing this way back in the 1950s, even before they sold their name and business to Ray Kroc. What is interesting, however, is how McDonald's has managed to rationalize both sides of the counter. This is where Ritzer comes in.

It is easy to see the production side of McDonald's efficiency. Specialized technology and a highly organized division of labor produce standardized menu items quickly and efficiently. Service may not be quite as fast as in the San Bernardino store, where orders were filled in 30 seconds, but the menu is much larger and competitive factors have forced McDonald's to permit customers to make some special orders. All in all, it is a highly structured, very efficient production line for food of reliably consistent quality and relatively low price.

What may be more significant, however, is how McDonald's has transformed the way that its customers behave. In traditional restaurants, customers are relatively passive participants in the food service operation. They arrive, are seated, and given menus. Wait staff deliver water and other beverages, take the order and deliver it, assuring that everything is exactly as requested. Staff typically check on the customers at several points during the meal, which may be multicourse and require changes in cutlery, glassware, and so forth. Finally, the bill is delivered and paid, change given, and table cleared and reset before it can be turned over to the next group of customers.

Compare this to a typical fast-food experience. Customers arrive and queue to give their orders at the counter, choosing from the standard items listed on the backlit overhead display. The order is given, payment made, and the customer waits for the food to arrive at the counter. (In fast food, customers, not staff, do the waiting.) The customer gets her own condiments and eating utensils, fills her own cup, finds her own table, and then clears it when finished. Customers do much of the work of running the restaurant, work that would otherwise be performed by paid staff. (Over at the drive-through window, customers are actually making their own home and office deliveries!) And they do this work rapidly, efficiently, and without apparent displeasure. Actually, customers don't seem to be aware that they are doing McDonald's work; they just go through the paces automatically. The miracle of the modern McDonald's is that its customers work for the firm but draw no wages. The experience of cooking a meal and eating it is thus transformed from an art to a highly engineered, precisely coordinated production process.

McDonald's is an excellent example of the process that the great German sociologist Max Weber (1864–1920) called "formal rationalization." According to Weber, Ritzer explains, "*formal rationality* means that the search by people for the optimum means to a given end is shaped by rules, regulations, and larger social structures. Individuals are not left to their own devices in searching for the best possible means of attaining a given objective. Weber identified this type of rationality is a major development in the history of the world." Weber's analysis of formal rationalization focused on bureaucracy as an institution that organized a certain segment of society to achieve certain goals quickly and efficiently. A successful bureaucracy is able to process large numbers of people relatively quickly and in a highly predictable manner. Individual variations are tightly controlled, with rules and regulations generally relied upon rather than variable (and therefore unreliable) human judgment within a tightly defined division of labor. There are few "surprises," especially unpleasant ones.

A successful visit to a modern health maintenance organization clinic illustrates a bureaucracy at work. The division of labor, both within offices and among specialties, is obvious. The steps of making appointments, gathering information, making diagnoses, planning treatment, performing tests, filling prescriptions, etc., are all discrete and handled by specialists. Information technology is used to share information and coordinate the stages. The patient (you) moves efficiently through the production line, through various locations, until you are discharged, instructions in hand, into the parking garage. The term *patient* is well chosen because, as in the fast-food restaurant, the customer does all of the waiting, while the assembly-line workers are kept in constant, efficient motion. Other public and private bureaucracies, including income taxation and pension and insurance systems, work much the same way.

George Ritzer gave the name *McDonaldization* to the way that formal rationalization organizes contemporary society, especially in the United States, I think. McDonaldization is characterized by efficiency, calculability, predictability, and the use of technology to control human behavior. McDonaldization is not about McDonald's, Ritzer says, it is about the transforming force of rationalization. Rationalization has many advantages, Ritzer notes. More goods and services can be made available to a larger segment of the population with greater convenience with respect to time and place. Lower cost increases affordability. Workers and customers alike confront a standardized process that is therefore stable and familiar. Uniform treatment means that discrimination due to gender, race, age, or ethnicity is reduced. Standardization means that many products are safer. A high degree of coordination means that technology is rapidly diffused.

McDonald's is a good example of each of these characteristics. When you go to McDonald's you know that there is little chance that you will have an unexpectedly good meal. The sandwiches, fries, and drinks will be just what you expect and no better. But no worse, either. The flip side of standardization is that bad surprises are systematically reduced (although the certainty of occasional human and equipment failures mean they can never fully be eliminated). If you've ever had an expensive meal with poorly prepared or unsafe food served (slowly) by a surly waiter, you know what I am talking about. There are few high points in a Big Mac value meal, but few lows, either.

I think this is why McDonald's is so popular in formerly Communist countries, despite prices that are high relative to weekly income. Under communism, people could be pretty sure of poor food and worse service in most cases, but sometimes they were pleasantly surprised. McDonald's is the other way around. The food is consistently decent. You provide most of the service yourself, so you are not dependent on the whims of a surly waiter. Not a bad deal, compared to the alternative.

If formal rationalization and McDonaldization were limited to McDonald's I don't think we would have very much to complain about. Ritzer's concern, which is shared by many others, however, is that what is true about McDonald's may also be true more generally. It's not about the burgers. It's about the lives behind the burgers and the limited and automatic roles we play as efficient producing and consuming agents. What is the final consequence as formal rationalism spreads from McRestaurant to McMall to McCinema to McHospital to McUniversity to . . . to what? To McChurch?

This is what seems to worry Benjamin Barber. Barber sees the rationalization process (and writes about it in *Jihad vs. McWorld*), but he is apparently more concerned with who has the power in the system (hence his misplaced concern with the infotainment telesector), not realizing that the power is the system. The power lies in the rationalization process itself. This is true even in the most unlikely places, such as the infotainment telesector.

Many people see increasing concentration in the print and electronic media and worry about the potential for abuse of influence. This is a legitimate concern, but it assumes that these firms want power, that they want to control what we believe, whereas I think they really want our money. What I see is increasingly fierce competition among the media giants, which drives them to ever bolder acts of rationalization. On television, for example, the reality show essentially gets audiences to produce their own shows just as McDonald's gets customers to fill their own drink cups. A true monopolist could become lazy and just show reruns or cheap game shows. It is competition and the quest for efficiency that drives them to extremes. It's not the manipulative power of the media giants that I fear, it is the possible effects of their drive to rationalize.

Thomas Friedman both recognizes the rationalization process inherent in globalization and, I think, embraces it. This accounts for Friedman's sunny but realistic attitude toward globalization. As a political reporter covering the Middle East and other troubled regions, Friedman has seen more than his share of irrational acts. I think he'd take economic rationalism over political or social irrationalism any day. He is hopeful that global capitalism will help people learn how to coordinate their actions and behave rationally—which means that they would try not to go to war, for example—even when they are not in a McDonald's. I sure hope he's right, but it is a long shot. Many people have argued that war is irrational because it is too expensive, but this doesn't seem to have stopped war. Perhaps McDonaldization—a deeper cultural process that starts with production and consumption and then eventually is absorbed into a society's DNA—will work where mere hunger for money has failed.

THE THREAT OF McNOTHING

If globalization is McDonaldization, where does that leave us? As you might expect, opinions differ. George Ritzer used to hold out hope for McDonaldization, not Thomas Friedman's hope that a rationalized world will be a rational one, but hope that standardization and rationalization could produce some good things along with mountains of mediocre mass-market stuff. He seemed to be taken with his experiences at Starbucks, for example.

At Starbucks, Ritzer noted in 1998, standardization and technology do more than just reduce cost and control human behavior, they also produce consistently high-quality products for which customers were willing to pay a premium. "Thus, Starbucks indicates that it is possible to McDonaldize quality . . . when there are technologies that ensure high and consistent quality, and when enough patrons are willing to pay large amounts of money for the product." Ritzer seemed to think that Starbucks and Ruth's Chris Steak House and a few other high-quality chains were the start of something important.

But now he's changed his mind. Ritzer's 2004 book *The Globalization of Nothing* looks at the proliferation of Starbucks in London and sees nothing to love. "Such a uniform chain is one of the prime examples of nothing and its proliferation in the most visited areas of the city tend to give it the feeling of nothingness." Ritzer has decided that meaningful content is difficult to globalize because it is too tied to time and place, too human, too special. To be successful, globalization has to bleach the authentic content out of products and services, make them standard, uniform, and meaningless. This, presumably, is why Nike's swoosh logo is so successful—it doesn't mean a thing.

What makes *something* different from *nothing*? You might think it is just a matter of taste—or lack of it—and I think there is something to this, but Ritzer proposes a sort of matrix of meaning to help separate content from void. Somethingness and nothingness form a continuum. Products or experiences closer to the something end of the spectrum are associated with these characteristics: unique, specific to time and place, humanized, and enchanted (capable of surprise). Nothingness, on the other hand, is characterized by its generic, timeless, placeless qualities and the tendency to be impersonal and disenchanted (rationally predictable). Dinner at a friend's apartment lies toward the something end of the continuum, even if you just order in Chinese food. Dinner at the local Ruth's Chris Steak House, on the other hand, is sort of nothing, even if it is delicious. Going trout fishing is something; going shopping at the mall is nothing.

This taxonomy helps us understand how Ritzer's reaction to Starbucks might have changed, although this is only speculation. Perhaps Ritzer was taken when the first Starbucks opened in his neighborhood, and he learned to order his special type of coffee drink ("I'll have a tall skinny vanilla latte, extra foam") and became a "regular," known by the staff and recognized by other customers. Perhaps this enchantment faded away as he saw his own special experience replicated almost endlessly by other "regulars" wherever he went. Or maybe it was that seeing Starbucks in London made him associate it with Americanization, and this offended him. Or maybe he just got tired of standing in line and switched to Diet Coke; I don't really know. In any case, the coffee drinks that were so "something" in 1998 have become "nothing" today.

The Globalization of Nothing is a very interesting book because, like the best globalization stories and metaphors, it appears at a time of social upheaval and uncertainty and tells us why we are so anxious and what will come to pass in the future. We are anxious, clearly, because globalization is stripping our lives of meaning as products and relationships are rationalized down to nothing. The more globalization proceeds, the more we have and the less it means to us. Existential questions inevitably arise.

But, while I share his anxiety, I am not convinced Ritzer is right. His Starbucks turnaround bothers me a bit as does the fact that he seems to find a lot of meaning in motion pictures, which seem to me to be the ultimate embodiment of nothingness, for the most part: mass-produced, centrally controlled, identical entertainment experiences supplied indiscriminately to millions at low cost in highly controlled artificial environments by cynical media oligopolists. It's just everything that Ritzer finds empty in other circumstances. But then I'm also a bit suspicious of Ritzer's tendency to find "something" in things that he personally likes (such as chrome and glass roadside diners) while he sees only "nothing" in things that he doesn't like, such as McDonald's. I worry that Ritzer has fallen into a sort of cultural elitism, which is hard to avoid when you are evaluating the content of culture.

A more serious criticism is that Ritzer distinguishes between something and nothing based upon the conditions of production. A McDonald's meal is nothing, for example, in part because it is standardized—they are all the same. But he thinks that a fine gourmet meal is something (and would be impossible to globalize) in part because of its variability—it is different each time the skilled chef makes it. But I find both sides of this division problematic.

I suspect that the customers at McDonald's are at least sometimes able to manufacture their own meaning, regardless of the rationalized environment. Standard-issue french fries can take on a life of their own when shared with grandchildren at Sunday lunch. If consumers are to be classified as part of the rationalized production process, then we must consider that they are full participants in the meaning creation business, too, and can sometimes make something out of nothing.

As for gourmet meals, I have eaten my share of them at wonderful restaurants. These meals were far from mass produced, but it would be a mistake to think that their pleasure comes from daily variation and inspiration. In my experience, great chefs work hard to find just the right recipe and then work even harder to see that it is prepared *exactly* the same way each time.

I am suspicious of the idea that globalization is the end of culture and meaning and hopeful, even confident, that authentic content can be preserved. To his credit, George Ritzer is hopeful, too. He ends *The Globalization of Nothing* with a brief discussion of a movement that tries to use globalization against itself, to preserve the local and the authentic. This is the Slow Food movement, which is the subject of a chapter of this book.

But I do take seriously the rationalizing force of capitalism and globalization that is driven by capitalism, so there are limits to my optimism. I am especially mindful of the argument made many years ago by the Austrian American economist Joseph Schumpeter in his book *Capitalism, Socialism, and Democracy*. Like Benjamin Barber, Schumpeter feared that capitalism would destroy democracy, but he was not worried about Jihad, McWorld, or the infotainment telesector. Rather, Schumpeter was worried about the effect of rationalization on society.

Schumpeter, you see, believed that society advanced due to the efforts of bold, heroic figures. This was especially true in business, where the figures are called entrepreneurs, but the idea also holds in politics, science, and the arts. Most of us take small risks with life and mainly play it safe. But a few people take bigger risks, and some of them achieve breakthroughs that really make a difference. These risk takers, even when they fail, are the real sources of social drive and change—he called it "creative destruction"—in Schumpeter's view. Without them, the world is a pretty stagnant, uninteresting place.

The problem, Schumpeter believed, is that capitalism's drive to rationalize is really quite intense, and he thought it would eventually destroy the culture that produces entrepreneurs. Capitalism, as a dynamic force, will slowly fade into stagnant socialism, Schumpeter thought, as rational calculation replaced entrepreneurial risk taking. Thus, he said socialism will overcome capitalism, just as Karl Marx predicted, but not through a worker revolt. Nope, the culture of calculation will swallow up capitalism from the inside out.

Schumpeter's view of politics is less well known, but he tended to see it in the same way he viewed the economy. He saw democracy as a competitive political marketplace. Like the economy, progress came through the actions of bold political entrepreneurs who took the risk of providing real leadership. And he thought that democracy, like capitalism, would be destroyed as a dynamic social force as bold political entrepreneurs were replaced by vote-calculating political managers, content to follow voters rather than leading them. Thus does democracy die, in Schumpeter's world, the victim of rationalism, not Jihad or McWorld.

* * *

Where does our study of globalization and McDonald's leave us? I don't know about you, but I feel like I have learned a great deal about McDonald's but not very much about globalization. This is the problem with using McDonald's or any single product or industry as a metaphor or image for something as complex as globalization. We quickly become caught up in the particular case and risk making false generalizations. Meanwhile, the true general globalization case, if it exists, remains unstudied for the most part.

McDonald's may in fact be an especially poor example to use in studying globalization. McDonald's seems to have a special meaning to Americans that it may or may not have to others. You can almost tell how an American feels about her country by what she has to say about McDonald's. We end up, as I have argued here, with an American view of America, not an objective analysis of globalization.

That said, studying McWorld is not entirely a waste of time. Ritzer's analysis of McDonaldization usefully highlights the rationalizing force of markets and makes us aware of the potential of cold calculation to benefit and to harm. What we need to do is to find a way to think about this process that isn't bound up in a particularly American set of values. That's what I try to do . . . by looking at globalization from a different angle—through the bottom of a glass of wine.

Thinking Critically

◆◆◆

1. Is it fair to describe rationalization/McDonaldization as "ugly"?

2. If so, is there not also a "pretty" side to rationalization/McDonaldization?

3. Which is more important, the ugly or the pretty side? Why?

4. What does Veseth mean by "McNothing"? Is it appropriate to fuse McDonaldization and Nothing in this way?

5. Did Ritzer really change his mind on Starbucks? Is it possible to both praise the quality of Starbucks' coffee and see it as "nothing"?

Part IV

1. How are cultural differentialism, cultural convergence, and cultural hybridization defined? Which one of these theories applies best to the current cultural conditions in the United States?

2. Samuel Huntington argues that the fundamental source of conflict in this new world will not be primarily ideological or economic but cultural. In that sense, does the economic cooperation between the United States and Saudi Arabia conflict with this theory? Discuss the authority of cultural norms and values in terms of global economy.

3. Does localization provide an antithesis to McDonaldization? If so, in what ways?

4. Does global culture promote convergence or divergence? Are local cultures the world over in decline? Are we witnessing the birth of a single global culture?

5. One of the causes of cultural change is diffusion, which is the spread of cultural traits from one society to another. Is cultural change a one-way process? Can you identify any elements of your way of life that are derived from other cultures?

6. How does globalization contribute to the transformation of the local?

7. How does McDonaldization operate on the structural-institutional level and on the symbolic-cultural level? Which one is more effective on the transformation of local cultures?

8. Do you think McDonaldization promotes uniformity or hybridity?

9. Are global homogenization and local heterogenization exclusive processes? Is there a third alternative?

10. Does McDonaldization necessarily relate to the proliferation of "nothing"? How does glocalization operate within the "something–nothing" continuum?

11. Although "nothing" tends to be less expensive than "something" for the individual in the short run, it proves to be more costly on social, environmental, political, and economic levels. Cite examples of the tension between "nothing" and "something" beyond those discussed in this part of the book.

12. Is it possible for "something" to be economically successful on a global scale?

13. Define grobalization and glocalization? Which one do you think is more influential on the creation and distribution of cultural products such as art and music?

14. Why is grobalization a more detrimental factor for local cultures than glocalization? Could glocalization be construed as an end product of grobalization or is it a different process?

PART V

Conclusion

This book closes with a set of my reflections on the future of McDonaldization. Although this book has focused on the continuing McDonaldization of various aspects of the social world, it is also possible to think about the possibility of de-McDonaldization. One is led to think about this possibility, in part, because McDonald's itself has been experiencing problems, especially in the American market. There are also a variety of countertrends, several of which have been discussed earlier (e.g., the Slow Food movement), that pose a threat to McDonald's. Even if its demise is far from imminent, there will come a time when McDonald's disappears from the world (after all, the Roman Empire eventually fell). While McDonald's will eventually disappear, the McDonaldization process will continue, even accelerate. With McDonald's gone, some future social thinker would need to come up with a different name for this process, but the underlying dynamics of rationalization will be stronger than ever.

The final chapter also discusses the fate of the highly rational, and therefore modern, process of McDonaldization in a postmodern world dominated by nonrationality or irrationality. There are various possibilities for McDonaldized systems—survival in the margins of an otherwise irrational world, disappearance under an avalanche of irrationalities, a fusion of McDonaldized and postmodern elements, and the ultimate triumph of McDonaldization and its rationalities over the irrationalities of postmodernism. Given its powerful history, the latter scenario, the triumph of McDonaldization, seems most likely.

39

Some Thoughts on the Future of McDonaldization

George Ritzer

THE DE-McDONALDIZATION OF SOCIETY?

Perhaps no idea would seem more extreme, at least from the perspective of the McDonaldization thesis, than the notion that we are already beginning to see signs of de-McDonaldization. (An even more heretical argument would, of course, be that the process did not occur in the first place. However, the social world has certainly changed and one of the ways of conceptualizing at least some of those changes is increasing rationalization. Furthermore, such a view would mean a rejection of one of the strongest and most durable social theories, one that has not only endured but grown through the work of such venerable social thinkers as Weber and Mannheim, as well as that of many contemporary social analysts.) If this is, in fact, the case, McDonaldization would seem to be a concept that may have made some sense at a particular time (and place) but that seems to be in the process

Editor's Note: Excerpts from "Some Thoughts on the Future of McDonaldization" by George Ritzer, pp. 46–57, in *Explorations in the Sociology of Consumption: Fast Food, Credit Cards and Casinos*, edited by George Ritzer, 2001, London: Sage. Copyright © 2001 by Sage, Ltd., London. Used with permission.

of being superseded by recent developments. If McDonaldization has already passed its peak, then its worth and utility as a fundamental sociological concept are severely, perhaps fatally, undermined. What evidence can be marshaled in support of the idea that we are seeing signs of de-McDonaldization?

The first is the fact that McDonald's itself, while still the star of the fast-food industry and continuing to grow rapidly, is experiencing some difficulties and does not quite have the luster it once did. If McDonald's is having problems, that may call into question the concept which bears its name and its imprint. The strongest evidence on these difficulties is the increasing challenge to McDonald's in the highly competitive American market. Indeed, the competition has grown so keen that McDonald's focus in terms of profits and future expansion has shifted overseas, where it remains an unparalleled success.

A second worrisome trend to McDonald's, and potential threat to McDonaldization, is the fact that McDonald's is becoming a negative symbol to a number of social movements throughout the world. Those groups that are struggling to deal with ecological hazards, dietary dangers, the evils of capitalism and the dangers posed by Americanization (and, as we will see below, many other problems) often take McDonald's as a symbol of these problems, especially since it can easily be related to all of them. Furthermore, these groups can mount a variety of attacks on the company as a whole (for example, national and international boycotts of McDonald's products), as well as the 30,000 (as of this writing) or so McDonald's outlets around the world. Such outlets make easy, attractive, and readily available targets for all sorts of dissident groups.

Much of the hostility toward McDonald's has crystallized in recent years around the so-called McLibel trial in London (Chapter 24).

As a result, at least in part, of the McLibel trial, McDonald's has become the symbolic enemy for many groups, including environmentalists, animal rights organizations, anti-capitalists, anti-Americans, supporters of the third world, those concerned about nutritional issues, those interested in defending children, the labor movement, and many more. If all of these groups can continue to see many of the problems of concern to them combined within McDonald's, then there is a real long-term danger to McDonald's. This problem would be greatly exacerbated if some or all of these groups were to come together and jointly oppose McDonald's. Once, and perhaps still, the model (in a positive sense) corporation in the eyes of many, McDonald's is now in danger of becoming the paradigm for all that is bad in the world in the eyes of many others.

Yet another threat to McDonald's stems from the difficulty any corporation has in staying on top indefinitely. McDonald's may well survive the two threats discussed above, but sooner or later internal problems (for example, declining profits, and/or stock prices), external competition, or some combination of the two, will set McDonald's on a downward course which will end in its becoming a pale imitation of the present powerhouse. While far less likely, it is also possible that these factors will even lead to its complete disappearance.

However, we must not confuse threats to McDonald's with dangers to the process of McDonaldization. McDonald's could disappear tomorrow with few if any serious implications for the continuation of McDonaldization. McDonald's will almost undoubtedly disappear at some point in the future, but by then the McDonaldization process will likely be even more deeply entrenched in American society and throughout much of the world. In the eventuality that McDonald's should some day be down or even out, we may need to find a new paradigm and even a new name for the process, but that process (generally, the rationalization process) will continue, almost certainly at an accelerating rate.

But isn't there a variety of countertrends that seem to add up to more that a threat to McDonald's, to a threat to the process of McDonaldization itself? Several such trends are worth discussing.

For one thing, there is an apparent rise of small, non-McDonaldized businesses. The major example in my area, the suburbs of Washington, D.C., is the opening of many small, high-quality bakeries. There seem to be a reasonably large number of people who are willing to travel some distance and to pay relatively high prices for quality breads made by highly skilled bakers. And there seems to be money to be made by such enterprising bakers. Of course bakeries are not the only example (various health conscious food emporiums would be another); there are many non-McDonaldized small businesses to be found throughout society.

Such enterprises have always existed; indeed they were far more commonplace before the recent explosive growth of McDonaldized systems. Under pressure from McDonaldized competitors, they seemed to have all but disappeared in many sectors, only to reappear, at least in part as a counterreaction to McDonaldization. While they exist, and may even be growing, it is difficult to see these alternatives as a serious threat to McDonaldization. The likelihood is that they will succeed in the interstices of an otherwise highly McDonaldized society. If any one of them shows signs of being more than of marginal importance, it will quickly be taken over and efforts will be made to McDonaldize it. It is difficult to envision any other scenario.

Recently, it has been argued that a "New Regionalism" has developed in the United States and that it constitutes a "quiet rebellion" against McDonaldization. Identified here is a series of distinctive regional trends, fashions, and products that are affecting the nation and ultimately the world.

One example . . . is a salsa originating in San Antonio, Texas, and manu-factured by Pace Foods. While certainly a non-McDonaldized, regional prod-uct, at least at first, the salsa, in fact the company, was purchased by Campbell Soup Company in 1995 for just over $1 billion. Over time, it will just become another McDonaldized product marketed by Campbell Soup. It will probably suffer the fate of Colonel Sander's original Kentucky Fried Chicken and many other products that at first were highly original and dis-tinctive, but over time turned into pale, McDonaldized imitations of what they once were.

Another example . . . is Elk Mountain Red Lager and Red Mountain Amber Ale. These sound like, and reflect the growing importance of, the products of local micro-breweries, but in fact they are produced by the Anheuser-Busch company. Furthermore, they are made from the same hops as Budweiser and Michelob. Anheuser-Busch is, of course, trying to capital-ize on the success of local and regional micro-breweries. What they are, in fact, doing is McDonaldizing micro-brewery beer.

[Then there is] the preservation of cities like Savannah, Georgia, as yet another example of the new regionalism, but [there is also] the development of "Disneyesque" simulacra like the Atlanta restaurant Pittypat's Porch, which is named after Scarlett O'Hara's aunt in the book and movie *Gone With the Wind* [as well as] the "movie-set" New York that . . . [emerged] in the resuscitation of Times Square (and in which Disney has a stake). Such examples seem far more supportive of the McDonaldization thesis (as well as of a postmodernist perspective, especially the emphasis on simulacra) than any counterthesis.

[It] is correct . . . that many of America's innovations flow from outly-ing regions [and that this is] evidence of a trend that runs counter to the ideas of homogenization and McDonaldization. However, [ignored is] the fact that regional creations that show any sign of success are quickly McDonaldized (examples include spicy New Orleans style cooking—Popeye's; southwestern Tacos—Taco Bell). McDonaldized systems do not excel at innovation: they are at their best in implementing and rationalizing ideas stemming from other sources. Thus, innovations are always highly likely to emerge outside of McDonaldized systems. This represents one of the dangers of McDonaldization. As we move closer and closer to the iron cage, where are the innovations of the future to come from?

McDonald's itself has developed a system for coping with its lack of inno-vativeness. After all, the creations that have generally flowed from the central office (for example, McDonald's Hula Burger—a bun with two slices of cheese surrounding a slice of grilled pineapple) have not been notably successful. It is the ideas that have stemmed from the franchises in the field (the Filet-O-Fish at McDonald's, for example) that have been the most important innovations.

Another countertrend worthy of noting is the rise of McDonaldized systems that are able to produce high-quality products. The major example is the large and fast-growing chain of Starbucks coffee shops. Until recently, virtually all successful McDonaldized systems have been noted for characteristics like low price and high speed, but not for the high quality of the goods and services that they offer. McDonaldization has heretofore been largely synonymous with mediocrity in these areas. Starbucks has shown that it is possible to create a McDonaldized system that dispenses quality products; on the surface, this poses a profound challenge to McDonaldization and, more generally, to the McDonaldization thesis.

However, Starbucks is, in many ways, an atypical chain. For one thing, it sells variations on what is essentially one simple product—coffee. For another, it is relatively easy, especially with advanced systems and technologies, to consistently produce a good cup of coffee. Third, the patrons of Starbucks are willing to pay a relatively large sum of money for a good cup of coffee. In fact, it may well cost as much to get a cup of "designer coffee" at Starbucks as to have lunch at McDonald's. Thus, Starbucks indicates that it is possible to McDonaldize quality when we are dealing with one (or perhaps a few) simple products, when there are technologies that ensure high and consistent quality, and when enough patrons are willing to pay relatively large amounts of money for the product. Clearly, most chains are *not* able to meet these conditions, with the result they are likely to remain both McDonaldized and mediocre. It is also important to remember that even with the kinds of differences discussed above, especially in quality, Starbucks continues to be McDonaldized in many ways (the different types of cups of coffee are predictable from one time or place to another). However, this is not to say that there are not more chains that will meet conditions enumerated above and follow Starbucks' model. We already see this in the first steps toward the creation of high-quality restaurant chains.

A variety of moderately priced restaurant chains based on the McDonald's model have long since sprung up, including Sizzler, Bonanza, The Olive Garden, TGIFriday's, and Red Lobster. In fact, such chains now control 35% of what is called the moderately priced casual market. In contrast, chains account for 77% of low-priced restaurant meals. Far behind, with only 1% of the market, are chains (actually, at this level they prefer to be called "restaurant groups") involved in the high-priced "linen tablecloth" business where the average patron's bill is in excess of $25. Notable examples include high-end steakhouse chains like Morton's of Chicago (33 restaurants) and Ruth's Chris Steak House (50 restaurants). The challenge in the future is to open high-end chains of restaurants that do not specialize in relatively easy-to-prepare steaks. Lured by the possibility of large profits, several groups are trying. For example, Wolfgang Puck, noted for his gourmet

Spago restaurant in Los Angeles, has opened branch restaurants in San Francisco and Las Vegas (in the highly McDonaldized MGM Grand Hotel) and plans another for Chicago. The problem is that such restaurants depend on a creative chef and it is not immediately clear that one can McDonaldize creativity; indeed the two appear to be antithetical. Said one restaurateur, "The question is, can . . . [one] take a chef-driven concept to a city without a chef?" The editor of *Gourmet* magazine raises another issue about such chains; one that goes to the heart of McDonaldization and its limitations:

> It's the homogenization of cuisine. Even something as good as Morton's Steakhouse is, nevertheless, still going to be the same meal in Chicago as it would be in Washington. There are some people who value that—the fact that you'll always get a good meal.

In the context of high-end restaurant chains, it is useful to discuss an analogy between Ford and Fordism and McDonald's and McDonaldization. In the early days of mass production of cars, people had little or no choice; there was virtually no variation in the number and quality of cars. Over the years, of course, and especially today in the era of post-Fordism, people have acquired a great deal of choice as far as their automobiles are concerned. There are many kinds of choices to be made, but one is certainly high-quality cars (Mercedes Benz or BMW) versus standard-quality (Ford Focus or Plymouth Neon) cars. However, they are all made using standardized parts and assembly-line techniques. That is, high-quality cars can be produced using Fordist techniques.

A parallel point can be made about McDonald's and McDonaldization. In its early years, the focus of fast-food restaurants was one of the most mundane, standardized products. While various fast-food chains competed for business, they all offered the same relatively low-quality, standardized product. Today, however, people are demanding more choices in foods, including higher-quality foods that do not cause them to sacrifice the advantages of McDonaldization. Just as we can produce a Mercedes Benz using Fordist principles, we can offer high-quality quiche using the tenets of McDonaldization. The only thing that stands in the way of a chain of restaurants that offers a range of high-quality quiches is the likelihood that there is insufficient demand for such a product.

As discussed in the case of Starbucks, it is possible to McDonaldize any product, even the highest-quality products, at least to some degree. The secret is to offer one product, or at most a limited number of products. What seems to defy McDonaldization is the essence of a fine restaurant—a range of well-prepared dishes changing from day to day on the basis of availability of high-quality ingredients and/or the whims of the skilled chef. This kind of creativity and variability continues to resist McDonaldization.

The move into high-quality products leads us to question one of the basic tenets of McDonaldization—calculability, or the emphasis on quantity often to the detriment of quality. This is certainly true of virtually all McDonaldized systems that we have known, but it is not necessarily true of Starbucks, or of similar undertakings that we are likely to see in the future. We will see businesses where large amounts of high-quality quiches (to take one possibility) will be purveyed. Don't get me wrong here: I think the most McDonaldized systems continue to forfeit quality in the pursuit of quantity (high speed, low cost, low price). However, McDonaldization, like Fordism, is changing and we will see more systems that are capable of combining quantity and quality.

Does this mean that just as we have moved into a post-Fordist era, we will soon be entering an epoch of post-McDonaldization? To some degree we will, but just as I think that the argument for post-Fordism is over-blown, I would not push the post-McDonaldization thesis too far. Just as today's post-Fordist systems are heavily affected by Fordism, tomorrow's post-McDonaldized systems will continue to be powerfully affected by McDonaldization.

Starbucks (and the fledgling high-quality restaurant chains) deviated from other McDonaldized systems largely on one dimension (calculability, or the emphasis on quantity rather than quality), but what of the other dimensions? Can we conceive of successful chains that deviate from the model in other ways? For example, could one build a chain on the basis of inefficiency? (In fact, as I write this, Chili's is running a nationwide televi-sion ad campaign claiming that it is *not* an assembly-line operation; that it is a monument to inefficiency.) Or unpredictability? Or on the use of human rather than nonhuman technology? All of these seem unlikely. But, there might come a time when most systems are so highly McDonaldized that a large market emerges among those who crave a respite. A chain of ineffi-cient, labor-intensive outlets offering unpredictable goods and services might be able to carve out a niche for itself under such circumstances. However, if such a chain was successful, it would quickly come under pressure to McDonaldize. The paradoxical challenge would be to McDonaldize things like inefficiency and unpredictability. Ironically, it could be done—a chain that efficiently manifests inefficiency, one which is predictably unpredictable, uniformly different, and so on. I even have a name for this proposed chain—"Miss Hap's." (Miss Hap's would be a burger-and-fries chain, but there could also be a steakhouse twin—"Miss Steak's.")

Imagine, for example, a chain of restaurants that rationalizes inefficiency—in postmodern terms, one that produces a simulated inefficiency.

A series of procedures to handle inefficiency would be created, procedures designed to attract customers fed up with efficient systems. These procedures would be broken down into a series of routine steps which would then be codified and made part of the company manual. New employees would be taught the steps needed to perform inefficiently. In the end, we would have a restaurant chain that has rationalized inefficiency. On cue, for example, a counter person at Miss Hap's would effortlessly spill an order of (perhaps fake) fries on the counter. Leaving aside the whimsical example, it is clearly possible to rationalize the seemingly irrational and to produce a system that well might have a ready-made market in a highly McDonaldized society. It would offer more "fun," more spectacle, than the run-of-the-mill fast-food restaurant. And spectacle is often seen as a key element of the postmodern world. It is certainly in the tune with trends like "Las Vegasization" and "McDisneyization."

Miss Hap's would also offer a range of products that were, or at least seemed, unpredictable. The shape of the hamburgers (Miss Hap's would certainly need to offer hamburgers) would be uniformly different. Instead of being perfectly round (or, in the case of Wendy's, square), the burgers would be irregularly shaped. The shape would *not* be left to chance. A variety of molds would be used to mass-produce several different types of burgers with slightly different shapes (this is the "sneakerization" principle to be discussed below). While the burgers would look different, the differences would not affect the ease with which they could be cooked and served: it would still be possible to produce and sell such burgers within the context of a McDonaldized system. For example, all burgers would fit within the same-shaped bun. While the bun might remain uniformly round, it could be made uniformly irregular in other ways (for example, the hills and crevices on the top of the bun). Similar irregularities could be built into the shakes (which could vary in texture), fries and chicken nuggets (which could vary in length without affecting uniform frying time), and so on.

Another potential threat to McDonaldization lies in the area of customization, or what has been called "sneakerization." There is considerable evidence that we have entered a postindustrial era in which the movement is away from the kinds of standardized, "one-size-fits-all" products, that are at the heart of McDonaldized systems. Instead, what we see is much more customization. True customization (for example, made-to-measure suits) is not easily amenable to McDonaldization, but that is not what is usually meant by customization in this context. Rather, it is more niche marketing, of which "sneakerization" is an excellent example. That is, instead of one or a few styles of sneakers or trainers, we now have hundreds of different styles produced for various niches in the market (runners, walkers, aerobic exercisers, and so on). This, of course, is not true customization; sneakers are not being made to measure for a specific user.

The central point is that sneakerization does *not* reflect a trend toward de-McDonaldization. Large companies like Nike produce hundreds of thousands or even millions of each type of sneaker with the result that each is amenable to a McDonaldized production (as well as marketing, distribution, and sales) system. In fact, one future direction for McDonaldization involves its application to products and services that are sold in smaller quantities. There is undoubtedly some absolute lower limit below which is not profitable to McDonaldize (at least to a high degree), but it is difficult to specify what that limit might be with any precision. In any case, that limit will become lower and lower with further technological advances. That is, we will be able to apply economies of scale to increasingly small production runs. More and different sneakers, more "sneakerization," do not represent significant threats to McDonaldization.

A similar argument can be made about what has been termed "mass customization." Take the case of The Custom Foot of Westport, Connecticut. There, a customer puts a foot into an electronic scanner that measures it on a computer screen with the aid of a salesperson. It is during this phase that the customer chooses things like style of shoe, type and grade of leather, color, lining, and so on. Computer software then translates all of this into a set of specifications that are transmitted to subcontractors in several cities in Italy. The shoes are cobbled and sent to the USA within two to three weeks. The cost ranges from $99 to $250, about the same price as ready-to-wear shoes for sale in good New York shoe stores. In contrast, traditional custom-made shoes might cost $1,200 and take several months to arrive. In short, Custom Foot is McDonaldizing the process of making and selling truly customized shoes.

Now clearly this is less McDonaldized than the mass production of thousands, or even millions, of the same shoe. Mass production is more efficient, it permits greater predictability, more of it is amenable to quantification, and it relies more on nonhuman technologies than the customized production of shoes, even the way Custom Foot does it. However, the procedures at Custom Foot are far more McDonaldized than the traditional methods of producing customized shoes. We are talking here, as is usually the case, about degrees of McDonaldization. Custom Foot has applied the principles of McDonaldization to the production and the sale of custom shoes. The nature of its product, especially in comparison to the mass production of identical shoes, limits the degree to which it can McDonaldize, but it does not affect the fact that it is being McDonaldized.

Thus, two of the directions in the future of McDonaldization are the production and sale of goods and services in increasingly small quantities and of goods that are higher in quality. While these are new directions, they do not represent de-McDonaldization. . . .

A MODERN PHENOMENON IN A POSTMODERN AGE

Let us re-examine McDonaldization and de-McDonaldization from the perspective that we are in the midst of the monumental historical change in which a postmodern society is in the process of supplanting modern society. The issue, in this case, is the fate of modern phenomena and a modern process in a postmodern world. Let us assume that we can consider the fast-food restaurant and the McDonaldization process as modern phenomena and that we are currently undergoing a transformation to a post-modern society. Can the fast-food restaurant survive, perhaps prosper, in a post-modern world? What is the fate of McDonaldization in such a world?

If rationality is the *sine qua non* of modern society, then nonrationality and/or irrationality occupies a similar position in postmodern society. Suppose the postmodernists are correct and we are on the verge of the emergence of a nonrational or irrational society. What are the prospects for McDonald's and McDonaldization in such a situation? For one thing, such rational phenomena could continue to exist in a postmodern world and coexist with the presumably dominant irrationalities. In that case, McDonaldized systems would be rational outposts in an otherwise irrational world. People would flock to McDonald's to escape, at least momentarily, the irrationalities that surround them. Visiting a McDonald's would be like frequenting a throwback to an earlier era (much like eating in a diner is today). But surviving in this way, in the interstices of an otherwise non-rational world, would be very different from being the master trend that McDonaldization, at least from a postmodern perspective, once was.

If one possibility is survival at the margins, a second is disappearance in an avalanche of irrationalities. This would be the scenario envisioned by many postmodernists. They would see rational McDonaldized systems as incompatible with the dominant irrational systems and likely, sooner or later, to be swamped by them. The long-term process of McDonaldization would finally come to an end as it grew increasingly unable to rationalize the irrational.

A third, and in many ways highly likely, possibility would be some sort of fusion of the irrational elements of postmodernity with the rational components of McDonaldization: in other words, the creation of a pastiche of modern and postmodern elements. While this appears, on the surface, to be a compromise, in fact such a pastiche is one of the defining characteristics of postmodernism. So this kind of fusion would represent another version of the triumph of postmodernity. Buttressing the case for this alternative is the fact that McDonaldized systems already are well described by many of the concepts favored by postmodernists—consumerism, simulacra, hyperspace, multinational capitalism, implosion, ecstasy, and many others. It could be argued that such systems are *already* pastiches of modernism and post-modernism and therefore already postmodern.

The fourth, and diametrically opposed, possibility, is that McDonaldization not only will resist the irrationalities of postmodernity, but will ultimately triumph over them. Thus, while at the moment we might be seeing some movement toward postmodernism and irrationality, this tendency is likely to be short-lived as it is repulsed by the master trend of increasing rationalization. In this scenario it is postmodernism, not rationalization, that is the short-lived phenomenon. This alternative would obviously be unacceptable to most postmodern thinkers, largely because it means that the advent of a postmodern world would be stillborn. The triumph of McDonaldization means, by definition, the continuation, even acceleration, of modernity.

The logic of the McDonaldization thesis would, needless to say, favor the last of these scenarios. After all, following Weber, the rationalization process has existed and flowered over the course of many centuries. In the process it has encountered a series of monumental barriers and counter-trends. In the end it has not only triumphed over them but emerged even stronger and more entrenched. Postmodernity *may* prove to be a more formidable opponent; it *may* do what no social change before it has done—alter, halt, or even reverse the trend toward increasing rationalization. While such things might occur, it is hard to argue against the continuation, indeed acceleration, of McDonaldization. If history is any guide, McDonaldized systems will survive, even proliferate, long after we have moved beyond postmodern society and scholars have relegated postmodernism to the status of a concept of little more than historical interest.

Thinking Critically

1. What is de-McDonaldization? Is American society undergoing de-McDonaldization?

2. Is McDonald's in trouble? What are the implications of its troubles for McDonaldization?

3. Are we moving into an era of post-McDonaldism?

4. What is the relationship between "sneakerization," "mass customization," and McDonaldization?

5. What is the relationship between McDonaldization and postmodernism?

Part V

1. What have you learned about McDonaldization to this point in this book?

2. Do any of the ideas raised in Chapter 39 change your thinking about any aspect of McDonaldization?

3. How do the ideas about McDonaldization raised throughout this volume relate to your own life?

4. How do the specific ideas discussed in Chapter 39 relate to your life?

5. Would you like to live in a more or less McDonaldized world? Why?

6. What would a less McDonaldized world look like? What would life in it be like?

7. What would a non-McDonaldized world look like? Is such a world possible given the complexities of contemporary society?

Index

About the Editor

George Ritzer is Distinguished University Professor at the University of Maryland, where he has also been a Distinguished Scholar-Teacher and won a Teaching Excellence Award. He was also awarded the 2000 Distinguished Contributions to Teaching Award by the American Sociological Association, and in 2004, he was awarded an honorary doctorate by LaTrobe University, Melbourne, Australia. He is perhaps best known for *The McDonaldization of Society* (translated into over a dozen languages) and several related books, including *Expressing America: A Critique of the Global Credit Card Society* and *Enchanting a Disenchanted World: Revolutionizing the Means of Consumption*. His latest effort in this domain is *The Globalization of Nothing* (2004). He recently edited *The Encyclopedia of Social Theory* (2005), and he is the founding editor of the *Journal of Consumer Culture*.

About the Contributors

Benjamin R. Barber is on the faculty of the School of Public Affairs, University of Maryland.

Barbara G. Brents is a member of the Department of Sociology, University of Nevada, Las Vegas.

Alan Bryman is a member of the Department of Social Sciences, Loughborough University, UK.

Melissa L. Caldwell teaches in the Department of Anthropology, University of California, Santa Cruz.

John Drane has taught in the universities of Stirling and Aberdeen in Scotland, and is an adjunct professor at Fuller Seminary, Pasadena, California.

Kathryn Hausbeck teaches in the Department of Sociology, University of Nevada, Las Vegas.

Ian Heywood is on the faculty of the Department of Environmental and Geographical Sciences, The Manchester Metropolitan University, UK.

P. D. Holley is a member of the Department of Social Sciences, Southwestern Oklahoma State University.

Suzanne S. Hudd is a member of the Department of Sociology/Criminal Justice, Quinnipiac University.

Uwe E. Kemmesies is a drug researcher and lecturer at Goethe-University in Germany.

Meyer Kestnbaum is a member of the Department of Sociology, University of Maryland.

Andrew J. Knight is a member of the Department of Criminology, Sociology, and Geography, Arkansas State University.

Mara Miele is a member of the Department of City and Regional Planning, Cardiff University, Wales.

Steven Miles is a member of the Department of Sociology, University of Plymouth, UK.

David Morse, a U.S.-based freelance writer, is author of *The Iron Bridge*.

Jonathan Murdoch is a member of the Department of City and Regional Planning, Cardiff University, Wales.

Joel I. Nelson is on the faculty of the Department of Sociology, University of Minnesota.

Alan Neustadtl teaches in the Department of Sociology, University of Maryland.

Jan Nederveen Pieterse teaches in the Department of Sociology, University of Illinois.

Sara Raley is a PhD student in the Department of Sociology, University of Maryland.

Uri Ram teaches in the Department of Behavioral Sciences, Ben Gurion University, Israel.

Matthew B. Robinson is affiliated with the Departments of Political Science and Criminal Justice, Appalachian State University.

Tony Royle is a member of the Department of Human Resource Management, Nottingham Business School, UK.

Bryan S. Turner is Professor in the Department of Sociology, Singapore University.

Malcolm Waters is on the faculty of Hobart University, Tasmania, Australia.

James L. Watson is a member of the Department of Anthropology at Harvard University.

D. E. Wright, Jr. is a member of the Department of Social Sciences, Southwestern Oklahoma State University.

Michael Veseth is Professor of Political Economy at the University of Puget Sound.